PERGAMON INTERNATIONAL LIBRARY
of Science, Technology, Engineering and Social Studies

The 1000-volume original paperback library in aid of education,
industrial training and the enjoyment of leisure

Publisher: Robert Maxwell, M.C.

P9-AQH-142

The Practice of
Behavior Therapy
(PGPS-1)

Pergamon Titles of Related Interest

Anchin/Kiesler HANDBOOK OF INTERPERSONAL
PSYCHOTHERAPY

Hersen/Barlow SINGLE CASE EXPERIMENTAL DESIGNS:
STRATEGIES FOR STUDYING BEHAVIOR CHANGE

Hersen/Bellack BEHAVIORAL ASSESSMENT: A PRACTICAL
HANDBOOK, Second Edition

Karoly/Kanfer SELF-MANAGEMENT AND BEHAVIOR CHANGE:
FROM THEORY TO PRACTICE

Papajohn INTENSIVE BEHAVIOR THERAPY

Walker CLINICAL PRACTICE OF PSYCHOLOGY: A GUIDE FOR
MENTAL HEALTH PROFESSIONALS

Related Journals*

ADVANCES IN BEHAVIOUR RESEARCH AND THERAPY
BEHAVIOUR RESEARCH AND THERAPY
CLINICAL PSYCHOLOGY REVIEW
JOURNAL OF BEHAVIOUR THERAPY AND EXPERIMENTAL
PSYCHIATRY
PERSONALITY AND INDIVIDUAL DIFFERENCES

*Free specimen copies available upon request.

PERGAMON GENERAL PSYCHOLOGY SERIES
EDITORS
Arnold P. Goldstein, *Syracuse University*
Leonard Krasner, *SUNY at Stony Brook*

The Practice of Behavior Therapy
Third Edition

Joseph Wolpe, M.D.
Temple University School of Medicine
Eastern Pennsylvania Psychiatric Institute

PERGAMON PRESS
New York   Oxford   Toronto   Sydney   Paris   Frankfurt

Pergamon Press Offices:

U.S.A.   Pergamon Press Inc., Maxwell House, Fairview Park,
                     Elmsford, New York 10523, U.S.A.

U.K.   Pergamon Press Ltd., Headington Hill Hall,
                     Oxford OX3 0BW, England

CANADA   Pergamon Press Canada Ltd., Suite 104, 150 Consumers Road,
                     Willowdale, Ontario M2J 1P9, Canada

AUSTRALIA   Pergamon Press (Aust.) Pty. Ltd., P.O. Box 544,
                     Potts Point, NSW 2011, Australia

FRANCE   Pergamon Press SARL, 24 rue des Ecoles,
                     75240 Paris, Cedex 05, France

**FEDERAL REPUBLIC   Pergamon Press GmbH, Hammerweg 6
OF GERMANY**   6242 Kronberg/Taunus, Federal Republic of Germany

Library of Congress Cataloging in Publication Data

Wolpe, Joseph.

The practice of behavior therapy.

Bibliography: p.
Includes index.
1. Behavior Therapy. I. Title. [DNLM: 1. Behavior
therapy. WM 425 W866p]
RC489.B4W6   1982   616.89'142   82-7547
ISBN 0-08-027165-0   AACR2
ISBN 0-08-027164-2 (pbk.)

Printed in the United States of America

To Allan and David

Lead me from the unreal to the real.
Upanishads

Contents

Preface to the Third Edition

In the eight years since the second edition of this book was published, the main technical advances in behavior therapy have been in the area of deconditioning methods based on *in vivo* exposure, and perhaps on the use of flooding techniques in particular. Cognitive-change procedures have received much more explicit attention but, on the negative side, we have seen the promotion of the absurd claim that changed thinking is the basis of all psychotherapeutic change.

Interest in behavior therapy has grown rapidly, as the greatly increased membership of the American Association for the Advancement of Behavior Therapy proves. The number of practitioners in this field has also expanded but since training opportunities are often below par, a great deal of the practice of behavior therapy leaves much to be desired.

A widespread lack of awareness of the distinctive character of behavior therapy has been alarmingly evident—even among some people who are prominent in the field. One manifestation of this lack is the ongoing "controversy" about the very definition of behavior therapy. Certain classes of unadaptive behavior have their origin in learning, and knowledge of the processes of learning and unlearning must have the greatest relevance to effecting change. Behavior therapy is the application of such knowledge. It is only secondarily a technology. Perhaps the emphasis placed on techniques in the didactic literature of behavior therapy, including the two earlier editions of this book, has played a part in deflecting attention away from principles.

I have included much more emphasis on matters of principle in the present edition; the result is that there are two new chapters. For a detailed exposition of the most basic principles relating to the neuroses, however, the reader must still be referred to *Psychotherapy by Reciprocal Inhibition* (Stanford University Press, 1958). The newcomer will find a painless introduction in my more recent book, *Our Useless Fears* (Houghton Mifflin, 1981).

The text has been largely rewritten or extensively revised and, where indicated, completely reorganized. Only Chapter 16 has survived relatively unscathed. All other chapters have incorporated what have seemed to me the

xi

most significant new contributions to theory and practice. It is obviously not possible to include everything.

I thank Stephen D. Lande and Paul R. Latimer for valuable commentaries on Chapters 3 and 11, respectively. I am most deeply grateful to Betty Jean Smith, my secretary, for her superlative help in every stage of the book's composition.

From the Preface
to the First Edition

Before the advent of behavior therapy, psychological medicine was a medley of speculative systems and intuitive methods. Behavior therapy is an applied science, in every way parallel to other modern technologies, and in particular those that constitute modern medical therapeutics. Therapeutic possibilities radiate from the uncovering of the lawful relations of organismal processes. Since learning is the organismal process most relevant to psychological medicine, the establishment of lawful relations relevant to the learning process is the main road to therapeutic power in this field.

However, the scientifically minded behavior therapist need not confine himself to methods derived from principles. For the welfare of his patients, he employs, whenever necessary, methods that have been *empirically* shown to be effective. Colchicum was a well-authenticated and widely used remedy for attacks of gout long before colchicine was isolated or the metabolism of gout understood (Stetten, 1968). In the same way, in present-day behavior therapy, we use mixtures of carbon dioxide and oxygen to alleviate pervasive anxiety without knowing the mechanism of their action. The criterion is the existence of compelling evidence of a relationship between the administration of the agent and clinical change.

A very special difficulty in evaluating how much a psychotherapeutic technique *per se* contributes to change resides in the fact that almost any form of psychotherapy produces substantial benefit in about fifty percent of cases, apparently because of anxiety-inhibiting emotional reactions that therapists evoke in patients (Wolpe, 1958). Therefore, a particular technique must be, *prima facie* at least, effective beyond that level if it is to be even provisionally recommended on empirical grounds. Failure to observe this rule can lead to the gullible acceptance of almost anything that is touted, and back to the pre-scientific chaos of recipes from which modern technological principles have extricated us.

Two themes have recently been prominent among the criticisms voiced by opponents of behavior therapy. One is that it is "mechanistic and nonhumanistic." The two adjectives are usually combined as though they belonged together like face and beard. Insofar as behavior therapy leans on mechanisms it is indeed mechanistic. But nobody can fairly call it nonhumanistic. No basis exists for the idea that others have more compassion than the behavioristic psychotherapist. Internal medicine is not dehumanized when penicillin replaces bloodletting as a treatment for infections; and no more is psychotherapy when conditioning replaces free association.

I am grateful to those who have helped in the literary side of the book's production—Mrs. Barbara Srinivasan, Mrs. Aviva Wanderer, and my wife; and to my old friend and colleague, Dr. L. J. Reyna, who, as so often in the past, has been a fount of information and ideas.

1

Behavioristic Psychotherapy:

Its Character and Origin

The central aim of all psychotherapy is to overcome, or at least significantly diminish, consistently recurring behavior patterns that an individual has learned and that are disadvantageous to him.

Consistently recurring responses to particular stimulus conditions are called *habits*. They are almost always a combination of motor, emotional, and cognitive responses. Most learned habits are adaptive—i.e., they subserve biological or acquired needs or avoid injury, pain, or discomfort. But habits that are unadaptive can also be learned; their effects are contrary to the welfare of the organism. Fortunately, these are much less common but some are very troublesome; they are the therapeutic problems. A great many of these habits are primarily emotional, and the emotion involved is usually fear. Fear is the centerpoint of the neuroses, whose treatment is the central focus of this book.

It follows that knowledge of the processes of learning and unlearning ought to be the most fruitful source of methods of eliminating unadaptive habits. Behavior therapy is based upon such knowledge; this is what distinguishes it from all other psychotherapies. The formal definition of behavior therapy is: *the use of experimentally established principles and paradigms of learning to overcome unadaptive habits*.

HISTORICAL ANTECEDENTS

There are many systems of psychotherapy, each based upon a theory. The theory of behavior therapy is quite straightforward: unadaptive habits that

1

are learned can be unlearned, and the most reasonable way to set about to achieve this is on the basis of knowledge of the learning process. Behavior therapists do many things, some of which—such as the gathering of information—are in a general way common to all psychotherapies. But a therapist can only be said to be doing behavior therapy when he is actually using methods that are derived from experimentally established principles. Such methods aim at weakening and eliminating unadaptive habits, or initiating and strengthening adaptive ones, or both.

The term "behavior therapy," which was originally introduced by Skinner and Lindsley (1954), owes its general acceptance as the label for this particular therapeutic discipline to Hans Eysenck (1960). Its chief advantage over the labels that competed with "behavior therapy" years ago—"conditioning therapy" and "behavioristic psychotherapy"—was that it seemed more likely to be found acceptable by clinicians than the other terms, which were redolent of the experimental laboratory. Another ostensible advantage was that the word "behavior" would draw attention to what was conceived as the cardinal distinguishing feature of this newcomer to the psychotherapies—its use of behavior to change habits. Behavior of one kind or another, however, is inevitably implicated in all systems of psychotherapy, most commonly verbal behavior of many kinds, that range through incantations, free associations, and "primal scream." Verbal interactions may, of course, lead to other behavior—such as the carrying out of suggestions or the following of advice. Thus, in retrospect, "behavior therapy" as a label was a poor choice; "conditioning therapy" would have been both more distinctive and more informative.

But "behavior therapy" is firmly established and we have to live with it. We can do this comfortably if we are reasonably vigilant. On the one hand, we must avoid the temptation to accept any method as behavior therapy *just because* it involves activity, and perhaps especially vigorous activity, such as running (Orwin, 1973). On the other hand, we must not exclude procedures whose impact is primarily cognitive on the mistaken ground that cognition is not "real" behavior. It is the latter error that has led to such travesties as "cognitive behavior therapy" (Beck, 1976).

In earlier editions of this book, I expressed the view that there is a generic similarity between behavior therapy and certain other treatments, including psychoanalysis, in which "the behavior itself is conceived as the therapeutic agent," and that these could be bracketed together as "behavioral therapies." But since, as indicated above, there is no psychotherapy in which behavior does not figure, the presumed behavioral therapies do not really fall into a class by themselves. If all psychotherapies are in a broad sense behavioral therapies, we must carefully specify what is distinctive about behavior therapy.

A HISTORICAL PERSPECTIVE

The history of behavior therapy is in general the history of psychotherapy, which consisted in the beginning of all the things that people through the centuries did to and for other people to relieve their emotional distress. Most of these activities were based on religious belief or superstition, or theories of magical influence. It was only when practices came to be based on consistent principles that they took on the character of psychotherapeutic disciplines as they are understood today.

The first important psychotherapist in this sense was Anton Mesmer (1779), an Austrian physician who had moved to Paris. He derived his therapeutic practices from the idea that emotional illness could be overcome by equilibrating the patient's "animal magnetism." To achieve this, he made use of a large troughlike arrangement of movable iron rods and mirrors that he called a "bacquet." To an assemblage of patients surrounding the bacquet and forming a closed circle by holding hands, Mesmer would make a dramatic appearance, clad in gaudy robes, holding in his hand his "magnetic wand," with which he would touch and stroke the patients at intervals in the seance. While his methods were highly esteemed by the public, they became the subject of investigation by a joint committee (in which Benjamin Franklin participated). In 1784, this committee issued a disparaging report; but this does not negate the fact that Mesmer had many well-documented therapeutic successes (Darnton, 1968). While the theory of animal magnetism did not stand up to scientific testing, Mesmer's procedures led to the modern practices of suggestion and hypnosis, and other modes of verbal behavior control.

Suggestion generally involves using words to arouse more desirable responses in a situation where undesirable responses are habitual. To the extent that this effort may be successful, it seems to be because the suggested response competes with the preexisting one effectively enough to inhibit it. There will be lasting diminution (or elimination) of the preexisting response to the extent that the inhibiting event results in *conditioned* inhibition (see Chapter 2). If standard practices of hypnotherapy have not had impressive long-term results, it may be because they have not brought the suggested responses into effective apposition with those meant to be eliminated.

An early example of a direct use of competing responses that is remarkably close to some modern practices was unearthed by Stewart (1961) in a book by Leuret (1846). The patient was a 30-year-old wine merchant with a 10-year history of obsessional thoughts that had become so insistent that he had become unable to carry on his business. After admitting the patient to the hospital, Leuret gave him daily assignments of songs to read and learn for recitation the next day. The patient's food ration was made contingent upon how much he had learned. In six weeks of this regimen, the patient's recitals steadily improved, while his obsessional thoughts became less and less troublesome. At the end of the six weeks, he announced that he had not had the thoughts for several days and felt much better. Leuret found work for the patient as a nurse and a year later noted that he was still well and had become a very efficient nurse. (For further examples of the innovations of this forerunner of behavior therapy, see Gourevitch, 1968; and Wolpe & Theriault, 1971.)

In the more conventional psychiatric setting, a large number of clinical experiments were performed and reported by Janet (1925), but unfortunately no usable rules emerged. The 19th-century therapist had some reason for confidence in the benefits of sympathetic support, advice, persuasion, and nonspecific suggestion. Sigmund Freud introduced the first system of therapeutic methods based on detailed and coherent theoretical principles. Psychoanalytic theory is imaginative and colorful, and Freud's presentation of it had an uncanny persuasiveness that brought an excitement into the field of psychotherapy that it had never previously had. The therapeutic methods that emerged from this theory did not, however, lead to the increase in favorable outcomes for which everybody had hoped (e.g., American Psychoanalytic Association, 1958). The theoretical propositions themselves were not empirically supported either (see, for example, Salter, 1952; Bailey, 1964). Despite the inadequacies of psychoanalysis, Freud's work had two important permanent consequences. He brought to the fore the overriding importance of emotional, as opposed to cognitive, events in the causation of neuroses, and he divested the subject of sex of its prudish social cloak.

Important as these contributions were during the first half of the 20th century, there was scarcely another field of knowledge more insulated from scientific advancement than behavioral therapeutics. No hypotheses were being put to the test, no lawful relations were being established, and no reliable methods for procuring therapeutic change entered the scene. There is an obvious explanation for this. Modern medicine is applied science. Modern psychotherapy could thus only develop when there was something to apply. There had to be a foundation in the form of data from the experimental laboratory.

THE DEVELOPMENT OF
AN EXPERIMENTALLY BASED PSYCHOTHERAPY

In the course of the 20th century, experimental studies, most particularly along the lines initiated by Pavlov and Watson, revealed more and more about the characteristics of habits and the factors determining their acquisition, maintenance, and decline. The lawful relations that had been established lent themselves to the development of hypotheses to account for the acquisition of patterns of unadaptive behavior, and to suggest methods that might be used to eliminate them.

Progress in this direction had its origin in Watson and Rayner's (1920) famous experiment on Little Albert.[1] This 11-month-old child, who was generally of a phlegmatic disposition, was observed to be disturbed by the loud noise made when an iron bar was struck behind him. By striking the bar each time the child touched a white rat, the experimenters quite soon conditioned a fear of this animal and, by generalization, of other furry objects. They proposed four possible strategies by which this conditioning might be overcome: (1) by experimental extinction, (2) by "constructive" activities around the feared object, (3) by "reconditioning" through feeding the child candy in the presence of the feared object, and (4) by stimulating erogenous zones in the presence of the feared object. Although Albert's departure from the hospital prevented the implementation of any of these suggestions, it is worth noting that the last three of them accord with the counterconditioning model which will be discussed in detail later.

A few years later, the third of these suggestions—reconditioning by feeding—was employed by Mary Cover Jones (1924a) in the treatment of children's phobias. She described her method as follows:

> During a period of craving for food, the child is placed in a high chair and given something to eat. The feared object is brought in, starting a negative response. It is then moved away gradually until it is at a sufficient distance not to interfere with the child's eating. The relative strength of the fear impulse and the hunger impulse may be gauged by the distance to which it is necessary to remove the feared object. While the child is eating, the object is slowly brought nearer to the table, then placed upon the table and, finally, as the tolerance increases, it is brought close enough to be touched. Since we could not interfere with the regular schedule of meals, we chose the time of the midmorning lunch for the experiment. This usually assured some degree of interest in the food and corresponding success in our treatment.

Jones (1924b) detailed the application of this method to the case of a three-year-old boy called Peter—"one of our most serious problem cases"—who recovered after daily treatment over a period of two months. That hunger had a role in the process of overcoming the fear habit was shown by the fact that the effectiveness of the method increased when hunger was greater. On the other hand, "the repeated presentation of a feared

---

[1]Even though Harris (1979) has pointed out that the magnitude and extent of Albert's fear conditioning has often been overstated in the literature, there is no doubt that some fear conditioning occurred. The relevant point is that the experiment provided a starting point for such later work as is described below.

object, with no auxiliary attempt to eliminate the fear, is more likely to produce a summation effect than an adaptation.'' The correspondence of these observations on the fears of a child with certain findings in experimentally neurotic animals (see Chapter 4) is worth noting. As the first to establish such lawful relations in a psychopathological content, Jones has earned an honored place in the history of behavior therapy.

At about the same time, Burnham (1924), starting from a mental hygiene orientation, was also proposing the use of counteractive behavior as the agent of habit change. The recommendation of graduated tasks in the treatment of neurotic patients did not reappear until years later in the writings of Herzberg (1941) and Terhune (1948), though neither of these therapists was aware of competing responses as the agent of habit change.

In the meantime, in the field of experimental psychology, the most studied habit-eliminating process was, and has continued to be, experimental extinction, the gradual decrement in strength and frequency of responses that are evoked without reinforcement; the mere absence of reinforcement weakens habits, by processes discussed in Chapter 2. Dunlap (1932) probed the therapeutic possibilities of this, and evolved the technique called ''negative practice,'' whereby undesirable motor habits are overcome as a result of their being deliberately evoked again and again. It was not long afterwards that Guthrie (1935) drew attention to the general applicability of counterconditioning methods such as those Jones had demonstrated, and concluded that the simplest rule for breaking a habit is ''to find the cues that initiate the action and to practice another response to these cues'' (Guthrie, 1935, p. 138). An indispensable ingredient of the formula was that the cue to the original response had to be present while the other behavior prevailed. The new response could then inhibit the original one and thereby weaken it.

An unequivocal demonstration of the therapeutic power of response competition was provided by its success in the treatment of experimental neuroses. These are persistent anxiety-response habits that can be deliberately induced in animals, first reported from Pavlov's laboratories (Pavlov, 1941) at the beginning of this century. A dog would be placed on a table in a small chamber, held in a harness that restricted its movements. A high level of anxiety was elicited in the animal either by noxious stimulation or by a strong motivational conflict. This anxiety was conditioned to the sights and sounds of the experimental situation. By repetition of the anxiety arousal, a rising level of anxiety conditioning developed to the experimental chamber and contiguous stimuli, a level that was eventually very high indeed. A striking feature of this anxiety was its extreme persistence; it was not in the ordinary course of events diminished in intensity either by exposure to the experimental cage or by prolonged removal from it. The calm behavior of the animals in their living cages contrasted with this most strikingly. Some anxiety was, however, manifest in environments that did include stimuli resembling those in the environment of the experimental cage, as might be expected. A notable series of experiments performed by Pavlov's pupil, W. Horsley Gantt (1941), showed that untreated animals would remain afflicted with their neuroses for the rest of their lives.

In experiments that I completed in 1948, I found that experimental neuroses could be overcome by employing the same response-competition concept that Mary Cover Jones had applied to children—using feeding to compete with small evocations of anxiety. These experiments led to formulation of the reciprocal inhibition principle of psychotherapeutic effects. In human adults, feeding is not an effective competitor with anxiety. Adult neuroses are, however, treatable by a very considerable number of other competing responses; and these and their manner of use are the main subject of this book. Much more will be said about experimental neuroses in Chapter 3 when we discuss the mechanisms and factors of neurotic conditioning and deconditioning.

LEARNED VERSUS
PHYSIOPATHOLOGICAL PSYCHIATRIC SYNDROMES

Psychiatry is the study and the treatment of unadaptive habitual behavior. Behavior is adaptive when its result is to satisfy the individual's needs, bring him relief from pain, discomfort, or danger, or avoid undue expenditure of energy (Wolpe, 1958, p. 2). Individual unadaptive acts are common in everybody's days, for not everything one does meets with success: the number one has dialed does not always answer; the shop one has entered does not always have the desired item. Only unadaptive acts that are *habitual* call for treatment.

The unadaptive habits that constitute psychiatric syndromes can be broadly subdivided according to two kinds of origins. Some are organically based (on lesions or biochemical abnormalities) and others are the result of learning. Behavior therapy, and indeed all psychotherapy, is generally only relevant to psychiatric syndromes that owe their existence to learning. These syndromes fall into five categories:

1. Neuroses[2]

Neuroses are persistent unadaptive habits that have been acquired in anxiety-generating situations and in which anxiety responses are almost invariably the central feature (see discussion below). They are ''pure'' learned habits in

---

[2]In giving this term its traditional role, I am, of course, disregarding its omission from DSM-II and DSM-III. The main reason given for that omission is that there is no consensus about the definition of the term (DSM-III, p. 9). But it is better to go where the evidence points than to

the sense that no special organic state is necessary for their occurrence. Almost everybody acquires some neurotic habits. Known predisposing conditions include high innate emotionality and previous learned anxiety in the relevant stimulus area.

2. Other "Pure" Learned Unadaptive Habits

Unadaptive habits that fall into this category lack the anxiety that characterizes neuroses. Examples are some tantrums, nailbiting, trichotillomania, enuresis nocturna, extreme stinginess, and chronic tardiness.

3. Psychopathic Personality [Antisocial Personality Disorder—DSM-III]

A diagnosis of psychopathic personality is applied to people who habitually perform asocial or antisocial behavior regarding which they feel no guilt or other anxiety, so that the rebukes, chastisements, and even the major penalties that society imposes have little or no restraining effect. While, quite possibly, a biological factor may predispose one to the development of psychopathic behavior (Eysenck, 1957), the particular patterns of behavior must be learned and are therefore subject to unlearning. Unfortunately, very little research into the therapeutic possibilities has so far been done.

4. Drug Addictions

A person may repeatedly take a drug to relieve pain, stress or anxiety, or for other reasons. If the drug-taking continues after the cessation of the stress, it is considered a drug addiction. Addiction is characterized by "cravings" that compel the person to seek the drug. Underlying a craving is a biological state that makes drug habits particularly different from other categories of unadaptive habits. Recent research (Lubeskind & Paul, 1977; Snyder, 1978) has shown that this difference is related to the effects of these drugs upon the binding of endogenous analgesics (endorphins) to pain receptors. Since the craving is a response to a biological state, I thought, some years ago, that it would be worthwhile to try to employ aversive stimulation to bring about its inhibition. An experiment is reported later in this book in which some evidence was obtained of the effectiveness of this measure (Wolpe, Groves, & Fischer, 1980). A particularly interesting finding of the experiment, how-

---

wait for a "consensus." As will be seen below, there is abundant experimental and clinical evidence of the existence of a large class of unadaptive behaviors united by the definition of *neurosis* given here; and it is useful to continue to employ the word to denote that class even if psychodynamically oriented clinicians ignore the evidence, and even though there are other theories about how these disorders develop.

ever, was that people who are addicted to narcotics are little motivated to be "cured." The addiction evidently results in gratifications that the subjects are reluctant to relinquish. No treatment program can be widely successful until some way is found to overcome this obstacle.

5. Learned Unadaptive Behavior of Schizophrenics

Although it is now clear that schizophrenia is at bottom a biological illness, some of the unadaptive habits that patients display are due to learning, and these can often be eliminated by operant conditioning schedules (Ayllon, 1963; Ayllon & Azrin, 1968; Paul & Lentz, 1977; Kalish, 1981).

Under the influence of psychoanalytic theorizing, the view that there is a continuum between neuroses and schizophrenia is still widely prevalent. It is assumed that schizophrenia is functionally related to the neuroses and that transitions occur between one and the other (see, for example, Arieti, 1955). These are often referred to as "borderline" states. In a survey of 13 different areas of comparative research that I made some years ago (Wolpe, 1970), I found that the evidence uniformly pointed to neurosis and schizophrenia being behavioral disorders whose etiologies and biological bases are separate and unrelated. For example, the genetic factors of schizophrenia do not coincide with those of neurosis (Eysenck and Prell, 1951); and a variety of physiological features that are present in schizophenics are absent in normal people and in neurotic subjects. What is particularly striking is that abnormal autonomic reactivity in schizophrenics persists even when they are in remission (Rubin, 1970). Other findings are that the early symptoms of schizophrenia are distinct from those of neurosis (Chapman, 1966), and that neurotic behavior is much more responsive to external stimulus conditions, and is lastingly modifiable by conditioning procedures in a way that schizophrenic behavior is not. It appears, in sum, that certain people inherit a biological abnormality that predisposes them to the development of schizophrenia if certain precipitating conditions occur. What these conditions are is unknown, but they are probably at least partly biological. The biology of fully developed schizophrenia is directly responsible for most of the symptomatology, but also sometimes predisposes to the selective learning of bizarre patterns of behavior. Such patterns are the only part of the psychosis that is modifiable by learning procedures (see Chapter 13). The underlying biological state can be altered by biological means, if at all.

THE MANIFESTATIONS OF NEUROSIS

Of the categories of unadaptive learned habits listed above, only the neuroses will be substantively dealt with in this book. The formal definition of neurosis is: *a persistent unadaptive habit that has been acquired by learning in an anxiety-generating situation (or a sucession of such situations) and in which anxiety[3] is usually the central component.*

A great many neurotic patients present themselves purely as having inappropriate fears; in others it is consequences of the fear that bring them to treatment. The most common neurotic fears are social—of criticism, rejection, and disapproval. Often bound up with the last is the idea of behaving unacceptably, which is the commonest basis of interpersonal timidity. Fears of public speaking or, more broadly, public scrutiny, are probably the most common of all neurotic fears. One step removed from these is the fear of taking responsibility.

Considerably less common—though one would not think so on the basis of their prominence in behavior therapy research—are the phobias. These include fears of a vast array of animals, such as dogs, mice, or spiders, and other configurations or aspects of things or places that objectively include no danger of any kind. Among these we have fears of darkness, blood, open wounds, injections, elevators, flying, deformities, hospitals and heights. Of special interst is agoraphobia. Patients who are given this diagnosis all share a fear of being separated from a safe place or safe persons or both; but as will be seen in Chapter 15, other kinds of fearfulness often lie behind the manifest agoraphobia. In addition to, but separate from, the specific fears, is pervasive ("free-floating") anxiety, in which anxiety is experienced continuously for days or months even in the absence of any specific anxiety-arousing stimulus. Apparently such anxiety has been conditioned to space, time, bodily sensations and other virtually omnipresent stimulus aspects (see Chapter 11).

Anxiety, especially if it is severe, and even more if it is both severe and either continuous or frequent, is a very serious source of human suffering. But in addition, anxiety often has secondary effects which in some cases are a more important source of suffering than the anxiety that causes them. For example, there may be shyness, blushing, or stuttering. Shyness, besides being an embarrassment in itself, hampers the initiation and development of relationships and may seriously thwart a person's lovelife. Anxiety is also the usual cause of sexual inadequacy in men (particularly in the form of premature ejaculation), as well as in women, who are affected in degrees that vary from total absence of sexual response to the inability to have coital orgasms. It is also the usual cause of such antisocial habit patterns as kleptomania, exhibitionism, and fetishism, and is the underlying cause of most obsessive and compulsive neuroses. I have left to the last, for emphasis, the fact that anxiety is the basis of neurotic depression (see Chapter 15).

Some of the consequences of anxiety are illustrated in Table 1.1.

[3]For a discussion of the definition of anxiety, see pp. 38–46.

Table 1.1. Consequences of Neurotic Anxiety.

Physiological Event	Common Clinical Consequences
A. Autonomic Event	
1. General autonomic response predominantly sympathetic	Feeling of anxiety, panic, dread, etc.
	Feeling of depression
	Feeling of threat of losing control or of insanity
2. Hyperventilation	Dizziness
	Fainting attacks
	Headaches
	Paresthesia
	Tachycardia
3. Automatic discharges especially channeled into one organ system	Psychosomatic symptoms, e.g.:
	Neurodermatitis
	Asthma
	Vasomotor rhinitis
	Peptic ulceration and peptic ulcer syndrome
	Irritable bowel syndrome
	Frequency of micturition
	Dysmenorrhea
	Hypertension
	Migraine
B. Motor Event	
1. Prominent muscle tension, general or localized	Motor disturbance, e.g.:
	Tremor
	Stuttering
	"Fibrositic" pain (e.g., backache)
	Ocular dyskinesia
2. Motor avoidance conditioning (may be conditioned to be either simultaneous with anxiety or secondary to it)	Avoidance of anxiety-evoking stimuli
3. Inhibition of complex functioning	Impaired vocational function
	Impaired social interaction
	Impaired sexual function
4. Complex motor behavior in combination with anxiety or related to anxiety reduction	Compulsions
	Character neuroses, e.g.:
	Promiscuity
	Aimlessness
	Sexual deviations, e.g.:
	Homosexuality
	Pedophilia

(continued)

Table 1.1.   (*continued*)

	Exhibitionism
	Voyeurism

C. Cognitive Event	
1. Cognitive focus on anxiety responses	Hypomnesia due to "nonregistration" of external events
	Impairment of learning and performance
2. Inhibition of a segment of experience by intense anxiety	Circumscribed amnesia (Wolpe, 1958, p. 94)

2

Stimuli, Responses, Learning, and the Nature of Cognition

STIMULI AND RESPONSES

As far as the nervous system is concerned, all behavior, even the most complex—what Pavlov called "higher nervous activity"—consists of stimulus-response sequences. A "response" is a particular neural activity or a consequence thereof. A "stimulus" is the antecedent of a response. A sensory stimulus is an extrinsic source of energy that produces activation of an afferent nerve. Each member of a sequence of responses can be regarded as a stimulus in relation to the responses that follow it. A movement can thus be regarded both as a response to the nerve impulses that have led to it *and* to the sensory stimulus that triggered those impulses (for a fuller discussion, see Wolpe, 1958, pp. 3–6).

For the sake of clarity of exposition, one may depict behavioral sequences in terms of the stimulus-response sequences in single chains of neurons, but one must remember that even the simplest reflex involves the activation of thousands of neurons. Every sensory stimulus has a multiplicity of neuronal consequences that culminate in various combinations of motor, autonomic, and perceptual responses, and each response has stimulus features that produce further responses—response-produced stimuli (Hull, 1943). Figure 2.1 purports to be a diagramatic representation of the network of simultaneous and successive stimulus-response events that go on incessantly during our waking lives. An exteroceptive stimulus—whether a simple flash of light or the sight of a beautiful woman—elicits a complex of perceptual, autonomic, and motor responses. A motor response not only produces proprioceptive stimuli, but also changes one's relations to the world around one. The mere change of one's bodily position changes the visual field, and introduces new potentialities for action. Autonomic responses may also produce new

13

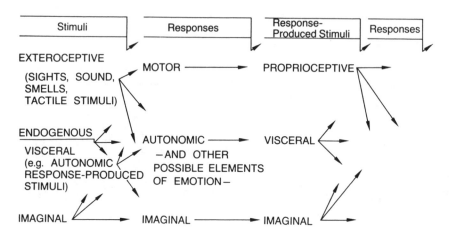

Fig. 2.1. A network of simultaneous and successive stimulus-response relations. (Courtesy of Graphic Communications, Eastern Pennsylvania Psychiatric Institute, Philadelphia.)

stimuli, such as a thumping heart or sweaty palms, whose very presence may affect subsequent behavior. The image of a stimulus object leads to further imagery, and autonomic and motor responses, all according to what has been connected to that image by previous learning. Responses that take place simultaneously may interact with each other and be mutually modified.

Despite the complexity, and granted that there is always a degree of variability, there is a general repeatability of the behavior of an organism to a particular stimulus situation within a certain range of physiological conditions. The empirical constancy of a stimulus-response relationship is what we call a habit. There are many kinds of habits. They may consist of simple movements in response to a stimulus, of dispositions (e.g., a set to listen or to look, or to imitate, or to solve problems) or of complex skills—to play tennis or chess, to perform eye surgery, to perform sonatas. Bandura (1969) has described some of the intricacies involved in the development of many social habits. Generally speaking, our habits favor our welfare; it is when certain of them are significantly disadvantageous that efforts to change them are made.

BASIC PRINCIPLES OF LEARNING AND UNLEARNING

Some readers will find it strange that this chapter deals with "learning" before dealing with cognition; but this is the correct sequence, because, as will be shown, cognition is based on perception, which is a product of learning.

The Role of Reinforcement[1]

Reinforcement is the process by which new responses are acquired and existing ones are strengthened. Pavlov's experiments systematically showed that the strengthening of a stimulus-response bond is related to the "reward," such as feeding, that follows the particular stimulus-response sequence (Pavlov, 1927). The amount of the reward and its timing in relation to the stimulus-response sequence are generally decisive in determining whether or not, and to what extent, functional bonding is established, so that the likelihood of the stimulus being followed by the response is increased (or decreased). This has been abundantly shown with respect to a great many motor habits and some autonomic habits (Pavlov, 1927; Skinner, 1953; Kimmel, 1967; Miller & DiCara, 1968). Conditioning of words, images, and ideas can also be facilitated by external rewards (Pavlov, 1955; Razran, 1971). External reinforcers are of many kinds; eating food and receiving tokens or praise are among the more commonplace.

There are a host of instances, however, in which learning occurs in the absence of any evident external source of reinforcement. One does not need an external reinforcement to learn from a dictionary that a podium is a high table used for lecturing, or that the German word for sky is *himmel*. The mere presentation of these pairs of symbols in juxtaposition may result in the one consistently evoking the other. Does this mean that reinforcement is absent in these instances? Actually, internal sources of reinforcement are apparently at work in such instances.

It has long been known (e.g., Dale, 1937; Lloyd, 1946; see also Eccles, 1975) that stimulus-response sequences depend on the particular functional connections that have been formed between neurons. A quarter of a century ago I showed how a simple neurological model facilitates and unifies the conceptualization of many instances and aspects of learning (Wolpe, 1949, 1950, 1952, 1952a, 1952b, 1953, & 1958, pp. 6–31). The model is based on the assumption that learning depends upon the development of conductivity (synaptic function) between neurons whose endings are in apposition—an assumption for which impressive evidence now exists (Culler, 1938; Olds et al., 1972; Olds, 1975; Woody & Engel, 1972). The processes involved in the development of synaptic function are just beginning to be defined (Huttunen, 1973; Olds, 1975; Young, 1973, 1975) (see pp. 25–26). One may legitimately use present knowledge as a framework for suggesting what *might* be happening at synapses during learning that accords with observations at the behavioral level.

To begin, we may ask how external reinforcement might influence events

---

[1]Much of the next 8 pages of this chapter has been modified from Wolpe (1978a).

at the synapse. As Hull (1943) observed, a feature common to all external reinforcements is that they reduce "drive"—states of central neural excitation that are due to the internal stimulation occasioned by states of bodily need, such as food or water deprivation, or to strong external stimulation, such as noxious stimulation. Central neural excitation beyond a certain level of strength results in overt motor activity. Reduction of this excitation (manifested typically by reduced motor activity) results from the reduction of the need-induced stimulation, or from the removal of the external stimulation. It seems that stimulation-reduction somehow produces a "cementing" effect at active synaptic points: real consummatory behaviors and brain rewards are both correlated with a cessation of firing in "a special kind of drive neuron" (Olds, 1975, pp. 386–387).

Given that external reinforcement is a source of drive reduction in much, *but not all,* learning, we must inquire whether other modes of drive reduction are at work when learning occurs in the absence of external reinforcement, as in the instances of cognitive learning given above. In fact, *every* response, even if it is only a perceptual response, must be correlated with some measure of central neural excitation, the cessation of which, as noted above, is drive reduction. Although of lower magnitude, this is an event of the same class as a drive reduction following the allayal of a need like hunger. The strength of cognitive learning will naturally be enhanced if there are concomitant arousals that are also reduced by the particular perception. For example, a greater measure of reinforcement of cognitive learning occurs when the perception allays curiosity (Berlyne, 1960). Learning is similarly enhanced to the extent that there are arousals secondary to the perceived stimuli, such as the aesthetic pleasure that the word "sky" might evoke (Berlyne, 1971). (Such pleasure is, of course, the subjective correlate of the neural excitations that are at the actual locus of learning.) These low-level reinforcements are the apparent basis of the fact that we are continuously learning throughout our waking lives, registering the sequences of our experience. In the mere fact of experience, there is drive, and the inevitability of drive reduction, and therefore of reinforcement.

While drive reduction at the behavioral level is perhaps the commonest correlate of reinforcement, drive increment may be one as well—as witness the experiments showing that raising the level of stimulation is reinforcing, for example, the addition of light (Hurwitz, 1956) or sweetness (Sheffield & Roby, 1950), and those showing reinforcement through hypothalamic stimulation (Olds, 1962, 1975). It is, thus, credible that in the formation of cognitive habits, reinforcement can be provided either by the cognition-arousing excitations, or by the reduction of these excitations, or both. Presumably, according to circumstances, either can lead to cessation of firing in Olds' (1975, p. 386) "special kind of drive neurons."

Unlearning

Unlearning has usually been studied in the context of the *procedure* called experimental extinction in which a learned response is repeatedly evoked without rewarding consequences. This results in the progressive weakening of the habit of response to that stimulus. For example, behavior in response to a bell that has been followed by food reinforcement becomes progressively weaker if its elicitations cease to be followed by food; and avoidance behavior elicited by a particular situation usually diminishes if it is not at least sometimes reinforced by a noxious event. Clearly, the performance of motor responses has consequences that weaken the operating habit when they are not countermanded by reinforcement. There is evidence of the involvement of two separate processes in the development of experimental extinction. One is the fatigue-associated reactive inhibition mechanism proposed by Hull (1943), for which I proposed a possible neurophysiological mechanism (Wolpe, 1958, p. 27). The second, which is probably more potent, is response competition—from "frustration" responses that compete with and inhibit the conditioned response (Gleitman, Nachmias, & Neisser, 1954; Amsel, 1962, 1972; see also Asratian, 1972).

Both of the foregoing mechanisms apply mainly to the extinction of unreinforced motor responses, which have been the special preserve of studies of operant conditioning. But many instances of unlearning cannot be accounted for in terms of nonreinforcement.

The extinction manifest in verbal forgetting is not the result of unreinforced evocations of the verbal response, but of the excitation of other verbal responses that compete with that response (see, for example, McGeogh, McKinney, & Peters, 1937). The process involved here is evidently reciprocal inhibition (Osgood, 1946, 1948), which is also the likely basis for the above-mentioned extinctive effects of response competition and the main basis for the deconditioning of anxiety (see Chapter 4). It is also worth noting in this context that in behavior therapy the elimination of undesirable behavior is very often achieved *without* the unreinforced elicitation of that behavior. For example, a woman's habitual shoplifting of 18 years' duration was revealed on behavior analysis to be based upon anxiety at surrendering anything of value; and the motor habit of shoplifting was lastingly eliminated by overcoming that anxiety response habit by systematic desensitization (p. 498). No elicitation of shoplifting behavior figured in the treatment. The shoplifting ceased because the anxiety that was its necessary antecedent was eliminated.

Either reactive inhibition or inhibition by a competing response (reciprocal inhibition) is the apparent basis of all of the above examples of response weakening. In relation to the elimination of unadaptive classically conditioned autonomic responses, it will be seen (p. 48ff) that other sources of response inhibition can also be the basis of deconditioning. It seems that inhibition of the response *is a necessary condition for the weakening of any habit,* just as excitation is necessary for conditioning it. Of course, it is the neural excitation that counts; peripheral inhibition of muscle responses does not prevent conditioning (Black, 1958).

COGNITION IN HUMAN BEHAVIOR

Our perception of things and situations in the world around us is undeniably a prime determinant of our actions. How we react to situations varies according to how we perceive them. In this sense, "thought" has a central role in human behavior. Nevertheless, thought obeys the same "mechanistic" laws as other behavior. There is no need for the invocation of an entity or a realm of activity independent of the mechanism-controlled organism. If there had been, Locke (1971) would have been right when he called the use of cognitions in behavior therapy nonbehavioristic. Not only the moment-to-moment content of thought but its very faculty is, as will be seen, comprehensible in behavioristic terms.

A necessary first step is to demonstrate the untenability of the popular belief that cognitive processes belong to a domain that is distinct from the physiological and beyond the sway of biological rules. What makes this demonstration important is the fact that the belief is shared by influential people in the behavioral field—some so-called "cognitive behaviorists" (e.g., Bandura, 1974; Beck, 1976; Mahoney, 1977; Meichenbaum, 1975). This separate domain, which they believe makes man "partially free" (Bandura, 1974, p. 867) from physical causality is what Ryle (1949) called "the Ghost in the Machine."

Ryle showed that the "ghost" is a product of the error of regarding different aspects of the same phenomenon as different entities. The dogma of the ghost in the machine maintains "that there occur physical processes and mental processes; that there are mechanical causes of corporeal movements and mental causes of corporeal movements" (p. 22). Nobody faces, let alone solves, the problem of explaining how a nonmaterial process can have effects on nerve tissue. No such problem exists when the physical and the mental are both seen as functions of the nervous system.

The following passages from Ryle's book crystallize some of the key points of his brilliant analysis of the relationship between the physical and the mental:

> When a person talks sense aloud, ties knots, feints or sculpts, the actions which we witness are themselves the things which he is intelligently doing. He is bodily

active and he is mentally active, but he is not being synchronously active in two different "places", or with two different "engines". There is the one kind of activity, but it is one susceptible of and requiring more than one kind of explanatory description. [Ryle, 1949, p. 50]

If we take the example of talking aloud, the need for more than one kind of explanatory description is plain. There may be no physical or physiological difference between one man gabbling and another talking sense, but the logical differences are enormous. It is not sounds, but the sequences of meaning that matter.

I discover that there are other minds in understanding what other people say and do. In making sense of what you say, in appreciating your jokes, in unmasking your chess-strategems, in following your arguments and in hearing you pick holes in my arguments, I am not inferring to the workings of your mind, I am following them. Of course, I am not merely hearing the noises that you make, or merely seeing the movements that you perform. I am understanding what I hear and see. But this understanding is not inferring to occult causes. It is appreciating how the operations are conducted. (Pp. 60–61]

A person's knowledge of the world consists entirely of private events. His first response to an object is his perception of it, and that is a private event. Images evoked in the absence of objects—for example, the architectural image evoked by the word "Parthenon"—are conditioned perceptions, in line with what Skinner called "conditioned seeing" (1953, p. 266). Together, immediate perceptions and conditioned perceptions make up cognition.

The Ontology of Cognition[2]

Since perceptions are the basis of cognitions, the ontology of cognition is at bottom the ontology of perception. This matter has received very little notice from psychologists, despite the long availability of a brilliant monograph on the subject by James G. Taylor (1962). He was the first to realize fully that perception is not just vision. Take a simple object like a teacup. It does not matter what aspect is held up before you, nor at what angle or distance—you always recognize it as a teacup. Clearly, from the different angles and distances, the stimuli impinging upon your retina are different, just as photographs from the various positions would be different. Yet you see the object as "the same." How does it happen? Why is there perceptual constancy? We take for granted what really should not be taken for granted.

Most psychologists regard perception as a kind of photographic process,

---

[2]This section has been adapted from Wolpe (1981c).

consisting of the following sequence of events: light rays from the seen object produce an inverted image of the object in the retina, where it arouses neural impulses that eventually excite the occipital cortex. That structure is then supposed to generate, right-way up, an image of the object. But how can neural activity generate imagery? It is easy to imagine how a nerve cell could secrete acetylcholine but not how it might secrete images. In any case, the above sequence of events does not explain why we see this object that is presented to us in many different ways as "the same" teacup.

Taylor showed that visual perception is the outcome of a very special sequence of events in the human organism—a complex sequence of conditionings. This is conveniently illustrated in the case of a patient who has suffered from bilateral cataracts and has had his crystalline lens removed. While light can now penetrate to the retina, the images are out of focus, and the pateint must be fitted with correcting lenses. When the patient looks through his eyeglasses for the first time, he will see objects magnified by 30 percent and will find that straight lines in the periphery of the visual field are curved. If he is not discouraged and makes the best of this peculiar visual world, the spherical aberration will disappear after a time. The true relationships of positions and the actual shapes of objects emerge, and ultimately the enlarged world contracts to its true size. Obviously, it is impossible to explain this change if you accept the theory that certain images going into the retina are reproduced in a faithful manner by the occipital cortex.

Certain experimental findings have bearing on this point. The first report was by Stratton (1897). He had a subject cover one eye and wear on the other a prism that reverses left and right. The effect of a visual world that is distorted in this way is to inhibit general mobility. If the subject does try to get around and adapt himself, things improve within about two weeks. Some time later, a remarkable transformation occurs: *the visual world rights itself even though the subject is still wearing the prism!* Here, again, it is quite futile to look for an explanation in the standard theory. But the fact that the correction occurs can be easily explained as a function of conditioning. For example, if I had a prism in front of my left eye, I would see the watch that is to my right on the table on the opposite side. If I wanted to pick it up I would reach out to the left, and it would not be there. I would move my arm around and eventually make contact with it. There is a neural coordination between the image I see and the action I take. Seeing the object on one side is reinforced by the successful contact made by a movement to the other side. If this happens again and again, such movement occurs with increasing readiness, and eventually the visual world changes, in conformity. This indicates that how we see things is a function of the success of our movements; it is a function of reinforcement, a function of conditioning.

An experiment which further illustrates the point was done by one of Taylor's collaborators. This man wore reversing prisms constantly for about two weeks. He walked about and did more and more things successfully, including riding a bicycle. He then started to ride the bicycle on alternate days with and without the prisms. After a few days he could ride the bicycle and see the world correctly, with *or* without the prisms. Obviously, there were still some differences (such as prismatic aberrations) that cued the different response systems.

Taylor started from the proposition that when a child is born it has practically no conditioned responses, only unconditioned responses. Conditioning occurs later. Taylor postulated that, at first, when the child can only lie on his back, he has a rather undifferentiated visual field and reaches out with his arms in an aimless fashion. Let us say that there is a horizontal bar in front of him. If, in his reaching out he by chance touches the horizontal bar while looking in its direction, he makes a grasping response to whose association with the visual stimuli the tactile sensations provide an element of reward or reinforcement. The movement thus becomes conditioned to the visual input of that moment. This process is repeated in numerous contexts. Besides the conditioning of the central visual stimulus, there is also some degree of conditioning of peripheral stimuli on each occasion. This means an involvement of the visual world within the limits of the visual field.

When the child is able to sit, objects which were previously out of reach become accessible to him. There is thus an extension of the world of potential conditioning. A still more dramatic expansion of the perceptual world occurs with the inception of locomotion. When the child crawls and later walks, he acquires responses to directions and distances of objects that were previously far beyond his reach. The most important visual effects of locomotion are related to the fact that the retinal image of an object changes as a continuous function of its distance. The visual angle subtended by a fixed object increases with positive acceleration as the child approaches it. During the approach, there are regularly occurring cycles of proprioceptive stimulation that are related to the stepwise character of locomotion inherent in both crawling and walking. The succession of locomotive cycles carves the continuously changing retinal stimulation into temporal slabs, each of which has a greater expanse than its predecessor had.

A whole crop of perceptual constancies emerges. Although there is a one-to-many relationship between the position of an external object (the teacup) and the patterns of stimulation to which it may give rise, conditioning establishes a one-to-one correspondence between the position of the object and the terminal response conditioned to it—the grasping of the object. Whenever there is a one-to-one correspondence between some property of objects and a terminal response appropriate to that property, a perceptual constancy will be found. To the neural process underlying this, Taylor applied the once popular term, "engram." The size of a stable object, such as a cup or a bowl, is such that the movements required to grasp it always require the same separation of the fingers or hands. The resulting tactile and proprioceptive constancies are the basis for the establishment of the engram.

The foregoing conveys only a soupçon of Taylor's profoundly important research. The interested reader should consult the original monograph (Taylor, 1962).

An interesting phenomenon that was recently brought to light seems at first glance to suggest that perceptual organization is developmentally established. It has been found that children around the age of two months show what appear to be precocious responses. They seem to recognize people, to smile, and to reach for objects. This behavior, however, fades out in a matter of weeks. It does not seem unreasonable to suggest that it has a phylogenetic explanation—a kind of recapitulation of the complex instinctual behavior of lower animals. After a few weeks, apparently, the responsible nerve structures atrophy or lose their function. Only much later, at the age of six to nine months, does one see the beginnings of learned perceptual behavior (Bower, 1976, 1977).

Our knowledge of the world is a function of the activation of engrams that are the product of repeated occasions of learning in varied spatial relations to objects. The engrams are complex integrated neural-response systems, arousable by systematically variable combinations of sensory inputs, providing, within specifiable limits, constancy of perception despite variations in sensory stimulation. Since there are constancies with regard to all parts of all perceptual fields, consciousness of the environment involves a simultaneous activation of engrams related to all objects present at a given time.

The learning process can connect any engram to any other in such a way that activation of the first leads to activation of the second. Imagery without perception is thus elicited; this is the basis of thinking.

3

The Causation of Neuroses

DEFINITION OF ANXIETY

In Chapter 1, neuroses were defined as persistent unadaptive learned habits whose foremost feature is anxiety. The word "anxiety" (for which "fear" is a synonym) must now be defined. I shall present the case for my continuing adherence to its operational definition as *the individual organism's characteristic pattern of autonomic responses to noxious stimulation* (Wolpe, 1958). A noxious stimulus is a painful stimulus, but it can be objectively characterized as a stimulus with physical effects that tend to evoke escape behavior.

A definition of anxiety with objective referents lends itself to practical application and provides a firm base for discourse. It is not affected by the presence or absence of motor and conscious correlates or their synchrony or desynchrony with the automatic events. A clear and unequivocal definition is in every way preferable to the prevailing fashion of conceiving of anxiety as a variable "entity," loosely tied to antecedents and made up of shifting autonomic, motor, and cognitive components. The definition has the additional virtue of allowing for the fact that the profile of autonomic responses to noxious stimulation varies from person to person, but is generally constant for the individual (Engel, 1972; Lacey, Bateman, & Van Lehn, 1953; Lacey & Lacey, 1958).

The contrary position has been clearly articulated by Lang (1970) and by Rachman (1974, 1978). Because the autonomic responses of fear are only imperfectly related to cognitive and motor aspects, Lang opines that "fear is not some hard phenomenal lump that lives inside people, that we may palpate more or less successfully."

One consideration that Rachman brings to bear is that despite marked behavioral improvements, such as a claustrophobic patient who becomes able to travel in underground trains, patients sometimes deny that they have benefited from treatment. Conversely, when the physiological reactions observed during the real and symbolic presentation of a feared object have diminished after treatment, some patients still complain of excessive fear (see Hersen, 1973). To the same effect is Fenz and Epstein's (1967) report of a lack of correspondence between the physiological measures of emotional distress and the subjective reports of fear of veteran parachute jumpers—in striking contrast to novices in whom the subjective and psychophysiological reactions correspond.

In response to the foregoing, a number of points can be made. First, on the basis of therapist demand or social expectation (Geer, 1965; Bernstein, 1973), patients will often do things they would otherwise refuse to do, but their experience of fear (the patient's central complaint) may be undiminished, as also are their psychophysiological fear responses. Second, it is an error to assume that the autonomic responses that are usually measured—heart rate, skin conductance, and respiration—are the totality of the autonomic nervous system's response of fear.

Besides a wide variety of peripheral vascular and muscle tension responses (see Martin, 1961; Lader, 1975), subjective anxiety has been correlated with elevations of blood pressure (Hall, 1927; Malmo & Shagass, 1952), alterations in gastrointestinal activity (Rubin et al., 1962), pupillary responses (Rubin, 1964), and characteristic changes in evoked electroencephalograph potentials (Shagass & Schwartz, 1963; Shagass, Roemer, Straumanis, & Amadeo, 1978). There are also variations of "autonomic balance" (Eppinger & Hess, 1915; Wenger, 1966), and an extensive array of endocrine changes (see Lader, 1976). The implication of this is that unless one has an unusually comprehensive knowledge of the individual's autonomic response profile, one cannot speak of the experienced emotion being present *in the absence* of autonomic activation. Like others involved in clinical psychophysiology, I have occasionally found subjects who either had no changes in skin resistance or no cardiovascular changes in response to stimuli that evoked strong subjective anxiety. There are probably subjects who respond in neither modality. It is difficult to believe that their feelings of anxiety have no physiological correlates.

With regard to Fenz and Epstein's (1967) study, it is likely that different people mean different things by the "experience of fear." It may be that the experienced parachute jumpers did not feel fear in the same way as the novices: to some extent, they may have been reporting their *evaluation* of the danger involved in the situation of jumping. It seems relevant that they were reported as seeming to enjoy the activity, and that "the absolute magnitude of fear of the experienced parachutists at no point approaches the magnitude of the fear experienced by novice parachutists shortly before a jump." In a somewhat similar way, a person who has a phobia may avoid the situation and report that he does so because he is "afraid," when what is actually happening is that he is anticipating the certainty of being afraid were he to enter the situation, but not actually *feeling* any fear.

On the strength of these rebuttals, there is good reason to maintain the physiological definition of fear given above. Rachman himself (1974, p. 20) concedes that a very substantial degree of cohesion does exist, and this despite the aforementioned limitations of conventional psychophysiological monitoring. Self-reports of fear correlate well with each other, and moderately well with the ratings of fear made by external judges and with the avoidance behavior observed in the fear test. Self-reports also correlate modestly with physiological indices of fear, and the usual physiological indices correlate modestly with each other. Sartory, Rachman, and Gray (1977) have obtained some indications that the correlation is greater at high than at low arousal, but according to Lande (1982), this is not invariably so.

HOW FEAR IS LEARNED

It is important to note that our definition of fear is based on an unconditioned response. The subject is usually not very aware of the autonomic responses that result from noxious stimulation because the simultaneous pain experience has overriding sensory intensity. Other unconditioned stimuli that also elicit anxiety are sudden loss of support (Watson, 1970, p. 153), very strong auditory stimulation (Watson, 1970, p. 152), and conflict (Fonberg, 1956). In addition, children show fear of unfamiliar faces when they first become able to distinguish them from their parents' faces, perhaps as a function of dissonance.

"Neutral" stimuli making impact on the person when fear is evoked may become conditioned to evoke fear. For example, if a mother's voice takes on a certain tone whenever she slaps her child, the fear stimulated by the slap will come to be conditioned to that tone of her voice. This conditioning can theoretically occur with any kind of contiguous stimulation—sounds, things, people, words, ideas—anything seen or heard or felt, anything perceived by the person. Then, by second- or multiple-order conditioning, fear may spread from one stimulus to another.

Stimuli are not, however, all equally susceptible to being conditioned to fear. Seligman (1971), building upon his important exposition (1970) of the limited generality of the laws of learning, put forth the proposition that only certain stimuli such as darkness and furry objects are readily connected to fear responses. He called these "prepared" stimuli, and suggested that their special liability to fear conditioning has a phylogenetic basis. His supposition is that such stimuli have had some kind of special significance in the evolutionary history of mankind. DeSilva, Rachman, and Seligman (1977) carried out a retrospective study of 69 phobic subjects and found that in the great majority of them the stimuli conformed to certain criteria of "preparedness." Öhman, Erixon and Löfberg (1975) exposed normal human subjects to pictures of supposedly "prepared" phobic stimuli (human faces) and supposedly neutral objects (houses) as conditioned stimuli in a classical conditioning experiment with shock as the unconditioned stimulus and skin conductance responses as the dependent variable. Equal acquisition of conditioning was shown to both sets of stimuli. During extinction, however, there were lasting conditioning effects only in the case of the "prepared" stimuli.

Clinical experience certainly supports the supposition that enclosed spaces, animals, insects, and darkness are much more likely to be phobic stimuli than are houses, flowers, clouds, and electric outlets; but a phylogenetic explanation cannot be taken for granted. Another possibility is, quite simply, that objects like flowers and houses in the normal course of life become strongly conditioned to pleasant and comforting responses, and that this "inoculates" them against anxiety conditioning. In contrast, there is nothing of this congeniality about most of the common sources of fear; and there is often, in relation to them, a history of unpleasant or fear-containing messages, from folklore, fairy tales, or the witnessed fearful behavior of other people. As Öhman, Eriksson, and Olofsson (1975, p. 626) put it, "The prepardness concept leaves us with the problem of determining the genetical or experiential basis for the preparedness. . . . It is only through knowledge of the background factors that we can explain this behavior."

There is no evidence that human beings have any purely developmentally based responses complex enough to be called "instinctive" (Gesell, 1946). The more complex the organization of an animal's nervous system, the less maturation has to do with complex stimulus response sequences (Carmichael, 1946). To take an example: whereas male rats raised from birth in isolation are able to copulate at their first encounter with a receptive female (Beach, 1942), chimpanzees have to learn how to copulate (Yerkes, 1939). The only example of complex human behavior that seems to be phylogenetically determined is the transitory perceptual responses of infants referred to above (p. 22). The absence of evidence of any lasting "instinctive" behavior in humans also renders implausible the suggestion of Marks (1969, p. 13ff) that some human fears are innately determined, regardless of the findings in chimpanzees or other animals.

In the above example about a child who becomes fearful of a certain sound in his mother's voice, the fear is the result of classical conditioning based on the contiguity of that sound and the autonomic accompaniments of pain. There are many incidents in the life of a growing child that result in the classical conditioning of fear responses. Approaching the stove becomes a conditioned stimulus to anxiety after the hand has been burnt; immersion in water becomes fearful after the child has inhaled some of it after falling into a pool; fears of thorny bushes or of stinging insects may follow the experience of being pricked or stung. We have already noted how Watson and Rayner (1920) deliberately induced in Little Albert a fear of a white rat and related stimuli—rabbits, fur, and fluffy masses of cotton—by repeatedly associating his touching of a rat with a frighteningly loud noise. As language develops, warnings or threatening statements become additional stimuli to which classical conditioning can occur.

Once a repertoire of conditioned fear responses exists in the young child, there is a basis for further spread of fears through second-order classical conditioning. This repertoire is also the foundation for the spread of fears in a new way—*on the basis of information*—a way that, as Rachman (1977) commented, "has been strangely overlooked—despite the fact that it is obvious, or perhaps because it is too obvious." A person fears lightning, or contaminated food, or being driven by a reckless driver, or having a pistol pointed at him, not because of classical conditioning but because of information. This is facilitated because the use of language results in the association of fears in general with ideas of "danger."

THE ETIOLOGY OF NEUROTIC FEARS

Much confusion about the etiology of neurotic fear emanates from the assumption that it is quite different from that of normal fear. As I shall show below, however, there is in fact no basic difference. Just as some normal (i.e., appropriate) fears develop on the basis of classical conditioning and some on the basis of information (cognitive learning), the same is true of neurotic fears. What differentiates normal and neurotic fears is the character of the stimulus situation to which the conditioning has occurred. If that stimulus situation is objectively either a source of danger or a sign of danger, the fear is appropriate or "adaptive"; if it is neither, the fear is neurotic.

Classically Conditioned Neurotic Fears

The classical conditioning of human neurotic fears may originate from a single occurrence (single-trial learning) or may be progressively built up in the course of a series of related events. The classic example of single-trial fear conditioning is the war neurosis. A soldier who is driven frantic by the carnage around him develops conditioned anxiety to surrounding stimuli. If in the causal situation a particular stimulus, such as the sound of machine-gun fire, is particularly prominent, that sound or anything that resembles it, such as a motorcycle at full throttle, will subsequently evoke anxiety. Other stimuli—the sight of blood, the sound of screaming, the pouring rain—would be less strongly connected with fear if they happened not to be at the center of attention at the critical time. The specificity of the reactions to the most prominent features of the individual's battle experience is well brought out by Grinker and Spiegel (1945, p. 16):

> Those who have withstood prolonged dive bombing and strafing from the air are intolerant of all aircraft, and in the worst cases, of the sound of any motor. The knowledge that all aircraft in the vicinity of the hospital are friendly planes is of no comfort. The patients react automatically to any plane overhead with fear and suspicion and seem to be continually listening for the sound of an airplane engine. On the other hand, those who have experienced adequate support from the air on the part of their own planes, but who have been subjected to heavy fire from artillery and mortar shells, have no fear of planes; however, they cannot tolerate sudden loud noises, such as the dropping of a dish or the banging of a door. In those who have had mortar shells land very close by and have seen the flash of the explosion and felt the concussion, almost any sudden stimulus will produce the fear and startle reaction. This is especially true of sudden flashes of light, such as are made by the striking of a match or a cigarette lighter, or by the opening of the blinds in such a way as to flood the room suddenly with light.

We may note that the anxiety is *automatically* aroused by the stimuli: no cognitive error is involved. The man does not for a moment believe that danger threatens in the sound of an engine or the sight of a friendly plane. Civilian examples of single-trial fear conditioning are also common.

Case 1

A 34-year-old man had a severe fear of being in an automobile. This had started four years previously when his car had been struck from behind while he was waiting for a red light to change. He had been thrust forward so that his head, striking the windshield, had sustained a small laceration. He had not lost consciousness, but a surge of panic had swept over him, brought on by the thought, "I am about to die." The fear became connected to the car's interior and spread to all car interiors. During these four years he had been unable to enter a car without great anxiety. Driving was out of the question. That fear was entirely due to classical autonomic conditioning. He had no expectation of danger when he sat in a motionless car.

Case 2

A 40-year-old businessman had been an enthusiastic spelologist until an incident seven years previously. During an expedition to a labyrinth of caves, while he was deep underground and separated from his companions, a gust of wind blew out his light. He had no matches and in the utter darkness was beset by a feeling of being entombed there forever. Terror engulfed him. He shouted for help, uncertain that he could be heard. When his companions arrived a few minutes later, his fear receded somewhat, but only subsided fully when he reached the open air. From that time onwards he had a fear not only of caves, but also of any situation in which he felt confined: traveling in an airplane, driving through a tunnel, riding on a train, and even lying in a tightly made bed.

Case 3

Agoraphobia in the male is relatively uncommon. Mr. S. was an industrial engineer, aged 52, who when first seen, had been severely afflicted with this condition for 16 years. He was almost completely unable to venture out of his apartment alone. He had adjusted to the problem in a way by moving to an apartment one block from his office, but he could not walk even that distance without becoming very anxious. His work naturally was seriously disrupted.

Twenty years earlier his wife, whom he had dearly loved, had died of lung cancer, and he had watched her literally suffocate to death. Gradually he had recovered from the trauma of that experience, and after a year had begun to form relationships with women. Three years later, his trouble started. At that time he had a steady girlfriend who would often spend the night at his apartment. One night, after an orgasm, she began breathing with difficulty and making movements that reminded him of his wife gasping when she was dying. Becoming extremely distressed, he told the woman to dress quickly so that he could take her home. In the car, Mr. S. began to notice that he was having dyspnea, which worsened to the point that he felt he was choking; and then he panicked. He dropped the woman at a taxi stand and drove home alone. With that single experience, his fear of being away from home began, and later generated a group of satellite fears, including fears of losing his mental stability, of meetings and social gatherings, of unfamiliar places, of being alone in a car, and of dead animals. (Mr. S.'s treatment is described in Chapter 11 as Case 39.)

Case 4

A 47-year-old housewife, Mrs. A., came for treatment for an extremely distressing fear of mice and rats. She had always been mildly fearful of them, but, in her opinion, "no more than many other women." Seven years previously, when her husband had retired, they moved from the city to a spacious old house in the country. One evening, while she sat in the living room with her husband and parents, a mouse appeared and walked slowly along the wall. She became extremely panicky and screamed loudly, and the mouse disappeared. From that moment she was extremely fearful of these creatures and constantly anticipated their appearance in every strange place. She dealt with the problem in her own home by having it fumigated monthly by a pest control company.

From a pilot study whose results are summarized in Table 3.2 (p. 36) it appears that multiple-event causation of classically conditioned fear is considerably less common than single-event causation. The following are examples of the former. In each case the initial incident resulted in only a moderate degree of anxiety conditioning.

Case 5

Miss S., a woman of 30, experienced a partial blackout while driving on an expressway, and guided her car on to the soft shoulder of the road, where she stopped. She felt dizzy and faint for about 30 minutes and also very anxious. She resumed driving when the dizziness and faintness stopped, but the anxiety continued. It gradually subsided during the half-hour drive home.

She avoided driving for a week, but after that she was nervous alone in the car or when she remembered blacking out or had any sensations that were at all suggestive of faintness when driving under any circumstances. The anxiety level was increased by two additional actual blackouts. These were later found to be due to paroxysmal tachycardia.

Case 6

A registered nurse of 35, Mrs. G. came for treatment of a severe fear of public speaking even to very small groups. This was a serious disability because she had to give reports to groups of doctors and nurses at the hospital where she worked.

A mild version of this fear had begun when she was nine years old. Her father, who was the principal of her elementary school, would often put her on display in front of adults to read or recite poetry. On one occasion, while reciting in front of the school board, she forgot her lines. She became confused, recited the wrong lines, and was greatly embarrassed, but managed to collect herself and finish the recitation. After this, she was always afraid of such performances, but did speak in front of the class. The fear was not severe enough to raise the question of therapy.

About a year before I saw her, Mrs. G. had accompanied her husband, a business executive, to a convention in a distant city. She had gone reluctantly, fearing his prominence would lead at some point to her being the center of attention. Despite his assurance that this would not happen, it did, and an enormous amount of anxiety was aroused in her. She was very much more fearful of any public performance and also afraid to speak to strangers or distant acquaintances on the telephone.

It is important to realize that anxiety need not be conditioned to an *external* stimulus.

Case 7

In a physician whose sexual interest and arousability had always been confined to women, a fear of homosexuality was conditioned in the following way. While reading a description of homosexual behavior in a novel, he became aware of a spontaneous erection (which quite frequently happened without any discernible relation to thoughts or circumstances). However, the thought now crossed his mind, "Does the fact that this is happening right now mean that I am unconsciously homosexual?" This thought, based on psychoanalytic "knowledge," aroused great anxiety, and he thereafter had instant anxiety when seeing a homosexual or reading about one, or when making physical contact with *any* male, as when sitting beside one on a bus or plane, even though except for that one fleeting thought he never believed he was homosexual.

Cognitively Based Neurotic Fears

As stated above, many of our *nonneurotic fears*—that is, those that relate to real threats—are cognitively based; they have been acquired through information. *Misinformation* can also bring about fears that are as powerful and enduring as those based on truth. A man may fear masturbation because he has been led to believe that it will injure his health, and a woman may be afraid of sexual arousal because her mother has told her it is bestial or because she has gathered from religious teaching that to be excited by any man who is not actually her husband is a "mortal sin." People may fear worms, flying insects, doctors, or hospitals because they have observed a parent consistently show fear to these things. A woman I once encountered who had fears of many kinds of insects reported that she had two sisters with similar collections of fears. All of these had originated from seeing their mother go distraught every time she saw an insect.

Some wrong beliefs are based on erroneous inferences, rather than on wrong messages. A person who has a bizarre and unusual sensation may infer that his personality is disintegrating.

Case 8

A 29-year-old married woman was afraid to venture out alone because she believed that her frequent attacks of dizziness and tingling of the hands were early signs of "going crazy." Because she had an aunt who had been in a mental hospital and two cousins who were "flaky," she had concluded that she was predisposed by heredity to mental instability. After I demonstrated to her that her dizziness and tingling were due to hyperventilation and then strongly assured her that there was no possibility of her going crazy, she rapidly lost her fearfulness. After seven sessions, she was able to go out comfortably on her own anywhere she wished. She was still well a year later.

Not infrequently, the very contiguity of the feared object to the cognitively aroused fear of it leads to the development of classical conditioning of fear of the object. When that happens, adequate treatment requires *both* cognitive correction and emotional reconditioning.

Case 9

A 31-year-old computer operator, who had for some time had intermittent showers of sparsely distributed rosy papules on her skin, one day chanced to read in a popular magazine that lupus erythematosus is characterized by rashes. She concluded that she had that dread disease and became profoundly anxious. After some months of ineffective insight therapy, she was sent to a dermatologist who thoroughly convinced her that she did not have that illness. Nevertheless, whenever she actually saw some papules she still automatically had an anxiety response, which necessitated systematic desensitization.

Fear also spreads by classical conditioning from one inappropriate stimulus to another. For example, a woman with a fear of crowds would go to the movies only in the daytime when few people were present. One afternoon the moviehouse suddenly filled with students, which sent her into a panic. After that she was afraid not only of crowds, but of moviehouses, of restaurants, and of churches, in fact, of any public building, even when it was empty.

Sometimes a patient's fear is found to have spread in several different ways.

Case 10

Mrs. B., an excessively submissive young woman, often endured harsh criticism from her husband, and began to dread his return from work. She tried to deal with the problem by working to improve herself so that she might silence his criticisms. Still, she became gradually more tense when the time approached for him to arrive home, and became increasingly aware of physical symptoms—rapid heartbeat, clammy hands, faintness, and lightheadedness. She did not relate these to her husband, but was frightened by them and consulted her physician. When the medication he prescribed failed to diminish her symptoms she decided that she "must be falling apart."

After about four months on the downward slope, when her husband was about to depart on a week-long business trip, Mrs. B. went to stay with her parents. Towards the end of the week, she visited a friend who was having a "nervous breakdown." Her friend looked exhausted and haggard, and Mrs. B. asked herself whether the same thing was happening to her. Dwelling on this idea, she became intensely anxious for the last two days at her parents' house. When she returned home, she immediately began to improve. But she could not visit her parents' house again because it had become a conditioned trigger to her intense fear.

Mrs. B.'s fear had spread in the following steps: first, the fear of her husband's criticisms gave rise to symptoms that included lightheadedness. These symptoms were a further source of fear because they suggested some strange illness. This new kind of fear was greatly intensified when she visited her friend, since she then connected her lightheadedness with the idea of having a "nervous breakdown," which it is quite reasonable to fear. Her preoccupation with this idea caused a continuous high level of anxiety while she was at her parents' house, so that she was afterward afraid of visiting them.

THE DISTRIBUTION OF CLASSICALLY CONDITIONED AND COGNITIVELY BASED FEARS

In order to get some idea of the distribution of classically conditioned and cognitively based neurotic fears, I asked an assistant to extract from my files the first 40 cases whose central complaint was unadaptive fear. In each case, I first decided whether the fear was automatically conditioned or cognitively based, and then whether its origin could be traced to single or multiple events. Twenty-six fears were found to be autonomically conditioned and 16 cognitively based. Both bases were manifest in two cases. The mean age of the subjects was 33.9 years; and the mean age at onset in those in whom it could be dated was 22.3 years. The data are presented in Table 3.1 and summarized in Table 3.2. As far as possible, similar cases are grouped together in Table 3.1.

It is worth noting that only two cases had to be discarded because the precise circumstances of precipitation could not be determined. This is in keeping with the findings of Symonds (1943) on war neuroses (see p. 36) and Ost and Hugdahl (1981), and of Lautch (1971) that every one of 34 cases with dental phobia reported having had a traumatic dental experience, such as fear from suffocation from an anesthetic mask, and it is in contrast to the inability of Marks (1969) to identify precipitating experiences.

Predisposing Factors

When a number of people are exposed to the same anxiety-arousing conditions, only some of them develop neurotic anxiety reactions. Clearly, then, individual differences are of the greatest importance in the etiology of neuroses. Yet, little research has been devoted to their elucidation. The most notable quantitative study is still that of Symonds (1943) on a consecutive series of 2,000 cases of war neuroses in Royal Air Force personnel. He found a his-

Table 3.1. Breakdown of 40 Cases of Unadaptive Fear.

Nature of fear	Present age	Age at onset	Fear basis		Single-event causation	Multiple-event causation
			Autonomically conditioned	Cognitively based		
1 Death	31	7		X		X
2 Death	43	39		X	X	
3 Death	10	8	X		X	
4 Death	14	8	X		X	X
5 Death	46	3	X	X		X
6 Death and loss of control	39	11	X		X	
7 Being alone	30	29	X		X	
8 Being alone	31	Childhood	X			X
9 Being alone	29	23	X		X	
10 Being alone	26	20	X		X	
11 Being alone	47	24	X			X
12 Driving	45	41	X		X	
13 Driving	36	34		X	X	
14 Driving	41	30		X	X	
15 Driving	25	16		X	(Undetermined)	X
16 Public speaking	28	25	X		X	
17 Public speaking	39	21	X		X	
18 Public speaking	28	18		X	X	

34

Item						
19 Related to health	36	22	X	X		
20 Self destruction	42	31		X	X	
21 Harming self	26	12			X	X
22 Blacking out	48	39	X	X		
23 Own blood	23	18	X	X		
24 People	31	11	X			X
25 Strange men	25	25	X	X		
26 Dentists	25	12	X	X		
27 Eye contact	30	8	X	X		
28 Automobiles	39	37	X	X		
29 Accidents	49	44	X	X		
30 Travel	36	25	X	X		
31 Agoraphobia	28	14	X	X		
32 Going to town	36	32	X		X	X
33 Flying	49	39	X	X	X	
34 Acrophobia	34	4	X	X		
35 Snakes	24	16	X		X	X
36 Mice	45	6	X	X		
37 Storms	58	Childhood	X		X	X
38 Examinations	22	20		X	X	(Undetermined)
39 Sexual inadequacy	25	20		X	X	X
40 War guilt	35	26	X	X	X	

Table 3.2.   Analysis of Bases of 40 Neurotic Fears. The Presence of Both Autonomic and Cognitive Bases in Two Cases Brings the Total to 42.

Autonomic conditioning		Cognitively based		
Single-event causation	Multiple-event causation	Single-event causation	Multiple-event causation	Undetermined
21	5	7	7	2
Total 26		Total 16		

tory of stress in 99 percent of the cases, and a reciprocal relationship between the degree of stress needed to precipitate the neurosis and the degree of predisposition in the form of preexisting emotional sensitivity.

A few specific facts are known which point to factors that may determine predisposition. First, people differ greatly in innate emotional liability. Shirley (1933) found marked differences of this character in very young infants. It is to be expected that an individual who is emotionally highly sensitive would have a greater intensity of anxiety aroused in him under given conditions than an individual who is relatively phlegmatic.

Second, preconditioning can increase sensitivity. Preexisting mild anxiety reactions to particular stimuli may have the result that the presence of these stimuli in the context of high arousal of anxiety will end up in a higher level of anxiety conditioning than would otherwise have eventuated. This is exemplified in Case 6 above. That anxiety which is unrelated to the particular stress may also predispose is indicated by Symonds' observations.

A third important factor seems to be the presence of factors that inhibit the arousal of *severe* anxiety by potentially stressful experiences. For example, children who are exposed to an alarming event, such as an air raid, are much less liable to be sensitized to such situations if they are with parents who behave calmly (John, 1941). It might be expected that a person who has previously received such reassurance from his elders will not be taken by surprise by later stress, but this remains to be investigated.

Information or a lack of information is a fourth factor. A large number of people who experience bizarre sensations in connection with the onset of a neurosis develop secondary fears that they interpret to mean they are "falling apart" or going crazy; these secondary fears are frequently much more severe and disabling than the original ones that caused them. To an important extent, lack of information or wrong information contributes to this. For example, physiological events such as paroxysmal tachycardia are a common basis for the conditioning of anxiety neuroses, notably agoraphobia. This is unlikely to happen in a physician because he understands the cause of the sensations and takes the tachycardia to be the innocuous event that it is. It is unfortunate that much more often than not, when people consult physicians for explanations of their strange feelings, they get very little help. Many patients recount that "he did not know what I was talking about," and this made the feelings more ominous.

It is quite likely that physiological factors may also have a role in predisposing people to neurotic conditioning—fatigue, infections, drugs, and special conditions of consciousness such as hypnagogic states. Properly designed studies of the relevance of such factors, as indeed of all the other factors mentioned above, are very much to be desired.

In the case of cognitively based fears, lack of information has obviously an even more crucial role. It is this that makes possible the acceptance of the anxiety-instilling misinformation.

THE EXPERIMENTAL MODEL
OF NEUROTIC ANXIETY

Among the most favorable areas for research in human illness are those in which the same illness occurs in small animals. We who are concerned with the causes and cures of neuroses are among the lucky researchers, for it is possible to induce states of fearful reactivity in animals that are indistinguishable from those of humans when allowance is made for differences among species.

Experimental neuroses have been a widely recognized phenomenon since they were first produced in Pavlov's laboratories at the turn of the century. They are stimulus-bound states of hyperexcitability, primarily of the autonomic nervous system. The bizarreness of some of the observed reactions led all the early experimenters to the erroneous conclusion that experimental neuroses were the result of some kind of lesion in the central nervous system. (For a comprehensive review, see Wolpe, 1952, 1958). Experiments that I performed between 1946 and 1948, described below, established beyond any reasonable doubt that these animal neuroses are basically conditioned anxiety reactions.*

There are two basic methods for producing experimental neuroses, both dependent on the elicitation of unconditioned anxiety responses (see definition, p. 9). The first is typified by Pavlov's (1927, p. 23a) circle-and ellipse experiment. At the beginning of the experiment, a luminous circle was projected before a dog that was held by a harness on the laboratory table. Each time the projection was followed by a piece of food placed within easy reach of the animal to condition an alimentary (food-approach) response to the cir-

---

*Mineka and Kihlstrom (1978) have argued that the basis for experimental neurosis is awareness of unpredictability and uncontrollability in the same way as in Seligman's "learned helplessness" experiments. This proposal is unacceptable for the same reasons reasons that learned helplessness is unacceptable as an analogue for clinical depression (see p. 273).

cle. After this, an ellipse with semiaxes in the ratio of 2 : 1 was conditioned as an inhibitory stimulus by being projected but not followed by food. And subsequently, the ellipse was made rounder in stages. At each rounder stage, the inhibitory effect of the ellipse was solidifed by interspersing its nonreinforcements with reinforced presentations of the circle. But a point arrived at which discrimination between the two shapes was no longer possible. When the ratio of the semiaxes was 9 : 8, the animal became increasingly agitated, and finally a state of severe disturbance developed. This disturbance was thenceforth always manifest when the animal was brought back to the experimental chamber.[1]

The other basic method for producing experimental neuroses consists of applying to the spatially confined animal either a large number of weak noxious stimuli (usually in the form of electric shocks) or a small number of stronger noxious stimuli. About 40 years ago, numerous experiments employing weak noxious stimulation were carried out by Liddell and his associates (Liddell, 1944; Anderson & Parmenter, 1941) at Cornell Animal Farm, employing a variety of domestic animals. (For an explanation of the rising titres of anxiety, see Wolpe, 1958, p. 63). Strong noxious stimulation was used by Masserman (1943) in an extensive and imaginative series of experiments on cats. Misled by certain features of their own experimental arrangements, these experimenters believed that the neuroses they had produced were due to conflict. Masserman, for example, ascribed the experimental neuroses he induced to conflict between food-approach motivation and avoidance-of-shock motivation, because the shock was inflicted on the animals when they were approaching food in response to a stimulus conditioned to feeding. In a similar experimental setting, however, I demonstrated (1952, 1958) that such neuroses could be produced by shocks administered to animals that had never been fed in the experimental cage. Subsequently, Smart (1965) made a comparative study of variations on this experimental model, and found very little difference on 16 measures of neurotic behavior between a "shock-only" group of cats and two groups that were shocked either while approaching food or while eating in the experimental cage.

The fact that at least some experimental neuroses can be induced without conflict in itself removes the grounds for the supposition that they result from neural damage or "strain" and provides a presumption that learning is their basis. In that case, the typical positive characteristics of learned behavior should be evident. If experimental neuroses are learned, they must have the following features in common with other learned behavior:

---

[1]The induction of neuroses experimentally in children by means of difficult discriminations has been described b Krasnogorski (1925).

1. The neurotic behavior must be closely similar to that evoked in the precipitating situation.
2. The neurotic responses must be under the control of stimuli that were present in the precipitating situation—that is, the responses must occur upon the impingement on the organism of the same or similar stimuli.
3. The neurotic responses must be at greatest intensity when the organism is exposed to stimuli most like those to which the behavior was originally conditioned and diminish in intensity as a function of diminishing resemblance, in accordance with the principle of primary stimulus generalization.

The first two of these features have been found in all experimental neuroses. All three were unequivocally evident in the neuroses I produced in cats by administering high-voltage, low-amperage shocks in a small cage following an auditory stimulus (Wolpe, 1952, 1958). The shocks evoked a variety of motor and autonomic responses (pupillary dilation, erection of hairs, and rapid respiration in all animals). After an animal had received between 5 and 20 shocks, it would be continuously almost as disturbed in the experimental cage as it was originally only in response to a shock, and then no further shocks would be given. The disturbance in each case consisted of just such responses as had been evoked by the shocks. Muscle tension, pupillary dilation, pilo-erection, and rapid respiration were found in all animals, and vocalizing and clawing at the netting as well as other autonomic responses were found in most. Some displayed special reactions which, invariably, had been previously observed in response to the shocks. For example, one cat who had urinated while being shocked always urinated subsequently within a few seconds of being put into the experimental cage. Another developed a symptom that would be called hysterical in a human being. He jerked his shoulders strongly every few seconds in the experimental cage. This jerking suggested an abortive jumping movement and seemed related to the fact that when he was first shocked he had jumped through an open hatch in the roof of the cage. This similarity between evoked behavior and acquired behavior satisfied the first of the stated criteria of learned behavior.

The control of the neurotic reactions by stimuli involved in the causal situation was evident in several ways. First, the reactions were always at their strongest in the experimental cage, where the animals strongly resisted intromission. Then, the sounding of a buzzer that had preceded the shocks could invariably intensify whatever reactions were going on. Finally, in the case of animals to whom the experimenter had been visible at the time of shocking, his entry into the living cage could at once evoke these reactions in the animal.

Primary stimulus generalization was evident on several continua. Each animal displayed neurotic reactions in the experimental room *outside the exper-*

imental cage, though at a lesser intensity than was observed when it was within the cage. Since stimuli from this room were acting upon the animal at a distance at the time of shocking, direct conditioning to them of neurotic reactions must have occurred. Now, if the animals were placed in any of four other rooms that had different degrees of physical resemblance to the experimental room, neurotic reactions in proportion to the resemblance would be aroused. Another instance of primary stimulus generalization was on an auditory intensity continuum. An auditory signal had always preceded the electrical stimulation. Presentation of that signal at close range would disturb an animal greatly, and the farther away he was from its sound, the weaker were his reactions.

Similarities and Differences between Experimental and Clinical Neuroses

All three of the above features are also found in human neuroses. The anxiety response, both in the war neuroses and the personal cases described above, is similar to the response that was present in the precipitation situation, and it is controlled by stimuli similar to those present in the causal situation. In almost all classically conditioned fears, there is primary stimulus generalization. For example, most fears of heights increase monotonically with increasing height, and claustrophobia varies in inverse relation to available space and in direct relation to span of confinement. Secondary generalization also occurs, in which the stimulus situations are not physically similar but produce a common mediating response (Osgood, 1953), of which anxiety is a consequent. For example, in a particular patient a tight dress and unremovable nail polish, though physically disparate, were placed in the same continuum of secondary generalization because both produced a closed-in feeling.

A fourth point of resemblance between animal and human neuroses is their resistance to extinction whether or not the subject is exposed to the anxiety-evoking situations. A neurotic cat shows an undiminished level of anxiety in the experimental cage for hours or days, and if, alternatively, if it is kept away from the cage situation for weeks or months. In a similar way, as an example, a person who is afraid of flying is unlikely to be improved over time, whether he keeps away from planes entirely, or for economic reasons, say, he makes repeated flights in which he may ameliorate the anxiety by doses of tranquilizers or alcohol. The reason for the failure of extinction is discussed below (p. 43).

Yet another point of resemblance is in the occurrence of second-order conditioning which was mentioned above (pp. 27, 32) with respect to human cases. The following experiment was done on each of two neurotic cats (Wolpe, 1958, p. 60): the animal's anxiety responses to visual stimuli had been deconditioned (by a technique described below), but were still elicted by the auditory stimulus. A piece of meat was dropped in a corner of the laboratory, and as the animal eagerly ran toward it, the buzzer was sounded. It recoiled, hair erect, pupils dilated, body rigid, and hesitated before again advancing; when it did advance again, the buzzer was again sounded. Repeating the procedure several times resulted in the establishment of anxiety and avoidance reactions to that corner of the room and also to the sight of food dropped on *any* floor (Wolpe, 1958, p. 60). A human example has been reported by Keltner and Marshall (1975).

The main *difference* between experimental and clinical neuroses is that, whereas in the former the original fear arousal is by an unconditioned stimulus such as electric shocks, in clinical neuroses it is a conditioned stimulus such as the comprehension of grave danger. Clinical neuroses originate in second-order conditioning. Jersild and Holmes (1935) found that as a child grows older, the incidence of autonomic arousal produced by painful or intense stimulation lessens progressively. This, plus the use of "unprepared" stimuli, probably explains the failure of attempts by Bregman (1934) and Hallam and Rachman (1976) to condition fear.

Can Neurological Stress Produce Lasting Changes in Nerve Cells?

Although the indications are strong that both experimental and clinical neuroses are to a very great extent phenomena of learning, it is necessary to consider the *possibility* that the causative stresses may also lead to lasting physiological changes in cell function under certain circumstances. A variety of clinical experiences make this question pertinent. First, the fact that endogenous depression is frequently precipitated by stressful experiences (Thomson & Hendrie, 1972) suggests in a general way that emotional events may have physiological effects that persist far beyond the duration of the stressor. More directly relevant to us are the occasionally encountered cases whose history and presenting symptoms point uncontestably to a diagnosis of neurosis, but whose neurotic responses are completely impervious to all the available procedures. This was the case with a 34-year-old man who had for five years after a wartime experience been in a state of high anxiety all his waking moments—anxiety that was exacerbated by guilty thoughts related to that experience. The failure of treatment does not prove that this anxiety had a basis other than learning, but compels the question.

Guensberger (1981) has argued that a parallel to this kind of case is to be found in certain instances of experimental neuroses that are characterized either by aggressiveness or by passivity, atonia, and lethargy. He suggests that overload of nerve cells produces some kind of physiopathology. Kandel

(1979) has reviewed a variety of experiments showing that repeated stimulation can have durable effects on synaptic function. For example, after repeated habituation sessions of a defensive reflex in the marine snail *Aplysia californica,* only 30 percent of sensory neurons showed detectable connections to the major motor cells, compared with 90 percent in control animals (Castelucci, Carew, & Kandel, 1978). The missing connections were only partially restored after three weeks. While it is hazardous to extrapolate such findings very far, they do, at the very least, show that noxious stimuli may produce lasting cellular effects under certain circumstances.

4

Mechanisms for Elimination of Classically Conditioned Neurotic Anxiety

THE RESISTANCE OF NEUROTIC BEHAVIOR
TO EXTINCTION

As noted in Chapter 3, neurotic behavior is remarkable for its persistence, often continuing for years and even for life, even though it is unadaptive. Under almost all other circumstances, unadaptive behavior is extinguished by the consequences of its own evocation (see p. 17, and Wolpe, 1958, pp. 24–31). Clearly, it is of crucial importance to know why the process of extinction is so egregiously ineffective in the natural history of *neurotic* responses.

Because of the striking similarities between animal and human neuroses, it seemed appropriate to me many years ago to look for an explanation in the experimental neuroses that I was then studying. I had noted at an early stage that the resistance of these neuroses to extinction was especially marked with respect to the *autonomic* responses. Related motor activity, such as clawing at the sides of the cage, was often extinguished relatively soon. One factor I was aware of that might account for the difference (Wolpe, 1952) was the small amount of fatigue generated by autonomic activity which is relevant insofar as reactive inhibition (Hull, 1943; Wolpe, 1958, p. 26) is a factor in extinction. Also, there was the fact that anxiety arousal (anxiety drive) was reduced each time the animal was removed from the experimental cage, and might be expected to reinforce the autonomic responses which, unlike the

43

motor responses, were continuously evoked in the experimental cage (see Miller & Dollard, 1941; Mowrer & Jones, 1945).

Today it is necessary to take into account the weight of evidence that the response-weakening effect of the nonreinforced evocation of a response depends less on reactive inhibition than on responses that compete with and inhibit that response (Gleitman, Nachmias, & Neisser, 1954; Amsel, 1962, 1972). We therefore also need to know under what circumstances other responses do compete successfully with anxiety, for this should indicate why ordinarily effective competition fails to occur in respect of neurotic responses. Our first recourse is to examine the circumstances in which competition is known unequivocally to succeed: the treatment of experimental neuroses.

THERAPY OF EXPERIMENTAL NEUROSES

Experimentally induced neurotic anxiety responses can reliably be weakened by systematically counterposing weak elicitations of them (by generalized stimuli) to an incompatible response (usually eating). The following is a brief description of the main procedure I applied to the cats that were made neurotic in the experiments described in Chapter 3. (For fuller accounts see Wolpe, 1958, pp. 55–60; 1976; pp. 44–80.)

I started from the observation that *inhibition of eating in the experimental cage was constant in all neurotic animals,* even after one or two days' starvation. This inhibition was also found in rooms that variously resembled the experimental room. An animal that had been starved for 24 hours would be offered food in these rooms in descending order of anxiety aroused until a room where generalized anxiety was low enough not to prevent eating was found. The eating was at first delayed and constrained, but subsequent portions of food were eaten with progressively greater alacrity, while at the same time manifestations of anxiety reciprocally diminished, eventually to zero. The animal would now eat in a room more similar to the experimental room, where he had previously refused to do so. There, successive feedings likewise eliminated all signs of anxiety. The same treatment was continued up the gradient. In the experimental cage itself, it took about 200 pellets of meat over several sessions to deprive the cage of its ability to evoke anxiety totally.

An alternative method succeeded in a few animals. Since the cats were accustomed to have food cast to them by the human hand in their living cages, it seemed possible that the hand had become a conditioned elicitor of approach responses to food. Consequently, a neurotic animal was placed in the experimental cage and pellets of meat were moved toward its snout on the flat end of a rod held in the experimenter's hand, in the hope that the presence of the hand would overcome the inhibition to eating. This succeeded in some animals. The responsive animals at first approached the pellets hesitantly, sometimes accepting and sometimes refusing, but after several pellets, they ate fairly freely from the rod, and soon after also began to eat pellets on the floor of the cage. As the number of pellets eaten in the cage increased, each of these animals ate more freely, moved about the cage with greater freedom, and showed decreasing anxiety symptoms. Insofar as the eating in this method was made possible by the introduction of an additional food-approach stimulus, we have a clear analogue to the therapist's exhortations which, when added to the patient's already present anger, make possible the initiation of assertive behavior (Chapter 7).

When all of the conditioned visual stimuli had lost their anxiety-evoking power, the sounding of the auditory stimulus that had preceded the shocks still elicited a high degree of anxiety, since that stimulus had not been included in the foregoing therapeutic procedures. One way of overcoming the auditory conditioning made use of an intensity dimension controlled by distance. It was necessary to determine by trial and error the closest distance at which an animal would eat with the conditioned auditory stimulus (usually a buzzer) sounding continuously. In one animal the distance was found to be 40 feet. Here, though continuously tense and mydriatic, he gulped down eight pellets but would not eat at a distance of 30 feet. The next day, after two pellets at 40 feet, he ate 10 at 30 feet. The distance at which he ate was reduced day by day. After consuming a total of 160 pellets at progressively decreasing distances, he was able to eat two feet away from the continuous buzzer, although he displayed considerable anxiety. By the end of four sessions at this distance, to a total of 87 pellets, he showed no further sign of avoidance or anxiety to the auditory stimulus.

Regardless of the procedure employed, the question remained whether the neurotic reactions had really been eliminated or had merely come to be dominated by a more strongly conditioned feeding reaction. The decisive experiment was *to extinguish the food-seeking response to the auditory stimulus* and then observe whether or not the neurotic reactions were reinstated. Each of the animals was given 30 irregularly massed extinction trials on each of three successive days. Long before the end of the third day's sessions they all showed almost complete indifference to the auditory stimulus. At the conclusion of the third extinction session the following test was made: a pellet was dropped on the floor of the experimental cage about two feet away from the animal, and as he began to approach it, the auditory signal was sounded continuously to see if extinction of eating had reinstated the anxiety. *In no instance was there any semblance of the restoration of an anxiety response or any inhibition of eating.*

Why Neurotic Anxiety is so Persistent

We are now in a position to see the likely reason for neurotic anxiety's characteristic resistance to extinction. The foregoing experiments showed that when anxiety is weak enough to permit a neurotic animal to eat in the presence of anxiety-evoking stimulation, the anxiety becomes progressively weaker. By contrast, if the anxiety is strong enough to inhibit feeding, no beneficial change occurs and, under certain circumstances, the anxiety spreads to continguous new stimuli. It seems probable that neurotic anxiety of any severity will inhibit the evocation of almost any response that might compete with it.

By contrast, low-intensity anxiety can be inhibited and can have its habit strength reduced through the competition of relatively low-level excitations. For example, in an experiment performed by Berkun (1957), rats that were mildly anxious in an alley lost their anxiety after repeatedly running in the same alley (in some cases at first in a somewhat different alley), even without any food reinforcement. It seems that because they too are of low intensity, most laboratory-induced conditioned emotional responses do undergo extinction (e.g., Black, 1958). In the same way, human neuroses that are relatively weak, most notably many of those in children, fade away seemingly "spontaneously." As even research on ordinary forgetting attests, time alone does not make learned responses fade. We may confidently postulate that such change is the result of weak fear arousals being inhibited by the normal emotional responses of daily life. Clearly, this is an area which is in need of empirical research.

RECIPROCAL INHIBITION AS A MECHANISM OF ELIMINATION OF ANXIETY

We have seen that strong evocations of anxiety were associated with inhibition of eating in food-deprived neurotic cats. On the other hand, eating took place when anxiety was relatively weak, and repeated eating resulted in manifest diminutions of the anxiety. A reciprocally inhibitory relationship between the two responses was thus apparent, and it seemed that the individual inhibitions of anxiety each resulted in a measure of lasting inhibition, that is, conditioned inhibition. The specific role of feeding in weakening fear responses in experimental animals has also been shown by Gale, Sturmfels, and Gale (1966), and by Poppen (1970).

The success of feeding as a reciprocal inhibitor of anxiety in the neuroses of animals led to a search for responses that might be similarly employed in humans. Feeding is effective only in children (Jones, 1924; Wolpe & Wolpe, 1981), but a score of other anxiety-competitive responses have been unearthed for use in both children and adults, as described in later chapters. Mention must also be made of the therapeutic impact of emotional arousal by the therapist (p. 326). In addition, there are the naturally occurring emotional responses of daily life which provide an intelligible explanation for the frequent cases of "spontaneous" cure of unadaptive fears, especially in children (Macfarland, Allan, & Honzek, 1954).

The recent tendency to disparage reciprocal inhibition as a therapeutic agent (e.g., Franks & Wilson, 1979; Goldfried, 1980) makes it necessary to redirect attention to its widespread role in the function of the nervous system. Sherrington (1906) was the first to demonstrate that the reflex excitation of a group of muscles is automatically coupled with the inhibition of antagonistic groups. Since that discovery, reciprocal innervation has been found to be constantly at work at all levels and modalities of nervous function (Gellhorn, 1967). Pavlov noted that the first response of a dog to an unfamiliar bell was to make listening movements—to turn its head in the direction of the bell and to prick up its ears—but when the bell was repeatedly followed by food, the dog came to respond to it by food-approach movements and the listening movements gradually disappeared. The role of reciprocal inhibition in complex human learning first appeared in research on verbal forgetting (Ebbinghaus, 1913). Osgood (1946) explicitly proposed reciprocal inhibition as the mechanism of forgetting.

Inhibitory conditioning of antagonistic responses is also part and parcel of the conditioning of operants. Consider an animal that has developed the habit of turning right in an alley because that response has been consistently followed by food. The right-turn habit will weaken if one stops delivering food after right turning, but it will weaken more rapidly if one rewards left turning at the same time. Presumably, with each left turn there is an inhibition of the right-turn tendency, and the old habit undergoes conditioned inhibition at the same time that the new habit is being reinforced.

In recent research, reciprocal inhibition has been increasingly studied. For example, in the study of "behavioral contrast," the reinforcement of one response has been found to have an excitatory effect upon that response, but also an inhibitory one upon another response (Catania, 1963, 1969, 1973). Similarly, the punishment of one response has an inhibitory effect upon that response, but also an excitatory one upon a second response (Deluty, 1976). A number of recent quantitative models of conditioning (e.g., Herrnstein, 1970; Wagner & Rescorla, 1972) have assumed the principle of reciprocal inhibition, although these theorists do not use the term "reciprocal inhibition." For a discussion of the similarity of these models with respect to a shared assumption of reciprocal inhibition see Deluty (1977).

In the therapeutic context, the operation of reciprocal inhibition is not confined to anxiety-response habits. It has a vital role in overcoming unadaptive cognitive habits as in Leuret's (1846) case described on p. 3. It is also the basis of the conditioned inhibition of obsessional and compulsive habits by aversive therapy (p. 258). A painful faradic shock, or other strong stimulus, inhibits the undesirable behavior, with the result that a measure of conditioned inhibition of the latter is established. Again, in the process of replacing an undesirable motor habit by a more effective one, the evocation of the new motor response involves an inhibition of the old. For example, when assertive behavior is being instigated, at the same time that the expression of "positive" feelings reciprocally inhibits anxiety, the new motor action inhibits the preexisting defensive motor-response tendency. To take a simpler example, if one is being taught to play a backhand tennis stroke by rotating on the right foot, each correct execution inhibits and diminishes the old inefficient response of playing off the left foot, and weakens its habit.

INHIBITION OF ANXIETY AS THE NECESSARY CONDITION OF ITS ELIMINATION

It was proposed in Chapter 2 that active inhibition of a response is necessary to weaken that response. We have considered above how fatigue-associated inhibition (reactive inhibition) and the inhibition of competing responses (reciprocal inhibition) may weaken anxiety-response habits. I shall now draw attention to some other ways of inhibiting anxiety that have the same result.

Intraresponse Reciprocal Inhibition

Competition can occur between the elements *within* a complex response, so that one element is strengthened and becomes dominant under one set of circumstances while another is weakened, and under opposite circumstances the reverse is the case. Freeman and Pathman (1942) and Haggard and Freeman (1941) long ago reported that motor responses diminished anxiety, an observation that has been confirmed more recently by Rauter and Braud (1969). Mowrer and Viek (1948) showed that conditioned anxiety gradually decreased if, in animals that were repeatedly shocked in a rectangular cage, the shock was consistently terminated when the animal jumped into the air, while greater and more persistent anxiety developed in "experimental twins" who received exactly the same duration of shock that was each time terminated without reference to what they were doing. In the group in which the jumping response was consistently reinforced, that response became progressively stronger. Presumably, upon attaining a certain strength, it produced inhibition and consequent weakening of the concurrent autonomic response. In the "twins," no particular response was reinforced because a different one would be going on each time the shock ended.

Therapeutic application of this idea has so far been made to only a very small number of patients. Once the patient has signalled that he clearly imagines a slightly disturbing situation, the therapist delivers a rather mild faradic shock to the forearm, stopping it when the patient briskly flexes his forearm. In the successful treatment of a particularly severe case of agoraphobia, about 20 forearm flexions were usually needed to reduce the anxiety response to a particular scene to zero (Wolpe, 1958, pp. 174–180).

External Inhibition

Experimenting with mild electrical stimuli on the basis of the published account of the foregoing case of agoraphobia, Philpott (1964) noted that by repeatedly administering weak galvanic stimuli to a patient's forearm, he could often progressively decrease pervasive ("free-floating") anxiety. Similarly, if a patient is asked to imagine a scene from a hierarchy (as in systematic desensitization), and if during the scene, two or three weak galvanic stimuli are delivered to his forearm, the anxiety-arousing effect of the scene may noticeably decrease with repetition. As a general rule, it takes between 10 and 30 presentations of a scene to reduce its anxiety-arousing effect to zero. There are some patients in whom very weak stimuli are ineffective, but in whom, if the stimulation is judiciously increased—sometimes to the extent of inducing local muscular contraction—the desired decrements of anxiety are obtained.

The mechanism by which this procedure produces change is seemingly *conditioned inhibition based upon external inhibition.* If this supposition is correct, then stimuli from other modalities should also be usable in this way for therapeutic purposes. The special virtue of electrical stimulation is the ease with which its strength and duration can be controlled.

Directly Conditioned Inhibition

It has been shown in a variety of contexts that the consistent presentation of a stimulus at each cessation of a response may lead to that stimulus becoming conditioned to the negative response. Zbrozyna (1957) produced conditioned inhibition of eating in this way. Similarly, there are experiments that suggest that a stimulus that coincides with the termination of a noxious stimulus acquires anxiety-inhibiting effects (Coppock, 1951; Goodson & Brownstein, 1955). Many years ago, I investigated the possibility of exploiting these observations clinically in a few patients. I applied a moderately painful faradic shock continuously to the forearm of the patient, who had been told that I would switch it off as soon as he said the word "calm." However, he was to try to bear it for at least 20 seconds. In some individuals the word became conditioned to an anxiety-inhibiting response, so that uttering, or even thinking "calm" in anxiety-arousing situations produced a decrease of anxiety (Wolpe, 1958, p. 181). This technique was called "anxiety-relief conditioning." In some cases, the systematic use of a word to which "anxiety relief" has been conditioned has the effect of gradually building a conditioned inhibition of anxiety to the stimulus situations involved. In an electroencephalographic study, Sommer-Smith et al, (1962) have demonstrated that schedules of this type produce conditioned inhibition of the characteristic responses to noxious stimulation.

CONDITIONED INHIBITION BASED ON TRANSMARGINAL INHIBITION

If a conditioned stimulus is administered to an animal at increasing intensities, it is usually found that the strength of the response increases until it reaches an asymptote—that is, it remains at its top level no matter how much stronger the stimulus is made. But in some circumstances, after the response has reached a maximum strength, its evocation paradoxically becomes weaker and weaker as the intensity of stimulation is increased. Pavlov (1927) called this kind of inhibition of response "transmarginal inhibition" or "protective inhibition." Gray (1964, p. 173), summarizing recent work in Russia by Rozhdestvenskaya (1959), redefines the phenomenon by saying that when the threshold of transmarginal inhibition is passed, response magnitude diminishes progressively as stimulation continues to increase in intensity.

This phenomenon has obvious possibilities as an explanation of the effects of flooding (see Chapter 12). Unfortunately, practically no research has been done on the lasting effects of transmarginal inhibition on habit strength. However, a fact that favors a transmarginal inhibition hypothesis for flooding is that its beneficial effects clearly depend on *insistent and prolonged* exposure to the anxiety-evoking stimulation.

It is clear from the foregoing that there are several ways in which anxiety can undergo inhibition, and in respect of most of these, there is evidence that such inhibition is followed by diminution and even extinction of anxiety-response habits. Nobody appears ever to have produced evidence that classically conditioned anxiety habits can be weakened, apart from the occurrence of such inhibition.

CRITIQUE OF OTHER THEORIES OF ELIMINATION OF CLASSICALLY CONDITIONED ANXIETY

There are at present several alternative theories for the deconditioning of anxiety: extinction, habituation, exposure, changed expectancy, and raised self-efficacy. All are inadequate.

Extinction

Extinction is the name for the procedure of repeatedly presenting a conditioned stimulus without reinforcement. It has a long history as a method for bringing about the decline and elimination of learned habits. Its chief present-day protagonists with respect to neurotic fears are Stampfl and Levis and their collaborators (Stampfl & Levis, 1967; Levis & Hare, 1977; Levis & Boyd, 1979) and Eysenck (1976, 1979).

The assumption behind the theory of extinction is that the weakening of the anxiety response is a function of the consequences of presenting the "CS alone." This is a defensible proposition in some cases—for example, where decrease of anxiety follows the subject's prolonged exposure to relatively strong anxiety-evoking stimulation. But weakening of anxiety responses does not always result from exposure to "CS alone." It never does, it seems, in animal neuroses, and often does not in human neuroses. Clearly, then, some other factor or factors must be at work to account for the inconstancy of the effects of what looks like exposure to "CS alone." Furthermore, as Eysenck (1976, 1979) discusses at considerable length, there are circumstances in which repeated and even prolonged presentations of the conditioned stimulus may result in *enhancement* of anxiety. This is found both experimentally (see p. 69; and Napalkov, 1963); and clinically (Campbell, Sanderson, & Laverty, 1964; Wolpe, 1958, p. 99).

Eysenck (1976, 1979) has put forward a theory to account for this paradoxical effect. He postulates that in the special case of nociceptive conditioning, the conditioned response acquires part of the character of the *unconditioned* response—in contrast to all other conditionings. He contends that conditioned anxiety is "painful." While this is true in the sense that it is unpleasant, the *physical pain* of the noxious conditioned stimulus is *not* present. Eysenck provides no evidence that any fraction of the *unconditioned* response is included that is not included in the case of other conditioned responses. The only "support" to which he points is in the build-up of strong conditioned anxiety responses on the basis of weak unconditioned responses (Liddell, 1944; see also Wolpe, 1958, p. 63) and the conditioned phenomena that follow repeated daily narcotic injections. But neither of these conditionings really supports his argument, since unconditioned responses are involved in both.

In any event, the supposed fraction of the unconditioned response would not be relevant to classically conditioned anxiety in humans, because its acquisition is almost always on the basis of second-order conditioning.

Absent from the accounts of Stampfl and Levis and of Eysenck is any *mechanism* for extinction. Eysenck points out that response enhancement is more likely when the anxiety is strongly and briefly elicited. But what does this mean in terms of the *process* of learning? The key question is, what happens in the topography of arousal to make the difference? Nothing is offered to parallel the answer proposed on pp. 43ff.

Habituation

Lader and Wing (1966) proposed that the anxiety-response decrements obtained by systematic desensitization were better explained by habituation than by reciprocal inhibition. Their theory was subsequently elaborated by Lader and Mathews (1968). Habituation is defined as the diminution of the response to a stimulus when the stimulus is repeatedly presented. *This definition is indistinguishable from that of extinction.* Contrarily, as Evans (1973) observed, in the experimental phenomenon called habituation, the response that has disappeared reappears after rest or stimulus change (Sokolov, 1963).

These considerations should suffice to dispose of the habituation theory. Attempts have been made, however, to argue for some kind of "deep down" difference from extinction. Gray (1976) has claimed to be able to set apart from other stimuli "novel stimuli that elicit orienting responses and stimuli that have been paired with punishing stimuli and arouse anxiety." They are supposed to share the property of inhibiting ongoing behavior and to increase arousal. Even if one could accept that they were distinctive in this way, it would not justify the inference that repetition acts on them by a process that is different from whatever effectuates "ordinary" extinction.

A still more complicated proposal is the dual-process habituation theory of Groves and Thompson (1970). This postulates that observable response decrement is the summation of two inferred processes: habituation and sensitization. Such speculations do not create a viable separation of habituation from extinction in their common meanings. The reader who is interested in the ins and outs of habituation theory should consult a scholarly review by Watts (1979).

"Exposure"

"Exposure" to the fearful stimulus has been vigorously promoted by Marks (1969, 1975, 1976, 1981), as the basis of psychotherapeutically induced diminution of anxiety. The result of the exposure is that the patient "gets used" to the stimulus, by a process that Marks does not specify. Since, as every psychologist knows, all classical conditioning and deconditioning necessarily involves the organism's exposure to the conditioned stimulus, to say that one is doing exposure treatment is to say nothing noteworthy at all.

Marks recognizes that not all exposure is therapeutic, and that sometimes sensitization is its result, but he has no explanation for this either. "Exposure" is thus nothing but a word that poses as a theory.

Expectancy

Kazdin and Wilcoxon (1976) have put forward changed expectancy as the basis of therapeutic effects, although they proffer no evidence that expectancy per se is ever therapeutically beneficial. They appear to ride on the suggestion of Rosenthal and Frank (1958) that behavior change can be "due to faith in the efficacy of the therapist and his or her techniques." But Rosenthal and Frank did not provide any evidence to back their suggestion either. Kazdin and Wilcoxon survey a number of experiments that were designed to examine the possible role of expectancy in successful systematic desensitization. These do not on the whole show expectancy to be much of a factor.

Two possible therapeutic roles for expectancy are discernible. Insofar as it implies a hopeful belief, it may displace contrary cognitions and therefore any fears attached to the latter. Then, the emotion expectancy arouses may compete with anxiety.

A more fundamental objection to their proposal is the fact that *expectancy is not a learning mechanism.* It is a behavioral event like retrospection, self-assertion, or autosuggestion. Any of these events may result in learning, but none of them is intrinsic to a learning process in the sense in which reinforcement or retroactive inhibition may be seen as intrinsic.

Raised Expectations of Self-efficacy

According to Bandura (1977), treatments that succeed in eliminating neurotic anxiety do so not by directly weakening anxiety-response habits but through the mediation of expectations of self-efficacy. This proposition must obviously be true of fears that are based on low coping expectations, such as certain fears of public speaking. But Bandura's contention is that it is true of *all* fears, that in effect there are no classically conditioned fears, no fears that are automatic responses to a particular perception! This flies in the face of both experimental and clinical data. For example, how could self-efficacy be relevant to the fear aroused by a bloodstained bandage, by a dead bird in a glass case, or by the patient's own tachycardia? "Coping" is not relevant to the reality of such instances. It is only possible not to see this if one is unshakably convinced that to feel fear implies awareness of a threat to be coped with. There is no such equation, though the two do often go together.

Bandura actually derived his theory of psychotherapeutic change from inferences he made from experiments in which phobic subjects were treated by having them observe fearless models (Bandura, Grusec, & Menlove, 1967;

Bandura, Blanchard, & Ritter, 1969). The most pertinent findings were as follows: in subjects with persistent behavioral patterns of fear and avoidance—for example, of harmless snakes—the repeated experience of observing a film of a person who is fearless of snakes (inappropriately called "symbolic modelling") was about as effective as systematic desensitization. In another form of treatment, called "modelling with guided participation," the subject, after watching the therapist handle snakes, was aided by the therapist to make progressively closer approaches to them. This was significantly more successful than the other two treatments. Bandura's (1977) explanation for this is that seeing others perform threatening activities without adverse consequences can generate expectations in observers that they too will improve if they intensify and persist in their efforts.

Within the narrow scope of Bandura's psychotherapeutic material, at first glance this explanation has plausibility, but careful scrutiny generates objections stemming from the inadequacy of his evaluation of his material and from his failure to note that more than modelling goes on in modelling treatments. He treats his fearful subjects as though they were all the same, showing no awareness of the dichotomy between classically conditioned and cognitively based fears. Though the "symbolic modelling" and systematic desensitization treatments achieved similar results, each was probably effective in different subjects. "Symbolic modelling" provides corrective information about harmless snakes; systematic desensitization provides little or no information but accomplishes reconditioning of classically conditioned fears. Thus, if Bandura's experimental population in fact contained, in more or less equal numbers, subjects who believed snakes to be dangerous, and subjects with classically conditioned fear of them, the two treatments would have fared about equally well (as they did). There might, however, have been some reduction of conditioned anxiety in some subjects receiving "symbolic modelling," based on the interpersonal anxiety-inhibiting impact of the therapist (p. 326).

Participant modelling treatment is the most effective of the three treatments because it clearly conveys even more information than "symbolic modelling," and also contains elements that might actively decondition conditioned anxiety. The subject interacts more closely with the experimenter, which would augment the interpersonal anxiety-inhibiting effect. Then, in its systematic gradual approach to the snake, participant modelling has all the ingredients of *in vivo* desensitization, with these interpersonal emotional responses as the counterconditioning agent.

In sum, these experiments do not provide the supposed support for Bandura's theory. They should be rerun with groups that have been subdivided by skilled behavior analyses. A later experiment (Bandura & Adams, 1977) purporting to show that systematic desensitization works by raising self-efficacy is subject to the same criticism (Wolpe, 1978).

Meanwhile, we must evaluate the self-efficacy theory of psychotherapy more broadly. The following statement (Bandura, 1977, p. 194) expresses its essence:

> People fear and tend to avoid threatening situations they believe exceed their coping skills, whereas they get involved in activities and behave assuredly when they judge themselves capable of handling situations that would otherwise be intimidating.

The phrase to note is "coping skills." A skill always involves motor performance, whether it is sawing logs or rebutting arguments. People certainly do avoid situations that exceed their skills, often and wisely. People who avoid *threatening* situations do not usually do so because they lack performance skills. They usually have the *motor capacity* to enter the situations and "get involved in activities." It is fear that prevents the activities. When a person does act in spite of his fear—does force himself (for business reasons, say) to fly, when he fears flying—then he is enduring the fear, and it could be said that, in a sense, he is coping with it. As long as the fear of flying is felt, a therapeutic problem remains. The compassionate solution is to enable the person to fly *without fear*.

And this is what psychotherapy should achieve—the elimination of the fears that cause the disabilities. Increases in self-efficacy expectations should and will *follow* fear diminution.[1]

---

[1]For a detailed critique of Bandura's theory, see Wolpe, 1978. At a more fundamental level of analysis, Smedlund (1978, 1978a) has observed that expectations of self-efficacy are *intrinsically* related to coping skills. The relationship is of the same logical type as "all normal elephants have trunks," when having a trunk is part of the definition of a normal elephant. Relationships that are definitional are not appropriate subject matter for empirical testing.

5

Behavior Analysis

GENERAL ORIENTATION
TO BEHAVIOR ANALYSIS

In the practice of behavior therapy objectivity, empathy, and sensitivity to suffering are pervasive from beginning to end. All these attitudes follow from the conception of human behavior provided in Chapter 2. The objectivity follows from the demonstration that all behavior, including cognitive behavior, is subject to causal determination no less than is the behavior of falling objects or of magnetic fields.

If a man pauses at crossroads, undecided which of two routes to follow, the route that he eventually takes is the inevitable one, the result of a balancing out of conflicting action tendencies. The strength of each action tendency is essentially a function of the stimuli tending to arouse it through preexisting habit structures.

The fellow feeling of the behavior therapist toward his patients accords with his deterministic outlook. He sees the patient as the product of physical endowment modified by experience. Each environment, each exposure to stimulation, has modified, through learning, the patient's character as a responding organism to a greater or lesser extent. Attitudes, thoughts, verbal behavior, and emotional behavior have all been shaped by his interactions with his environment. It is the misfortune of the patient to have had experiences that have caused him to learn unadaptive habits.

While a behavior therapist may sympathize with the patient for unhappy state he never blames or disparages him in any way. On the contrary, he goes out of his way to dislodge any self-blame that may have been engendered by social conditioning and perhaps magnified by statements from friends, relations, and previous therapists. Later on, when he has heard the patient's story, he can increase conviction by retracing the learned origins of the patient's own neurosis. To some sophisticated patients he may describe how similar reactions are induced in animals who remain neurotic indefinitely, until the experimenter chooses to cure them by methods that are guided by principles of learning, and how the same principles are used to overcome human neuroses.

Behavior analysis is the process of gathering and sifting information to be used in the conduct of behavior therapy. The therapist's central focus is on the distress and disablement that have brought the patient to seek treatment. The first question concerns the realm of broad diagnosis—whether the distress is learned or organically based, for behavior therapy is appropriate only if it is learned. If the stressful behavior patterns are due to psychotic illness or in any other way organically based, a biological form of treatment is indicated, and not behavior therapy.

The vast majority of patients who are likely to find their way into the behavior therapist's office do in fact have problems that are attributable to learning, and the bulk of these problems are neuroses. The patient's primary complaints consist of unadaptive anxiety responses, or else of secondary effects of such anxieties. The anxieties have been established through learning, and the therapeutic aim is to undo or reverse this learning. A behavior therapist will generally set about this by applying the principles discussed in Chapter 4. But he will first need to extend the behavior analysis by identifying precisely what stimuli trigger the anxieties.

People are infinitely varied, and so are their complaints and the ways in which these are tied to stimulus conditions. That is why it is of cardinal importance for the therapist to be able to question probingly, to repeat questions in several different ways if necessary in order to establish particulars beyond any reasonable doubt. The best way to develop this skill is on the basis of supervised work with patients. Formulas and schedules for behavior therapy assessment (Mash & Terdal, 1976) can be helpful, but they can never suffice. They are counterproductive if they lead the student to regard them as a comprehensive guide.

ESTABLISHING STIMULUS-RESPONSE RELATIONS OF UNADAPTIVE BEHAVIOR

Having obtained from the patient such personal details as his name, address, telephone number, age, and occupation, the therapist proceeds to explore his fears and other complaints. The circumstances surrounding the onset of each of these are meticulously examined in order to obtain a coherent picture of its determinants. We try to identify not only the circumstances in which a fear was originally conditioned, but also what later events may have modified its form or led to its "spread" to other stimuli by second-order conditioning.

The conditioning history of each unadaptive habit is traced in the same essential way.

This historical information provides a background for subsequent steps. At the very least, it gives the therapist a perspective on the case; but it may also provide important clues to the stimulus-response relationships that are currently relevant. These *current* relationships will usually be the chief subject of therapy. The most intensive scrutiny is therefore given to them. If the patient is anxious in social situations, it is necessary to find out exactly what aspects of these situations upset him. Perhaps he has a conditioned anxiety reaction to being looked at. Then, with what factors does it vary? It may increase with the number of people looking at him, or depend on the degree of speaking-performance-demand that the situation seems to hold, or on a fearful feeling of not being able to get away. The correct identification of the stimulus antecedents of reactions, which is indispensable to effective behavior therapy, depends mainly on the questioning. Cases 12, 13, and 14 provide examples of this. A list of consequences of anxiety is given in Table 1.1 above.

It is easy to be led astray either by the patient's assumptions or by one's own too facile interpretations. For example, one patient attributed her severely disabling anxieties to the anesthesia for an operation she had undergone. Close questioning revealed that social stresses were their true cause and that the anesthetic was irrelevant. The two etiologies pointed to two totally different treatment strategies. The following is an example of therapists' countertherapeutic preposessions.

Case 11

A man's fear of symptoms had started after an occasion when he had felt an insufferably strong urge to defecate while driving through a suburban area. He had stopped at a house where his request to use the toilet had been granted. On resuming his journey, he felt very tense and became aware of rapid heartbeat and tremor, which led him to think that some bodily damage might have resulted from his severe stress. Thus began a chronic cycle of symptoms and fears. A succession of treatments, including one that was behaviorally oriented, focused on the physiological events but yielded little benefit. Only several years later, when he came to the Behavior Therapy Unit, was a detailed analysis made of the precipitating event. This revealed that the cause of the man's great emotional upset was his embarrassment at having to ask for the use of a toilet. The overcoming of social anxiety thus emerged as an indispensable first goal of treatment. The physiological responses were secondary.

The task of stimulus-response analysis is further complicated when there is a presenting complaint other than anxiety—for example, a stutter, a compulsion, or a "psychosomatic" illness. In asthma and other presumed psychosomatic conditions, the possibility of a purely organic etiology must not be forgotten. Apart from such cases, psychosomatic reactions are consequences of neurotic anxiety responses in predisposed individuals (see p. 11). We want to know how the anxiety is related to the stutter, the compulsion, or the asthmatic attack. Usually the relationship is clear and straightforward. For example, a stutter may be found to increase as a function of intensity of felt anxiety, which in turn depends upon features of the audience—their strangeness, their number, and their demeanor. But sometimes it may be more difficult to detect the relationship between the emotional upset and the psychosomatic reaction. I once treated a person with asthma whose attacks took place regularly four hours after a stressful event. This became apparent only after the patient had kept an hour-by-hour diary for several weeks.

One of the first decisions a therapist must make about any fear is whether it is based on classical conditioning or on misinformation (see Chapter 3). With reference to Figure 5.1, consider a person who has a fear of harmless snakes. When a snake (S_1) comes into his line of vision, it produces the neural effects that yield a perception (image) of the snake (rS_1), and that eventually excite the efferent processes shown as r_a that lead to anxiety and avoidance (R_a). There are two pathways through which rS_1 may lead to R_a. The perception of the snake may evoke a secondary image of danger or death (rS_2) to which anxiety and avoidance responses have already been conditioned in almost everybody. To eliminate this anxiety response habit would entail breaking the connection between rS_1 and rS_2.

The other possibility is that the perception (rS_1) immediately and without

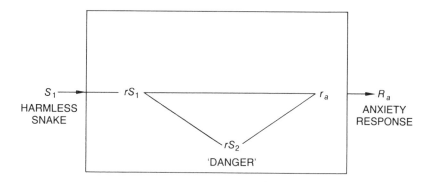

Fig. 5.1. The harmless snake (S_1) causes the perceptual response (rS_1) which may lead to the molecular responses for anxiety (r_a) either immediately or through the intermediary of the conditioned concept "danger" (rS_2). (Courtesy of Graphic Communications, Eastern Pennsylvania Psychiatric Institute, Philadelphia.)

any cognitive intermediary evokes the anxiety response because of classical conditioning. In that case, cognitive correction will be of no avail in overcoming the fear of harmless snakes. Deconditioning will be necessary. But sometimes the patient has *both* a misconception of the implications of the perceived object *and* an automatic, nonrational anxiety response to it.

BACKGROUND HISTORY

When the patient's presenting reactions have been sufficiently explored, the therapist obtains the basic facts of his past and present life. The first topic is the patient's early family life. He is asked how many siblings he had and by how many years he was separated from each. What kind of person did his father seem to him to be? Did the father show personal interest, did he punish, and if so, did it seem just or not? Is the father still alive? If not, how did he die, and what was the effect of his death? The same questions are asked about the mother. How well did the parents get on with each other? Were there any other important adults in the patient's early home life? Who were they and what was their influence upon him? How did he relate to his siblings? How important was religious training, and how much of an influence upon him does religion retain? Did he have any childhood fears or nervous habits, and what became of them?

The next group of questions relate to the patient's education. Did he enjoy school? If so, what did he like about it; if not, for what reason? How well did he do academically? Did he take part in athletics, and how well did he perform? Did he make friends and were any of the friendships intimate? Were there any people, either among teachers or students, whom he grew to fear or to dislike especially? At what age did he leave school? Did he graduate from high school? What did he do next—embark on a life of leisure, go to work, or continue his studies at a university or other institution? How did he get on at the institution, academically and socially? Upon graduating, what work did he do, how did he function at it, and how satisfying did he find it? Have there been changes of employer, and if so for what reasons? How does he get on with employers, underlings, and peers?

The patient's sex life is then traced from his first awareness of sexual feelings. At what age and in what context was he first aware of sexual arousal? What were the experiences that followed? Did he masturbate, and was this associated with any feelings of fear or guilt? At what age did he commence dating? When did he have his first important relationship? What attracted him to the girl, and what brought the association to a close? The same questions are asked about subsequent associations. What attracted him to his wife? How did the courtship go? Were there obstacles from the families of either party? How have they got on together over the years? How has the sexual side of the marriage been? In general, as much attention is given to love and emotional warmth as to sexual behavior as such.

What are his present social relationships? Does he have difficulties with any of his friends? Does he have any particularly intimate friends? How does he get on with people with whom his association is casual?

After the anamnesis, the patient is given three inventories to fill out—the Willoughby Schedule (a short form of the Clark-Thurstone Inventory), a Fear Survey Schedule, and the Bernreuter Self-Sufficiency Scale. These inventories, which are reprinted in appendixes, will be briefly discussed.

The Willoughby Schedule (original form, Appendix A) consists of 25 questions that are answered on a five-point scale (0–4). About half of the questions yield information about common areas of neurotic reactivity, mainly interpersonal, and the other half indicate degrees of general emotional sensitivity. This questionnaire is a highly significant indicator of neuroticism (Wolpe, 1958, p. 110). A psychometric study by Turner, DiTomasso, and Murray (1980) has shown that the items of the schedule converge to the unitary construct of hypersensitivity to interpersonal situations. Decreases in the score are correlated with the patient's improvement (Wolpe, 1958, p. 221). But it is possible for a person to have a low Willoughby score and yet be highly neurotic in areas not covered by the schedule. To insure against ambiguity the therapist explains each question to the patient. A revised Willoughby for self-administration is given in Appendix B.

The Fear Survey Schedule (Appendix C) Wolpe and Lang (1964) lists a large number of stimulus situations to which fear is unadaptive. The patient indicates on a five-point scale how disturbed he becomes in each situation. This schedule is an exceedingly useful clinical instrument that frequently brings to the therapist's attention neurotic sensitivities that would not otherwise have been suspected. A revised schedule containing 108 items (Wolpe & Lang, 1969) is commercially available.[1]

The Bernreuter Self-Sufficiency Inventory (Appendix D), which is a list of 60 questions, is used less consistently than the two foregoing schedules. A normal score is generally between 24 and 42. A score of less than 20 shows marked lack of self-sufficiency. Low scores are found in cases of overdependency, many of whom present themselves as agoraphobic. People who are low in self-sufficiency frequently find it difficult to carry out instructions for self-assertion. Very high scores (45 and over) are obtained by some normal people and by some psychopaths.

When there is a question of psychopathic personality and when there are

---

[1] From Educational and Testing Materials, P.O.Box 7234, San Diego, California 92107.

ambiguous manifestations of hysteria, the introversion-extraversion scale of the Maudsley Personality Inventory (Eysenck, 1962) often provides decisive information.

If there is the slightest suggestion that organic disease may be playing a part in the patient's illness, a medical investigation should be undertaken. One of the strongest indications for this is the presence of episodic anxiety attacks to which no constant stimulus antecedents can be attached. Common organic causes of anxiety are paroxysmal tachycardia, hypoglycemia, including relative hypoglycemia (Salzer, 1966), and hyperthyroidism. Among less common causes are limbic lobe seizures and pheochromocytoma.

When the initial information gathering is concluded, therapeutic goals and strategies are discussed with the patient. The therapist must decide which areas of disturbance should be given priority. The degree to which a neurotic habit is detrimental to the life economy of the patient is usually a prime consideration. Thus, in a particular case, agoraphobia may be treated first because of its profoundly incapacitating consequences, even though other neurotic reactions have predated it, and in a sense spawned it.

SOME EXAMPLES OF INITIAL INTERVIEWS

Behavior therapy is always an individual program. A few general rules, however, will be stated in order to make the examples of initial interviews given below more comprehensible:

1. The emotional climate is at all times a blend of objectivity and permissiveness.
2. The patient must be assured that his unpleasant reactions are reversible. If they have been learned, they can be unlearned. The therapist can usually illustrate the learning process from the patient's own history.
3. Misconceptions must be corrected as soon as possible. This applies both to socially conditioned misconceptions (e.g., "masturbation is dangerous") and iatrogenic misconceptions (e.g., "I need my symptoms"). How important this can be is illustrated in Case 18.
4. Assertive behavior (Chapter 7) should be instigated at an early stage whenever indicated unless there are severe phobic reactions to some aspect of it, such as being the center of attention (see Case 13).

The cases whose first interviews are given here are quite varied. The first presented itself as a phobia for sharp objects, the second as a problem of interpersonal anxiety, and the third as one of inadequate sexual response. Yet the same line of action is apparent in all three: a concentrated effort to secure the greatest possible definition in relating stimuli (situations) to the responses that constitute or underlie the complaints that brought the patient to treatment.

Case 12. *First interview in a case of phobia for sharp objects* (Mrs. P., age 32)

The interview with Mrs. P. shows that the behavior therapist does not settle for the circumscribed phobia for knives which the patient initially presented. He follows his routine of uncovering broad areas of the patient's history. The reader should attend to the manner and content of the questioning procedure. In particular, he should note how the therapist went out of his way to be permissive, to condone acts and attitudes that the patient seemed to believe it natural to deplore, and how he took pains to define with precision features that he thought might be significant for therapeutic action.

The one benefit obviously expected from therapy was the removal of the phobia. An outsider might therefore have expected a behavior therapist to proceed with systematic desensitization, but the *second* interview (not given here) led in another direction. Exploration of factors currently controlling Mrs. P.'s fear of knives revealed that it became particularly strong when other people's children were unruly inside her house. This was related to the fact that she was extremely inhibited in almost all interpersonal situations, and how she habitually suppressed her anger for fear of disapproval. (Note that direct questioning during the first session failed to elicit the suppressed anger.) In keeping with this, her Willoughby score was 66. The first therapeutic undertaking was, accordingly, *not desensitization, but assertiveness training*. It was postulated that by developing an ability to express her feelings freely and appropriately, she would remove the major stimulus antecedent of her phobia. Assertiveness training was rapidly effective, but although the phobia then became less troublesome, desensitization eventually had to be carried out.

THERAPIST: Dr. N. has written to me about you, but I want to approach your case as though I knew nothing about it at all.[1] Of what are you complaining?

MRS. P.: I'm afraid of sharp objects, especially knives. It's been very bad in the past month.

THERAPIST: How long have you had this fear?

MRS. P.: It began six years ago when I was in the hospital after my first child was born. Two days later, my husband brought me some peaches and a

[1]It is always a mistake to rely upon the version of a case provided by a psychiatrist or psychologist whose orientation is not behavioristic, since a good deal of information that interests them may not interest us, and vice versa.

sharp knife to cut them with. I began to have a fear that I might harm the baby with it.[2]

THERAPIST: How long had the knife been with you when it occurred to you that it might harm the baby?

MRS. P.: I don't believe I let him leave it overnight, that night; I think you could say I told him to take it home. I can't remember exactly; I know I just didn't want it around. From that day to this, I don't mind using knives as long as I'm with someone, but when I'm alone with the children I just don't want them around.

THERAPIST: Can you remember in what way the thought first came into your mind that you might hurt the baby?

MRS. P.: I can't remember.[3]

THERAPIST: Now since that time, generally speaking, has this fear been the same all along, or has it got better or worse?

MRS. P.: Well, right after we moved to Richmond about five months ago I felt a little better about it. At first, when I got home from the hospital I made my husband take all the knives away from the house. I didn't want them around, so he took them to my mother's. I brought a couple back from her house when we moved to Richmond. But I couldn't—after I brought them—I couldn't use them. I couldn't keep them out where I could see them and might pick one up and, you know, use it sometime.

THERAPIST: So what do you say in general—that the fear has been much the same?

MRS. P.: It seems the same. In fact, mostly I think it's gotten worse.[4]

THERAPIST: Is there anything—any situation—that you can associate with it getting worse?

MRS. P.: No. Only it just seems to be on my mind I guess. If you don't mind me going back to something that Dr. N. said that I just didn't want them around, that it was a habit, and I mean I guess I've just been thinking about that and—it's hard to admit—the children, I don't know why they make me nervous and I just am afraid that—that sometime it may get the better of me.

THERAPIST: Are the children making you more nervous—in the past month?

MRS. P.: Well, you know in the summertime they stay outside; but in this

---

[2]One does not have to be a Freudian to suspect from this that the baby might have been a resented intrusion in her life—and, as will be seen, it was.

[3]It did not seem advisable to exert pressure on her memory at this point when she was not yet comfortable with the therapist.

[4]Frequent recurrence of emotional disturbance owing to the destructive idea could have resulted in the conditioning of various new stimuli to that disturbance.

kind of weather they can't get out, and, of course, they like to run and when they run in the house it does kind of get me.[5]

THERAPIST: When you were in the hospital that time after your baby was born, what was your general feeling about the situation?[6]

MRS. P.: Well, I wasn't too happy in the first place because we had just built a house. I had just started to work and had been working about six months when I got pregnant and I wasn't too happy about it, because I liked my job and, building a house, we wanted new furniture and all. Well, I guess neither one of us was happy about it. And then just before the baby was born I said, "If it's a girl, a dark-headed girl with brown eyes it will be fine"; but it turned out that it was blonde and a boy. (*Laughs*)

THERAPIST: Was that important?

MRS. P.: That it was a girl or boy?

THERAPIST: Yes. Or were you just joking?

MRS. P.: Well, no, I don't think I was joking, because I really didn't much want it to look like my husband and his side of the family (*laughs*). But it turned out to be the image of his Daddy.[7] But I think that was a selfish . . .

THERAPIST: Well, that's all right.

MRS. P.: . . . on my part. It's probably a selfish way to look at it. I wanted a dark-headed girl.

THERAPIST: Well, you were expressing how you felt about the child at that time. It was just your feeling, and there's no question of right or wrong. It was your true feeling.[8] . . . Don't you like the way your husband's family looks?

MRS. P. (*laughing*): I could never like their looks. I know they like me because of the way they act and . . . I wouldn't do anything against them.

THERAPIST: It is quite possible not to like the way some people look.

MRS. P.: I must have liked the way my husband looked or I wouldn't have married him.

THERAPIST: Then why was it important to you to have a child look like your family?

MRS. P.: Well, as I said, I think it was just selfish on my part.

THERAPIST: But you had a preference. It is not a matter of being selfish. You had a preference.[9]

---

[5]The worsening was related to the noise and activity of children.

[6]A return to the quest for information regarding the circumstances of the onset of the phobia.

[7]Not only had the pregnancy been unwelcome, but when the child arrived, it was physically displeasing.

[8]Note the matter-of-fact acceptance of her account and the strong rejection of the suggestion of moral turpitude implied in her use of the word "selfish."

[9]The idea of selfishness was again combatted.

MRS. P.: Well, I felt I had to go through having and caring for the baby and all, and I felt like I sort of wanted it to look like me since I had to go through it all.

THERAPIST: Sort of reward for your trouble?

MRS. P.: That's right.

THERAPIST: Did you ever have this kind of feeling before this child was born?

MRS. P.: Never.

THERAPIST: Well, when I said that, I wasn't thinking only about this feeling about knives, but has it ever happened before that you had a feeling of wanting to smash up things, maybe, if you were cross about them?[10]

MRS. P.: I've always been sort of, you know, perfectionist, I guess you'd say, particular about my things. I had two younger sisters and I know if they meddled with any of my things . . . I would get awfully mad about that . . . but I never wanted to hurt anybody.

THERAPIST: Would you ever want to hit them?

MRS. P.: I don't think so.

THERAPIST: Would you ever want to hit anybody who annoyed you? Or when situations worked out the way you didn't like?

MRS. P.: I don't think so. I can't remember it. . . .

THERAPIST: Well, it doesn't have to be a matter of hurting anybody physically, but just a feeling of anger and expressing anger towards people. Well, now let's get your background. Where were you born?

MRS. P.: Norfolk.

THERAPIST: How many brothers and sisters?

MRS. P.: Four sisters and one brother.

THERAPIST: And where to you come?

MRS. P.: I'm in the middle. There's two sisters and a brother older and two sisters younger.

THERAPIST: Will you just tell me how much older than you your eldest sister is?

MRS. P.: She was 47 in October . . . and I've got one who will be 45 in January and my brother will be 43 in December, and then 18 months younger there's a sister, and one 2 years younger than her.

THERAPIST: Are your parents alive?

MRS. P.: Yes.

---

[10]This raised the question whether, in general, she had a tendency toward anger and aggression when thwarted. According to her statements, she did feel angry but did not react violently. The possibility of verbal expression of anger was not pursued at this point, though it might well have been.

THERAPIST: What kind of person is your father, especially as you remember him in your childhood?

MRS. P.: Sweet and easy-going.

THERAPIST: Did you feel he was interested in you?

MRS. P.: You mean what I did at school and like that?

THERAPIST: Was you father interested in you personally and in what you were doing?

MRS. P.: Not too much.

THERAPIST: Did he ever punish you?

MRS. P.: No.

THERAPIST: And what about your mother?

MRS. P.: Well, I could say the same about her. They were both good—you know—provided. She . . . well she was interested, did things like driving us to school. She didn't seem to be too interested in how we got along or what we did; or if I failed; and I made awful grades in school. She never talked to the teacher to find out if I could have done better. She never helped with homework or anything like that. Of course, I guess she always had too much else to do.[11]

THERAPIST: Aside from the fact that your parents were rather similar people, would you say they liked each other and also behaved towards you as though they liked you?

MRS. P.: Well, they tried to see that we did right and I can remember they always took us to Sunday School and to church.

THERAPIST: Did they get on well together?

MRS. P.: Well, yes. As far as I know. They had arguments.

THERAPIST: Did they have lots of arguments?

MRS. P.: Well, no; after all they lived together some 40 years.

THERAPIST: Were there any other adults who played any important part in your early home life—like grandmothers, aunts, or nurses?

MRS. P.: No, I don't remember any grandmothers or aunts.

THERAPIST: How did you get on with your brother and sisters?

MRS. P.: Well, pretty good, I guess. Of course, when you are children I think you fuss and fight lots of times. Now I think we all get along good.

THERAPIST: Did you have any particular fears when you were a child?

MRS. P.: Well no, not that I know of. But when I was eight years old our house burned down. I was on my way home from school and the fire trucks passed us. It was in January and it was snowing like anything and somebody told us that our house was on fire. And there was a fear. . . . My parents lost

[11]Having had such uninvolved parents, it is hardly surprising that Mrs. P. was unenthusiastic about having children.

almost everything they had. For . . . five or six years after that, every time I would hear a fire engine I would get so nervous if I was in school I would have to get up and leave. I wouldn't leave the school, but I would have to get out of the class—but things like that don't bother me now.[12]

THERAPIST: Did you have any other such experiences, or any other fears at all when you were a child?

MRS. P.: No.

THERAPIST: Well,now, you said that you didn't get on very well at school. Apart from the fact that your studies were difficult, how did you like school?

MRS. P.: I liked it fine. I mean I just played right along.

THERAPIST: Well, did you always do badly at your classes?

MRS. P.: Yes.

THERAPIST: What about sports? How were you at them?

MRS. P.: I might have taken after father in sports. I did well.

THERAPIST: Did you make friends at school?

MRS. P.: Yes, I had plenty of friends at school.

THERAPIST: Did you have any close friends?

MRS. P.: Well, yes. There were about six or eight of us that always chummed around together, girls and . . .

THERAPIST: Were there any people at school you were afraid of? I mean either among the girls or teachers?

MRS. P.: No.

THERAPIST: How far did you go in school?

MRS. P.: I finished high school.

THERAPIST: How old were you then?

MRS. P.: 18.

THERAPIST: And then what did you do?

MRS. P.: I worked for a doctor for three years.

THERAPIST: As a receptionist?

MRS. P.: I did his lab work and typing, shorthand . . . helped with his patients.

THERAPIST: Did you like that work?

MRS. P.: Yes, very much.

THERAPIST: And then what did you do?

MRS. P.: I worked for a power company for five years, as a clerk-stenographer. I liked that too.

THERAPIST: And then?

MRS. P.: Got married. I didn't work for about ten months. Then I worked for a plastic firm in Norfolk until the first child was born—as I told you.

---

[12]It is usual for childhood phobias to be deconditioned by the experiences that life provides, and without formal treatment.

THERAPIST: And since then?

MRS. P.: Housewife.

THERAPIST: How do you like being a housewife?

MRS. P.: Fine.

THERAPIST: Is there anything you don't like about it?

MRS. P.: That things don't stay clean when cleaned. (*Laughs*) No, I like it fine, I wouldn't go back into public work for anything. Unless I could work in a hospital, something like that. I should get something like that when my children are through school.

THERAPIST: How old were you when you first had any kind of sexual feelings?

MRS. P.: Well, I . . . (*Desperate gesture*)

THERAPIST: Well, roughly—were you ten, or fifteen, or twenty? More or less?

MRS. P.: Well, I can't remember. I have no idea.

THERAPIST: Well, then, was it before ten?

MRS. P.: I wouldn't think so.

THERAPIST: Was it before 15? . . . Before 20?

MRS. P.: Well I would think it was before 20.

THERAPIST: Say about 17?

MRS. P.: Well, yes, maybe.[13]

THERAPIST: In what kind of a situation did you have your first sexual feeling? Was it out with boys, or at the movies, or what?

MRS. P.: Well, I never dated too much. And when I was in school, well, in my class in school there just wasn't any boy. And . . .

THERAPIST: So, you started to date when you were 18 or so, after you left school?

MRS. P.: That's right.

THERAPIST: At that stage did you go out with lots of different boys or just one at a time? Did you go to parties? What was the pattern?

MRS. P.: Well, I went around with several. I belonged to the choir at church and whenever there were things like Sunday School parties we'd usually take somebody with us.

THERAPIST: Well . . . when did you first become especially interested in anybody?

MRS. P.: Well, let's see. I started going with my husband, Charles when I was 24. And after I started going with him I never did go out with anybody else.

THERAPIST: There has been nobody else ever in whom you have been really interested?

---

[13]Note the therapist's insistence on at least an approximate answer, and that, once it has been obtained, details are pursued.

MRS. P.: Well, when I was working at my second job, there was a boy there, but he was married, and I never did go out with him.

THERAPIST: What did you like about him?

MRS. P.: Well, just everything. (*Laughs*) And, ah, well he showed me a lot of attention too. Then he quit and went to Richmond to work and I never did see him again.

THERAPIST: So you didn't have any kind of going out with him or any physical contact?

MRS. P.: I know a lot of people wouldn't believe this, but it's absolutely true.

THERAPIST: I believe it. What did you like about Charles?

MRS. P.: My husband is just . . . the way he . . . well, just everything I guess. He was nice and the thing that impressed me with him most was the way he treated his mother. His father had been dead for a few years and he was good to her, and he always phoned her, and I felt like anybody who would be that good to his mother might be a good husband.

THERAPIST: Well, when did you feel that you were ready to marry him?

MRS. P.: I don't know if I ever did feel like I was. I went with him for seven years.[14]

THERAPIST: Well, was he interested in marrying you earlier?

MRS. P.: Uh-huh. Every time I would put it off. And I would say okay and then I would get nervous and upset and couldn't sleep and would say, well, I can't go through this again. so we would put it off again, until he got fed up with that. He was working, and when he got fed up he said he was going to quit his job and go to college. And he did.

THERAPIST: He went to college?

MRS. P.: Uh-huh. From January '53 to June '56. And then he went to Tennessee and got a job at ____. When he left, of course, it left me sitting at home by myself and I nearly died. I lost 20 pounds; I couldn't eat; I couldn't sleep.

THERAPIST: Well, can you tell me what the other man you mentioned had that Charles didn't have? What points were important as far as your feelings were concerned?

MRS. P.: Oh, he was good looking. But I was thinking of my husband's blonde hair and blue eyes. He had dark hair and dark eyes.[15]

THERAPIST: When you had the prospect of marriage to Charles before you, and you felt nervous, what did you feel nervous about? Was there any particular aspect of the relationship that made you feel nervous?

---

[14]It seems that the choice of a husband made on rational grounds, and not because of his emotional appeal—in contrast to the married man previously mentioned.

[15]Further evidence of the emotional importance to her of the appearance of close relatives, which accounted largely for the strength of her negative reaction to her newborn child.

MRS. P.: The whole thing, I guess. I just wasn't ready to get married.

THERAPIST: In 1954 Charles went to study?

MRS. P.: Yeah, he went to Baltimore.

THERAPIST: So eventually you got married. When?

MRS. P.: In August of 1956.

THERAPIST: At that stage, were you satisfied about being married?

MRS. P.: Well, he first of all, he called me from Tennessee and said, "If you don't marry me now," he says, "we're through. I'm leaving the country." So it was then or never, so I said, "Okay." So we got married the next autumn.

THERAPIST: Well, how do you get along together?

MRS. P.: We get along fine. I knew I would never marry anybody else. Well, I guess I'm just the type of person, you know, someone sort of has to say well, we are going to do it now or never.

THERAPIST: How is the sexual side of your marriage?

MRS. P.: Fine; I hope he'd say the same (*laughs*).

THERAPIST: At this moment I'm only interested in your side.[16] Do you have climaxes?

MRS. P.: Yes.

THERAPIST: Always?

MRS. P.: Well, no, I don't always, but I do at least part of the time.

THERAPIST: So you're quite happy in general about the marriage?

MRS. P.: Well, I wouldn't be any other way.

THERAPIST: What do you mean by that?

MRS. P.: Well, I mean I wouldn't be single again.

THERAPIST: But you have no complaints about the marriage?

MRS. P.: No.

THERAPIST: How many children have you now?

MRS. P.: I have two. The girl will be three on the 16th of this month.

THERAPIST: Do you like your children?

MRS. P.: Well, I should say I do.

THERAPIST: Except when they make a lot of noise and get on your nerves?

MRS. P.: Well, that's to be expected. I wonder sometimes what my mother did when there were six of us. Of course, we weren't all there at the same time.

THERAPIST: Your children are quite well?

MRS. P.: Yes.

THERAPIST: Do you like living in Richmond?

MRS. P.: Better than I expected. I'd heard that the people were not too friendly, but I found out that they are.

---

[16]This statement expresses the central orientation of a behavioristic history. Everything has to be seen from the standpoint of the sufferer, for it is she who needs to be changed.

THERAPIST: Is there anything you're not satisfied with?

MRS. P.: Well, I would like to have a new house. We had to buy an old house and there wasn't anything to rent or to buy right when we had to move so we bought this old house and it still needs a lot done to it.

THERAPIST: What's your religion?

MRS. P.: Methodist.

THERAPIST: Is religion important in your life?

MRS. P.: Yes, it is.

THERAPIST: Well, in what way?

MRS. P.: Well, I don't think you can get along without it.

THERAPIST: Do you spend a lot of time with church activities?

MRS. P.: Oh, no, no. I haven't been to church in Richmond. We have taken the children to Sunday School.

THERAPIST: Well, do you worry much about what God is thinking about what you're doing?

MRS. P.: I do the best I can.

THERAPIST: Well, I've got enough of the important background information. I will give you one or two questionnaires to do as homework and then next time you come here we'll talk of the treatment procedures.[17] We'll probably be doing a special kind of treatment, called desensitization. It involves deep muscle relaxation and other special procedures. That is all for now.

Case 13: *First interview in a case of interpersonal anxiety* (Miss G., age 21)

This is the transcript of the first of two interviews in a filmed demonstration of basic procedures in behavior therapy of neurosis.[18] The reader should note the therapist's insistent endeavors to define the stimulus sources of the anxiety reactions that the patient reported in certain kinds of social situations. After some initial probing, he turned his attention to that patient's life history, but interrupted the chronicle repeatedly to follow clues that promised to throw further light on anxiety-eliciting stimuli. Toward the end of the interview, he abandoned the uncompleted life history to renew his investigation of these stimuli. Finally, he made an examination of some situations in which self-assertive behavior (see Chapter 7) would be appropriate; but it emerged that the anxiety that Miss G. would have in response to the consequences of

---

[17]Already, at this interview, the patient was given the message that active therapy would begin very soon. As noted on p. 63, however, the first active treatment was assertiveness training.

[18]A film, which is technically excellent, and which consists of excerpts from these interviews, is available from Psychological Cinema Register, Penn State University, State College Pa., under the title *Behavior Therapy Demonstration*. The viewer should, however, know that it is a 35-minute condensation of almost two hours of interviewing which gives it a misleading impression of cursoriness.

assertion was so great as to render futile any attempt at assertive training at this stage. It would first be necessary to desensitize her to being looked at and to disapproval.

THERAPIST: So your name is Carol Green? How old are you?

MISS G.: 21.

THERAPIST: What is your complaint?

MISS G.: I am very very nervous all the time.

THERAPIST: All the time?

MISS G.: Yes, all the time.[19]

THERAPIST: How long has this been so?

MISS G.: Since I was about 14.

THERAPIST: Can you remember what brought it on?

MISS G.: No, not really. I wish I could.

THERAPIST: But, are you not saying that before you were 14 you were not nervous?

MISS G.: Well, I was, but not to this extreme. I remember being . . . especially in elementary school when I would have to read something in front of the class, then I would get very nervous about that—giving speeches or answering in class. That would bother me.

THERAPIST: Well, that is a special situation.

MISS G.: Yes, but now all the time. When I go out of the house, or walk out the door.

THERAPIST: Well, let's try to build up a picture. You say in elementary school you were only nervous when you had to get up and speak in front of the class. Only then?

MISS G.: Yes.

THERAPIST: And then in high school?

MISS G.: It got worse. When we would go out with boys I would be very nervous.

THERAPIST: Do you mean that you became more nervous in front of the class?

MISS G.: I wouldn't sleep for nights worrying about giving a speech in front of class or something like that.

THERAPIST: And you also said you became nervous about going out with boys.

MISS G.: Yes. You know, I was afraid, especially if I would have a blind date I would be scared to death.

---

[19]It is important to establish the presence or absence of continuous anxiety. Its sources are various—the most common being ongoing conflicts, ruminations about possible catastrophes, and pervasive anxiety (see Chapter 11). Here, it turned out later that Miss G.'s statement about being always anxious was incorrect.

THERAPIST: Well, isn't that to some extent natural?[20]

MISS G.: I guess so, but not to the extremes that I would go to.

THERAPIST: And if you went out with somebody you knew. What about that?

MISS G.: Well, after a while I would be a little calmer, but still nervous.

THERAPIST: And what about if you went out with girl friends?

MISS G.: Not as much. I wouldn't be quite as nervous, but still a little bit.

THERAPIST: Were there any other situations in which you developed nervousness while you were in high school?

MISS G.: No others that I can think of, just basically when I would walk out of the house everything would just bother me.

THERAPIST: Everything? Like what?

MISS G.: Well, you know I was afraid to take tests or things like that or make speeches like I said before. Just to be with people would scare me.

THERAPIST: Just being with any people?

MISS G.: Yes, it would bother me more if I was with people I didn't know too well.[21]

THERAPIST: What about at times of vacation?

MISS G.: Vacation? I don't understand what you mean.

THERAPIST: Well, I mean you have to take tests and so on at school, but during vacation there are no tests. So would you still be nervous going out of the house?

MISS G.: A little bit. But not quite as much.[22] Because I wouldn't be thinking of that.

THERAPIST: What year did you graduate from school?

MISS G.: 1963.

THERAPIST: And what did you do then?

MISS G.: I went to school and became a technician.

THERAPIST: What kind of technician?

MISS G.: X-ray.

THERAPIST: Do you like this work?

MISS G.: Not really. It's just because I didn't know really what else to do. I thought it would be interesting and the only reason I went into it is because I thought it was interesting, but once I got there I was very nervous about everything. It scared me to be with patients.

THERAPIST: Patients scared you?

MISS G.: Well, especially the sick ones. If something would happen to them.

---

[20]This was said to imply that her reaction was really not so "far out."

[21]This tells us that her interpesonal anxiety *varies* directly with the strangeness of other persons.

[22]When the threat of tests was present the general level of anxiety was increased.

THERAPIST: You were scared that something might happen to them?

MISS G.: Yes, like they would have an attack or something.[23]

THERAPIST: Has this ever happened?

MISS G.: No, not really.

THERAPIST: Well, it is now about five years since you became a technician.

MISS G.: It is about four.

THERAPIST: During those four years, did you become more nervous or less nervous or stay the same?

MISS G.: Definitely more.[24]

THERAPIST: You have been getting gradually more nervous?

MISS G.: Yes.

THERAPIST: All the time?

MISS G.: Yes. My mouth tightens up all the time.

THERAPIST: I see. Now, are there any special things that make you nervous nowadays?

MISS G.: Special things?

THERAPIST: Well, let's start off by considering your work situation.

MISS G.: Yes.

THERAPIST: You said that sick patients make you more nervous.

MISS G.: And my boss.

THERAPIST: Yes?

MISS G.: He makes me extremely nervous. I am afraid of him.

THERAPIST: Why, is he very strict?

MISS G.: Um, yes, he gives that appearance.

THERAPIST: Does he carry on? Does he scream and so on?

MISS G.: Never at me. But I am always afraid that will happen.

THERAPIST: And what about nurses?

MISS G.: Not really. I am not in too much contact with them.

THERAPIST: And who else scares you?

MISS G.: Men.

THERAPIST: Men?

MISS G.: If I go out with them.

THERAPIST: Yes. What about men who come in where you are working, like medical students?

MISS G.: Yes, they scare me, too. They do.

THERAPIST: They scare you, how?

MISS G.: I am afraid to . . . I don't know. I am not afraid of them really. I am just afraid of how I'll act . . . that my nervousness will show through. And I think about it so much.

---

[23]Here we have anxiety from an entirely different source.

[24]This makes it important to know in what directions reactivity has spread.

THERAPIST: Well, is it correct to say that you are sort of scared of being watched?[25]

MISS G.: Yes. I think everybody is always watching me.

THERAPIST: Now, that is at work. What circumstances scare you when you are away from work?

MISS G.: Just going out. I am afraid, you know, that they'll see the way I am. I am afraid to pick something up, because I am afraid that I am going to shake, and my mouth is all tightened up. I am afraid to look at people directly in the eye.[26]

THERAPIST: Are you only afraid of looking at your escort in the eye, or anybody?

MISS G.: Anybody.

THERAPIST: So looking at a person face to face increases your nervousness?

MISS G.: Yes.

THERAPIST: Suppose that you were walking down the street and there was a bench across the road with some people waiting for a bus. Now those people would be sort of vaguely looking across the street. Would you be aware of their presence?

MISS G.: Yes, definitely.

THERAPIST: Even though they might not be particularly looking at you?

MISS G.: Yes.

THERAPIST: Now, supposing we take people away altogether. Suppose that you are just walking all by yourself, say in a park. There is no one else at all there. Are you then completely comfortable?

MISS G.: Yes.

THERAPIST: I must be quite certain of this.[27]

MISS G.: Yes.

THERAPIST: If you are completely by yourself, are you absolutely calm and comfortable?

MISS G.: Yes, I am. The same way I am at home. I feel all right.

THERAPIST: Well, that means there are some people who can look at you and not bother you.

MISS G.: Yes, at times. But I don't know why this happens.

THERAPIST: Well, what about your mother?

MISS G.: No, it doesn't bother me at home.

THERAPIST: You mother can look at you as much as she likes?

MISS G.: Yes. It's silly but . . .

---

[25]Being watched by people means greater contact than when they are not watching.

[26]This maximizes the effect of the being-looked-at stimulus.

[27]Many patients will initially report moderate distress as "completely comfortable."

THERAPIST: Well, that's not silly.[28] It is just the way things have developed.

MISS G.: I know.

THERAPIST: And who else can look at you without bothering you?

MISS G.: My whole family.

THERAPIST: Who is in your family?

MISS G.: My father, my mother, my sister, my grandmother.

THERAPIST: Besides these people, are there any others at all who can look at you without disturbing you?

MISS G.: No.

THERAPIST: What about a little baby?

MISS G.: No, that doesn't disturb me. And an older person who is senile or something—that doesn't bother me.

THERAPIST: What about a little boy of four?

MISS G.: No.

THERAPIST: Six?

MISS G.: No.

THERAPIST: Eight?

MISS G.: No. It's when they get older, I get nervous.

THERAPIST: Twelve?

MISS G.: Around in their teens.

THERAPIST: About twelve? They sort of begin to bother you?

MISS G.: Yes.

THERAPIST: I take it that a boy of twelve wouldn't be as bad as one of eighteen?

MISS G.: No.

THERAPIST: Let's go back to the street where you are walking and there are three people sitting on a bench across the road. Would it make any difference to you whether they were three men or three women?

MISS G.: No, it wouldn't. I would feel worse if I would see somebody very handsome.

THERAPIST: When you see him, even if he is not looking at you?

MISS G.: Yes, that's correct.[29]

THERAPIST: If you go to a movie and see a very handsome film star, does that bother you?

MISS G.: No, not really, because I know he is not there looking at me.

THERAPIST: And if there is a handsome actor on the stage?

[28]The patient is to accept her reactions as matters of fact. They are neither "wrong" nor "stupid."

[29]At first glance this is an exception to her rule. But on the indications of the succeeding conversation, it seems clear that she was reacting to the anticipation of being looked at by this potentially strongly anxiety-evoking figure.

MISS G.: Yes, it would.

THERAPIST: It would bother you even though he was not looking at you?

MISS G.: Unless it is very dark and he could not see me.

THERAPIST: Well, then, it is only if he can see you that you feel afraid—because you think that he might see you.

MISS G.: I think he might.

THERAPIST: Besides looking at you, what else can people do to make you nervous? You have, I think, mentioned one thing. They can be critical of you. You are scared of your boss criticizing you.

MISS G.: Any criticism gets me upset even if I know that I am right. I can't talk back and tell them that I am right[30] in this case; I just get all choked up and feel like I am going to cry.

THERAPIST: Is there anything else that people do to upset you?

MISS G.: Well, let them just tell me I'm wrong—if I am wrong or if I'm right, it still bothers me. It upsets me.

THERAPIST: That's a kind of criticism. Supposing people praise you?

MISS G.: That makes me feel good.

THERAPIST: It makes you feel good. Okay. Who is older, you or your sister?[31]

MISS G.: I am.

THERAPIST: By how much?

MISS G.: Three years.

THERAPIST: What sort of person is your father?

MISS G.: He's on the quiet side, and both of my parents are on the nervous side. My sister, too. The whole family really.

THERAPIST: Was your father kind to you when you were a little girl?

MISS G.: Yes.

THERAPIST: And your mother?

MISS G.: Yes, she's the stronger one. I'm more like my father and my sister is more like my mother.

THERAPIST: In what way is your mother stronger?

MISS G.: Well, things don't bother her, at least outwardly, as much as they do my father and me. She sort of makes decisions.

THERAPIST: What does your father do?

MISS G.: He sells insurance.

THERAPIST: Did either of your parents punish you when you were young?

MISS G.: They used to hit me once in a while. My mother did. My father hardly ever did.

---

[30]Another major anxiety source.

[31]This begins the questioning about general background.

THERAPIST: Did your mother hit you often?

MISS G.: Not that often.

THERAPIST: Well, did she do anything else to discipline you?

MISS G.: No, that's all. She would have little talks.

THERAPIST: Did you feel when your parents punished you that it was unreasonable?

MISS G.: Sometimes I did.

THERAPIST: Were there any other adults who played any important part in your home life—grandmothers, aunts, nurses?

MISS G.: Yes, my grandmother—she lives with us.

THERAPIST: Okay, well now—what about her? What kind of a person is she?

MISS G.: She is very good to me. I am her first grandchild, so she pays more attention to me than to my sister, but she doesn't understand a lot of things because she wasn't born in America and she did not have an education.

THERAPIST: How do you get along with your sister?

MISS G.: We used to fight an awful lot, but lately we have been getting along better than we used to, but we are not really close because she is completely different.

THERAPIST: What is she like?

MISS G.: She's more talkative than I am—more outgoing. I'm on the quiet side.

THERAPIST: Did you go to school in Philadelphia, Carol?

MISS G.: Yes, I did.

THERAPIST: Did you like school?

MISS G.: Not really.

THERAPIST: What did you dislike about it?

MISS G.: I was afraid of getting up in front of the class.[32]

THERAPIST: Yes, is that all?

MISS G.: Yes.

THERAPIST: How well did you do?

MISS G.: I was a B average.

THERAPIST: Did you take part in sport?

MISS G.: No.

THERAPIST: Did you make friends?

MISS G.: Yes, I have a lot of friends.

THERAPIST: Any close friends?

MISS G.: Yes, one in particular.

THERAPIST: You say that you don't like being an X-ray technician. What would you like to be?

---

[32]This has already been noted and partly explored. It will shortly be pursued further.

MISS G.: I would like to be a kindergarten teacher. I like to be with children.

THERAPIST: Apart from this fear of getting up and speaking, did you have any other fears when you were small?

MISS G.: No.

THERAPIST: Like, maybe, insects, darkness?

MISS G.: I was afraid to take a shower because I had claustrophobia.[33]

THERAPIST: When was that?

MISS G.: It was about 12 or 13. I was afraid to be closed in. Somebody locked me in a closet and I couldn't stand it. It scared me.

THERAPIST: How old were you when that happened?

MISS G.: I really don't remember. I guess about 10 or 11.

THERAPIST: After you were 12, that fear disappeared?

MISS G.: Well, I would still be afraid if someone would lock me in a closet. I am not afraid to take showers.

THERAPIST: Do you like going into elevators?

MISS G.: I used to be afraid; I am not anymore.[34]

THERAPIST: You're quite okay now?

MISS G.: Yes, I take the elevator.

THERAPIST: Do you remember any experience at all when you were at school that was particularly frightening in relationship to getting up and talking in class?

MISS G.: Yes, when I was in sixth grade I had to read something in front of the class. I was holding the paper and I started shaking. And the teacher said "What's the matter?" and I couldn't really talk.[35] And from then on if I had to read something I'd put it down on the desk and look at it. I would still be nervous.

THERAPIST: Before this happened were you already nervous?

MISS G.: Yes.

THERAPIST: And after this, you were much worse?

MISS G.: Yes.

THERAPIST: Let me ask you how you would react to certain everyday situations.[36] Supposing you were standing in line and somebody got in front of you, how would you feel and what would you do?

---

[33]Once again the therapist's persistence yielded some fruit.

[34]Especially in childhood, many fears are overcome by life experiences. Miss G. still had some degree of claustrophobia (in closets), but it was not evidently related to her present serious neurosis.

[35]This seems to have been a critical conditioning event. The tremor of her hands suggests that there may have been a preexisting anxiety conditioning, but since it had not happened before in this situation, some intercurrent physiological cause such as hypoglycemia seems more likely.

[36]The answers to these questions throw light on interpersonal anxieties of the kind calling for assertive training (see Chapter 7).

MISS G.: I wouldn't do anything, but I would feel I would be ready to explode because I would think it was wrong.

THERAPIST: Yes, certainly it would be wrong.

MISS G.: But I can't say anything about it. I can't get up the nerve to say anything.

THERAPIST: And does that apply to every situation of that type?

MISS G.: Yes. There's a man who gets on the same bus and he limps and he hasn't gotten in front of me, but he pushes and slides and nobody says anything to him and it really upsets me because everybody always complains, but nobody says anything.

THERAPIST: Well, why would you not say something to him?

MISS G.: I would be afraid to. He has a mean temper.

THERAPIST: Well, supposing it wasn't him? Supposing you were standing in line at the Academy of Music box office and somebody you don't know got in front of you?

MISS G.: I probably still wouldn't say anything.

THERAPIST: Why not?

MISS G.: Just because I'm afraid to. I'm afraid to open my mouth.

THERAPIST: Does this have anything to do with the idea that if you were to say something, people would start looking at you?

MISS G.: Maybe.

THERAPIST: Let me try to put the question in another way. I would like you to think very carefully before you answer. Supposing you didn't care if people looked at you, would you say something?

MISS G.: I really don't know. It's just that I can't get it out. The words just won't come out.

THERAPIST: Well, all right. You realize that if somebody does a thing like that, getting in front of you, he is doing you a wrong. One of the things you are going to learn to do when you are treated here is to take action about that kind of thing—to stand up for yourself and not allow people to do you wrong.

MISS G.: How do you go about planning that?

THERAPIST: Essentially what you do is to express the annoyance that you rightly feel.[37] It is very hard at first, but if you make a special point of doing it, you find that it gets easier and easier.

MISS G.: I have tried but I can't; if the situation arises, the words just don't come out and I start stuttering.

THERAPIST: Well, I will help you. Later on, each time you come here, I will say, "Carol, did you have any situations of this sort last week?" You will say, maybe, "Yes," and I will want to know what you tried to do about it; and we

---

[37]A basic principle in assertive training (see Chapter 7).

will play-act what you ought to have said and done. But in the meantime, I know it is difficult for you because of the very special fear you have of being the center of attention. If you told someone to get back in line, he would look at you and other people would look at you. And that makes it more difficult.[38]

MISS G.: Yes.

THERAPIST: So one of the things we will have to do is to break down this fear that you have of being looked at. In order to do this, we need to know more about it. Let's use as a kind of basic situation the one we mentioned in which you are seen from a bench across the road.[39] Now, would it make any difference to you how wide the street was?

MISS G.: Yes—if they were closer to me I would feel worse.

THERAPIST: I see. Now I find it very useful to have some kind of quantitative way of expressing how much afraid a person would be. One way to do it is to ask you to think of the worst fear that you ever had and call that 100; and then you think of being absolutely calm, as when you are at home, and call that zero.[40] Now, consider that the street is as wide as Broad Street (about 100 feet) and there is just one person sitting on that bench; how much anxiety would you feel? Would it be 5, 50, or 20 or what?

MISS G.: I guess around 50.

THERAPIST: Now, supposing that the street was twice as broad as Broad Street and there is just this one person?

MISS G.: I guess about 25.

THERAPIST: Now, if you see two persons, would it still be 25?

MISS G.: Yes.

THERAPIST: It doesn't matter how many?

MISS G.: Well, if there is a whole group it's worse.

THERAPIST: Supposing that you are standing at one side of a football stadiium that is twice as wide as Broad Street, and there is one man sitting on one of the stands right across the other side; how much anxiety would that cause you?

MISS G.: Around 25.

THERAPIST: And if, instead of being a man, it is a boy of 12?

MISS G.: It wouldn't be as large . . 5, 10.

THERAPIST: With a boy of 15, would it be in between 10 and 25?

MISS G.: Yes.

THERAPIST: Well, we can use that information in your treatment. But first we have to prepare you. Your problem, as you know, is that you have anxiety where you shouldn't have it. In order to combat the anxiety, we have to use

---

[38]Assertiveness training is for the time being precluded by her reaction to being looked at.

[39]What follows is the beginning of a hierarchy construction (see Chapter 8).

[40]For a discussion of this scale, see p. 141.

emotions within you that can fight anxiety. One very convenient one is the calmness brought about by muscle relaxation. Now, you have probably never learned how to relax your muscles, have you?

Miss G.: No.

THERAPIST: Next time I will start to show you.

In the first of the foregoing two interviews we saw that the basis of a woman's fear of knives lay in interpersonal dissatisfactions, for which, (eventually) assertiveness training was the first and foremost therapeutic need, and not systematic desensitization, as might at first glance have been expected. In the second, widespread social fearfulness called in the first place for desensitization to social scrutiny. Both cases were relatively simple, yet without the details that the interviews provided, treatment could very easily have been misdirected.

These cases were selected as demonstrations of initial interviews precisely because the directions of therapy were so easily apparent. It is by no means always so easy. Sometimes a dozen sessions or more are needed to unravel a patient's web of reactions. And sometimes, as therapy proceeds, new information changes the therapeutic strategy. This information may arise from the patient's day-to-day experiences, or from the therapist's observations of his response or lack of response to the measures being applied. The following cases illustrate this.

Case 15

For two years Mr. D., a lawyer, aged 44, had had difficulty in achieving or maintaining an erection though for the previous 12 years he had had an excellent sexual relationship with his wife, to whom he was strongly attracted. Working at first from the information he had supplied that his first failures had occurred on occasions when he had been unusually tired, I treated him by the *in vivo* method of gradual approaches described in Chapter 10. At first he seemed to improve, but after a few weeks, his sexual performance was quite erratic. He continued to have "a nagging feeling of uncertainty" about his capacity to make love. This made me examine his relationship with his wife more closely. What emerged was that she had for the first ten years of the marriage subordinated her life to his. Then she had become dissatisfied with her situation, and two years before her husband's sexual difficulties began, had consulted a therapist who encouraged her to be her own person instead of an appendage. After some months, she had begun to rebel in various ways. For example, she had started to resist catering and playing hostess at the very frequent parties he had her give in order to make and consolidate his professional contacts. This resistance gave him a feeling of having been rejected and abandoned. It was this feeling that interfered with his erotic responses and impaired his sexual function. (The subsequent treatment of this patient is described under Case 32.)

Case 16

Miss E. was an attractive 33-year-old research worker in the field of sociology. She came for treatment because of an absolute inability to make a marital commitment despite many opportunities, and despite a number of intense and prolonged affairs. The initial behavior analyses, though they revealed some unadaptive social anxieties, seemed to indicate the existence of the usual basis for this complaint—a fear of being tied down (which is often intertwined with claustrophobia).

When some tests of this hypothesis proved fruitless, however, I went into an exceptionally detailed probing of her lovelife from childhood onwards. From this probing, it emerged that her parents had instilled in her a great fear of doing the wrong thing, and her avoidance of marriage was bound up with this in a rather complicated way. It became clear from an examination of Miss E.'s relationships with men that the obstacle to her forming permanent relationships was a *fear of disappointing someone.* Her social inadequacies and her avoidance of marriage were really one problem. If she merely had to refuse a request to borrow a coat, the person would be only slightly disappointed, and Miss E.'s anxiety would be relatively little. This fear was miniscule in comparison to the terror she would feel if she disappointed someone in an important love relationship. If she met a man whom she could envisage as her life's partner, she would at the same time feel, "I really can't be certain; I might have to back out later. Then I'll be disappointing him. . . ."

Treatment consisted of desensitization to a hierarchy of situations in which Miss E. disappointed people, starting with mild kinds of social refusals. With respect to relationships with marriage-worthy men, the strength of the fear varied according to two factors: how deeply the man cared about Miss E., and how long the relationship had lasted. It was the latter that chiefly determined how strongly she felt committed to him, and consequently, how much stress there would be in disappointing him. After 16 sessions, all known areas of useless anxiety had been covered, and therapy was completed.

A year later she reported being almost entirely free of her inappropriate anxieties and the resulting inhibitions. She had been having a very satisfying affair with a man she intended to marry after solving some financial problems. She no longer feared involvements that might lead to marriage (for a full account of this case, see Wolpe, 1976, p. 199ff).

Case 17

Miss Y., a 21-year-old psychology student, complained of a lifelong fear of spiders for which she sought treatment because it had become much more severe during the past few months. The larger the spider, the greater her fear.

At least once a week she had nightmares in which spiders were involved; for instance, they were thrown at her or surrounded her on a beach.

Miss Y. would often feel that there was a spider on her when there was none. No other creature affected her in this way. She had been married two years before, and during the five unhappy months of the marriage, her nightmares had ceased. On her return to her parents' house, they had recurred. The significance of this piece of history was not immediately clear. I decided to treat the spider phobia by systematic desensitization in parallel with a variety of social anxieties.

It became apparent some weeks later that the spider fear and nightmares were due to her mother's relentless grip on her life. What finally overcame the fear of spiders was not its direct desensitization, but the overcoming of her fear of rebelling against her mother through a combination of assertiveness training and systematic desensitization. That the spiders had in a sense become equated with the mother, was shown by the fact that the same feelings were aroused by the dream spiders and the real mother. The equation was confirmed by the disappearance of the peripheral (symbolic) fear when the central one was eliminated.

The occasional occurrence of such symbolism does not justify dream interpretation as it is commonly practiced. Nor does it provide a warrant for incorporating psychoanalytic practices into behavior therapy, as suggested by Feather and Rhoads (1972). These authors reported some cases in which, as in the case of Miss Y, the true source of disturbance was something other than the main complaint. In one case, a woman's fear of cockroaches was found to be mainly an expression of severe marital tensions. There is really nothing psychoanalytic about this and, in fact, in Feather and Rhoads' own thoroughly appropriate therapeutic interventions, no procedures of a psychoanalytic type were actually involved.

6
Cognitive Therapeutic Procedures

The behavioral basis of cognition was discussed in Chapter 2. Cognitive responses are interwoven into practically all human activities, and therefore into all psychotherapy. The patient is aware of the therapist and may be thinking of him as "the man who may help me." He notices the furniture and decor of the office, perceives the therapist's gestures and words, and responds by movements, emotions, and words. If little was said of these natural reactions in the early writings of behavior therapists, it was because to do so seemed as superfluous as to state that a syringe was used when recording that a patient received an injection. I mention this to show the inaccuracy of the allegation of "cognitivists" (for example, Beck, 1976) that behavior therapists try to dispense with cognition (see below).

But besides the presence in the interview situation of the kind of cognitive activity that is part and parcel of human interaction in general, cognitive *procedures* have always been part of the stock-in-trade of behavior therapy as a matter of common sense. To begin with, there is the gathering and organizing of information described in Chapter 5. Then there is the routine of preparing the patient for the specific procedures of behavior therapy.

Behavior therapists have always been mindful that many human problems are due to wrong information or errors of judgment (see Chapter 3). For these they have taken the appropriate cognitive action (Wolpe, 1954, 1958). This means chiefly correcting misconceptions, but there are a number of other behavior therapy techniques that are directed to changing cognitive habits: for example, Taylor's (1959) thought-stopping technique and Cautela's (1967) and Homme's (1965) covert conditioning procedures. All of these were developed on conditioning principles, in accordance with the realization that cognitions are a subclass of behavior.

PREPARING THE PATIENT FOR
BEHAVIOR THERAPY

To introduce the patient to the practices of behavior therapy, the central role of fear (anxiety) in the neurosis must be brought to the fore at an early stage. Most patients are already quite aware that they are hamstrung by fear. No so many recognize that it is the essence of their disturbed reactions (as shown in Table 1.1); but most can accept it when the therapist points it out. The distinctive features of neurotic fears are brought out in statements on the following lines:

> You know that your trouble is having too much fear. It is an emotion that is normal in everybody's life whenever a real threat arises—for example, walking alone and unarmed at night in an unsafe neighborhood, learning that one's firm is about to retrench its staff, or being confronted by a poisonous snake. It is a different matter when fear is aroused by situations that contain no real threat—such as seeing somebody receive an injection, entering a crowded room, or riding in a car—to take examples other than your own. To be fearful in such situations is obviously inappropriate, and this is what we call neurotic fear. It is the task of therapy to detach this from the stimuli or situations that provoke it.
>
> Let us consider how neurotic fears originate. The process is really what common sense would lead you to expect. A severe fear reaction that is aroused in the presence of a particular sight or sound becomes "attached" to it. As a result, the later occurrence of the sight or sound under any circumstances automatically triggers the fear reaction. For example, an American lieutenant "went through hell" in the bursting of high explosive in a pass in Vietnam. A few weeks after he returned to the United States, when he and his wife were walking to a wedding in New York City, a truck backfired near them. He reacted with instant panic, "rolled up next to a parked car, cringing in the gutter."
>
> Your own fears were likewise acquired in the course of unpleasant experiences, which we touched upon in your history. The unpleasant emotions you then had became conditioned, or connected, to aspects of the situation that made an imprint on you at the time. This means that subsequent similar experiences led to the arousal of these same unpleasant feelings. Now, just because this happened as a result of a process of learning it is possible to eliminate the reactions by the application of principles of learning. If, as in the case of the Vietnam lieutenant, your fears are automatic emotional habits, we will have to use other emotions to break down those habits. If any of your fears are due to misinformation, we will provide corrective information.

It is not possible to decondition anxiety from a situation that the patient believes, however wrongly, embodies real danger. No amount of desensitizing effort is likely to make a person indifferent to handling a snake which he believes to be poisonous. Misapprehensions are particularly common in fears of the "hypochondriacal" kind. A patient with recurrent pains in the chest needs to be convinced that the pains do not signify heart disease. If, as in Case

9, there is *in addition* a classically conditioned fear of the symptoms, desensitizing operations can only be effective after the patient has fully realized their lack of significance.

IDENTIFYING FEARS BASED ON MISINFORMATION

It is usually quite easy to decide whether a fear or family of fears is based on classical conditioning or on misinformation, but in many cases it is a very difficult matter that calls for a great deal of perceptiveness on the part of the therapist. This is a faculty that only experience can bestow.

Lande (1981) has shown, however, that it is possible to construct inventories that can be extremely helpful to inexperienced therapists. Lande has exemplified this in the areas of two fears in which classically conditioned and cognitive bases are both common: fears of enclosed spaces, and fears of ominous sensations. In respect of each of these the patient is provided with a list of relevant stimuli in relation to each of which he answers the following questions on a five-point scale (from zero, meaning "not at all," to four, meaning "very much" or "almost always"). The questions are:

1. How much do you become anxious, upset, or fearful either while in the situation or when you think of going into the situation?
2. How often do you *say to yourself* that the situation is physically dangerous either while in the situation or when you think about it.
3. How much do you *truly believe* the situation presents an actual danger?

Examples of items in the enclosed-spaces category are:

1. Stopped in a closed elevator
2. Stopped in a closed subway
3. Closed in a small room
4. Closed in a crowded room
5. Closed in a closet
6. Riding in an airplane
7. Using an oxygen mask.

Examples of "ominous" sensations are:

1. A sense of spinning or rotation
2. A panic attack
3. Prickly sensations in the skin
4. A sense of unreality
5. Dizziness

6. Pain or pressure in the head
7. Pain or pressure in the chest.

Obviously, this kind of questionnaire could be applied to a wide range of unadaptive fears.

COMBATTING COGNITIVELY BASED FEARS

If the therapist has decided that some or all of the patient's fears are cognitively based, he may introduce corrective measures by a general statement like the following:

> Your fears are based on faulty thinking. In the instances where this is a matter of incorrect information, I will point this out and provide correct information, in as much detail as is necessary. To the extent that, even with correct information, you are in the habit of making self-defeating, fear-arousing statements to yourself, I will attempt to reveal this, and will help you to break the habit.

The corrective information will of course be determined by the particulars of the wrong thinking. For example, the patient who fears suffocation in elevators will require appropriate education about elevators. In most cases, verbal information suffices, but in others, actual demonstrations of the ventilation systems of elevators by an elevator technician may be necessary. What is more difficult is the cognitive distortion that may be part of a complex system of faulty thinking woven into the patient's life. A great deal of instruction and argumentation will be needed to overcome it. This is illustrated in detail in the transcribed material from the case of Lisa.

Case 18

Lisa was a very intelligent 35-year-old woman who had suffered greatly for more than ten years from marked irritability, severe depressions, and frequent tantrums, which were sometimes violent. She had never had a coital orgasm, and had accepted the consensus of friends, relations, and doctors that she was constitutionally incapable of normal sexual function, a view that was confirmed in her mind when almost ten years of psychoanalysis had failed to produce any change. This view of herself, coupled with her impression that her husband, Ed, had lost interest in her, filled her with despair, and was behind the depressions and tantrums.

Since the erroneousness of this view was quickly apparent to me, I began, during the history taking, to undermine it at every opportunity. I used the facts Lisa provided to argue that she was a well-integrated person who had, through learning, picked up some unadaptive habits—most notably a fear of trusting people, that was particularly manifest in the context of the most deeply felt sexual experience—the orgasm.

Once she accepted this, Lisa experienced tremendous emotional relief, and was never again subject to depressions or tantrums. Their conceptual basis had been demolished. She subsequently cooperated eagerly in the measures that were instituted to normalize her sex life, measures that are summarized on p. 108.

The following transcript is comprised of excerpts from Lisa's first three interviews. During the first half of the initial interview, I saw Lisa alone and at several points disputed that her disability was a "sickness," and that she was to blame for the marital trouble. Ed participated in the second half, to give him the opportunity to correct Lisa's impression that he did not care for her. At the conclusion of the interview, they were both given the Willoughby Schedule to answer at home. A few days later, Ed called to say that Lisa was in an emotional crisis and had taken 30 tablets of Librium the previous day. I at once arranged a brief emergency session with her, during which she stated that her Willoughby score of 51 in contrast to Ed's 16 had convinced her that she must be hopeless. As the excerpts from the session show, I persuaded her that the difference was due purely to emotional conditioning. After this, she never looked back. The third session continued to dwell on conceptual clarification. The excerpts from it include some of Lisa's background history.

First Session

THERAPIST: I gather from Ed that there is a lack of harmony in certain ways between you.[1] The question is whether there is any practical possibility of straightening out your relationship and making it mutually desirable.

LISA: I think we're very different people. Of course, most people are different, but I think that I married my husband for very neurotic reasons, and I'm sure there had to be something like that on his side too. I've spent ten years in therapy. You're the third doctor my husband has made me come to—not made me come to. I shouldn't phrase it that way.

THERAPIST: Well, sometimes it's not a matter of therapy.[2] Anyway, before we make any decisions, let's get some facts. When did you first meet him?

---

[1]The statement referred to a telephone conversation I had had with Ed before the interview. It was deliberately phrased in these extremely general terms so that the patient could state the issues as she saw them without constraint.

[2]Some marital incompatibilities cannot be resolved by psychotherapy. This is true, for example, of intellectual differences and wide divergencies of interest. This idea was now introduced in order to suggest to the patient that she might, after all, not be "sick," as had always been assumed. As it turned out, this was the key move in the treatment of the case.

LISA: I guess I knew him casually when we were in our teenage years. I was a freshman at college when he was a senior. I didn't start dating him until after my first marriage dissolved.

THERAPIST: What did you like about Ed?

LISA: He was entirely opposite from my father.[3]

THERAPIST: How old were you when your first marriage dissolved?

LISA: 20.

THERAPIST: You liked the fact that Ed was different from your father.[4] Well, what was the difference?

LISA: He was quiet and more stable, certainly emotionally more balanced. He was the type of man that I've always been attracted to—protective, I guess.

THERAPIST: Well, he was stable and elicited a feeling of protectiveness. Is that the essence of it?

LISA: I don't know. I never thought about it that way.

THERAPIST: Did you feel very strongly attracted to Ed at that time?

LISA: Yeah.

THERAPIST: How long after this did you get married?

LISA: Six months.

THERAPIST: And how did you get along with him during those six months?

LISA: Ah—it was sort of a topsy-turvy relationship.

THERAPIST: What do you mean?

LISA: Well, there were certain periods of stress and strain. It was never what I would call a quiet courtship period.

THERAPIST: What were the causes of the stresses and strains?

LISA: Me, I guess. I was a very emotionally sick person at the time and I—

THERAPIST: Something must have upset you.[5]

LISA: I don't know. I guess his background.

THERAPIST: I'm not asking you in that sense. I'm not asking you what caused the upset. I'm just asking what upset you.[6]

LISA: Oh, I don't know. I guess I was demanding and insecure and jealous of the amount of time he spent with me. I never go along on an even keel. I'm always up or down or—

THERAPIST: Still, what are the kinds of things that upset you?[7]

LISA: When he gives attention to another woman, that upsets me.

---

[3]The importance of this became very clear later.

[4]The history of the first marriage was passed over at this point in order to avoid breaking the flow of the story of her relationship with Ed.

[5]Further deflecting from the idea of "sickness" and suggesting accountable reactivity.

[6]Patients who have had psychoanalytically oriented therapy are characteristically more ready to provide causal hypotheses than facts.

[7]The pressure on her continued as she had still offered no facts, only explanation. Her next response had factual content, but it was unrelated to the time in question.

THERAPIST: Well, that's clear enough. Was that the sort of thing that used to happen?

LISA: It's so long ago, I can't remember. I was in such a state of complete unreality when Ed and I were dating. I don't even remember what my behavior was like.

THERAPIST: But you liked to be with him and you were happy with the relationship.

LISA: Yeah.

THERAPIST: But there were just some things that upset you?

LISA: Yeah. Well, I was living at home with a small baby[8]—not exactly an ideal set-up.

THERAPIST: What was the sexual relationship[9] like at that period?

LISA: I don't know. For me there never has been any sexual satisfaction, but I guess I have tried very hard because I want to hold on to him.

THERAPIST: So there wasn't any real sexual enjoyment for you?

LISA: There never has been with anyone.

THERAPIST: You know some women will say they don't reach a climax, but they enjoy sex. You don't even enjoy it?

LISA: Oh, I guess I enjoy it. Yeah, to a point.

THERAPIST: Yes?

LISA: Yes, I guess I never really tore it apart like that.

THERAPIST: Well, do you get stimulated up to a point and then feel left high and dry. Do you feel frustrated?

LISA: No, the anger has completely faded out of it for me. I'm no longer angry about it or demanding of it. I become very irritable and hostile toward Ed.

THERAPIST: Well, that's what I mean.

LISA: But I don't feel that this is my fault because—

THERAPIST: It's not important whose fault it is.[10]

LISA: No, but I mean, there isn't any sexual relationship—unless it comes from me, there isn't any.

THERAPIST: I see. Anyway, going back to that time. At that time, you were having some sex with him?

LISA: Yeah.

THERAPIST: And, you were enjoying it up to a point—

LISA: Oh, yeah.

THERAPIST: And then you were left irritated afterwards?

---

[8]The offspring of her first marriage.

[9]It should be noted how casually this crucial topic was introduced.

[10] I seized every opportunity to assuage guilt and diminish self-blame. It does not matter that in this instance the patient's next remark showed me that I had missed her intent.

LISA: Yeah.

THERAPIST: So that tended to make you keep away from him because it was sort of punishing.

LISA: Well, I think eventually, yes. Especially after you're married and you're legally bound to one another, you're safer and you can turn it off, so to speak, emotionally. When I went to the first psychiatrist, and Ed found out there was a problem, he completely dropped sexual approaches. In the last ten years—if I didn't initiate it, there was nothing. Last year, we went the entire year without any sex at all. But I do feel that my therapy has been—it's been long, but it has served the purpose.

THERAPIST: What purpose has it served?

LISA: Well, I have found out, I think, the reasons for my problems. I consider myself a controlled neurotic[11] now. I'm afraid to do anything.

THERAPIST: You're afraid to do anything?

LISA: Right. I don't do anything—at all. If I know it's dangerous to my—

THERAPIST: This is very important. Take this sexual situation. If you find that sex leaves you very upset and irritated, then it's reasonable to avoid it. It doesn't necessarily mean that your failure to respond sexually is itself neurotic. It may be; I don't know. But it may not be.[12]

LISA: Well, it's a different feeling now. But since I returned to Ed—I'm sure he explained to you—following the circumstances of last fall,[13] he made an effort and I made an effort. But he has backed off and this makes me more irritable—

THERAPIST: He has backed off in what way?

LISA: He doesn't make advances toward me any more. He tried for a while —I never rejected him in this entire period; and I was cooperative and enjoyed it and—

THERAPIST: So today you would like him to make advances?

LISA: But he doesn't. And this is when I started questioning him. I said, "Ed, I am not going to any more psychiatrists because it's a two-way street." And I said, "I am tired of always being the aggressive one in our relationship." I can never be subordinate in my mind if I'm the only one who's aggressive.

THERAPIST: In the beginning, you were the one to avoid intercourse and now he avoids it.

[11]By whatever route her therapy had led to this conception, it boiled down to an acceptance of intractable inferiority. This was the purpose that therapy had served!

[12]Like the referent of footnote 2, a thrust in the direction of throwing doubt on the assumption of the patient's "sickness."

[13]The reference was to an affair with a student that Ed had described to me on the telephone and that she later detailed.

LISA: Well, he avoided it during the entire eight-year period. The doctors questioned about it.[14] They felt that Ed had dropped it much too quickly when he found out that I had a mental block concerning—well, they called it an oedipus complex, a father complex, you don't have the ability to have an orgasm.[15] It's so beyond me. A lot of girls adore their fathers—so what? After ten years of therapy, there certainly should have been some change.

THERAPIST: I agree with you.[16]

LISA: Here we are in the same situation and, for some reason, these women are still very upsetting to me—his mother, his sister—it doesn't make any difference; it's just women in general. My mother was my competitor, so any woman is my competitor.[17]

THERAPIST: Well, do you think you would feel this as much if Ed were making advances to you?

LISA: No, I wouldn't. I would feel more secure.

THERAPIST: That makes sense.

LISA: As it is now, I feel very insecure. I feel any woman is a threat to me. There are certain kinds of women that are very feminine, who seem secure enough in their own life. They don't pose a threat. But then there are those that all of a sudden bleach their hair and are dissatisfied with their home situations. To me they are threatening.

THERAPIST: But there's a basis for this. Ed is a person and has needs. If he doesn't come to you, maybe he feels these dissatisfied people are more accessible.[18]

LISA: Well, if it's that, I've disguised it to myself. Perhaps that would be too horrible for me to face.

THERAPIST: But you are acting as if you were feeling that way, aren't you?

LISA: I guess.

THERAPIST: Apart from this sexual business, how do you get along?

LISA: Terribly. I'm constantly irritable—we're just like two people grating against each other.[19] I do love Ed and we have three of the loveliest children. They're very stable, healthy in body and spirit. It's amazing to me. I look at them and think, "With my mental condition, how could these children possibly be the way they are?" Ed has never been around for 12 years. I guess to es-

---

[14]Without, however, dispelling the belief that the primary blame was Lisa's.

[15]This dogmatic equation would preclude any exploration of the evolution of Lisa's sexual behavior on the part of the analysts.

[16]Reinforcing her questioning of the analytic theory, and augmenting the statements referred to in footnotes 2 and 5.

[17]The reason being, as it emerged, that no other woman suffered from her "abnormality."

[18]Because they are looking around outside of their home situations.

[19]In the light of what has been said, it could scarcely be otherwise.

cape me, he throws himself into work. I don't know. I guess a lot of men do. Maybe it's just a pattern of behavior. It runs in his family. His own sister never stays home and she has four children; and she is constantly going. And his brother has been through three divorces at 38. I look at all these things and I think, "Is it all me?" I've said to Ed, "I'm through with the therapy. I feel like I've been placed under doctor's care so I couldn't make waves[20] so you could go on your merry way and enjoy life while I was trying to keep the lid on, plus raise the children." I guess you get to a certain point where you just don't care.

THERAPIST: Have your thoughts ever turned to other men?

LISA: Last year, I went away with a college student for a few days. He was unhappy with his personal life. His family are our neighbors. He came to speak to me and I got involved. Reality just seemed to leave me. I look at it now and I think it couldn't possibly have happened. But it did.

THERAPIST: Was it an emotionally satisfying situation?

LISA: Emotionally satisfying, yes. It fulfilled a need. I guess I've been looking and looking for years, but I just didn't think it would be a boy of 20.

THERAPIST: Well, that doesn't matter.[21] Did you have orgasms?

LISA: No.

THERAPIST: Well, did you get close to them?

LISA: No.

THERAPIST: What do you think is lacking—preventing you from having an orgasm?

LISA: Well, I've been told it's an oedipus complex.

THERAPIST: Never mind that.[22] What do you think?

LISA: I just don't think that I feel adequate. I don't know.

THERAPIST: Can you picture any circumstances in a relationship that would let you—

LISA: Oh—I feel that I have a fear of losing touch with reality.

THERAPIST: Sort of a fear of letting go, is it?

LISA: This is what it is. I don't trust anyone enough.[23]

THERAPIST: Of course, really, if you have an orgasm, you're not losing touch with reality. You are engrossing yourself very very much in reality.[24] I can see that you might feel the other way, though. We find people who are afraid even to relax.

---

[20]While this was not the purpose of "doctor's care," it was certainly a consequence of it.

[21]A few words to dispel any thought of censure.

[22]A further rejection of the "sickness" diagnosis and a suggestion of self-exploration.

[23]This remark opened a new direction of investigation. What did she mean by "trust"? How did fear of it begin? What factors were involved?

[24]I reverted to this topic because, before going further, I wanted the basic facts of sexual responding to be clear in her mind.

LISA: Well, I never relax either. I don't mean just in sex, I mean in anything. And they tell me, "Don't be nervous." It's very fine to tell somebody, don't be nervous, but—

THERAPIST: Well, I would like to ask Ed to come in and see if we can get some further clues.

(*Ed is summoned and enters.*)

ED: Good morning, sir.

THERAPIST: Do sit down. We've had a brief conspectus of the marital problem from Lisa's point of view and it seems to me that there are both general and situational factors. One situational factor that seems very important to me is that, according to her account, you don't make any sexual approaches to her. Can you comment on that?

ED: I'd say that generally it's true.

THERAPIST: Uh-hum. Well, there must be a reason for it. What prevents you?[25]

ED: There's been a particularly bad spectacle, so to speak, between us over this thing. I was just turned off somewhere along the line.

THERAPIST: Perhaps there has been some bad communication between you. Long ago,[26] Lisa became negative towards sex because she was irritable after not having orgasms. But her feeling is different now. She now looks for signs of affection from you and would respond to them. I guess that you're not aware of that.

ED: Well, she's told me that. Perhaps I have a block now, because of past bad experiences with her.

THERAPIST: Well, do you like her?

ED: I love her.

THERAPIST: Do you like to be close to her?

ED: Very much so.

THERAPIST: Well, how do you get there without approaching her?

ED: I'm not following your question.

LISA: He means how to get to first base, honey, if you don't try.

ED: Oh, I see. Well, it's a good question, but I don't have an answer.

THERAPIST: It's very understandable that you've become scared, like a child who has had his knuckles rapped quite a number of times. To be perfectly frank with you, a situation can become so powerfully aversive that the approach movement cannot be made.[27] There will then be a therapeutic prob-

---

[25]This is a characteristically behavioristic question, seeking the antecedents of behavior. It is to be contrasted with other kinds of therapist responses at a juncture like this—moralizing, directing, interpreting, "reflecting," etc.

[26]A thumbnail resumé of the history as background to discussing the present situation.

[27]By raising the possibility that emotional factors might render action impossible, I freed Ed from the belief that I was pointing an accusing finger at him.

lem. But, before trying therapeutic solutions, I want to see if I can persuade you to make approaches. The fact that the three of us have been discussing the matter openly may already have facilitated action, because you now know in advance, Ed, that you are going to be accepted. Would you welcome it, Lisa?

LISA: I think it would take some effort. I've become angry to the point that I just can't predict an answer. I mean, you can become so completely turned off that it would take a longer period of time to be aroused. But I'd welcome it, sure.

THERAPIST: I think, Lisa, a lot depends on what we mean by an approach. An approach can take many forms. It can be just holding your hand. It can be walking into the kitchen and giving you a hug. At this stage, Ed is sort of hesitant and you are sort of resentful. But since affection is mutual, action should start.[28]

LISA: I think that I would be very suspicious. I would feel that he was initiating it because you told him to.

THERAPIST: Well, that's true, but he also wants it.

LISA: I'm not convinced of that.

THERAPIST: Well, how can we find that out?

LISA: I don't know. I've spent ten years in therapy and I haven't found out.

THERAPIST: I really don't see how that therapy could have helped you find this out. You said that you would be pleased if he were to approach you. If he didn't want you, he could just leave you, couldn't he?

LISA: Yeah. Sure.

THERAPIST: What would be the point in his lying? Why should he pretend he wants you? Why should he endure the dissatisfaction, unless he really hopes that someting will work out?

LISA: Well, I think this is true.[29]

THERAPIST: Therefore, I think there's a primary reason for accepting him. There is what we might call ground for an experiment. I would like to see him making approaches, small approaches, many approaches. He would be uncertain at first, but you would reward him. Then it would become easier for him to do it.

LISA: I have been forthcoming since Christmas time, since I went back to Ed.

THERAPIST: Yes, but I mean when he makes an approach.

LISA: I have.

THERAPIST: But you said he never makes an approach.

LISA: He tried. He read this book by Masters and Johnson, and then he dropped it again.

---

[28]The degree of affection was, of course, questionable.

[29]The purpose (and evident result) of the foregoing argument was to shake Lisa's firmly held conception of Ed's attitude toward her.

THERAPIST: Why did you drop it again, Ed? Did you feel unwelcome or what?

ED: Yes, to a great extent, I did. I felt that it was a failure, although at first we did have a good relationship on occasion. But then after that, if I did reach an orgasm—it was premature and Lisa said, "Why are you so fast?" Sometimes the act just was a failure.

THERAPIST: What is foremost here is not sex, but love of which the sexual act is an outward expression, but not the only one.[30] There are also many small things that happen between people—small approaches where sex needn't happen, and perhaps couldn't happen. If Ed will do these things and Lisa responds positively, a strong feeling of mutual assurance will build up, from which sex is a natural offshoot, though it will not necessarily be an enormous success from the beginning. Lisa's fear of letting go may make it impossible now for her to have coital orgasms. But I'm pretty sure she will eventually have orgasms with you.[31]

LISA: I don't think we accept each other as individuals.[32] Therefore, I don't see how we can possibly have a satisfactory sexual relationship.

THERAPIST: Let's consider that. Sometimes people don't accept each other because they really are terribly different and incompatible. Sometimes they don't accept each other because of a succession of wrong messages. I don't really know what the situation between you is. Let's explore these things. I'll ask each of you some questions. Do you, Ed, feel attracted to Lisa physically?

ED: Yes.

THERAPIST: Do you feel attracted to Ed physically?

LISA: Yes, definitely.

THERAPIST: Do you have a substantial number of common interests?

ED: We have a number of them; we have golf, we have our children.

LISA: I took up golf to be with you.

THERAPIST: But it's there now.

ED: It's there, yes.

LISA: We enjoy it.

THERAPIST: What else are you interested in?

LISA: Not very much anymore.

THERAPIST: What could you be interested in?

---

[30]The expression of affection solely in the context of sexual intercourse is amazingly common, and a major source of marital trouble.

[31]This speech exaggerated the potentialities of the situation in order to encourage the approach experiment as much as possible, and to reveal the obstacles.

[32]Now, though granting mutual goodwill, she expressed the idea that a fundamental incompatibility comes between them.

LISA: Creative things. Anything creative; I sew a lot. Things that Ed isn't interested in.

THERAPIST: Well, you don't have to share everything.

LISA: Don't you have to share some things?

THERAPIST: Some things.[33] You have golf and you have the children.

LISA: But golf only came about in the last four years.

THERAPIST: That doesn't matter. It's here now. What about movies and books and so on?

LISA: We don't like the same movies at all.

THERAPIST: I think the most important thing is a feeling of mutual participation in living itself. That is more important than movies and books, to the extent that you can feel yourselves capable of building a life together, in which your house and children are an important part. Do you have any such general feeling?

ED: Of being able to build a life together?

THERAPIST: Yes.

ED: Oh, certainly I have.

LISA: I thought you said "participation."

THERAPIST: Yes. I mean emotional participation in building a life together.

ED: Well, I think that—I think we both really want than. I think this is—

THERAPIST: All right, Lisa, what are the things that you would like that Ed doesn't provide?

LISA: Well, I think the most important thing is to be able to see somebody's needs. And when they need you, you've got to be there.[34]

THERAPIST: I'll tell you what I'd like you to do. Would you each make a list of the things that you feel come between you? As many as you can. Then I would like you to give each other these lists and indicate whether you think that anything can be done to reconcile each particular objection. I would also like each of you to fill in one of these Willoughby Questionnaires.

Second Session This was an emergency session that took place four days later, three days before the next one scheduled. Ed telephoned to tell me that Lisa had been in a state of great emotional distress, because of which she had swallowed 30 tablets of Librium the previous day. I asked him to bring her to see me without delay. The following is the relevant part of the brief, but important, interview that followed:

THERAPIST: You seemed rather hopeful at the end of the last session. Then there was a collapse. What happened?

---

[33]There was a reasonable amount of mutual interest to build on.

[34]She saw Ed as insensitive and unresponsive to her needs.

LISA: Those Willoughby tests we did showed that I am the sick one and that Ed is the normal one. My answer to practically every question is the opposite to his. He was right all along. His answers show stability and mine show instability. I feel hopeless.

THERAPIST: That test measures social neuroticism. That means the extent to which there is excessive anxiety or nervousness in relation to other people. Your score of 51 in contrast to his of 16 shows that you are much more vulnerable than Ed is to people's statements and their attitudes toward you. But this anxious reactivity is not organic. It is not inherited. It was acquired by learning. It is a matter of emotional learning. What has been learned can be unlearned.

LISA: But how? All these years of psychotherapy!

THERAPIST: Well, we have methods that are based on our knowledge of how learning takes place. Your previous therapists did not use such methods because they operated on the theory that your troubles are caused by emotional complexes deeply buried in your supposed unconscious mind. Since that theory, though very widely held, has no scientifically acceptable support, it is not surprising that their efforts have not helped you.

LISA: I never could understand how all the analyzing of my childhood was supposed to help. But what else would help?

THERAPIST: If we take a laboratory animal and make him fearful by means of a mild electric shock in a particular room or in the presence of a particular sound, such as a gong, that room or that gong will become attached to the fear—associated with it. It acquires independent power to arouse fear. The fear reaction to the gong can last for years even if the animal is never again given a shock in its presence. But we can do things with him that we know will break that habit. I am sure that when we examine your history we will find that you have had experiences that led to your reacting fearfully to various social situations, including certain aspects of sex. Different kinds of experiences can be arranged here that can disconnect fear from these situations.

LISA: I get the idea.

THERAPIST: We'll begin to develop that kind of program when you come here on Thursday as arranged. How do you feel now?

LISA: Happier. Very encouraged.

Third Session

THERAPIST: How have you been feeling in the last three days?

LISA: I felt very, very good. Better than I've felt in a long time. It's a strange feeling when somebody offers you a hug and you're ready to grab it.[35] I feel like some sort of halfway home.

---

[35]The elucidation of the nature of her illness at the second interview had given her a feeling of

THERAPIST: Well, we have to proceed systematically now. What have your complaints been?[36]

LISA: All of them? You mean my complaints of my marriage or of my personality?

THERAPIST: You had psychiatric treatment. What has been the trouble in that area?

LISA: The fact that I haven't been able to produce since I was about 13 years of age. My studies started to fail. I was a very bright student—bright enough to have skipped sixth grade. Then I started to slip. I became grossly overweight, and then I was sent to a fine girls' school, but it wasn't fine for me. I became heavier and my work failed. I was taken out and sent to public high school for the last year where I didn't produce either. I was accepted at the Philadelphia Museum School of Art, but I wasn't permitted to attend. I was sent to Penn State University. I still could not produce.

THERAPIST: Okay, you were unproductive. What do you think was the reason for this?

LISA: I refused to compete because I didn't want to fail. My father only has one measuring stick, and that's the top; there's no in-between. It's either A + or nothing. And I was tired of my mother as a competitor. I always came out second-best anyway.

THERAPIST: Now, there was a time when you were doing very well.

LISA: Uh-hum.

THERAPIST: And then you stopped doing very well. Something must have changed. What changed?

LISA: I don't know. Me. I had a sexual attitude, I guess. I don't know.

THERAPIST: Why do you say a "sexual attitude"?

LISA: I don't know. It must have been. Isn't that the age when you start to have—[37]

THERAPIST: Maybe, but I want to know what actually happened to you.

LISA: Nothing. Not a thing.[38] It was just a period of—I started to change.

THERAPIST: Well, there was a time when you did your work and a time when you didn't. What was it that prevented you from doing your work?

LISA: A lack of desire.

THERAPIST: You lost interest in work?

---

my complete acceptance and convinced her that her troubles were not only understood, but also remediable. The emotional crisis that preceded that interview was the last of its kind to date. She subsequently had "normal" upsets to ordinary frustrations and difficulties, but no more of the helpless distress that had previously been more or less constant.

[36]It was necessary to pose this question anew because we had previously concentrated on the sexual problem and its repercussions.

[37]The "explanation" presumably came from her psychoanalytic mentors.

[38]This is not credible. Something *must* have happened. The patient may truly be unable to recall it. The therapist must do all he can to jog her memory—but gently, not derogatorily.

LISA: It was a way of getting complete attention because I didn't do it.[39]

THERAPIST: No, that's theory. Don't give me any theory. We have lots of theories.

LISA: I don't know. I can't tell you. It was so many years ago. I was so nervous. Maybe I couldn't concentrate.

THERAPIST: What made you nervous? What were you nervous about?

LISA: Maybe of being accepted into a world I didn't want any part of. I don't know. I guess I had seen a bad relationship between my mother and father. Maybe I didn't wish to grow up.

THERAPIST: You are full of psychoanalytic indoctrination, and when I ask you to tell me what happened, you give me theory. I don't want theory.

LISA: But I don't know what happened.

THERAPIST: I'm just asking you what were the events. I don't want to know motives or things like that. I want you to give me a kind of story. The details will be yours. The kind of story I'm expecting from you now is this: "I was doing fine until the age of 15 and then my grandmother began to live with us. There are things about her that I find disturbing and I got into a nervous state and I couldn't do my work." These would be facts; that's the kind of story I want.

LISA: There had been a great big Halloween Party in fourth grade and we had all run off in the woods.[40] And I can remember the boys starting to tease us and call us by dirty names, you know. And then in junior high school, boys who had also transferred from the other school continued to ride me.

THERAPIST: They continued to ride you?

LISA: Yeah, about these episodes that had happened when we were in fourth grade. They kept calling me names. I can remember how tremendously upsetting it was. Some days I didn't even want to go to school.

THERAPIST: You were very distressed by the attitude of these boys?

LISA: Mortified. Just absolutely horrified.[41]

THERAPIST: This went on all through the seventh grade?

LISA: Eighth grade and part of ninth.

THERAPIST: Now you're telling me the kind of thing I want to know. Were you sensitive to other things that people might say?

LISA: Oh, yes. I had my nose straightened a few years ago. I had a pug nose, not large, but enough that I looked like my mother. They used to tease me about this nose and it upset me.

---

[39]She had either been told this or deduced it from standard psychoanalytic thinking. I continued to press for facts from her own experience.

[40]Lisa having finally understood what I meant by *facts,* we began to get some.

[41]Possibly a key conditioning experience in the development of the "fear of trusting," one of whose results was the inhibition of her sexual response.

THERAPIST: How would you defend yourself?

LISA: By retaliating or saying something harsh about some other person—which I didn't do.[42] I usually was so wounded that I never said anything. There was also no doubt about my parents being critical of me. I mean it was a life of criticism: "Sit straight"—"Put your napkin on your lap."

THERAPIST: Are your parents alive?

LISA: Yes.

THERAPIST: What sort of a person is your father?[43]

LISA: Brilliant—unfortunately. He's always a perfectionist.

THERAPIST: How did he treat you when you were a little girl? Was he good to you?

LISA: Oh yes—yes, very good—very generous. He didn't have very much time, because of his business, to give to me, but he was very generous materially. He never doled out any punishment—my mother gave it all. He always wanted to be the good guy.

THERAPIST: And he always wanted to see high standards from you?

LISA: Oh yes—completely. He gave me everything he lacked when he was raised in the semislums of Philadelphia.

THERAPIST: What about your mother?

LISA: Possessive—critical—domineering—competitive—negative—but she tried to do everything for me. I mean I never lacked anything. She was always there to drive me or take me or pick me up.

THERAPIST: Well, what was your general feeling towards her?

LISA: I didn't like her—I still to this day can't bear to have her near me or touch me. I didn't want either of them to touch me as a child.[44] It even distresses me to think about it—that's how hostile I was towards both of them.

THERAPIST: Something must have happened to make it unpleasant.

LISA: She was just critical—it was just one constant criticism.

THERAPIST: What in particular did she criticize?

LISA: I don't mean criticizing me as a person—I mean critical of my actions—if I didn't put my napkin on my lap at dinner time—corrective measures. It was just a constant sort of thing. My father had a very destructive side. He used to get me pets and if they didn't please him, then he would have them given away or destroyed, which was extremely upsetting to me as a child.[45]

---

[42]Patients are often aware that they should behave assertively, but usually cannot do so without help.

[43]This began the formal background questioning. Topics previously covered were, of course, not repeated.

[44]It is possible that this negative conditioning to touching was a factor in the development of her sexual inhibitions. She had, however, always enjoyed erotic touching.

[45]It is easy to see how this would have increased her fear of trusting people close to her.

THERAPIST: That extraordinary.

LISA: It's a little cruel, isn't it? When I went away to school and wasn't a good student, when I came home for vacation my dog was gone. When I first got married, I had played the piano for 14 years. I came back and my piano was gone. There were lots of little things like that. When I wouldn't divorce my first husband during a very rocky marriage, I was disowned. It's amazing to me that I've lasted 12 years with Ed. To me it's just incredible; that he's seen all of me and he still doesn't hate me.

THERAPIST: Well, why should he?

LISA: I guess because maybe I hate myself and I'm sure everyone else will, too. I mean in total picture; oh, there are lots of things I don't desire to change at all.

THERAPIST: You mean you expect to be hated?

LISA: Maybe, yes—disliked.

THERAPIST: But you might be quite wrong in thinking that you should be.[46]

LISA: I don't know.

THERAPIST: Well, I rather think that's true. At what age did you have your first sexual feelings?

LISA: Towards boys—I guess about—

THERAPIST: Did you have them towards girls?

LISA: No. I guess around nine—eight or nine.

THERAPIST: Did you engage in masturbation?

LISA: Yes.

THERAPIST: At what age?

LISA: About nine.

THERAPIST: Did you have any feelings of guilt about it?

LISA: Yes.

THERAPIST: What did you think would happen?

LISA: I was afraid someone would discover me.[47]

THERAPIST: You didn't think it would do anything terrible to you?

LISA: I didn't know.

THERAPIST: Well, some just enjoy themselves and don't care.

LISA: Oh, really?

THERAPIST: And some have been given some sex instruction and they—

LISA: I was given none—ever about anything.

THERAPIST: So you had a sort of fear of discovery. But did you have any fear that you might be doing harm? Did you think that God might punish you?

---

[46]Putting a spoke in the wheel of this belief.

[47]This early fear was another etiological factor in the development of her sexual inhibition, in which the production of fears of being revealed and of trusting seemed to have combined.

LISA: There wasn't any God in my life. I had never been taken into the Church.

THERAPIST: When did you start dating and all that sort of thing?[48]

LISA: Well, I went to dancing class when I was about nine years of age—but dating—maybe twelve, thirteen—you know, little parties where your parents drove you, picked you up—stupid little tea dances.

THERAPIST: Well, when did you become interested in any person?

LISA: I was interested very definitely in one boy when I was—from about the age of nine on till about twelve or thirteen maybe. I thought he was perfectly marvelous.

THERAPIST: What did you think was marvelous about him?

LISA: He was just bright and blond and handsome and athletic.

THERAPIST: Was there anyone important before your first husband?

LISA: No—none.

THERAPIST: What was your first husband's name?

LISA: Sid.

THERAPIST: What did you like about him?

LISA: He was blond and charming and quiet, pleasant and handsome—all the men in my life were quiet.

THERAPIST: Well, what happened?

LISA: It was one constant harangue—one violent fight after another.

THERAPIST: What were the causes?

LISA: I guess I was hostile and irritable. Sexually we weren't compatible—I knew something was wrong with me.

THERAPIST: With you?

LISA: Yes—I mean I couldn't achieve orgasm and, of course, this started to disturb me greatly.

THERAPIST: Was this the main thing that disturbed you?

LISA: Oh, I think so, yes.

THERAPIST: This is terribly important. Are you telling me that if you had had orgasms no trouble would have arisen in this marriage?

LISA: I think I would have been able to adapt. I really don't know. I mean if you're irritable and hostile because your sexual relations aren't right—how do you know how you'd react to everyday living?

THERAPIST: Well, tell me, actually what used to happen?

LISA: It just was a tempestuous sort of relationship. I think he was a perennial sophomore college type and, of course, I was trying to do all the little things to make a marriage hold together. He wanted a playmate and I wasn't it.

THERAPIST: Before you married did you get on well?

---

[48]Further inquiries into her sexual history were now begun in a very open-ended way.

LISA: Oh, yes. I can never remember one bad fight that we ever had.[49]

THERAPIST: Then, when you got married and there were attempts at sex, you would get roused and you wouldn't have an orgasm?

LISA: We had sex a few times before we were married and of course, when I didn't have any orgasm he said, "Well, that's all right because it's unnatural circumstances and you're not relaxed," etc. Of course, after you get married, you're supposed to be relaxed, aren't you?

THERAPIST: Are you saying that not having orgasms had a very strong physiological disturbing affect?

LISA: Definitely it did. It was so disturbing I went to see a strange doctor down in Memphis, Tennessee. All he did was look at me and say, "Well, I'm sure it will right itself in time—don't worry about it."

THERAPIST: Can you say why you didn't have orgasms? Could it have been anything to do with him?

LISA: No—it's me.

THERAPIST: No, wait a minute—that's sort of—

LISA: An assumption—I shouldn't—

THERAPIST: I'd just like to know why you say that—could it be that if he had handled you differently, you might have had orgasms?

LISA: No. There have been many men in my life since my first husband. It's me.

THERAPIST: Has your pattern of response to each of them been the same?

LISA: Exactly.

THERAPIST: What is that pattern of response?

LISA: Pleasure to a certain degree and wanting to be closer to somebody; and yet when it comes to the act of intercourse—nothing. You know I've always made a joke, saying I want somebody to hold my hand—period. Maybe I'm still waiting to go back to adolescence.[50]

THERAPIST: That's rubbish.

LISA: Well, I don't know—may not be.

THERAPIST: You say you get pleasure up to a degree. Tell me what the pattern is in detail?

LISA: I don't dislike it. I find the intimacy pleasurable and I like to be close to Ed—but there's no sensation there at all. I become a little edgy about it—uncomfortable—it makes me feel bad—sad—melancholy—not irritable, as in the past—I accept the pleasure that I do get to a certain degree, and accept the fact that there is nothing else. I have accepted this.

[49]This strongly suggests that they might have "made out" if there had been no sexual problem.

[50]Even if there had been some evidence to support this proposition, it had no practical implications, suggested no direction of action for change.

THERAPIST: Well, what actually happens—first of all, there's petting, etc. Do you find that pleasurable?

LISA: Yes—I find everything pleasant.

THERAPIST: Do you get excited?

LISA: Oh, yes.

THERAPIST: Do you get really strongly excited?

LISA: Yes.

THERAPIST: And then it's only during the actual act of intercourse that you get no sensation?

LISA: No sensation whatsoever.

THERAPIST: What happens if your clitoris is stimulated?

LISA: Nothing.

THERAPIST: Nothing at all?

LISA: No.

THERAPIST: But you said to me at an earlier stage that you had masturbated.

LISA: Yes.

THERAPIST: Does that mean that an orgasm can be induced by digital stimulation?

LISA: It hasn't so far—no.

THERAPIST: And by you yourself?

LISA: No.

THERAPIST: When you were a child?

LISA: No.

THERAPIST: You never had an orgasm?

LISA: Yes I have, but I don't touch myself.[51]

THERAPIST: How do you have an orgasm?

LISA: By crossing my legs and applying pressure on my muscles.

THERAPIST: Well, what does that stimulate?

LISA: I guess my clitoris, I don't know. I mean medically I don't know.

THERAPIST: I'll try not to impose the answer on you.

LISA: Well, I don't know the answer.

THERAPIST: But if it's compressed by hand, that doesn't have any effect?

LISA: No.

THERAPIST: How often can you have an orgasm that way?

LISA: How often? What do you mean how often?

THERAPIST: Well, can you do it every day?

LISA: Oh, certainly.

THERAPIST: Can you do it repeatedly?

LISA: Four or five times in a row.

---

[51]Once again demonstrating the value of insistent questioning. Her ability to have masturbatory orgasms was crucially important.

THERAPIST: You regularly do that sort of thing?

LISA: Not every day—no, but when I do I can maybe four times in a row. So I'd say I'm a pretty healthy woman. But for some reason I cannot build up an intimacy with another person. And it's not just Ed. It's anybody.

THERAPIST: Why do you say it that way? You say you can't build up an intimacy. Do you mean that in a general way or just in a physical sense.

LISA: I mean in any way.

THERAPIST: You spoke of this kind of thing happening when you were at school. There was sort of a fearfulness about persons. Do you still have the feeling that way?

LISA: Yes.

THERAPIST: Well, that might be the clue. Let me just pursue it one step further. Suppose you have been stimulated sexually and you haven't had an orgasm in the usual way, can you or do you then go ahead and give yourself one by compressing your thighs?

LISA: No.

THERAPIST: Now, why is that?

LISA: Because Ed is there.[52]

THERAPIST: Oh, I see.

LISA: I told you it was an embarrassing thing with me when I was a child and it still is. I guess it became a personal withdrawn sort of action.

THERAPIST: How terribly interesting. Next week we'll begin treatment.

LISA: You mean there's treatment for this?

THERAPIST: Oh, yes. We do have to have a little more history—but not much.

The first target in the domain of sex was to overcome Lisa's fear of being observed having an orgasm. Further questioning revealed that if she planned to masturbate, even Ed's geographic proximity made her anxious. She would feel it if he was visiting three houses away, and it increased when he was nearer. Accordingly, desensitization on a proximity dimension was planned. But the first time she was asked to close her eyes for the purpose of relaxing, she became very anxious—another manifestation of her fear of trusting people. Through periods of *in vivo* eye closing for as long as she was comfortable, she came to tolerate long eye-closure in the course of a single session indefinitely, and then desensitization overcame the anxiety related to Ed's proximity during masturbation in several further sessions.

Once Lisa was able to masturbate imperturbably in Ed's presence, it was

---

[52]This answer was the "open sesame" of the case. It was now plain that all efforts directed at giving Lisa coital orgasms must fail as long as she could not bear to be seen having even masturbatory orgasms.

possible to organize a series of steps through which the masturbatory orgasm was integrated into coitus in a way that both of them found satisfying. The jealousy reaction faded out as sexual progress continued. Five months later, Lisa wrote: "My days continue to be filled with sunshine and my evenings begin with a million stars." There has not been even the shadow of recurrence of serious emotional disturbance in a nine-year follow-up.

Lisa's chronic distress and violent emotional storms resulted from a misconception of a rather unusual kind. False beliefs of dire physical or mental illness are probably the most frequent souces of cognitively based neuroses.

Baseless fears of heart disease are usually associated with tachycardia, palpitations, or pain in the front of the chest. It is necessary in every case to eliminate the existence of actual pathology by a thorough medical investigation. In some cases this alone will put an end to the fear (see, for example, Case 19). Other patients, not unreasonably, require in addition a positive explanation for the pain, which is usually caused by gastrointestinal distension or skeletomuscular conditions of the chest wall. In many gastrointestinal cases the characteristic pain can be convincingly elicited by drinking a glass of orange juice to which a teaspoonful of sodium bicarbonate has been added. This experience is more effective in quelling such a fear than verbal assurances. But in some cases, no amount of cognitive correction suffices, because a classically conditioned fear reaction to the pain also exists; and being a function of subcortical conditioned connections, it is impervious to logic (see, for example, Case 9), so that systematic desensitization or an equivalent procedure must also be instituted.

As noted earlier, when anxiety is exceptionally severe or prolonged, it may cause sensations that are strange to a person. Sometimes there appears to be a mutual inhibition of anxiety and some other simultaneously aroused emotion, producing a feeling of "deadness" or "unreality" (see Wolpe, 1958, p. 82). These bizarre or unusual sensations may cause the patient to suspect that he is in some way "cracking up," and he may view the commonly encountered inability of physicians to provide reassurance as confirmation of his suspicion. A vicious circle of mounting fear in response to symptoms that become unceasingly severe is thus set up. The behavior therapist must provide the strongest reassurance. Quite often he can cause some or all of the bizarre sensations to be evoked by having the patient voluntarily hyperventilate. I often tell the patient who fears that he is on the brink of mental collapse that he is simply not of the "right" constitutional type, and that I am willing to give him a written guarantee. Some sophisticated patients may be given the varied evidence of constitutional predisposition (Wolpe, 1970), and some may have to be offered the ultimate reassurance of a pupillography investigation that detects predisposition to schizophrenia (Rubin, 1970).

The following cases are examples of the treatment of anxiety-response habits based on incorrect cognitive associations.

Case 19

Mr. S., a 43-year-old car dealer, was sitting in an office doing routine work, when suddenly he felt flushing of his face, shortness of breath, and a constriction in his chest. He became very anxious, thinking that he was about to die, because his father and brother had both died of heart attacks, and his sister had died of high blood pressure. Even though a medical checkup showed that he was in perfect health, he was left with the feeling that something was wrong. From then on, he was continuously anxious whenever he was alone. He also occasionally had inexplicable, frightening attacks like the first one. These were very likely due to paroxysmal tachycardia.

When I first saw Mr. S., this fear had been with him for five years. I began by carefully explaining to him that the major attacks were typical of a kind of rapid beating of the heart that occurs in normal people. It starts suddenly, stops just as suddenly after minutes or hours, and produces strange sensations like those he had experienced. While it is an unusual state of heart function, it is not harmful. It took six sessions and the help of medical textbooks to convince him that he was in no danger. Through losing his fear of these symptoms, he lost his fear of being alone. On a later occasion I saw Mr. S. during an attack and confirmed the diagnosis of paroxysmal tachycardia.

Case 20

Mrs. T., 60 years old, had had an obsessional fear of cancer for 20 years, that had not been helped by numerous treatments, including psychoanalysis and insulin-shock treatment. When she was 17, her parents had persuaded her to marry a kindly man of "good family" to whom she was not attracted and who was not as bright as she. The marriage was an emotional disaster, but she was unable to leave her husband because she was afraid that her parents would disapprove. As time went on, the anxiety caused by her conflicting emotions increased, generating "terrible depressions and attacks of panic."

When Mrs. T. was 51, she had a hysterectomy for benign myomata of the uterus. On coming around from the anesthesia, she asked the nurse, "Did I have cancer or didn't I?" The nurse replied, "A friend of mine had cancer and lived to be 70." Mrs. T. was terrified, and even when the surgeon showed her reports that the tumors were not malignant, she remained unconvinced. She began probing for cancers, especially in her breasts, and then, as time passed, she moved to suspecting other parts of her body at the slightest provocation. When Mrs. T. came to see me, she was obsessed with the thought that she had cancer of the intestines. She scrutinized her bowel movements and panicked at any slight diarrhea or constipation. She was under the impression that cancer could develop in a day or a week; consequently, she had had repeated x-rays and other examinations.

Realizing that it was her wrong thinking that had to be changed, I presented her with pathological evidence that cancer of the bowel takes a year to double its size. She had recently had a sigmoidoscopy that had shown no abnormality of the bowel wall. "If," I reasoned with her, "you have a cancer of the bowel now that is so small that it cannot be seen with this instrument, it will still be of neglible size a year from now. Even then it may be too small to be detected. And a cancer of the bowel that small cannot produce diarrhea or any other symptoms. So cancer is the one thing that *cannot* be their cause. A once-a-year checkup with this instrument is more than enough." This argument repeated in different ways over several sessions markedly diminished her fear. (Her social fears needed to be treated by a combination of assertiveness training and systematic desensitization.)

It is often not enough just to reason with a patient if his thinking is to be changed. An activity in which he participates can play a vital role in changing what he perceives to be the source of fear. The activity may be quite elaborate, as illustrated in the unusual case of Mr. E. who had an all-engulfing fear of rabies.

Case 21

Mr. E.'s fear of rabies had begun two years previously when, having been scratched by a stray cat, he had seen a doctor who had asked him, "Do you reckon that cats may be rabid"? Two months before he came to see me, the fear had become much worse after he had read of a child who had died of rabies after being bitten by a bat in daylight. Because he knew that bats fly most often after dark, Mr. E. had long been afraid at night. He had blocked the chimney and locked all the doors and windows; but since reading about the boy, he had become reluctant to go out even during the day.

I therefore had to convince him that he had an impregnable defense against rabies. At the time, only a painful and temporarily effective vaccine was available, but he was willing to put up with the discomfort of the vaccine in order to become free of his fear. Since serum examination at the university's laboratories showed no antibodies to rabies, we went ahead with the vaccination. A few days later a second examination showed significant antibodies. Both reports were shown to Mr. E., who, upon reading them, felt very relieved. His family doctor in his home town agreed to provide booster injections as often as necessary. Mr. E.'s belief that he now had nothing to fear from any rabies-infected bite (no matter how remote the possibility), put an end to his fearful obsession. Nevertheless, he was enjoined to consult his doctor at once if by chance he were bitten because of the danger of sepsis.

Follow-up information was obtained through the family doctor over a period of eight years. The phobia did not recur, and the treatment was later facilitated by the development of a less painful vaccine with more durable effects. The case affords a striking illustration of the enormous power of belief, first in causing a severe useless fear, and then in overcoming that fear.

Thought Stopping

Thought stopping is a method of changing cognitive behavior that, unlike the foregoing, does not depend on changing the meanings of words or the implications of situations. It is a way of eliminating day-to-day preoccupations with useless thoughts. It consists of training the patient to exclude at the earliest moment—even, if possible, before its formulation—every undesirable or unproductive thought.

Thought stopping was introduced to me by James G. Taylor in 1955 (see Wolpe, 1958), but, unknown to him, it had already been described by Alexander Bain (1928). Rosen and Ornstein (1976) have recently discovered a still earlier usage by Lewis (1875). Lewis treated a man who was preoccupied with thoughts of nude women by having him change the contents of his thoughts whenever a sexual idea entered his mind, a program that proved very effective.

Taylor regarded the method as parallel to his successful treatment of a case of compulsive eyebrow plucking of 31 years' duration by training the patient to inhibit the chain of movements leading to the compulsive act (see Taylor, 1963). If motor habits can be overcome by inhibiting the relevant response, so can thinking habits.

Unrealistic, unproductive, and anxiety-arousing, perseverating trains of thought are a common clinical problem. If chronic, they are called obsessions. Many are only episodic. A businessman, for example, constantly brooded upon the possibility of a fire breaking out in one of his warehouses after a friend of his suffered a severe financial loss.

An essential preliminary to training in thought stopping is to reach agreement with the patient that particular categories of thought are indeed futile and therefore worth the trouble necessary to eliminate them. The training typically begins by asking the patient to close his eyes and verbalize a typical futile thought sequence. During the verbalization the therapist suddenly shouts, "Stop!" and then draws the patient's attention to how the thoughts actually *do* stop. This is repeated several times, and then the patient is urged to try stopping the thoughts by saying "Stop!" himself, subvocally. He is warned that the thoughts will return, but every time they do, he must interrupt them again. Effort is later directed at trying to stifle each unwanted thought at its birth. The moment it looms, the patient must quickly inhibit it by concentrating on something else. The thoughts in many cases return less and less readily and eventually cease to be a problem.

Modifications of the method are applied to patients with whom the standard procedure fails. A fairly uncomfortable faradic shock accompanying the "stop" signal may successfully disrupt the negative thought sequence. Or the patient may be asked to keep his mind on pleasant thoughts and to press a button which activates a buzzer each time a uselsess thought intrudes. Whenever the buzzer sounds, the therapist instantly shouts, "Stop!" Usually, in the course of the session, there is a progressive decline in buzzer pressing, which may be steep, e.g., from 20 times per minute to once every two minutes in the course of a 15-minute treatment period.

Some years ago, I took advantage of an opportunity to observe the effects of this procedure on myself. I had been involved in a legal dispute that was finally settled at a meeting of principals and lawyers. Later that day, reflecting upon the proceedings, I became very disturbed when I realized how ineptly I had handled an important interchange. Dwelling continuously on the matter, I became increasingly distressed. I decided to try the thought stopping that I so readily recommended to patients who had this kind of problem. I found it very difficult to do, for the thoughts were seemingly borne along by the anxiety that they themselves had stirred up; but I worked at it assiduously, and after an hour, I noticed that the general anxiety level was distinctly lower. After two more hours, I was no longer troubled by these thoughts. Even when my anxiety was high, it seemed that the successful exclusion of a thought slightly diminished it, but when the anxiety was low, this effect was quite marked.

While thought stopping has its most frequent use for episodic preoccupation or brooding, it is also occasionally of great value in the treatment of true obsessions. In an obsessional neurosis of eight years' duration reported by Yamagami (1971), it was the sole agent of recovery. The patient was a 24-year-old male graduate student whose obsession consisted in verbalizing in thought the names of colors, counting numbers, and typing words in fantasy. The color obsession was predominant, occurring an average of 110 times per day. Colored sticks, which could trigger the color obsession, were placed in front of the subject. He was told to look at them and not to try to suppress whatever obsessional thinking came to mind. He was to signal the onset of the obsessive thoughts by raising a finger. At this point the therapist would shout, "Stop," which he was instructed to repeat. By the fourth session, the obsession had diminished by about 80 percent. Treatment was continued for a total of 17 sessions, in the course of which 3 variations of the technique were used. In one of them an electric shock was substituted for the shouting of the word "Stop." At the time of the 17th weekly session the obsession had decreased to about five occurrences per day; and the patient could control it easily by saying, "Stop," subvocally, on any occasion. A month after the end of treatment, the color obsession disappeared completely. At a seven-month follow-up, it had not recurred, and the other obsessions were reported to be progressively decreasing.

From the personal experience described above, as well as the testimony of patients, there is reason to believe that thought-stopping procedures work by reinforcing thought inhibition by the anxiety-reducing consequences of each successful effort at thought inhibition. This hypothesis could be tested by psychophysiological monitoring.

COGNITIVISM: A RETROGRESSIVE THEORY OF THERAPY

Through most of human history, mental events—perceiving, feeling, thinking and deciding—were regarded as functions of the "mind," an entity that is supposedly separate from the body and that obeys its own rules, our old friend, the "Ghost in the Machine" (p. 18). Only with the emergence of an objectively based science of human behavior could psychology be integrated with biology. As the result of investigations that began with Sechenov (1965) and culminated in the work of Taylor (1962) (surveyed in Chapter 2), it became apparent that even the most complex human behavior could be understood in organismal terms. *This was for psychology a revolution and a rebirth.* In psychotherapy, behavior therapy was the logical offspring of this revolution, and the logical successor to the preexisting mentalistic theories.

Recently, it has been proclaimed with an air of discovery, that cognitive errors or distortions are, after all, the sole cause of neuroses (see, for example, Beck, 1976; Ellis, 1974; Goldfried & Goldfried, 1975; Mahoney, 1977; Meichenbaum, 1975; Raimy, 1970). Mahoney (1977) has labeled this retrogressive viewpoint "the cognitive revolution." If neurotic problems are all due to wrong ways of thinking, then thought correction must always be what is needed to overcome them. While the cognitivists unflinchingly assert that this is the case, it should be noted that in practice they frequently use behavioral procedures such as assertiveness training and systematic desensitization, while they minimize their import (e.g., Beck, 1976). They also project on to the patient the irrational beliefs they suppose he ought to have (see, for example, Ellis, 1962, pp. 126–128).

For the cognitivists, emotional conditioning, and specifically, learned automatic triggering of fear responses, do not exist. To take the example of a person who has a fear of being the center of attention, they presume that between the perception of the situation of being the center of attention and the fear that follows, some kind of thought-out basis for the fear is necessarily interposed, e.g., the idea, "being the center of attention is dangerous." Essentially, then, they propose that some kind of idea of danger is the universal mediator of fear. As I have shown however, (e.g., pp. 27–31), responding to situations with fear can occur directly, unmediated by thoughts of danger. Further reasons for my rejection of the cognitivist position are detailed below.

Facts that are Incompatible with the Cognitivist View of Psychotherapy

I reject the view that the psychotherapeutic task is a matter of nothing but cognitive correction, both because it is contrary to established facts about autonomic responses, and because it is substantially contradicted by clinical data. The specific points are as follows:

1. Cognitive responses are a subset of behavioral responses. Therefore, cognition-directed treatment procedures must be a subset of behavioral procedures and not the other way around, as claimed by Beck (1976, p. 320).

2. When a situation that is encountered in reality evokes anxiety, *imagining* it also usually evokes anxiety (Wade, Malloy, & Proctor, 1977), though the subject can scarcely be *believing* that the image is dangerous. This fact contradicts the cognitivist theory. On the other hand, if anxiety is a conditioned response, it is arousable by both real and imaginary images.

3. Most neurotic patients are afraid of situations that they clearly know are not objectively dangerous, and this is usually the case, contrary to Beck's (1976) contention, even *while* they are anxious. The stimulus to a neurotic anxiety response may be such that one cannot understand how it could be regarded as a threat; for example, a woman's lifelong fear of mice began when, at the age of five, her brother chased her all over the yard with a mouse he held in his hand. She knew very well that mice were harmless, but even *the picture* of one aroused fear.

4. An extensive literature shows that, in order for a conditioned response to be weakened, its evocation must always in some way be involved in the operations that weaken it (Pavlov, 1927; McGeogh, 1932; Hinde, 1966). Cognitive events can change autonomic habits only if they have autonomic effects. False feedback experiments at one time seemed to suggest that systematic desensitization might diminish anxiety on the basis of cognitive change (Valins & Ray, 1967). Better-controlled experiments subsequently revealed that information is followed by decrements of anxiety *only* when it is veridical— that is, when it actually reduces anxiety responding (Sushinsky & Bootzin, 1970; Gaupp, Stern, & Galbraith, 1972; Kent, Wilson, & Nelson, 1972; Rosen, Rosen, & Reid, 1972).

5. Standard desensitization does not include feedback of the foregoing kind. Nor does it provide any corrective information. It has been argued that the patient gets better because he "realizes" in the course of the procedure that he is having little or no fear, but such realization is secondary to the fact that the procedure produces less and less fear to the given stimulus. This is quite different from the elimination of fear *secondary* to a realization that what was thought to be dangerous is not so. Assertive training affects cognitions in a similar way. Rachaim, Lefebvre, and Jenkins (1980) showed that changes in behavior altered cognitions, rendering unnecessary adjuvant cog-

nitive strategy. Strict cognitivists tend to strain the facts to fit their explanations. This is reminiscent of Weitzman's (1967) efforts to explain the effects of systematic desensitization on the basis of psychoanalytically derived propositions. As I pointed out in a critique of Weitzman's article (Wolpe, 1971), it is always possible to "explain" particular phenomena on the basis of almost any theory that one chooses. One might, for instance, explain gravity as the action of angels who are seizing heavy objects and pulling them downwards.

6. A patient who is continuously anxious may be found to have a specific persistent fear, for example, of going insane. Strong reassurance may convince him to the contrary, yet his anxiety may not materially diminish. A few inhalations of a mixture of carbon dioxide and oxygen (Wolpe, 1973, pp. 157, 183) may lastingly remove that anxiety (e.g., Latimer, 1977; Steketee & Roy, 1977). This cannot be explained as a matter of cognitive correction. (See also Chapter 11.)

7. A clinical experiment that inadvertently provided some data contradicting the "pure cognitive theory" was reported by Seitz (1953). He encouraged 25 patients with psychocutaneous excoriation syndromes to express, during his interviews with them, their hostile feelings toward other people, while explicitly discouraging them from "acting out" their aggressions in their life situations. Eleven of the 25 disobeyed him, *and in these eleven alone the skin cleared up.* As we so often also find when we are teaching assertive behavior, emotional change does not follow understanding, but requires outward behavior based on that understanding.

8. Beck (1976) has claimed that cognitive therapy is effective in the treatment of depression. Most of his patients were also given such behavioral procedures as systematic desensitization and assertive training, but the benefit was ascribed to the cognitive interventions. This will be discussed in detail in Chapter 15. In a prospective study of a large number of subjects, Lewinsohn et al. (1981) found no evidence that depression-related cognitions are causally related to depression.

When some of the above criticisms appeared in a journal article (Wolpe, 1978), they evoked responses from several cognitivists. These responses almost entirely skirted the content of the criticisms. For example, Beck and Mahoney (1979) made the self-contradictory claim that "freedom of choice *requires* determinism"! They quoted a poll that showed that cognitivists are skeptical of free will as an argument that cognitivism is deterministic! (They themselves viewed thoughts as only partially determined.) They disregarded the data I had presented that showed learning to be a function of the nervous system and expressed their disagreement with the behaviorist position as a matter of opinion—"a paradigm clash" (quoting Kuhn, 1962), with each "competitor" formulating issues on his own terms. The fact is that the proposition that cognition *is* behavior cannot be rebutted without specifically addressing its supporting evidence (see Chapter 2).

On the clinical issue of the pervasiveness of misconceptions, Beck and Mahoney referred to a study by Teasdale and Rezin (1960) in which each depressed patient had negative cognitions. It is hardly remarkable that such cognitions should be found in depression, but it is as likely for them to be effects as causes, in fact more likely in the light of the study of Lewinsohn et al. (1981) mentioned above (p. 116). To answer the question whether the addition of cognitive techniques to behavioristic practices improves on the results of the latter, they appealed to a comparison by Shaw (1977) between the effects of "pure" cognitive therapy and "behavior therapy." The cognitive group did better than the "behavior therapy" group, but the difference was not spectacular. Moreover, there were only eight patients in each group; the "behavior therapy" was of the Lewinsohn variety which, as I shall show (p. 281), is inappropriate for neurotic depression, and there was no prior behavior analysis.

With reference to the last point, it is relevant that Taylor and Marshall (1977) found that depressed college students who were treated with a combination of cognitive therapy and behavior therapy did better than those who were treated by either modality separately. Apparently, the combination did take care of *both* classically conditioned and cognitive cases (see Chapter 15).

The loose thinking that is manifest in the above paragraphs is very common in cognitivist writing. But when the temptation to regard oneself as at least "partially free" is endorsed by so prestigious a psychologist as Bandura (1974), it is not surprising that some are persuaded (e.g., Marzillier, 1980; Wilson & O'Leary, 1980).

7

Assertiveness Training

This is the first of several chapters that deal with specific methods of eliminating classically conditioned anxiety-response habits. Although systematic desensitization is the most widely used method, assertiveness training will be considered first because it is frequently introduced at a very early stage. It can frequently be initiated on the basis of relatively simple instructions, leading, in suitable cases, to significant change in a matter of weeks.

Assertive behavior is the appropriate expression of any emotion other than anxiety toward another person. Assertiveness training is mainly used to decondition unadaptive habits of anxiety response to other people's behavior, exploiting the appropriate expression of other emotions that the same people evoke. These emotions are quite varied. Another person may arouse approval, affection, admiration, irritation, or anger. To the extent that these emotions are subserved by bodily responses that are different from those of anxiety, they are potentially competitive with it. When these emotions instigate motor behavior, their intensity is enhanced, with the result that any anxiety that is simultaneously present is more likely to be inhibited.

The contexts in which assertiveness training is an appropriate therapeutic method (although not necessarily the only one) are numerous. In almost all the contexts we find that the patient is inhibited from the performance of "normal" behavior because of neurotic fear. He is inhibited from saying or doing things that seem reasonable and right to an observer. He may be unable to complain about poor service in a restaurant because he is afraid of hurting the waiter's feelings; unable to express differences of opinion to his friends because he fears that they will not like him; unable to get up and leave a social situation that has become boring because he is afraid to seem ungrateful; unable to ask for the repayment of a loan or to administer a legitimate reproof to a subordinate because he is afraid of losing his image as a "nice guy"; or unable to express love, warmth, admiration, or praise because he finds such expression embarrassing. Besides the behaviors that fear prevents, there may be others that a person cannot restrain because of it. For example, he may compulsively reach for the lunch check on every occasion to ward off a fear of incurring an obligation, or he may talk too much because silence makes him anxious.[1]

Interpersonal anxiety responses of the kinds exemplified above sometimes lead to the channeling of innate drives into unadaptive paths. Fear that is evoked by heterosexual peers may deflect the patient from normal sexual partnerships, to engage in such deviations as homosexuality, pedophilia, or exhibitionism. Frequently, the suppression of action that would give outward expression to feelings results in prolonged inner turmoil, which may generate psychosomatic symptoms and even pathological changes in predisposed organs. The correct target of treatment is not the primary presenting problem (such as the sexual deviation), but the causative interpersonal anxieties, in whose overcoming assertiveness training has a prominent role (see Cases 59 and 60).

A very common history in patients who have difficulty in asserting themselves is of early teaching that has overemphasized social obligations, engendering the feeling that the rights of others are more important than their own. An extreme, but not very unusual example, was a 36-year-old man whose parents had strongly insisted on polite submissiveness. During World War II, at the age of eight, he had gone to live for two years with an uncle and aunt who had encouraged self-expression. The behavior learned while with the aunt and uncle was severely punished when the patient returned to his parental home, which led to an enduring habit of timidity, espcially toward authority figures.

The therapist's interventions are aimed at augmenting every impulse toward the elicitation of such anxiety-inhibiting responses as the expression of legitimate anger. The expectation is that on each occasion this will result in some degree of weakening of the anxiety-response habit. Meanwhile, the motor behavior by which the anger is expressed will be reinforced by its favorable consequences, such as the attainment of control of a social situation, reduction of anxiety, and, later the approbation of the therapist. Thus, the counterconditioning of anxiety and the operant conditioning of the motor act take place simultaneously, facilitating each other. (For a fuller discussion, see Wolpe, 1958). Operant conditioning of assertive behavior is employed alone in certain people who lack it not because of anxiety but because they simply have not acquired the appropriate motor habits for certain social situations.

---

[1]In the context of such anxieties as the latter two, assertiveness training is almost certain to fail without prior systematic desensitization.

Like all other methods of behavior therapy, assertive training is applied only in relevant contexts. Some patients are unassertive in a very wide range of personal interactions, and to these, Salter's (1949) appellation, "the inhibitory personality," is descriptively appropriate. In them, almost any social interaction might provide grounds for assertive training. In other people, the indications for assertiveness are circumscribed. There are those who are able to handle tradesmen and strangers competently, but who are timorous and submissive with anybody who is important to them, like a mother, a wife, or a lover. Others are comfortable with close associates and may even dominate them, but are fearful, awkward, and in various degrees ineffective in their dealings with the "outgroup."

The quintessence of assertive behavior is to do toward others what is reasonable and right. It is well brought out in the following extract from a statement written by a journalist (Wolpe, 1958, p. 118):

> I have been given the assignment of winning emotional victories in daily life. . . . This is the important discovery I have made—and it is a satisfying one emotionally. Other people's opinions and feelings count—*but so do mine.* This does not mean that I have become aggressive, unpleasant, or inconsiderate to other people. . . . This new method of coping with interpersonal situations simply boils down to doing the things which, if you were an onlooker watching the situation, would seem fair and fitting.

The interrelations between assertive and other categories of behavior are illustrated in Figure 7.1. Assertiveness involves many categories of emotional behavior. The most common of these categories is oppositional behavior (e.g., standing up for reasonable rights). Types of oppositional behavior outside the assertive category are the provocative, the aggressive, the violent and, often, the sarcastic. A second major category of assertiveness is the expression of affection of all kinds and degrees. There is a wide group of miscellaneous assertive responses that include admiration, gratitude, the expression of opinions and questions, and various modes of humorous expression.

There has been relatively little psychophysiological research on the interrelations between the various emotional states since the early survey by Leschke (1914). Arnold (1945) marshalled the evidence of physiological antagonism between anger and anxiety. Ax (1953) expressed doubts about this, although his own data to some extent supported it. Arnold (1960) later collected further supporting data. Soviet research (Simonov, 1967) has yielded impressive evidence of the existence of separate and reciprocally inhibitory centers for anger and anxiety in the midbrain. When either of these sources of emotional response is put out of action by drugs or by ablations, the other is facilitated.

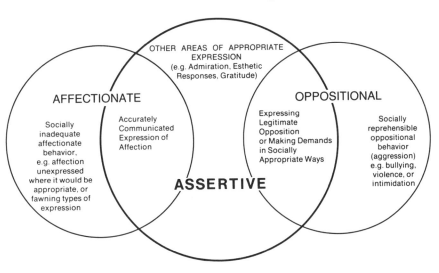

Fig. 7.1. Interrelations between assertive, oppositional, and affectionate categories of behavior. (Courtesy of Graphic Communications, Eastern Pennsylvania Psychiatric Institute, Philadelphia.)

PRELIMINARIES TO ASSERTIVENESS TRAINING

Before assertive training can begin, the patient must accept its reasonableness. Sometimes submission to the needs of others is bound up with the general philosophy that it is morally good to place the interests of others ahead of one's own. An extreme example of this is the person who, on religious grounds, makes a practice of turning the other cheek. I tell him that this policy is practical only for rare saintly individuals, and that from everybody else biology exacts its toll for behavior contrary to the interests of the organism. I add that most people who turn the other cheek do so because they are socially anxious.

There are, however, patients who raise doubts about the morality of assertive behavior. A reasoned response to them may start by pointing out that any one of three principles may guide a person's approach to interpersonal relations. One possible principle is to consider one's self only and ride roughshod over others to get what one wants. The psychopathic personality is the extreme embodiment of this. While he may get away with it to a considerable extent, sooner or later he usually falls foul of society. A second possible principle is always to put others before oneself. People who follow this policy are frequently emotionally upset, their feelings fluctuating between guilt at falling short of their own standards of selflessness and annoyance at the frustrations of self-abnegation. It is this kind of person the Talmudist had in mind when he wrote, "If I am not for myself, who will be for me?" This question expresses an awareness of the reality that the welfare of the organism begins with its own integrity. But the Talmudist went on to ask, "But if I am for myself alone, what am I?" The addition of the latter question leads on to the third possible principle of conduct: the individual puts himself first, but takes others into account. He conforms to the requirements of social living while yielding to the demands of his own biology.

Most patients can readily be brought to recognize the need for appropriate assertiveness. Some have always been aware of it. The insight as such,[2] however, produces no change (see p. 116 above; and Rathus, 1972). The therapist must help the patient to translate the insight into action. Simple coaxing and directing are often all that is necessary. This consists in part of emphasizing the disadvantages of nonassertion—its inevitable winlessness, its frequently unpleasant emotional consequences, and the unfavorable image it gives to others—and in part, of promising increasing ease of execution of assertive acts as anxiety diminishes. I tell patients that the power to assert grows with action like a snowball rolling down a slope. Sometimes it is helpful to tell the story of a successful previous case.[3]

A suitable context for starting assertiveness training often emerges in a very natural way from the patient's narration of some recent incident. An alternative starting point may be found in the patient's responses to the Willoughby Personality Schedule (Appendix A)—particularly if there are high numerical responses to the following questions: Are your feelings easily hurt? Are you shy? Does criticism hurt you badly? Are you self-conscious before superiors?

To take the first of these as an example, the therapist asks for an actual situation that hurts the patient's feelings, and follows this up by inquiring how he would handle the situation. If the handling was unassertive, the therapist proposes an assertive substitute. Another route to the initiation of assertion in "outgroup" contexts takes off from asking the patient how he behaves in one or more set situations, such as the following:

1. What do you do if, after having bought an article in a shop, you walk out and find that your change is a dollar short?

---

[2]Pegging away at the patient's "illogical self-verbalizations," which Ellis (1958) conceives as the cause of neurotic behavior, is futile here. That is presumably why Ellis (1970) added assertiveness instructions to his treatment.

[3]If assertion results from these interventions, it can be seen as being due to a summation between an already-present action tendency (to protest, for example) and the similar impulse

2. What do you do if, arriving home after buying an article on the way, you find it slightly damaged?
3. What do you do if somebody pushes in front of you in line (e.g., at the theater)?
4. At a shop, while you wait for the clerk to finish with the customer ahead of you, another customer arrives and also waits. What do you do if the clerk subsequently directs his attention to that third customer?
5. You order a steak rare and it arrives well done. How do you handle the situation?

In all these situations, a person ought to be able to stand up for himself and right the wrong. If he is unable to do so, a context for assertiveness training exists. A very useful inventory for identifying areas of inadequate assertiveness has been provided by Gambrill and Richey (1975).

THE CONDUCT OF ASSERTIVENESS TRAINING

Let us trace how assertiveness training may begin out of the third of the above questions:

THERAPIST: What do you do if you are standing in line for theater tickets and somebody gets in front of you?
PATIENT: I don't do anything.
THERAPIST: Well, how do you feel?
PATIENT: I feel mad. I boil up inside.
THERAPIST: So, why don't you do anything?
PATIENT: I'm afraid of hurting the other person's feelings.
(*Thus, it is the fear of distressing the intruder which prevents the patient from taking action. But at the same time, he is angry. The therapist must try to get him to augment this anger by giving vent to it in a socially appropriate way. Then the level of anger may rise to a level sufficient to inhibit the anxiety.*)
THERAPIST: People are taking advantage of you. This person is taking advantage of you. You should not allow it. You must say to him, "Will you kindly go to the back of the line?" In doing this, you will be expressing your anger in a way that is appropriate to the situation and socially acceptable.

Each time the patient, by expressing his anger, inhibits his anxiety, he weakens in some measure the anxiety habit. But emotion is not the only com-

---

prompted by the attitude and words of the therapist (in parallel to the experimental therapy described on pp. 44–45).

ponent of the instigated behavior. There is also new verbal behavior: the patient for the first time tells another person to go to the back of the line. He will usually be rewarded by the approval of others in the line, and by the interloper moving to the rear. These rewards will reinforce the patient's tendency to speak up, not only in this specific situation, but in all similar ones.

Progress in assertion depends on success. Therefore, the therapist must be aware of the details of the situations in which he is counselling assertive action. He would not, for example, advise the patient to insist on his rights standing in line in a tough neighborhood.

Case 22

The following transcript provides a more detailed example of the initiation of assertiveness, taking off from another of the set situations on p. 123. Dorothy, a schoolteacher, was 40 years old.

THERAPIST: Suppose that you went into a shop to buy a pair of gloves and when you came to the glove counter there was somebody else standing there. Naturally you would wait. Now suppose that while you were waiting, another customer arrived. After a time the assistant finished with the customer who was there before you and turned her attention to the one that came after you. What would you do?

DOROTHY: It happens all the time. I would not say anything.

THERAPIST: What would your reason be?

DOROTHY: Well, I remember as a child my mother being very hard on salespeople and I was always embarrassed, and I tend to be the opposite. I'll stand there forever sometimes.

THERAPIST: Well, what does this actually mean? How would you feel?

DOROTHY: I would be angry. Probably more than anything angry with myself for not speaking up.

THERAPIST: So, you think that really you ought to speak up?

DOROTHY: Right.

THERAPIST: Then what prevents you?

DOROTHY: I feel tense and unhappy at making a scene.

THERAPIST: Well, I certainly agree that you should speak up. Obviously, it's a fear that is preventing it. There's the anger that you feel at the same time because of the injustice. But the fear is dominant, and that is why you've never spoken up. Now, if you do speak up, if you make it your business to speak up, you will express the anger. And each time you do that, you will push the fear down a little and each time as a result somewhat weaken the fear habit.

DOROTHY: I see.

THERAPIST: Gradually, through repetition, you will find that you don't have this fear any more and then you will naturally and easily stand up for yourself. Of course I'm not just talking about this single situation. There are all kinds of similar ones. So I would like you to go out of your way to try to do things like that—expressing your legitimate feelings towards people. What we have been talking about is the expression of angry feelings that are appropriate. Do you have any difficulty with the expression of appropriate *positive* feelings?

DOROTHY: Yes. Sometimes I do. I notice it with my children. When they were tiny it was very easy to cuddle them. Now I find that although I love them as much as ever, it's hard to give even a little hug.

THERAPIST: As we saw in the situation where you wanted to buy gloves, it was fear that prevented the expression of feelings. In the same way, we usually find that when a person doesn't express affectionate feelings or feelings of admiration, it's also because of a kind of fearfulness. I want you to make an effort to express your affection. To the extent that you do, you'll find that it gets progressively easier, as the fear lessens. What about another kind of expressiveness? Sometimes you have a need to ask for somebody's help. Do you have any difficulty in doing this?

DOROTHY: No. I have some close friends and we reciprocate. It works out well.

THERAPIST: And you don't have any problem?

DOROTHY: No.

THERAPIST: You can make reasonable demands of people?

DOROTHY: Yes I can.

(At the next session it was seen that the instructions were already having an effect.)

DOROTHY: I more or less followed your advice and said what was on my mind on a few occasions without holding back.

THERAPIST: Very good. Give me an example.

DOROTHY: I have a very good example. I was chaperoning a swim party of 90 junior-high-school children, with 5 mothers to cook their meals and everything. I was the only mother who was a member of the club. So, during dinnertime a lifeguard came up to me saying the children weren't behaving very well—you're a member—do something about it. So I said, "Well, you're the lifeguard—you were hired to take care of the people in the pool, not to oversee the children's behavior."

THERAPIST: Very good. That's a very encouraging performance.

DOROTHY: Yes.

THERAPIST: Any other examples?

DOROTHY: I noticed a number of small things that occur daily—for instance, driving the car and being overly polite and letting five cars getting into line when one is sufficient really. So I put a stop to that.

THERAPIST: Well, you certainly have the idea, and you are commendably on the lookout.

The examples of Dorothy dealt mainly with strange persons in public places. The following is an example of the initiation of assertiveness with significant figures in the patient's life.

THERAPIST: Let us talk about your mother-in-law.

MRS. A.: She is a bully, says a lot of things and does a lot of things to me that I sit back and take. I really should open my mouth and not be big about it. Personally, I don't care if the woman does not like me. I feel more for the guy in the line than I do for her, because she has done a lot of things that I feel are not right. She steps all over me and I let it boil up inside.

THERAPIST: Now what would happen if you let it out on your mother-in-law—which is what you really want to do, isn't it? Let us take an actual example.

MRS. A.: Well, she is always telling me for instance that my mother did not raise me properly.

THERAPIST: That is an insulting remark.

MRS. A.: Yes, it is, and I never say anything.

THERAPIST: Well, do you mind the remark?

MRS. A.: It cuts me, like you would stab me.

THERAPIST: And you let her get away with it. What should you do?

MRS. A.: I should say, "It is my mother. Please don't talk about her."

THERAPIST: Right. And the effect will be to increase her respect for you.

MRS. A.: My in-laws don't like the way I behave, by the way; they really don't.

THERAPIST: That's not surprising. Let me give you a contrast. Suppose you are visiting at somebody's house and you notice two men there. They are your hosts' two sons-in-law. One of them is meek and ingratiating all the time, while the other one speaks up to his in-laws. Which one gives you a better impression?

MRS. A.: The one that speaks up. You don't have to make up an example. This new fiancee of my sister-in-law is living at my in-law's house right now with them and he speaks up. They love him.

(*A little later in the interview, Mrs. A. expressed concern that her husband might object to her new behavior to his mother.*)

MRS. A.: Suppose my husband starts up with me, "You shouldn't talk like that to my mother. You are not cementing relationships; you are putting them farther apart." How do I handle that situation?

THERAPIST: You have to say, "If your mother makes unjust remarks I have to tell her and I will tell her. If your mother makes reasonable criticisms, I will be very interested in what she has to say. But she is always at me, and she has gotten into the habit of it because I have been allowing her to say whatever she likes. I am not going to have it any more.''

The following are two random lists of assertive statements; the first is a list of statements that express opposition, the second of commendation. The former are more numerous because they are more frequently used in assertiveness training.

Oppositional Assertive Statements

1. Would you please call me back. I can't speak to you now.
2. Excuse me. You're obstructing my view.
3. Will you kindly stop talking during the play/movie/music.
4. This is a line. Please go to the back of it.
5. You have kept me waiting 20 minutes.
6. Do you mind turning down the heat in the restaurant?
7. It's too cold for me to go outside.
8. Please put those heavy packages in a *double* bag (at a supermarket).
9. Your behavior disgusts/annoys me.
10. I hate your duplicity/intolerance/unreasonableness.
11. Your nagging bores me.
12. If it is not inconvenient, will you pick up my parcel?
13. I'm sorry, but it won't be possible.
14. Would you ask the pilot to radio ahead to my connecting flight? (To the stewardess on a flight that is late for a connection.)
15. I would rather not wait.
16. Why are you late?
17. If you persist in coming late, I shall stop making appointments with you.
18. I insist that you come to work on time.
19. How dare you speak to me like that.
20. Pardon me, I was here first.
21. I enjoy talking to you, but please be quiet while I am reading/writing/ thinking/listening.

Commendatory Assertive Statements

1. That's a beautiful dress/brooch, etc.
2. You look lovely, terrific, ravishing, glamorous.
3. That was a clever remark.
4. What a radiant smile.
5. I like you.
6. I love you.
7. I admire your tenacity.

8. That was brilliantly worked out/well expressed/right on target.
9. You handled him very skillfully.

With a reasonable amount of pressure and encouragement, most patients begin to be able to assert themselves in a matter of days, or a week or two. At each interview, they report what they have done in the intervening time, and the therapist commends their successes and corrects their errors. They must be warned not to rest on their laurels, but to be alert for every opportunity for appropriate assertion. One rule must always be observed: *Never instigate an assertive act that is likely to have punishing consequences.* As the interpersonal anxiety decreases in consequence of efforts, acts of assertion become easier to perform.

For patients who have a great deal of anxiety about assertion, it may be necessary to grade the tasks in a way that parallels desensitization. On the whole, it is good practice to make this a general rule.

Some patients have great difficulty performing any assertive acts at all. The therapist must ascertain why. He may discover a "phobic" reaction to some aspect or implication of assertion. For example, the patient may have a strong conditioned anxiety response to perceiving himself behaving aggressively or to the idea of *having* behaved aggressively (i.e., guilt about aggression).[4] A preliminary program of systematic desensitization to the relevant stimulus configurations is then needed (Chapter 8). Marked fear of hostility from others (which is always a possible response to assertiveness) similarly requires desensitization.

When the patient finds assertive behavior difficult even though no such inhibiting fears are evident, more vigorous direct efforts are made toward eliciting assertion. It may suffice simply to increase the patient's motivation by strongly contrasting the negative and unprepossessing effects of timidity with the benefits that assertion is expected to yield; or the therapist may refuse to see the patient until he can report some action. Another possibility is behavior rehearsal.

BEHAVIOR REHEARSAL

In the great majority of subjects, satisfactory assertive behavior (and consequent diminution of interpersonal anxiety) results from instructions followed by monitoring of reports of performance from session to session. There are,

---

[4]There are also those who have no difficulty assertively expressing themselves, but nevertheless feel guilt afterwards or because fear of such guilt prevents assertiveness. Such reactions also usually lend themselves to desensitization.

however, a considerable number of people who find it difficult or impossible to carry out their assignments. In some cases, although the requisite words are uttered, it is with inadequate expressiveness; in others there is so much anticipatory anxiety that the performance of assertive behavior cannot even be initiated. Behavior rehearsal has its most important role in the treatment of such cases, although it is also often used to accelerate assertiveness training in run-of-the-mill cases.

Behavior rehearsal was originally called "behavioristic psychodrama" (Wolpe, 1958). It consists of the acting out of short exchanges between the therapist and the patient in scenes from the patient's life. The patient represents himself, and the therapist someone toward whom the patient is unadaptively anxious and inhibited. The therapist starts with a remark, usually oppositional, that the other person might make, and the patient responds as if the situation were "real." His initial response will usually be variously hesitant, defensive, and timid. The therapist then suggests a more appropriate response, and the exchange is run again, in a revised form. The sequence may be repeated again and again until the therapist is satisfied that the patient's utterances have been suitably reshaped.

It is necessary to take into account not only the words the patient uses, but also the volume, firmness, and emotional expressiveness of voice, eye contact, and the appropriateness of accompanying gestures and other bodily movements. Serber (1972), who placed great importance on these features of assertive behavior, advocated giving the patient videotaped feedback of his behavior—a device that I have occasionally used with excellent results in difficult cases. The aim of such modelling, shaping, and rehearsing is to prepare the patient to deal with his real "adversary" so that the anxiety the latter evokes may be reciprocally inhibited and the requisite motor assertive habits established.

Case 23

This case affords a typical example of the shaping that is done during behavior rehearsal. (Wolpe, 1970). The patient had been brooding over having been unfairly criticized by her father for lacking in family feeling, and wanted to rectify the matter.

THERAPIST: Well, let's do an experiment. Let's sort of act it out. Suppose you just go ahead and pretend I am your father and say to me what you think you would like to say to him.

PATIENT: About the other night, I would like to say that I think you were exceptionally unfair in assuming that I did not want to come up and that I was the one who was being unjust or the villain because I wasn't coming up to make the family happy. The family hasn't been much of a family actually for a number of years and when it comes down to it, the family doesn't mean that much to me. I would be much happier spending Christmas by myself. And then he would probably say, "Well, you just go ahead and do that."

THERAPIST: Wait a minute. Don't you worry about him. I am he, so don't put words in my mouth. Besides this, in general I would like to correct your approach. You are doing it in a way that leaves you too vulnerable. First of all, it is very unsatisfactory for you to complain to somebody that he is *unfair*, because if you do that you are really in some sense putting yourself at his mercy. A better line would be: "I want to tell you that you had no right to assume the other night that I had no intention of coming for Christmas. You know very well that I have always come. You accused me of lacking feeling. I have a great deal of feeling, and perhaps too much. Your attack was absolutely unwarranted." In saying this, you are not asking for justice or fairness, you are simply stating what you feel was wrong in his behavior. Now, do you think you could redo it in some fashion?

PATIENT: Okay. I would like to set some matters straight—about your call the other night. When you called me I just couldn't think of this right away. I was so taken by surprise, but I have been thinking about it and I would just like to say a couple of things.

THERAPIST: I must interrupt you again. You started fine—the first sentence was fine, but when you begin to explain why you didn't say it the other night, that weakens your position. For example, it might invite him to say "Yes, that is like you, isn't it? You never answer at the right time. You always have to brood for three days before you can say anything." He *could* say something of that sort. But in any case, it is a kind of underdog statement, and we don't want that.

PATIENT: All right. About the call the other night, I had not entirely given up on the idea of coming up to have Christmas with you and Mom. I was doing what I thought was best according to what I gathered from the conversation I had with Mom. I felt that Mom wanted me to have Christmas with Grandma and Grandpop—have Christmas dinner, and I wanted to be both places, but I just felt that the drive might be too much.

THERAPIST: I am sorry, but I must interrupt you again. You see, you are explaining yourself. You are giving a kind of excuse. Actually, the important part of this conversation is to bring out the point that it was not right for him to plunge into a criticism that assumed that you had made up your mind not to come.

PATIENT: How about—I don't think it was right for you to call me last night, and say what you did, because I don't think you had the facts straight from Mom. I think you should have checked with her first and be sure you understood the situation. I had talked with Mom earlier and felt that this was what we had worked out and I think you should have checked with her and made sure that—

THERAPIST: That's enough. The fact that you keep on suggests that you are not very confident; so stop. Now, let him say something.

Actually, a *good deal of deconditioning of anxiety frequently takes place during the behavior rehearsal itself.* For example, a librarian of 42 had so much anxiety at the idea of inconveniencing people that she could not be persuaded to make even the most miniscule demands of anybody except her closest friends. In behavior rehearsal with her, I took the role of one of her office colleagues who lives near her, and told her to ask me for a ride home (that would only take me one block out of my way). She had difficulty in even formulating this request. I therefore gave her this sentence to use: "If you are going home after work, would you mind giving me a ride home?" Her first enunciation of this was very awkward, and she stated that it had evoked a good deal of anxiety (70 *suds*). My reply was, "I will take you with pleasure." With repetition, she articulated the sentence with greater ease and better expression, while the level of her anxiety progressively fell. After a total of eight repetitions in two sessions, she could request that ride with practically no anxiety. During subsequent sessions, the distance she was taking me out of my way was progressively increased. These "rehearsals" enabled the patient comfortably to make reasonable requests in reality.

The ability of "put on" behavior to bring about real therapeutic change is in accord with some observations on actors reported by Simonov (1967). Especially (but not only) when the actor has been trained by the Stanislavsky method (which requires him to try to *live* each part), he evinces autonomic responses in the direction of the emotions that he is simulating. Simonov states, "The actors were asked to pronounce certain words under various mentally reproducible conditions. . . . The changes in the heart rate, recorded in the actor when he was fulfilling the task, confirm that he was actually reproducing an emotionally colored situation and was not copying intonations formerly noticed in other people. This conclusion was confirmed by comparison with the results of analyzing speech in natural situations." However, there are differences, too, because if the actor is doing his part well he gets a pleasurable feeling intermixed with the anxiety or anger that he is enacting. A detailed account of this work is, unfortunately, available only in manuscript form (Simonov, 1962).

LIFEMANSHIP

There are circumstances in which direct assertion is inappropriate, but in which it is nevertheless desirable for the patient to achieve some kind of control. For example, it is not often advisable for an employee to give his employer "a piece of his mind." If assertion is necessary, it calls for subtle tactics. These are sometimes suggested by special knowledge of the other person's weaknesses, but there are gambits that may be applied to almost anybody—statements that automatically put the recipient at a disadvantage, without revealing an aggressive intent on the part of the speaker. A widely usable example is, "Is anything wrong? You don't seem to be quite your usual self today."

A large variety of clever instances of behavior of this kind are described in a series of little books by the late Stephen Potter, who referred to them as "oneupmanship." They were fairly recently published in a single volume (Potter, 1971). Although Potter's aim was humor and not psychotherapy, there is much that can be used by the psychotherapist. For example, Potter (p. 13) describes how one day he and Professor Joad were playing tennis against two Oxford University students—fine, upstanding young men, Smith and Brown. Smith's first service, delivered to Joad, was an ace which Joad did not get near. He then served to Potter with the same result. At the next service, Joad managed to get his racket to the ball, which went flying over the net and hit the bottom of the back netting on the students' side. Then, as Smith was crossing over to serve the *coup de grace,* Joad called across the net, in an even tone: "Kindly say clearly, please, whether the ball was in or out."

SMITH: I'm so sorry—I thought it was out. (*The ball had hit the back netting twelve feet behind him before touching the ground.*) But what did you think, Brown?

BROWN: I thought it was out—but do let's have it again.

JOAD: No, I don't want to have it again. I only want you to say clearly, if you will, whether the ball is in or out.

This slight suggestion of unsportsmanlike behavior was sufficient to upset the students' performance and make them lose the game.

A film of the complete treatment of a patient, *Behavior Therapy in a Case of Overdependency,*[5] has sections that illustrate assertive training. A good demonstration of assertiveness training is to be found in a sector of a film entitled *Behavior Therapy: An Introduction.*[6]

---

[5]Available from Behavior Therapy Presentations, Eastern Pennsylvania Psychiatric Institute, Philadelphia, Penna.

[6]Available from MTI Teleprograms, Inc., Northbrook, Illinois.

8
Systematic Desensitization

Systematic desensitization is one of a variety of methods for breaking down neurotic anxiety-response habits in piecemeal fashion, modelled on the therapy of experimental neurosis. A physiological state that is inhibitory of anxiety is induced in the patient by means of muscle relaxation; he is then exposed to a weak anxiety-arousing stimulus for a few seconds. If the exposure is repeated, the stimulus progressively loses its ability to evoke anxiety. Successively "stronger" stimuli are then introduced and similarly treated. This method has given us the power to overcome a great many neurotic habits, often in a short time. It has enabled us to treat these habits in almost any order that we choose, and as far as we choose.

Employing a counteracting emotion to overcome an undesirable emotional habit *step by step* has a precedent in everyday experience: a child becomes accustomed to a situation he fears by inadvertently being exposed to small doses of it in circumstances in which other emotions are also present. For example, if a child fears a visitor's long black beard, he is quite likely to become reconciled to it by deconditioning events that may occur if he sits on his father's lap while the latter speaks to the visitor. The child may at first briefly glance at the beard so that the anxiety arousals are small each time. Since they occur against a background of warm and pleasant responses to the father, these small fear arousals are presumably inhibited, and gradually, as the fear subsides, the child tolerates lengthening inspections of the beard.

Besides being inadvertent agents to such spontaneous therapy, parents quite often "instinctively" treat their children's established fears in an essentially similar way (deliberately and fairly systematically). When a child is afraid of bathing in the sea, the parent will, at first, take him by the hand to the very fringe of the approaching waves and lift him up when a wave approaches; then, when the child has become comfortable about this, the parent encourages him to dip his foot into a wave, and later his ankle, and so on.

Conquering his fear by degrees, the child eventually becomes able to play in the sea with pleasure. This is very much like the routine followed in primitive societies to prepare individuals to undergo ceremonial ordeals, and in our own world in the training of mountaineers and trapeze artists. The first example of the deliberate use of counteracting responses to overcome neurotic anxieties by gradually approaching the peak stimulus was in the use of feeding to overcome children's phobias in the cases of Mary Cover Jones (1924) described in Chapter 1.

THE HISTORY OF SYSTEMATIC DESENSITIZATION

The systematic desensitization technique has its roots in the experimental laboratory (Wolpe, 1948, 1952, 1958). Having produced experimental neurosis in cats confined in a small cage by administering to them high-voltage, low-amperage shocks (as described in Chapter 3), I found that the neurotic anxiety responses to the cage and related stimuli and to an auditory stimulus that had preceded the shocks were extremely resistant to the normal process of extinction. Neither prolonged nor repeated exposure of the animals to the environment of the cage led to decrement in the intensity of the anxiety responses even though the animals were never again shocked. This failure to extinguish is, of course, also regularly found in the neuroses of man. Furthermore, the experimental animals, however hungry they were, could not be tempted to eat pellets of fresh meat scattered on the floor of the experimental cage. In other words, the anxiety produced total inhibition of eating in very hungry animals. It seemed likely that this depended on the greater relative strength of the anxiety.

If, therefore, one could arrange for the feeding impulse to exceed the anxiety in strength, one might expect the anxiety to be inhibited reciprocally. The animals showed less anxiety in the experimental laboratory outside the cage and still less in other rooms, according to how closely the rooms resembled the laboratory. There was always a room where the anxiety was not great enough to inhibit feeding. The animal ate successive pellets of meat there with increasing readiness while anxiety receded and finally disappeared. The same then happened in the room next in resemblance to the experimental laboratory. By advancing stage by stage, eating behavior eventually reappeared in the experimental cage itself, and by its repetition totally eliminated all anxiety there (see pp. 44–45).

While these observations led to a search for methods by which the neurotic habits of humans might also be broken down bit by bit, they did not immediately suggest the technique of systematic desensitization. This emerged only after a succession of further experiences. Since 1947, I had been trying to overcome anxiety in patients through getting them to perform behavior that was antagonistic to anxiety in their life situations. The most common enterprise was the instigation of assertive behavior. I was greatly encouraged in these activities by their buoyant advocacy in Salter's *Conditioned Reflex Therapy* (1949); and, in fact, was moved by its optimism to apply instruction in self-expressive behavior to all patients. I did this even though it was not clear to me how it could ameliorate those neuroses in which the stimuli controlling the neurotic reactions were not present in the interpersonal situations in which the assertive behavior was induced.

I soon realized, however, that certain neuroses were not responding to assertive behavior training, precisely in accordance with theoretical expectations. Conditioning theory requires that, in order to eliminate or change a habit of reaction to a stimulus, that stimulus must be present in the deconditioning situation. If a patient has a fear of being alone, this will not be diminished by assertive behavior, if only because assertion implies the presence of another person. Certainly, now and then, benefit is noted in special cases in which a chain of other habits may be secondarily altered when interpersonal fear has been diminished (for example, in certain cases of agoraphobia). In general, however, assertion toward persons is irrelevant where anxiety responses are to such nonpersonal stimulus constellations as enclosed spaces, animals, heights, the sight of blood—in short, in most classical phobic reactions. It is also irrelevant in the much more common case of anxiety responses that other people elicit in contexts where action on the part of the patient would be inappropriate—for example, where the fear is evoked by the mere presence of particular persons, by being the center of attention, or by a feeling of "rejection," or by being in a social situation where the patient believes that too little attention is being directed at him.

A case which starkly displayed the irrelevancy of interpersonal expressiveness was that of a woman who was severely anxious at manifestations of illness in other people. Successful schooling in expressive behavior failed to diminish her anxiety and she was sorrowfully abandoned as a failure. At that time I knew of no way to inhibit anxieties that were aroused by stimuli to which no relevant *action response* could be proposed for the patient.

Soon afterwards I had the good luck to come across Edmund Jacobson's *Progressive Relaxation* (1938). Here was a description of an anxiety-inhibiting response that did not call from the patient *any kind of motor activity toward the source of his anxiety*. I began to give relaxation training to patients for whose neuroses assertion was not applicable. However, an enormous relaxation potential was necessary to inhibit the anxiety evoked by a major real-life phobic stimulus. I conjectured that some of Jacobson's patients were enabled to inhibit *high* levels of anxiety because of prolonged training and diligent practice.

Since treating patients once or twice a week did not result in such marked ability to relax, I began to experiment with programs of exposure to graduated phobic stimuli *in vivo* for patients who had acquired some facility in relaxing, usually after six to ten sessions. But it was often difficult to arrange for the required graded real-life situations. I therefore began to explore the possibility of making use of imaginary situations in place of real ones, being encouraged in this by the writings of practitioners of hypnosis. I was delighted to find that magnitudes of experienced anxiety diminished progressively when I repeatedly presented imaginary situations that were weakly anxiety arousing. Increasingly "threatening" imaginary stimuli could, one by one, be divested of their anxiety-evoking potential, and most important, there was transfer of the deconditioning of anxiety to the corresponding real situations. At first, influenced by certain of Pavlov's experiments, I presented only one stimulus of any class at a session, but cautious trials of multiple presentations revealed no adverse effects. This opened up the prospect of greatly accelerating therapy.

GENERAL STATEMENT OF
DESENSITIZATION PARADIGM

Just as feeding can counteract an anxiety response in the neuroses of animals only if the anxiety response is weak, so the autonomic effects of relaxation in humans can counteract only relatively weak anxiety responses. I have found again and again that a stimulus that evokes a *strong* subjective anxiety response may be presented many times to the relaxed patient without diminishing the strength of anxiety. By contrast, if the anxiety response is weak, almost invariably, from one presentation of the stimulus to the next, the anxiety diminishes until at last there is none.[1]

Once a stimulus to weak anxiety has ceased to arouse any anxiety, a somewhat "stronger" one is presented to the fully relaxed patient, and this "stronger" stimulus evokes less anxiety than it would have done before. Successive presentations will bring that anxiety also down to zero. Increasingly potent stimuli are thus brought within the anxiety-inhibiting capacity of the subject's relaxation. To illustrate this: if there are ten stimuli which in their variations along a dimension evoke quantities of anxiety that vary from one to ten, and if through the inhibiting effects of relaxation the anxiety aroused by the stimulus evoking one unit is reduced to zero, the stimulus originally evoking two units of anxiety will be found to be evoking only one unit. This is illustrated in Figure 8.1. Thus, in an acrophobic subject who has one unit of anxiety produced by looking out of a second-floor window, and two units by looking out of a third-floor window, reduction of the amount of anxiety from the second-floor window to zero would have the effect that the amount of anxiety evoked at a third-floor window would be diminished to one unit.

---

[1]In contrast to this, many observations, including those of Wolpe and Flood (1970), indicate that response decrement often does occur if stronger stimuli are administered insistently enough. This will be discussed under the rubric of flooding (Chapter 12).

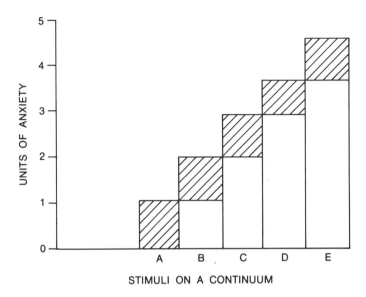

Fig. 8.1. Illustrating desensitization process. When A's ability to evoke anxiety goes down from 1 unit to 0, B evokes 1 unit in place of an original potential of 2 units; and when B's evocation is 0, C evokes 1 unit, and so forth.

Then, when anxiety at the third floor is zero, there is only one unit at the fourth floor, two at the fifth, and so forth. (This linear relationship is used for clarity of exposition. The actual relationship is a simple power function; see p. 161ff.)

It is appropriate at this point to note that although it has been usual to refer to the weaker anxiety-evoking stimuli as "generalized stimuli," this does not accurately apply to all instances. A generalized stimulus incorporates some feature, usually diminished, of the conditioned stimulus, and the magnitude of the shared feature is the basis of a generalization gradient (Hull, 1943). But sometimes, weaker anxiety evocation is a function of stimuli that have been conditioned to anxiety through being *on the recognized pathway* to the central conditioned stimulus. These pathway stimuli owe their anxiety-evoking power to their location, and not to their resemblance to the central conditioned stimulus. The difference is illustrated in Figure 8.2.

The Anxiety-Inhibiting Role of Deep Muscle Relaxation

The autonomic effects that accompany deep relaxation are diametrically opposed to those that are characteristic of anxiety. Jacobson (1939, 1940) long ago showed that pulse rate and blood pressure were diminished by deep muscle relaxation. It was subsequently demonstrated (Drvota, 1962; Clark, 1963;

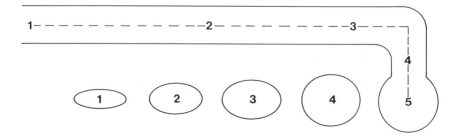

Fig. 8.2. *Two stimulus continua: shape generalization and pathway stimuli.* If there is a conditioned anxiety response to a circular enclosure, less anxiety is evoked by exposing the subject to a shape that is less than circular, or by placing him at points on the accustomed pathway to the enclosure. In the latter case, anxiety increases with decreasing distance. (Courtesy of Graphic Communications, Eastern Pennsylvania Psychiatric Institute, Philadelphia.)

Wolpe, 1964a) that skin resistance increases and respiration becomes slower and more regular during relaxation.

More thoroughgoing studies subsequently appeared. Paul (1969) showed that muscle relaxation produces effects opposite to those of anxiety on heart rate, respiratory rate, and skin conductance. Obvious effects were obtained even by simple instructions to relax; but they were significantly enhanced if the instructions were given in a hypnotic setting and even more significantly if they followed relaxation training. Van Egeren, Feather, and Hein (1971), in an elaborate psychophysiological study involving skin conductance, heart rate, digital pulse amplitude, and rate of respiration, found that relaxed subjects showed less decrease in skin resistance to phobic stimuli than subjects who were not relaxed. These calming effects of Jacobsonian relaxation appear to be concomitants or consequences of the voluntary efforts made by the subject to diminish the tonus of his muscles. They cannot be secondary to the relaxed state of the muscles: the complete or almost complete relaxation induced by drugs like curare may elicit severe anxiety (Campbell, Sanderson, & Laverty, 1964). The inhibition of aversively conditioned autonomic responses by relaxation responses has been directly demonstrated by Grings and Uno (1968) and Grings and Schandler (1977).

Not only are the effects of relaxation opposite in kind to those of anxiety, but, if counterposed to anxiety-evoking stimuli, they diminish the anxiety responses that these stimuli are able to evoke. A pilot investigation by Wolpe and Fried (1968) provided evidence that the galvanic skin response (on Lathrop's [1964] variability measure) decreases during desensitization in parallel to the decrements of anxiety that are reported by patients. Figure 8.3 shows the averaged changes of four patients to whom hierarchical phobic scenes were each presented three times in each of two sessions. The decrease of response from one presentation to the next should be noted, as well as the "savings" between Session 1 and Session 2 on the same scene.

Van Egeren (1970) reported that with repetitions of the phobic stimuli, the magnitude of effects decreased progressively in relaxed subjects, but remained much the same in the unrelaxed. In a nontherapeutic experiment comparing the effects of presenting hierarchical stimuli in a standardized repetitive way to relaxed and nonrelaxed subjects (Wolpe & Flood, 1970), a consistent downward trend of autonomic arousal as measured by galvanic skin response was noted across sessions with respect to each stimulus in the case of relaxed subjects but not in the nonrelaxed. In a clinical context, Paul (1969) demonstrated that autonomic arousal by a stressful stimulus decreases with repetition as a function of the degree to which relaxation has anxiety-inhibiting effects. Conner (1974) made the interesting observation that even when muscle relaxation is insufficient to lower autonomic baseline levels, it can still diminish the anxiety response to a conditioned stimulus.

In the practice of standard systematic desensitization there is also evidence of the potency of relaxation. Working on spider and snake phobias respec-

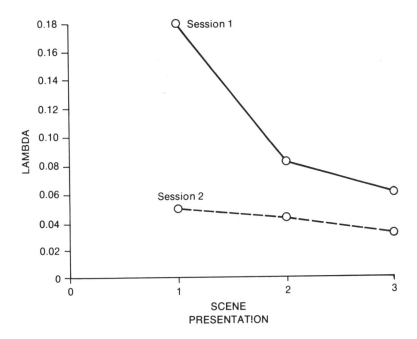

Fig. 8.3. Showing the lambda values for three presentations of the same scene during two successive desensitization sessions. The figure averages the readings for four different patients. Note that reactivity not only declines during each session but the decrement obtained at the end of Session 1 is maintained at the beginning of Session 2.

tively, Rachman (1965) and Davison (1965) found that subjects to whom the whole desensitization sequence of procedures was applied showed significantly more improvement than either those who received relaxation training without scene presentations or others to whom scenes were presented without relaxation. Farmer and Wright (1971) subjected snake-phobic subjects to desensitization under either muscle relaxation or directed muscle activity. Muscle relaxation was significantly effective in reducing fear; muscle activity was less so. An observation of incidental interest was that subjects showing high body-image scores in Fisher and Cleveland's (1958) personality test did particularly well with relaxation and very poorly with muscle activity. The finding of Davis (1960) that muscle tension is higher in high scorers both at rest and under stress may be relevant.[2]

WHEN TO USE SYSTEMATIC DESENSITIZATION

Generally speaking, systematic desensitization is used for the treatment of fears evoked by situations that do not lend themselves to "being handled"— in contrast to those social fears that are accompanied by motor inhibitions and in whose treatment changed verbal and motoric action is the vehicle for overcoming the fear-response habit, as exemplified in assertiveness training.

In relation to the kind of fear to which desensitization is applicable, the patient is a passive responder to the stimulus. One cannot "handle" darkness or an elevator in the same sense in which one can "handle" an unfair remark or an unattentive waiter. What applies to darkness and elevators also applies to all the other classical phobias—harmless animals, enclosed spaces, and such impersonal human stimulus situations as crowds. Systematic desensitization is, however, much more widely applicable to social fears of the many kinds for which assertiveness training is not suitable. Everybody recognizes the value of systematic desensitization for phobias, but even though social fears are much more common, not many therapists adequately exploit systematic desensitization in treating them.

THE TECHNIQUE OF
SYSTEMATIC DESENSITIZATION

The problems of the patient will have been carefully studied by the therapist. Misconceptions will have been corrected if indicated by the behavior analysis, and assertiveness training, if required, will have started. If systematic desen-

[2]A critique of recent research appears at the end of this chapter.

sitization is indicated, it will be initiated as soon as possible and may go on concurrently with assertiveness training and any further cognitive measures that may prove necessary. The technique involves four separate sets of operations:

1. Introduction of the subjective anxiety scale.
2. Training in deep muscle relaxation.
3. The construction of anxiety hierarchies.
4. Counterposing relaxation and anxiety-evoking stimuli from the hierarchies.

Introduction of the Subjective Anxiety (*sud*) Scale

Knowledge of the magnitude of the patient's anxiety responses to specific stimuli is indispensable to desensitization in several different ways: in the grading of stimulus situations for their relative anxiety-arousing effects, in judging the efficacy of relaxation training, in determining the anxiety baseline prior to and during the main procedure, and in assessing the anxiety aroused by presented stimuli. Verbal descriptions are not very informative. A subjective anxiety scale is therefore used, by which the patient reports his anxiety levels on a private scale of 0 to 100, where 100 represents the highest anxiety that he has or could have experienced.

The scale is introduced by addressing the patient as follows: "Think of the worst anxiety you have ever experienced, or can imagine experiencing, and assign to this the number 100. Now think of the state of being absolutely calm and call this zero. Now you have a scale of anxiety. On this scale how do you rate yourself at this moment?" Most subjects give a figure without much hesitation, and with practice come to be able to indicate their feelings with increasing confidence in a way that is much more informative than the usual adjectival statements can be. The unit is the *sud* (subjective unit of disturbance).

Training in Relaxation

The method of relaxation that is routinely taught is essentially that of Jacobson (1938), but instruction is completed in about six lessons, in contrast to Jacobson's very prolonged training (generally 50 sessions or more).

In introducing the subject of relaxation, I tell the patient (who by this time usually has a general idea of the nature of conditioning therapy) that relaxation is one of several available methods for combating anxiety. It is a skill that I will teach him, and that like other skills improves with practice—to which he will be expected to devote 10 to 15 minutes twice a day. I continue as follows:

Relaxation works by producing emotional calmness. Even the ordinary relaxing when one lies down often has quite a noticeable calming effect. There is a definite relationship between the extent of muscle relaxation and the production of calmness to oppose to anxiety. I am going to teach you how to relax far beyond the usual level, and with practice you will be able to "switch on" at will.

There is no sacred sequence for training the various muscle groups in relaxation, but the sequence adopted should be orderly. My own practice is to start with the arms because they are convenient for purposes of demonstration and it is easy to check their relaxation. I go on to the head region next because the most marked anxiety-inhibiting effects are usually obtained by relaxation there; and then I move downwards.

The patient is asked to grip the arm of his chair with one hand to see whether he can distinguish any qualitative difference between the sensations produced in his forearm and those in his hand. He is told to take note of the quality of the forearm sensation because it is caused by muscle tension in contrast to the touch and pressure sensations in the hand. The gripping action tenses both the flexor and extensor muscles of the forearm. The patient must note the exact location of the tensions. Next, the therapist grips the patient's wrist and asks him to bend his arm against resistance, thus making him aware of tension in his biceps. Then, by having him straighten his bent elbow against resistance in the opposite direction, he draws attention to the extensor muscles at the back of the arm. He goes on to say:

> I am now going to show you the essential activity that is involved in obtaining deep relaxation. I will again ask you to resist my pull at your wrist so as to tighten your biceps. I want you to notice very carefully the sensations in that muscle. Then I will ask you to let go gradually as I diminish the amount of force exerted against you. Notice, as your forearm descends, that there is decreasing sensation in the biceps muscle. Notice also that the letting go is an activity, but of a negative kind—it is an "uncontracting" of the muscle. In due course, your forearm will come to rest on the arm of the chair, and you may then think that you have gone as far as possible—that relaxation is complete. But although the biceps will indeed be partly and perhaps largely relaxed, a certain number of its fibers will still, in fact, be contracted. I will then say to you, "Go on letting go. Try to extend the activity that went on in the biceps while your forearm was coming down." It is the act of relaxing these additional fibers that will bring about the emotional effects we want. Let's try it and see what happens.

Gripping the patient's wrist a second time, the therapist has him tense and then gradually relax the biceps. When the forearm is close to the horizontal, he releases the wrist, allowing the patient to complete the movement on his own. He then exhorts him to "go on letting go," to "keep trying to go further and further in the negative direction," to "try to go beyond what seems to you to be the furthest point."

When the patient has shown, by successfully relaxing his biceps, that he fully understands how to proceed, he is asked to put both hands comfortably on his lap and try to relax all the muscles *of both arms* for a few minutes. He must report any sensations that he may feel. The usual ones are tingling, numbness, and warmth, mainly in the hands. After a few minutes the therapist palpates the relaxing muscles. With practice, he can judge in a rough way between various degrees of muscle tension.

Most patients have rather limited success when they first attempt to relax, but they are assured that good relaxation is a matter of practice, and told that whereas, initially, 20 minutes of trying may achieve no more than partial relaxation of an arm, one can eventually become able to relax one's whole body in a few minutes. However, there are some fortunate individuals who from the beginning experience a deepening and extending relaxation, radiating, as it seems, from particular muscles such as those of the arms or the jaws, and accompanied by marked calmness.

I customarily begin the *second lesson* in relaxation by telling the patient that because, from the emotional point of view, the most important muscles are situated in and around the head, we will deal with them next. We begin with the muscles of the face, demonstrating the tensions produced by contracting the muscles of the forehead. These muscles lend themselves to a demonstration by the therapist of the "steplike" character of deepening relaxation. The therapist simultaneously contracts the eyebrow-raising and the frowning muscles in his own forehead very intensely, pointing out that an anxious expression has thus been produced. He then says: "I am going to relax these muscles in a controlled way to give you an impression of the steplike way in which decrements of tension occur during attempt at deep relaxation, although, when you are learning to relax, the steps take much longer than in my demonstration." The therapist then relaxes his forehead, making an obvious step down about every five seconds until, after about half-a-dozen steps, the forehead is quite smooth. At this point he states that the relaxation is continuing, and that this relaxation "beneath the surface" is the part that matters for producing the desired emotional effects. The patient is then told to contract his eyebrow-raising muscles and is given a few minutes to relax them as far as possible. The same routine is applied to his frowning muscles. (It is much better to train the forehead muscles separately than together, as I used to do in the past.) Many patients spontaneously report sensations of tingling, warmth, or a feeling of thickness, as though the skin were made of leather. These sensations are indicative of relaxation beyond the normal level of muscle tone.

This lesson usually concludes by drawing attention to the muscles in the region of the nose by getting the patient to wrinkle his nose, and to the muscles around the mouth by making him purse his lips and then smile. All these muscles are relaxed in turn.

At the *third lesson* the patient is asked to bite on his teeth, thus tensing his masseters and temporales. The position of the lips is an important indicator of relaxation of the muscles of mastication. When these are relaxed, the lips are parted by a few millimeters. The masseters are definitely *not* relaxed if the mouth is resolutely closed. On the other hand, an open mouth is no proof of relaxation.

At the same lesson, I usually also introduce the muscles of the tongue. These may be felt contracting in the floor of the mouth when the patient presses the tip of his tongue firmly against the back of his lower incisor teeth. Relaxing the tongue muscles may produce such local sensations as tingling or a feeling of enlargement of that organ.

The *fourth lesson* deals with the two muscle groups in the eye region that have been postponed because of their delicacy while the patient practiced with larger muscles. They are the circumorbital muscles, which are felt by closing the eyes tightly, and the extrinsic eye muscles, identified by turning the eyes sharply to the right, left, up, and down in turn. Relaxation of these muscles can be profoundly calming, but it is also difficult and may be omitted in patients who are doing well without it.

The *fifth lesson* deals with the neck and shoulders. The main target in the neck is the posterior muscles that normally maintain the head's erect posture. Most people become aware of them merely by concentrating on sensations at the back of the neck. Relaxing these muscles makes the head fall forward, but because in the unpracticed individual the relaxation is incomplete, the head's whole weight is imposed on the few muscle fibers that are still contracted, producing discomfort and perhaps pain in the neck. As Jacobson pointed out, persistent practice, despite the discomfort, leads to a progressive yielding of these muscles; and usually in a week or so the patient finds that his neck is comfortable when his chin is resting on his sternum. Those who find the discomfort of the forward-learning head too great are instructed to practice relaxing the neck muscles with the back of the head resting against a high-backed chair.

Shoulder muscle tensions are demonstrated by the following routine: the deltoid is contracted by abducting the arm to the horizontal, the lateral neck muscles by continuing this movement up to the ear, the posthumeral and scapulo-spinal groups by moving the horizontal arm backward, and the pectorals by swinging it forward across the chest. In relaxing these muscles, the patient is directed to observe their functional unity with those of the arm.

The *sixth lesson* deals with the muscles of the back, abdomen, and thorax. The procedure with respect to the first two areas follows the usual pattern. The back muscles are contracted by backward arching of the spine. The abdominal muscles are tensed as if in anticipation of a punch in the belly. After contracting these muscles, the patient lets them go as far as he can. The thoracic muscles, or, more accurately, the muscles of respiration, are necessarily in a different category—for total inhibition of breathing is not an achievement to be promoted! But the respiratory rhythm can often be used to augment relaxation. Attention to the musculature during a few fairly deep breaths soon reveals that while some effort is involved during inhalation, expiration is essentially a "letting go." Some patients find it very helpful to coordinate relaxation of various other muscles with the automatic relaxation of the respiratory muscles that takes place with the exhalation of *normal* breathing.

In making patients aware of the muscles to be relaxed in the lower limbs, during the *seventh lesson,* it has been my custom to start with the feet and work upwards. The flexor digitorium brevis is felt in the sole by bending the toes within the shoe, the calf muscles by placing some weight on the toe, the peroneal and anterior tibial muscles by dorsiflexing the foot, the quadriceps femoris by straightening the knee, the hamstrings by trying to bend the knee against resistance, the adductors of the thigh by adduction against hand pressure on the inner aspect of the knee, and the abductors (which include some of the gluteal muscles) by abduction against pressure. These muscles are quite a load of new information, and the patient should be allowed enough time for relaxing them.

The assessment of a patient's ability to relax depends partly upon his reports of the degree of calmness that relaxing brings about in him, and partly upon impressions gained from observing him. By the second or third lesson, most patients report ease, tranquility, or sleepiness. A few experience little or no change of feeling. It is an advantage to have objective indicators of relaxation. Jacobson (1939, 1964) has used the electromyogram, but mainly as a corroborative measure. Recently, more convenient equipment has become available that translates muscle potentials into auditory signals whose pitch drops as tension decreases (Budzinski, Stoyva, & Adler, 1970). This also facilitates relaxation by providing feedback to the patient. Fortunately, the reports of patients are usually a sufficiently reliable guide to their emotional state, especially with the help of the subjective anxiety scale. Quite a number of them, especially those who start with little or no ongoing anxiety, report a positive feeling of calm after only one or two sessions of relaxation training. In some of these, it is possible to base desensitization on relaxation training of only the upper half of the body or less.

The Construction of Hierarchies

An anxiety hierarchy is a thematically related list of anxiety-evoking stimuli, ranked according to the amount of anxiety they evoke. It has always been my practice to place the stimulus that evokes the greatest anxiety at the top of the list. While hierarchy construction is sometimes an easy matter, it can also be very complicated, as Case 58 in Chapter 16 illustrates.

The theme, or common core, of a family of anxiety-evoking stimuli most often consists of something that is extrinsic to the patient, such as spiders or criticism; but it may be internal, like a feeling of losing control. Sometimes a number of physically disparate extrinsic stimulus situations all induce a common internal response. For example, a case of claustrophobia (Wolpe, 1961) had the same kind of trapped feeling when she had irremovable nail polish on her fingers or when she wore a tight ring, as she had when she was physically confined. Such commonality of response is the basis of secondary generalization (Hull, 1943, p. 191).

Hierarchy construction usually begins at about the same time as relaxation training, but is subject to alterations or additions at any time. It is important to note that both the gathering of the data and their subsequent organizing are done in an ordinary conversational way and not under relaxation.

The raw data from which hierarchies are constructed come from four main sources: (a) the patient's history (see Chapter 5); (b) responses to the Willoughby questionnaire (Appendix A or B) which reveals anxieties mainly in certain interpersonal contexts; (c) a Fear Survey Schedule[3] (Wolpe & Lang, 1964) (see Appendix C); and (d) special probings into situations in which the patient feels unadaptive anxiety. If needed, further information may be sought by assigning to the patient the homework task of listing all situations, thoughts, or feelings that he finds disturbing, fearful, embarrassing, or in any other way distressing.

When all the identified sources of neurotic disturbance have been listed, the therapist classifies them into themes. Usually, there is more than one theme. In a good many cases, the themes are fairly obvious, but there are frequent exceptions. For example, a fear of going to movies, parties, and football games may suggest a fear of public situations and yet turn out to be really a claustrophobia or a fear of scrutiny. Frequently, fear and avoidance of social occasions turn out to be based on fear of criticism or rejection; or the fear may be a function of the mere physical presence of people, varying with the number to whom the patient is exposed. One patient's ostensible fear of social situations was really a conditioned anxiety response to the smell of food in public places. A good example of the importance of correct identification of relevant sources of anxiety is to be found in a previously reported case (Wolpe, 1958, p. 152) in which the anxiety underlying a man's impotence turned out to be due, not to any aspect of the sexual situation as such, but to the idea of inflicting physical trauma. (An attempt at defloration had aroused high anxiety in this patient, and this anxiety had been conditioned to the sexual act.) The strategy of treatment was shifted by this revelation from *in vivo* use of the sexual response to systematic desensitization to tissue damage.

It is not necessary for the patient actually to have experienced each situation that is included in a hierarchy. The question posed is, "If you were today

---

[3]A more extensive inventory (Wolpe & Lang, 1969) is commercially available. (Educational & Industrial Testing Service, San Diego, California).

confronted by such and such a situation, *would you expect* to be anxious?"
To answer this question he has to *imagine* the situation concerned, and it is
generally almost as easy to imagine a supposed event as it is to imagine one
that has at some time occurred. The temporal setting of an imagined stimulus
configuration scarcely affects the responses to it. A man with a phobia for
dogs will usually have about as much anxiety at the idea of meeting a bulldog
on the way home tomorrow as he will when recalling an actual encounter with
one of this breed.

The following list of fears supplied by a patient will be used to illustrate
some of the intricacies of hierarchy construction. This list is reproduced exactly as the patient presented it.

Raw List of Fears

1. High Altitudes
2. Elevators
3. Crowded Places
4. Church
5. Darkness—Movies, etc.
6. Being Alone
7. Marital Relations (pregnancy)
8. Walking any Distance
9. Death
10. Accidents
11. Fire
12. Fainting
13. Falling Back
14. Injections
15. Medications
16. Fear of the Unknown
17. Losing My Mind
18. Locked Doors
19. Amusement Park Rides
20. Steep Stairways

With the help of a little clarification from the patient the items were sorted into categories, thus:

A. ACROPHOBIA
  1. High Altitudes
  19. Amusement Park Rides
  20. Steep Stairways
B. CLAUSTROPHOBIA
  2. Elevators
  3. Crowded Places
  4. Church
  5. Movies (darkness factor)
  18. Locked Doors
C. AGORAPHOBIA
  6. Being Alone
  8. Walking any Distance (alone)
D. ILLNESS AND ITS ASSOCIATIONS
  12. Fainting
  13. Falling Back
  14. Injections
  15. Medication
E. BASICALLY OBJECTIVE FEARS
  7. Marital Relations (pregnancy)
  9. Death
  10. Accidents
  11. Fire
  16. Fear of the Unknown
  17. Losing My Mind

Before considering the truly neurotic groups A–D to which desensitization is relevant, some remarks must be made about group E. The patient's fears of pregnancy, accidents, death, and fire were all in contexts in which fear can be reasonable, but in her case, apprehension about these matters was somewhat more than normal. I considered that this might be a function of a generally elevated level of anxiety—which is quite often found in neuroses—and would probably disappear when the major neurotic anxiety sources had been removed by therapy. Her fear of the unknown was bound up with the idea of death. Her fear of losing her mind, an inference from the bizarre and uncontrollable feelings that characterized her neurosis, was overcome by strong assurance that her condition was not related to insanity and could *never* lead to it. The assurance was reinforced by demonstrating that hyperventilation could precipitate many of her symptoms. (There are people in whom *all* fears would belong to group E, in which case, of course, desensitization would not be relevant; supplying corrective information, with the addition, sometimes, of thought stopping would be indicated. See Chapter 6.)

On scrutinizing the stimulus groups A–D, the reader should observe that the items are not suitable for hierarchical ranking. The items of each group are merely exemplifications that can lead to more numerous stimulus situations, specific enough to be ranked, through further communication between patient and therapist. This is not always immediately obvious to newcomers to behavior therapy. They often attempt to arrange such exemplifications into hierarchies. One day, I asked a group of 25 members of a class (none of whom had previously treated more than two or three patients) how they would proceed to build a hierarchy out of the five claustrophobia items of group B. The majority of them were disposed to ask the patient to rank elevators, churches, movies, etc., hierarchically, and to assume that the influence of modifying factors, like *size* of elevator, would automatically be included in the hierarchical ranking. But these five items were merely settings with potential for space constriction. Further questioning of the patient showed, as expected, that the claustrophobic anxiety was an inverse function of the size of the enclosing space and a direct function of duration of confinement. Desensitization, accordingly, involved two hierarchical series: first, confinement for a constant length of time in progressively smaller rooms, and then confinement in a very small room (four feet square) for increasing periods.

Similarly, in a group A, acrophobia, each of the three items refers to a whole range of concrete situations. They do not have the specificity that would permit them to be used in desensitization; but particularizing within the areas they encompass provided a range of concrete situations evoking responses of different intensities. It emerged that increasing heights were increasingly fearful, starting from about 20 feet (or a second-floor window), and that motion aggravated the fear at all heights. Group D yielded a fairly extensive hierarchy, some of whose items, ranked in order of diminishing anxiety, were:

1. Feeling of being about to lose consciousness.
2. Feeling of falling backwards.
3. Marked dizziness.
4. Feeling of lightness in head.
5. Moderate dizziness.
6. Smell of ether.
7. Receiving an injection.
8. Racing heart (anxiety increasing with rapidity of heart beat).
9. Weak knees.
10. Seeing syringe poised for an injection.
11. Sight of bandages.

It may be observed that the stronger stimuli (1–5) are all endogenous, and most of the weaker ones exogenous. What is common to all is the arousal of a feeling of personal threat.

In other cases, besides multiplicity of hierarchies, one encounters multiple "dimensions" within a single hierarchy. For example, in a patient having claustrophobic reactions in social situations, five variables controlled the intensity of the reaction. The reactions were the *stronger*:

1. The greater the number of people present.
2. The more strange the people.
3. The greater the difficulties in the way of leaving the room (both physical factors and social propriety being relevant).
4. The shorter the time since her last meal (this factor determining the measure of a fear of vomiting).

They were *weaker* if she was accompanied by

5. Protective persons—husband, mother, or close friend (in descending order of effectiveness).

Sometimes, the inadequacies of a hierarchy become evident only after attempts at desensitization have begun, when it may be seen that the anxiety level does not diminish after repeated presentations of the weakest scene contained in the hierarchy, even though relaxation is manifestly good. The problem is then to seek still less disturbing stimuli whose evoked anxiety is weak enough to be inhibited by the patient's relaxation. In many cases, it is obvious where to look for weaker stimuli. For example, in a patient who had an anxiety hierarchy on the theme of loneliness, the weakest item in the original hierarchy—being at home accompanied only by her daughter—was found to evoke more anxiety than was manageable. In order to obtain a weaker starting point, all that was needed was to add to the situation two or more companions. But it is not always so easy, and the therapist may have to put on his thinking cap to find a way of procuring weak stimuli.

For example, following an accident three years previously, a woman patient had developed severe anxiety reactions to the sight of approaching automobiles. I had been led to believe that the patient noticed the first glimmerings of anxiety when a car was two blocks away, and that the anxiety increased gradually up to a distance of half a block, and then much more steeply with further approximation. This seemed straightforward enough; but at the first desensitization session an imagined distance of two blocks from the car aroused anxiety too great to be inhibited by the counteraction of relaxation. Further questioning revealed that the patient had considerable anxiety at the very prospect of even the shortest journey by car, since the whole range of threatening possibilities was already present the moment a journey became imminent; but she had "not thought this amount of anxiety worthy of report." Desensitization could not begin to succeed until the "danger" contained in scenes from the hierarchy was removed. What was required was a sharp delimitation of the implications of each situation. Accordingly, an imaginary enclosed field, two blocks square, was drawn on paper. The patient imagined that she sat in her car "placed" in one corner of the field while a trusted person drove his car up to an agreed distance from her car, and then to ever-closer agreed points as the patient progressed. The "danger" was thus always circumscribed. This, and later steps in the treatment of the case are described in some detail in Chapter 16.

Another instance of difficulty in obtaining sufficiently weak anxiety-evoking stimuli was a patient with a death phobia, whose anxiety-arousing contexts in descending order were human corpses, funeral processions, and dead dogs. Presentation of scenes of dead dogs produced marked and undiminishing anxiety, even when they were imagined at distances of two or three hundred yards (where they were hardly visible). A solution was found in the use of a temporal dimension, beginning with the historically inaccurate sentence, "William the Conqueror was killed at the Battle of Hastings in 1066."

A third example concerns a woman who had very severe reactions to the idea of anybody fainting or "losing power." Imagining even the most trivial sign of weakness in a person or an animal produced more anxiety than her relaxation could counteract. The first scene to be successfully used in her desensitization was in the context of her being conducted around a campus. Her imaginary escort pointed to a platform and said, "That is where, five years ago, an animal was given an injection that paralyzed it for five minutes." Desensitization involved first making the incident more recent and then increasing the duration of the paralysis.

In constructing hierarchies one always aims for a reasonably evenly spaced progression. If items are too similar, time will be wasted; if adjacent items differ too widely in anxiety-evoking potential, progress will be halted upon moving from the lesser to the greater. Occasionally a patient may even be further sensitized, i.e., conditioned to higher levels of anxiety as the result of severe anxiety being evoked. (It is not clear why, but this hardly ever happens with social stimuli to anxiety.) When a hierarchy is based on a directly measurable dimension such as distance, a well-spaced progression is relatively easy to obtain. However, this is not a linear function: a simple power function is involved, whose index exceeds unity in some cases and is fractional in others (see p. 162ff). In phobias in which anxiety increases with proximity to the feared object, small changes in the physical dimension affect anxiety more with increasing closeness of the object. The opposite applies to acrophobia and agoraphobia. Where fear is a function of number of feared objects, small increments are more potent at low numerical levels. This whole topic is discussed below (pp. 162ff).

The above considerations render it desirable for a hierarchy to be in quantifiable form, an objective for which the subjective anxiety scale is of the greatest value. The standard procedure is to ask the patient to rate the items of the hierarchy according to the amount of anxiety he would have upon exposure to them. If the differences between items are similar, and, generally speaking, not more than five to ten *suds,* the spacing can be regarded as satisfactory. On the other hand, if there were, for example, 40 *suds* for item number 8, and 10 *suds* for item number 9, there would be a need for intervening items.

Case 24

Sometimes efficiency requires a context for desensitization that is to outward view remote from the presenting problem. In a 42-year-old woman who for 21 years had a fear of traveling alone, it became evident that the center point of her disability was a fear of *being alone* away from home. It would certainly have been possible to deal with this in the context of traveling, but her sensitivity was extreme and aloneness would have been difficult to quantify in terms of distance. It was possible to obtain much better control of her reactions by using an elevator as the vehicle of her separation from the outside world. The weaker items of the hierarchy were set in a completely open elevator in which she ascended an increasing number of floors up to 100. Then she was "placed" in an elevator that had a single one-foot-square window, and in this a similar sequence was followed. The same was then done in an elevator with a window whose dimensions were 9" × 2", an elevator with a 2-inch peephole, and finally, a completely opaque one. Desensitization to these items was attended by a progressive increase in her capacity to travel afield, even though distance had not figured at all in the desensitization up to this point. Then a new series was started embracing anxiety-conditioned stimuli belonging to journeys of various kinds.

SOME EXAMPLES OF HIERARCHIES

A Cluster of Hierarchies Involving People

Case 25

Miss C. was a 24-year-old art student who came for treatment because marked anxiety at examinations had resulted in repeated failures. Investigation revealed additional phobic areas. The hierarchies are given below. All of them involve people, and *none belongs to the classical phobias.* Note, in the examination series, that the hierarchical order of the top five items does not correspond with the temporal order. Emotional conditioning does not always fit in with logic. (Freedom from anxiety to the highest items of each of these hierarchies was achieved in 17 desensitization sessions, with complete transfer to the corresponding situations in actuality. Four months later, Miss C. passed her examinations without anxiety.)

Hierarchies in Descending Order of Reaction Intensity
(suds in parentheses)

A. *Examination Series*
    1. On the way to the university on the day of an examination. (95)
    2. In the process of answering an examination paper. (90)
    3. Standing before the unopened doors of the examination room. (80)
    4. Awaiting the distribution of examination papers. (70)
    5. The examination paper lies face down before her. (60)
    6. The night before an examination. (50)
    7. One day before an examination. (40)
    8. Two days before an examination. (30)
    9. Three days before an examination. (20)
    10. Four days before an examination. (15)
    11. A week before an examination. (10)
    12. Two weeks before an examination. (5)

B. *Scrutiny Series*
    1. Being watched working (drawing) by ten people. (85)
    2. Being watched working by six people. (70)
    3. Being watched working by three people. (55)
    4. Being watched working by one expert in the field. (Anxiety begins when the observer is ten feet away and increases as he draws closer.) (25–55)
    5. Being watched working by a nonexpert. (Anxiety begins at a distance of four feet.) (5–20)

C. *Devaluation Series*
    1. An argument she raises in a discussion is ignored by the group. (60)

2. She is not recognized by a person she has briefly met three times. (50)
3. Her mother says she is selfish because she is not helping in the house when studying. (40)
4. She is not recognized by a person she has briefly met twice. (30)
5. Her mother calls her lazy. (20)
6. She is not recognized by a person she has briefly met once. (10)

D. *Discord between Other People*
1. Her mother shouts at a servant. (50)
2. Her young sister whines to her mother. (40)
3. Her sister engages in a dispute with her father. (30)
4. Her mother shouts at her sister. (20)
5. She sees two strangers quarrel. (10)

A Variety of Hierarchies on the Theme of Sickness and Injury

The following examples illustrate individual differences in the content, order, and number of items that make up hierarchies of the same theme in different patients. In each of the cases there was fear of both external and internal stimuli. All three required and received training in assertive behavior in addition to desensitization.

Case 26

Mrs. D., aged 35, was agoraphobic in addition to the fears of illness shown in these two hierarchies. She had never actually experienced any of the possible events in the endogenous series.

External Series (Illness in Others)

1. Sight of a fit. (100)
2. Jerky movements of another's arm. (90)
3. Sight of someone fainting. (85)
4. An acquaintance says, "That man across the street has some form of insanity." (80)
5. The word "insanity." (70)
6. The word "madness." (65)
7. Insane-sounding laughter. (60)
8. An acquaintance says, "That man across the street has an anxiety state." (50)
9. The sound of screaming (the closer, the more disturbing. (25–40)
10. A man with a fracture lying in bed with ropes and pulleys attached to his leg. (35)
11. A man propped up in bed short of breath because of heart disease. (30)
12. An acquaintance says, "That man across the road is an epileptic." (25)

13. Seeing a man propped up in bed short of breath because of pneumonia. (20)
14. A man walks by with a plaster cast on his leg. (15)
15. A man with Parkinson's disease. (10)
16. A man with blood running down his face from a cut. (7)
17. A person with a facial tic. (5)

Endogenous Series (Illness in Self)

1. Having a fit. (100)
2. Fainting. (80)
3. Tremor of her hand. (50)

Note that the large *sud* differences in the endogenous series were acceptable because in the actual desensitization these items could be coordinated with those of the external series.

Case 27

Mrs. E., aged 32.

External Series (Illness in Others)

1. The sight of physical deformity. (90)
2. Someone in pain (the greater the evidence of pain, the more disturbing). (50–80)
3. The sight of bleeding. (70)
4. The sight of somebody seriously ill (e.g., heart attack). (60)
5. Automobile accidents (50)
6. Nurses in uniform. (40)
7. Wheelchairs. (30)
8. Hospitals. (20)
9. Ambulances. (10)

Endogenous Series (Illness in Self)

1. Tense (explosive) sensation in head. (90)
2. Clammy feet. (80)
3. Perspiring hands. (75)
4. Dry mouth and inability to swallow. (70)
5. Dizziness. (60)
6. Rapid breathing. (50)
7. Racing heart. (40)
8. Tense feeling in back of neck. (30)
9. Weakness at knees. (20)
10. Butterflies in stomach. (10)

Case 27a

Mrs. F., aged 52, also had a severe phobic system on the theme of death.

External Series (Illness in Others)

1. Child with two wasted legs. (85)
2. Man walking slowly—short of breath owing to weak heart. (80)
3. Blind man working lift. (70)
4. Child with one wasted leg. (65)
5. A hunchback. (55)
6. A person groaning with pain. (50)
7. A man with a club foot. (40)
8. A one-armed man. (30)
9. A one-legged man. (20)
10. A person with a high temperature owing to a relatively non-dangerous disease like influenza. (10)

Endogenous Series (Illness in Self)

1. Extrasystoles. (80)
2. Shooting pains in chest and abdomen. (70)
3. Pains in the left shoulder and back. (60)
4. Pain on top of head. (55)
5. Buzzing in ear. (50)
6. Tremor of hands. (40)
7. Numbness or pain in fingertips. (30)
8. Shortness of breath after exertion. (20)
9. Pain in left hand (old injury). (10)

It will be noted that the content of each of the foregoing hierarchies is heterogeneous. It is impossible to abstract a common feature that can be varied quantitatively. Consider in contrast, the following example taken from the literature, in which there was a heterogeneity on the surface, and a common factor to be discerned on close inspection:

1. At large university cocktail party talking with strangers.
2. At departmental luncheon with friends.
3. Entering common room of residents where people glance up.
4. People look at you walking down street.
5. Reading in library, glanced at by two men at opposite table.
6. At library, conscious of girl looking at you.

The essence of this hierarchy was anxiety at scrutiny on a numerical dimension. It could have been treated in a single arbitrarily chosen setting, for example, in a library, being looked at by increasing numbers of people. If it eventually turned out that different settings added their own anxiety, these could have been dealt with in a new hierarchy, keeping the persons present at a constant large number.

Although most hierarchies vary in a single dimension, many have two or more factors. It is the rule to find multiple dimensions in fears of the attitudes and opinions of other people. The fear varies in magnitude with the nature of the opinion and also with the identity of the person. The hierarchy is then set out in the tabular form illustrated by Table 8.1 in which a woman's fears of the negative opinions of others varied according to adjectives applied to her and the person expressing them. It should be noted that the hierarchical order of the adjectives varied somewhat from speaker to speaker. The usual way of treating hierarchies of this kind is to have the patient imagine herself overhearing the named person attributing an "undesirable" quality to her while unaware of being overheard.

Desensitization Procedure: Counteracting Anxiety by Relaxation-Induced Calmness

The stage is set for the desensitization procedure when the patient has attained a capacity to calm himself by relaxation, and the therapist has established appropriate hierarchies. Many patients can be adequately calmed when relaxation training has gone halfway or less. While a desensitization program makes it highly desirable for the patient to achieve a positive feeling of calm —i.e., a negative of anxiety—it is not mandatory, and one can be well satisfied with zero subjective units of disturbance. In a fair number who have considerable levels of current anxiety (whether or not this is pervasive—"free-floating"—anxiety) it has been found that a substantial lowering of the level —say, from 50 to 15 *suds*—may afford a sufficiently low anxiety baseline for successful desensitization. Apparently, an anxiety-inhibiting "dynamism"

Table 8.1. **Bidimensional Hierarchy Set Out According to the *sud* Score Resulting from the Interplay of Pairs of Factors.**

	Uncle Charlie	Florence	Sharon	Geraldine	Shopkeeper She Barely Knows
Uses People	95	65	70	50	20
Irresponsible	90	75	50	40	20
Selfish	90	75	40	50	20
Unreliable	80	60	30	40	10
Lazy	60	50	10	20	0
Untidy	50	40	20	10	0
Awkward	40	30	10	10	0

can inhibit small quantities of intercurrent anxiety even when it does not fully overcome current anxiety. However, desensitizing effects are very rarely obtainable with levels in excess of 25 *suds,* and in some individuals a zero level is obligatory for change to occur.

The therapist naturally hopes for a smooth passage, and such is often the case, but there are many difficulties that may encumber the path. I shall first describe the technique and the characteristic course of uncomplicated desensitization.

The first desensitization session is introduced by saying, "I am now going to get you to relax; and when you are relaxed I will ask you to imagine certain scenes. Each time a scene is clear in your mind indicate this by raising your index finger about one inch."

While the patient sits or lies comfortably with his eyes closed, the therapist proceeds to bring about as deep a state of relaxation as possible by the use of such words as the following: "Now, your whole body becomes progressively heavier, and all your muscles relax. Let go more and more completely. We will give your muscles individual attention. Relax the muscles of your forehead and your lower face. (Pause 10 to 20 seconds.) Relax the muscles of your jaws and those of your tongue. (Pause.) Relax the muscles of your eyeballs. The more you relax, the calmer you become. (Pause.) Relax the muscles of your neck. (Pause.) Let all the muscles of your shoulders relax. Just let yourself go. (Pause.) Now relax your arms. (Pause.) Relax all the muscles of your trunk. (Pause.) Relax the muscles of your lower limbs. Let your muscles go more and more. You feel so much at ease and so very comfortable."

At the first desensitization session, which is always partly exploratory, the therapist seeks some feedback about the state of the patient, asking him to state on the subjective scale how much anxiety he feels. If it is zero or close thereto, scene presentations can begin. If the patient continues to have some anxiety despite his best efforts at direct relaxation, various imaginal devices may be invoked. Those most commonly used are:

1. "Imagine that on a calm summer's day you lie back on a soft lawn and watch large, fleecy clouds move slowly overhead. Notice especially the intensely brilliant edges."
2. "Imagine an intense, bright spot of light about 18 inches in front of you just above eye level." (This image is attributable to Milton Erickson.)
3. "Imagine that near a river's bank you see a leaf moving erratically on little waves."

The introduction of the scenes at the first desensitization session follows a standard routine. Observations of the patient's responses at this session frequently lead to modifications of technique to fit in with him.

The first scene presented is a "control." It is neutral in the sense that the

patient is not expected to have any anxious reaction to it. I most commonly use a street scene. Sometimes it is "safer" to have the patient imagine himself sitting in his living room reading a newspaper, but there is no guarantee
of safety unless the subject matter has actually been explored beforehand.
At one time I used to employ a white flower against a black background as
a control scene. One day, a patient evinced considerable anxiety to it, because he associated it with funerals, and, as it turned out, had a neurosis
about death.

There are two reasons why a control scene is used. First, it provides information about the patient's general ability to visualize. Second, it provides indications of possible contaminating factors: for example, the patient may
have anxiety at relinquishing control, or about the "unknown." In either
case, that anxiety, which has nothing to do with the target of the desensitization, must be removed before therapy can continue.

For many years, the standard method of introducing scenes was the one
that I first described in detail in 1954. The patient was asked to imagine the
scene, and then instructed to desist after "sufficient" time had passed (usually 15 to 20 seconds). He was then invited to raise his finger if the scene had
caused even the slightest rise of anxiety. That procedure had the disadvantage
that the therapist could not tell when visualization had actually begun. Consequently, there could have been wide variations in the actual duration of
scenes. In addition, the procedure was usually unnecessarily time-consuming. The following method, which is free from these disadvantages, has been
consistently used and taught since 1968.

The patient is asked to imagine scenes as indicated by the therapist. He is
told to raise his left index finger about one inch when the image is clear. The
therapist then presents a scene and lets it remain for exactly as long as he wants
—usually 5 to 7 seconds. He terminates it by saying, "Stop the scene," and
then asks the patient to state how much it disturbed him in terms of *suds;* i.e.,
by how many *suds* did the scene raise his *sud* level? After a few sessions, many
patients get into the habit of stating the number of *suds* automatically upon
the termination of the scene. While a verbal report may possibly disrupt relaxation more than would the raising of a finger, the adverse effects have in
no case to date seemed to be important. Any disadvantages are certainly out-
weighed by dispensing with the need to allow "long enough time" to be sure
that the patient has visualized the scene, and by the immediate and precise
feedback of amount of disturbance.

In order to illustrate what is typically said and done, let us make use of the
cluster of four hierarchies of Miss C. (p. 152).

THERAPIST: I am now going to ask you to imagine a number of scenes. You
will imagine them clearly and they will interfere little, if at all, with your state

of relaxation. If, however, at any time you feel disturbed or worried and want to draw my attention, you can tell me so. As soon as a scene is clear in your mind, indicate it by raising your left index finger about one inch. First, I want you to imagine that you are standing at a familiar street corner on a pleasant morning watching the traffic go by. You see cars, motorcycles, trucks, bicycles, people, and traffic lights; and you hear the sounds associated with all these things.

(After a few seconds the patient raises her left index finger. The therapist pauses for five seconds.)

THERAPIST: Stop imagining that scene. By how much did it raise your anxiety level while you imagined it?

MISS C.: Not at all.

THERAPIST: Now give your attention once again to relaxing.

(There is again a pause of 20–30 seconds, with renewed relaxation instructions.)

THERAPIST: Now imagine that you are home studying in the evening. It is the 20th May, exactly a month before your examination.

(After about 15 seconds Miss C. raises her finger. Again she is left with the scene for 5 seconds.)

THERAPIST: Stop that scene. By how much did it raise your anxiety?

MISS C.: About 15 units.

THERAPIST: Now imagine the same scene again—a month before your examination.

At this second presentation the rise in anxiety was five *suds* and at the third it was zero. The numbers given vary with the individual and with the scene. When the initial figure is over 30, repetition is unlikely to lower it. But there are exceptions. There are also occasional patients in whom an initial rise of ten is too great to be diminished by repetition.

Having disposed of the first scene of the examination hierarchy, I could have moved on to the second. Alternatively, I could have tested Miss C.'s responses in another area, such as the discord hierarchy, which I did:

THERAPIST: Imagine you are sitting on a bench at a bus stop and across the road are two strange men whose voices are raised in argument.

(This scene was given twice. After the patient reported on her response to the last presentation I terminated the desensitization session.)

THERAPIST: Relax again. Now I am going to count up to five and you will open your eyes, feeling calm and refreshed.

The responses of this patient were commonplace. Since visualization was clear, and there was evidence of decrease of anxiety with each repetition of a

scene, it seemed likely that we would make our way through all four hierarchies without much trouble, an expectation that was borne out by the course
of events.

Procedure at later sessions takes much the same course as at the first, but
there is a tendency for the preliminaries to take less and less time. Whenever
the patient is judged sufficiently relaxed, he is informed that scenes will be
presented to his imagination. Only at the earliest sessions is he reminded that
if anything should disturb him unduly he should at once communicate this
fact to the therapist. Exposure to a very disturbing scene can seriously increase
phobic sensitivity.[4] If at the previous session there was a scene for which repeated presentations diminished anxiety, but not to zero, that scene is usually
the first to be presented. But if at the previous session, that scene ceased to
arouse any anxiety, the scene next higher in the hierarchy will now be presented. There are, however, some patients who, though they have had no anxiety
at all to the final scene at a session, again show a small measure of anxiety to
that same scene at the next session—a kind of "spontaneous recovery" of
anxiety. The scene must then be repeated until the anxiety is entirely eliminated, before continuing to ascend the hierarchy. In some of these patients, the
need for backtracking can sometimes be eliminated by overlearning at the
earlier session, i.e., presenting a scene two or three times more after it has
ceased to arouse anxiety.

All relevant occurrences during the desensitization session are noted on a
card by a concise notation. The following is the record summarizing Miss C.'s
desensitization session as described above:

S.D. by rel. Scene 1—corner ([× 1] 0). 2—studying at home one month before
exam ([× 3] 15,5,0). 3—two strange men argue across road ([× 2] 15,10).

"S.D. by rel." stands for "systematic desensitization by relaxation." The
numbers in square parenthesis show how many presentations were given.
Those to their right are the *sud* scores for the successive presentations.

The usual plan followed in assigning numerical indices to scenes is to use
an integer to indicate the class of subject matter, and letters for variations of
detail. For example, in Miss C.'s case, the imaginary situation of being at
home working two weeks before the examination was given the index 1 a, one
week before the examination was 1 b, and so forth. The advantages of employing these indices are: (1) they obviate repeatedly writing out the features
of scenes; (2) they make it easy to find particular scenes when one consults the
record; and (3) they facilitate later research work.

---

[4]This is generally true of brief exposure but not true of the prolonged exposure that is part of
a flooding program (Chapter 12).

QUANTITATIVE CONSIDERATIONS

There is great variation in *how many themes, how many scenes from each,* and *how many presentations are given* at a desensitization session. Generally, up to four hierarchies are drawn upon in an individual session, and not many patients have more than four. Three or four presentations of a scene are usual to bring the responses to zero, but ten or more may be needed. The total number of scenes presented is limited mainly by availability of time, but sometimes by the endurance of the patient. On the whole, available time increases as therapy goes on, and eventually almost the whole interview period may be devoted to desensitization, so that whereas at an early stage eight or ten presentations may be the total at a session, at an advanced stage the number may be 30 or even 50. The usual duration of a desensitization session is 15 to 30 minutes. However, Wolpin and Pearsall (1965) reported totally overcoming a phobia in a single session conducted continuously for 90 minutes.

While the foregoing generalizations apply to the great majority of patients, there are rare individuals who manifest marked perseveration of even the mild anxiety aroused by a single scene presentation. Yet, anxiety decreases from session to session. In such individuals only one scene should be given at a session. Marked perseveration of anxiety can also occur in the usual run of patients after the presentation of an unduly disturbing scene. When this happens, the session should be terminated.

It has hitherto been the accepted principle in systematic desensitization to use only weakly anxiety-evoking stimuli. While this is obviously prudent when one depends on reciprocal inhibition for change, it is not necessarily always the most economical thing to do. There are clinical reports suggesting that more rapid progress sometimes follows larger steps (Rachman, 1971). It is conceivable that there is some personality factor that determines responsiveness to change, ranging from "desensitizability" at one extreme to "floodability" at the other.

The *duration* of a scene is usually of the order of five to seven seconds, but it may be varied according to several circumstances. It is quickly terminated if the patient indicates strong anxiety. Whenever the therapist has special reason to suspect that a scene may evoke a strong reaction he presents it with cautious brevity—for one or two seconds. By and large, early presentations of scenes are briefer, later ones longer. A certain number of patients require 15 or more seconds to construct a clear image of a verbally triggered scene. The character of the scene also necessarily plays a part in determining the time allowed for it. A clap of thunder takes less time than making a speech.

The *interval* between scenes also varies. It is usually between 10 and 30 seconds, but if the patient has been more than slightly disturbed by the preceding scene, the interval may be extended to a minute or more, during which time he may be given repeated suggestions to be relaxed and tranquil. Until the therapist is well acquainted with the patient's reactions, he should frequently check the basal relaxation level between scenes. For this purpose, the *sud* scale is invaluable.

The *number* of desensitizing sessions required depends on the number of scene presentations necessary to overcome the phobic constellations of the patient. Relevant factors are the number of such constellations, the severity of each, and the degree of generalization or involvement of related stimuli in the case of each. One patient may recover in half a dozen sessions, another may require a hundred or more. The patient with a death phobia (p. 150), on whom a temporal dimension had to be used, also had two other phobias and required a total of about a hundred sessions. To remove the death phobia alone, a total of about 2,000 scene presentations were given.

The *spacing* of sessions does not seem to matter greatly. As a rule, sessions are once or twice a week, but may be separated by many weeks, or take place daily. Some patients, visiting from afar, receive two sessions a day, and occasionally as many as four. Whether sessions are massed or widely dispersed, there is practically always a close correlation between the extent to which desensitization has been accomplished and the degree of diminution of anxiety responses to real stimuli in the phobic areas. Except when therapy is almost terminated and nothing remains of a phobia but a few weak reactions that may be overcome by the competition of emotions arising spontaneously in the ordinary course of living (Wolpe, 1958, p. 99), very little change occurs, as a rule, between sessions. In one case of severe claustrophobia, a marked but incomplete degree of improvement achieved by a first series of sessions remained almost stationary during a 3½-year interval, after which further sessions led to complete elimination of the phobia. The patient mentioned earlier, who had a disabling fear of cars, had daily sessions for a week or two every five weeks or so, and improved greatly during the treatment phases, but not at all during the intervening weeks (see Case 58).

Rate of change is neither haphazard nor a purely individual matter. At least in the case of desensitization of the classical phobias, it follows consistent quantitative laws. A study of 20 phobias of 13 patients (Wolpe, 1963) was prompted by the casual observation that during densitization the number of presentations of a scene required to bring the anxiety level down to zero is not uniform, but tends to increase or decrease on the way up the hierarchy. An attempt was made to establish quantitative relations by a study of those phobias that vary along a physical dimension. It was found that in claustrophobia and those phobias in which the patient becomes more anxious with increasing proximity to the feared object, the cumulative curve relating number of scene presentations to therapeutic progress is a positively accelerating function. In agoraphobias, acrophobias, and those in which anxiety depends on the number of objects, the cumulative curve is a negatively accelerating function. No exceptions were found, as may be observed by studying Figures 8.4 through 8.7, each of which contains the curves of a particular group. In

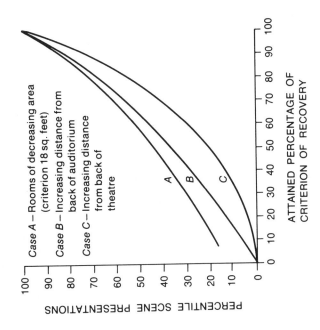

Case A – Rooms of decreasing area
(criterion 18 sq. feet)

Case B – Increasing distance from
back of auditorium

Case C – Increasing distance
from back of
theatre

PERCENTILE SCENE PRESENTATIONS

ATTAINED PERCENTAGE OF
CRITERION OF RECOVERY

Fig. 8.5. Percentile cumulative curves: Desensitizing operations in claustrophobia.

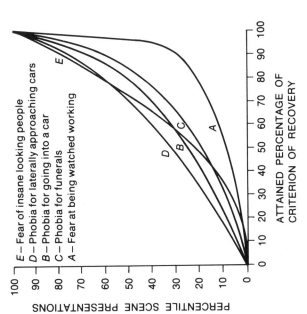

E – Fear of insane looking people
D – Phobia for laterally approaching cars
B – Phobia for going into a car
C – Phobia for funerals
A – Fear at being watched working

PERCENTILE SCENE PRESENTATIONS

ATTAINED PERCENTAGE OF
CRITERION OF RECOVERY

Fig. 8.4. Percentile cumulative curves: Desensitizing operations in proximation phobias in different subjects.

163

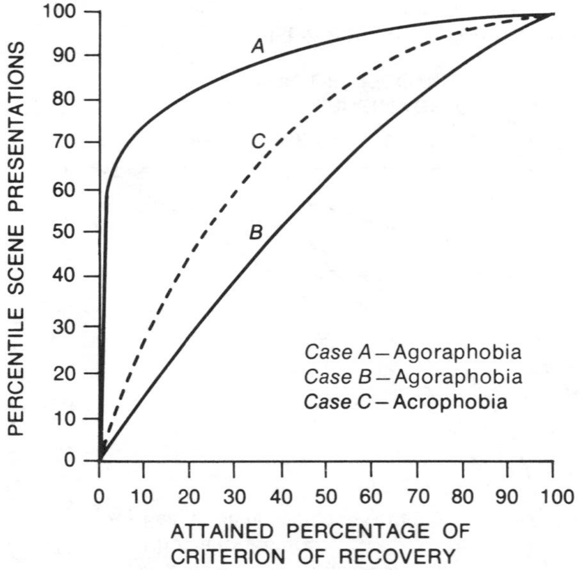

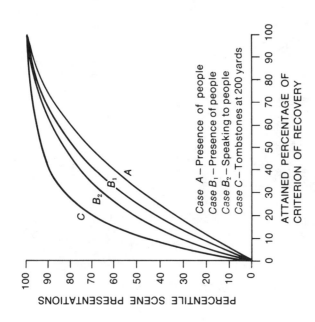

Fig. 8.7. Percentile cumulative curves: Desensitizing operations in phobias increasing with numbers of phobic objects.

Case A – Presence of people
Case B₁ – Presence of people
Case B₂ – Speaking to people
Case C – Tombstones at 200 yards

Fig. 8.6. Percentile cumulative curves: Desensitizing operations in phobias involving increasing distance from a safe point: Agoraphobia or acrophobia.

Case A – Agoraphobia
Case B – Agoraphobia
Case C – Acrophobia

order to make them comparable, the curves were subjected to percentile transformations. The horizontal axes show attained percentage of criterion of recovery, and the vertical axes scene presentations as a percentage of the total number employed to overcome the whole hierarchy.

Figure 8.8 illustrates that it is not the personality of the patient but the type of phobia that determines the shape of the curve. The three curves in this figure were obtained from a single patient. That displaying negative acceleration (*B*) delineates the desensitization of the anxiety response to an increasing number of tombstones at 200 yards. The positively accelerating curves belong respectively to proximation phobias to a dead dog (*A*) and to a stationary automobile (*C*), and are strikingly concordant.

Mathematical analysis of the curves reveals that, with the exception of that for agoraphobia Case *A,* and Curve *C* in Figure 8.7 (which will be commented upon subsequently), they express the same kind of functional relation as has been found by Stevens (1957, 1962) in relating the physical magnitude of a stimulus to its perceived intensity—the "psycho-physical law." According to

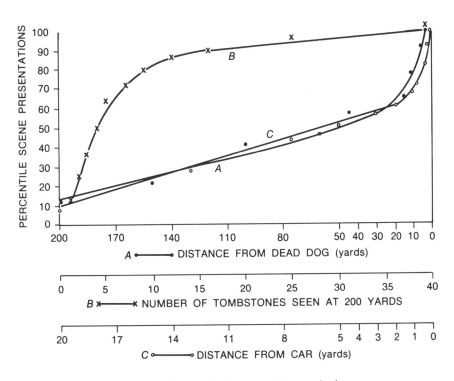

Fig. 8.8. Percentile cumulative curves from a single case.

this empirically based law, psychological (subjective) magnitude is a power function of stimulus magnitude. This means that to make one stimulus seem twice as strong as another, the physical energy must be increased at a fixed ratio, no matter what the initial intensity level. The relationship is expressed by the formula:

$$P = kS^n$$

where P stands for perceived intensity (psychological magnitude), S for stimulus magnitude, k is a constant, and n the exponent of the relationship. The exponent is determined empirically by the formula:

$$n = \frac{\log 0.5}{\log r}$$

where r is the ratio between the physical magnitude of a given stimulus and the physical magnitude of the stimulus that appears twice as strong as the given stimulus.

Insofar as the desensitization curves portray this kind of functional relation, it may be deduced that the amount of work required for each measured unit of progress in overcoming these phobias is a function of the correlated magnitudes of the subject's pretreatment responses. The relevant indicator of response should be *autonomic response magnitude* rather than perceived magnitude. To test this presumption, it would be necessary to compare the curve of directly measured autonomic magnitudes of response at different points in hierarchies *before treatment,* with the desensitization curves subsequently obtained. No direct comparison has as yet been attempted, but Lang et al. (1970) found that the curve correlating pulse rate change with hierarchical position of the stimulus in snake phobias is very similar to the proximation phobia curves in Figure 8.4.

For several of the curves, the value of the exponent n was determined by Stevens' formula (v.s.), the value of r being derived from the point on the x axis at which $y = 50\%$ (0.5). Among the proximation phobias (Fig. 8.4) the exponent of the middle curve, C, is about 3.0. Among the phobias varying with numbers of phobic objects (Fig. 8.7) the value for Curve B_2 is 0.43. The middle curve, C, in the remoteness phobia group (Fig. 8.6) is almost identical with this.

As mentioned above, curve A of the remoteness group does not conform to a power function but the case was unusual in that the desensitization distances reflected in the curve ranged from 20 yards to 100 miles. It is obvious that a person's perception of differences of yards may vary in quite a dissimilar way from differences of miles. It was found upon plotting separate curves for 0–1 and for 1–100 miles that two power function curves were obtained, the first (0–1) being similar to the theoretical curve $n = 0.44$, and the second (1–100) conforming almost exactly to the theoretical curve $n = 0.26$ (Wolpe, 1963). Curve C in Figure 8.7 fits an exponential function $[(P = 76.11 \ (1-0.85^n)]$ a good deal better than a power function, but remains close enough to the power curve $n = 0.3$ not to constitute a damaging exception to the rule.

Awareness of these quantitative relations makes it possible both to predict in general at what stages, in cases of this class, progress will be slowest, and, more specifically, to calculate, after treatment has proceeded long enough to provide the essential data, how much more treatment will be needed to overcome a particular phobia. Furthermore, the curves characterizing different dimensions help the therapist to decide which dimension to work with first in a multidimensional hierarchy. For example, in a woman with a dread of being seen vomiting, the fear increased with numbers of witnesses and with proximity. The knowledge that the numbers curve accelerates negatively and the proximation curve positively led me first to present increasing numbers at a hundred yards. This allowed the number dimension to be mastered with very little effort. Then the numerous witnesses could be gradually brought closer. If the reverse order had been adopted I would ultimately have had to work at the steep ends of both curves simultaneously.

Some Snags and Pitfalls

Sometimes, despite having carried out the preliminaries conscientiously and apparently successfully, the therapist is chagrined to find that desensitization is not proceeding according to his expectations. Either the patient experiences no decrement of anxiety to successive presentations of scenes, or reports no improvement in his reactions to real situations to correspond with progress during sessions. Human variations are so complex and subtle that even the most extensive experience can provide no absolute insurance against disappointments. What the therapist must be able to do is to retrieve the situation. To do this he must first find out what accounts for his failure. The usual reasons are of three kinds, which will be discussed in turn.

1. Difficulties of relaxation.
2. Misleading or irrelevant hierarchies.
3. Inadequacies of imagery.

Difficulties of Relaxation When relaxation is inadequate, it may sometimes be enhanced by giving doses of such drugs as diazepam or codeine an hour before the interview. Which drug to use is a matter of trial and error. When pervasive ("free-floating") anxiety impedes relaxation, the use of carbon dioxide–oxygen mixtures by La Verne's single inhalation technique (see p. 225) is of the greatest value, and with some patients comes to be used before every desensitization session. Inhalations are given until anxiety stops decreasing—usually by the fourth inhalation. In a few patients who cannot relax but who are not pervasively anxious, attempts at desensitization may nonetheless succeed, presumably because therapist-induced emotional responses (see p. 326) inhibit the anxiety aroused by the imagined stimuli. This is a supposition that current experimental testing has tended to support.

Relaxation is sometimes enhanced by hypnosis. Most often, I employ the levitation technique described by Wolberg (1948). The patient may have been hypnotized in an exploratory way during one or more earlier interviews, but more often the first attempt at hypnosis is made during a desensitization session. In those who are difficult to hypnotize, the procedure is soon abandoned. But some patients certainly relax better in a formal hypnotic context.

Another kind of difficulty arises when the therapist has the impression that the patient is well relaxed when in fact he is not. The patient may say that he feels relaxed when he is in fact moderately tense. This may happen for various reasons. He may not yet be sufficiently aware of the internal indications of tension, or he may not think them worth reporting, or it may be so long since he last experienced a true state of calm that any substantial drop in tension *seems* like relaxation to him. The use of the quantitative subjective anxiety scale decreases the likelihood of miscommunications of this type (though it does not eliminate them). The diagnosis can often be made by psychophysiological monitoring, for which the simplest indicator is auditory feedback from muscle potentials (Budzinski, Stoyva, & Adler, 1970; Leaf & Gaarder, 1971). It often takes very careful questioning of the patient to reveal the true state of affairs; and then, of course, the therapist can take whatever action seems appropriate to improve relaxation.

There is an important group of patients who find it difficult to relax because of a general fear of "letting go." Some of these are afraid even to attempt to relax their muscles. Others make the effort and succeed to an extent, but remain afraid. The autonomic excitations that comprise the anxiety response are unchanged, and may even increase. The solution to this problem varies. Sometimes it is possible to achieve a physiological state adequate for desensitization simply by telling the patient to get calm and comfortable in his own way, without attempting to "let himself go." In other cases, one may attempt prior desensitization of the fear of letting go by an *in vivo* method (Chapter 9) or else to resort to one or other of the electrical methods of counteracting anxiety, such as "anxiety relief" or the nonaversive sensory interference technique (Chapter 9).

Misleading or Irrelevant Hierarchies Even with seemingly appropriate and well-constructed hierarchies, the therapist occasionally finds himself making no headway. One possibility is that his hierarchies are off the track. Sometimes this happens because the patient's fears are frequently aroused in contexts that generate or contain the cause of the fear, though quite distinct from it. For example, after a man had been treated for 20 sessions with minimal benefit for claustrophobia and agoraphobia it was found that both were occasions for eliciting a fear of dying. He was anxious when his freedom of movement was restricted or when he was far from home because both of these circumstances implied difficulty in getting help if he should collapse. While I was struggling misdirectedly with this patient, another man with very similar presenting phobias was responding to desensitization in classical fashion; in him, the space-related stimuli were the true antecedents of his anxiety.

A common kind of case in which the hierarchies obtained are not amenable to desensitization occurs in unhappily married women who are low in self-sufficiency (see p. 284). Apparently simple phobias that have originated in the course of the marriage turn out in reality to be fear reactions to stimulus situations that are related to some aspect of the marriage that evokes tension and aversion. This has been independently noted by Fry (1962). These cases frequently present as agoraphobia, and possibly comprise a majority of agoraphobia cases.

Case 28

This is a nonagoraphobic example. A 34-year-old woman complained of a feeling of being closed in and an urgent need to escape when engaged in conversations with adults, except in interchanges of the casual kind, such as asking the time. The problem had begun eight years previously during the patient's first pregnancy. When I first saw her, I could elicit no satisfactory precipitating cause. I trained her in relaxation and took the phobic stimuli at their face value. The first hierarchy I used was based on the theme of being stared at, in which her reactions increased with the proximity of the starer. The scenes I presented to her imagination aroused very little anxiety until a distance of 15 feet was reached, and then there was a *severe* reaction. Various other dimensions were then tried in turn—number of people at a distance, age of starer, duration of stare, and intensity of illumination—in each instance with the same consequence. It was obvious that something was being missed, but I could not tell what. I was about to abandon the case when the patient, for whom tranquilizers had only helped a little, asked, "Is there *nothing* that could diminish my distress?" I replied, "At times of special stress you might try a little alcohol." After a long pause she said, "My husband doesn't let me drink." This was the first time I had heard her make an adverse remark about him, but it was the thin end of a wedge that pried open long-suppressed anger and frustration at his absolute domination over her. The first pregnancy had precipitated the neurosis because it had seemed to block forever a way out of the marriage, which to the outer world and partly to herself she had pretended was a great success.

The phobia was now seen to be primarily a fear of peering or prying. In relevant situations this summated with the impulse and feeling of wanting to escape, chronically engendered by the marriage. Thus, an unacknowledged tension in her life was the real basis of the phobia. Teaching the patient assertion with her husband now became the foremost therapeutic tactic.

Since some might infer that in this case of hidden information, psychoanalysis might have been the treatment of choice, it must be said that the patient had previously had two years of psychoanalysis without any success. The truth about the marital situation had not emerged during its course, in which major attention was given to oedipal attitudes and the like. The guiding rules of psychoanalysis often prove to be a straitjacket prohibiting the full and free exploration of a case. In any event, the insight about the marriage was not of itself therapeutic.

Inadequacies of Imagery Most patients are able to project themselves into imagined anxiety-evoking situations in a way that evokes something of the reality of the situations and a corresponding amount of anxiety. I have found this in about 85% of patients in both South Africa and the United States. In England, the percentage is probably considerably lower, according to my impression during a year of behavior therapy practice in that country and according to the comments of Meyer (1963). Perhaps traditional English training that encourages underplaying manifestations of feeling also impairs the ability to associate emotion with imagery.

Some patients are unable to conjure up either visual or auditory images—at any rate—in response to the requirements of the therapist. Far more commonly, the trouble is that while images *can* be formed, they have no sense of reality for the patient. Occasionally, the therapist can overcome this difficulty by certain interventions: providing much verbal detail of the situation to be imagined, inducing a ''deep'' trance in good hypnotic subjects, or getting the patient to verbalize what he imagines. Darwin and McBrearty (1969) found that in speed-anxious subjects, significantly more rapid progress was made during desensitization if the patient described the scenes out loud instead of merely imagining them. An apparently effective program for the deliberate training of the capacity to imagine realistically has been put forward by Phillips (1971). If such efforts fail, therapeutic change will require the use of the real stimuli, or their physical representations.

Occasionally patients who have visualized satisfactorily cease to do so when they have reached an advanced point in the hierarchy. They then seem to detach themselves from the imagined situations, viewing them as if they themselves were only disinterested spectators. An example is Case 61, who had an extreme form of cleanliness compulsion, based upon a fear of contamination with his own urine. When imaginary situations lost their usefulness, his relaxation was counterposed to real stimuli instead. On this basis, his neurosis was fully overcome.

RESULTS OF SYSTEMATIC DESENSITIZATION

In evaluating the effectiveness of desensitization applied to appropriate cases, one should bear in mind that it is not a method *sui generis,* but a particular application of a principle.

A Clinical Study

In a statistical study (Wolpe, 1961a), I used as subject matter 39 patients whose case records were extracted in random fashion from my therapeutic files. Many of these patients also had other neurotic habits that were treated by other methods deemed more appropriate.

The details of the study are tabulated in Table 8.2, in which outcome of treatment is indicated on a five-point scale ranging from four-plus to zero. A four-plus rating means complete or almost complete freedom from the fear of the relevant class of stimuli *encountered in actuality.* A three-plus rating means an improvement of response such that the fear class is judged by the patient to have lost at least 80 percent of its original strength. A zero indicates that there is no definite change. It will be noted that only four-plus, three-plus, and zero ratings were applicable to the patients in this series.

Table 8.2. Basic Patient Data

Patient Sex, Age	No. of Sessions	Hierarchy Theme	Outcome	Comments
1 F,50	62	a Claustrophobia	+ + + +	
		b Illness and hospitals	+ + + +	
		c Death and its trappings	+ + + +	
		d Storms	+ + +	
		e Quarrels	+ + + +	
2 M,40	6	a Guilt	+ + + +	
		b Devaluation	+ + + +	
3 F,24	17	a Examinations	+ + + +	See Case 25
		b Being scrutinized	+ + + +	
		c Devaluation	+ + + +	
		d Discord between others	+ + + +	
4 M,24	5	a Snakelike shapes	+ + + +	
5 M,21	24	a Being watched	+ + + +	
		b Suffering of others	+ + + +	
		c "Jealousy" reaction	+ + + +	
		d Disapproval	+ + + +	
6 M,28	5	Crowds	+ + +	
7 F,21	5	Criticism	+ + + +	

(continued)

Table 8.2. (*continued*)

Patient Sex, Age	No. of Sessions	Hierarchy Theme	Outcome	Comments
8 F,52	21	a Being center of attention	0	No disturbance during scenes
		b Superstitions	0	Was in fact not imagining self in situation
9 F,25	9	Suffering and death of others	+ + +	
10 M,22	17	Tissue damage in others	+ + + +	
11 M,37	13	Actual or implied criticism	+ + + +	
12 F,31	15	Being watched working	+ + +	
13 F,40	16	a "Suffering" and eeriness	+ + + +	This case has been reported in detail
		b Being devalued	+ + + +	(Wolpe, 1959)
		c Failing to come up to expectations	+ + + +	
14 M,36	10	a Bright light	+ + + +	
		b Palpitations	+ + + +	
15 M,43	9	Wounds and corpses	+ + +	
16 M,27	51	a Being watched, especially at work	+ + +	No anxiety while being watched at work.
		b Being criticized	+ + + +	Anxious at times while playing cards
17 M,33	8	Being watched at golf	+ + +	
18 M,33	8	Talking before audience (stutterer)	0	No imagined scene was ever disturbing
19 M,40	7	Authority figures	+ + + +	
20 M,23	4	Claustrophobia	+ + + +	
21 F,23	6	a Agoraphobia	0	Later successfully treated by conditioned motor response method
		b Fear of falling	0	
22 M,46	19	a Being in limelight	+ + +	
		b Blood and death	+ + + +	
23 F,40	20	Social embarrassment	+ + + +	
24 F,28	9	Agoraphobia	0	
25 F,48	7	Rejection	+ + +	
26 M,28	13	a Disapproval	+ + +	
		b Rejection	+ + + +	
27 M,11	6	Authority figures	+ + + +	

Table 8.2. (*continued*)

Patient Sex, Age	No. of Sessions	Hierarchy Theme	Outcome	Comments
28 M,26	217	a Claustrophobia	+ + + +	
		b Criticism (numerous aspects)	+ + +	Finally overcome completely by use of
		c Trappings of death	+ + +	flooding
29 F,20	5	Agoraphobia	+ + + +	
30 M,68	23	a Agoraphobia	+ + + +	
		b Masturbation	+ + + +	
31 F,36	5	Being in limelight	+ + + +	
32 M,26	17	a Illness and death	+ + +	
		b Own symptoms	+ + +	
33 F,44	9	a Being watched	+ + + +	
		b Elevators	+ + + +	
34 F,47	17	Intromission into vagina	+ + +	
35 M,37	5	a Disapproval	+ + + +	
		b Rejection	+ + + +	
36 F,32	25	Sexual stimuli	+ + + +	
37 M,36	21	a Agoraphobia	+ + + +	
		b Disapproval	+ + + +	
		c Being watched	+ + + +	
38 M,18	6	a Disapproval	+ + +	
		b Sexual stimuli	+ + + +	Instrumental in overcoming impotence
39 F,48	20	a Rejection	+ + + +	Stutter markedly improved
		b Crudeness of others	+ + + +	

Table 8.3 summarizes the data given in Table 8.2. There were 68 anxiety-response habits among the 39 patients, of whom 19 had multiple hierarchies. The treatment was judged effective in 35 patients. Forty-five of the anxiety-response habits were apparently eliminated (four-plus rating) and 17 more markedly ameliorated (three-plus rating), making 90 percent in all. It is probable that many of the latter group would have reached a four-plus level had there been additional sessions. In patients 16 and 29, progress had diminished when sessions were discontinued, but not in any of the others.

Among the failures, patients 8 and 18 were unable to imagine themselves within situations; patient 21 could not confine her imagining to the stated scene and repeatedly exposed herself to excessively disturbing images. She was later treated with complete success by the conditioned motor response method outlined on page 188. Patient 24 had interpersonal reactions that led to erratic responses and, having experienced no benefit, sought therapy elsewhere.

Table 8.3.   Summary of Data in Table 8.2.

Patients	39
Number of patients responding to desensitization treatment	35
Number of hierarchies	68
Hierarchies overcome	45
Hierarchies markedly improved	17
Hierarchies unimproved	6
Total number of desensitization sessions	762
Mean session expenditure per hierarchy	11.2
Mean session expenditure per successfully treated hierarchy	12.3
Median number of sessions per patient	10.0

The mean number of sessions per fear was 11.2; the median number of sessions per patient 10.0. It should be noted that a desensitization session usually takes up only part of a 45-minute interview period, and some of the cases also had other neurotic problems for which there were interviews in which a desensitization session did not occur, and these are not included in the tally.

An important point to note about this data is that of the 68 fears treated, *only 14 can be classed among the classical phobias.* That number includes five cases of agoraphobia which, as will be seen in Chapter 15, is frequently based on *social* fears. The others are claustrophobia (4), snakelike shapes, bright light, crowds, storms, and tissue damage in others. The inclusion of the last as a phobia is probably questionable. Although in clinical practice the predominating use of desensitization is in the treatment of social fears, the popular belief continues to be that its applicability is confined to phobias.

CONTROLLED OUTCOME STUDIES

In a brilliantly designed experiment, Paul (1966) compared desensitization with two other methods in the treatment of students with severe fears of speaking in public. He enlisted the services of five experienced psychotherapists whose "school" affiliation ranged from Freud to Sullivan. Nine subjects were allotted to each therapist so that he could use three different methods, each in three subjects. The methods were: (1) the therapist's own customary type of insight therapy, (2) a stylized procedure involving suggestion and support called "attention-placebo" therapy, and (3) systematic desensitization, which the therapist had to be trained to administer. Each patient had five therapeutic sessions. The results showed significantly superior effectiveness for systematic desensitization on a variety of measures: cognitive, physiological, and motor performance. On the conventional clinical criteria, 86 percent of the patients treated by desensitization were much improved and 14 percent improved (Table 8.4). This compares with 20 percent much improved and 27 percent improved for the insight group, and with none much improved and 47 percent improved for the attention-placebo group. In a follow-up two years later (Paul, 1968), it was found that the differences had been maintained.

Lang was the chief architect of an excellent series of controlled studies beginning with Lang and Lazovik (1963) and Lang, Lazovik, and Reynolds (1965). Their subjects were students who had severe phobic reactions to harmless snakes. They treated some groups by systematic desensitization, and compared the results with those obtained in control groups who either received no treatment or else "pseudotherapy" (i.e., relaxation training followed by interviews focusing on problems of "living," with the subject in a state of relaxation). The desensitized students improved much more than either of the control groups, as shown by a snake avoidance test, and by the patient's self-rating of fear reactions to snakes (Table 8.5). The difference was significant at the 0.001 level when 15 or more hierarchy items had been desensitized.

Moore (1965) described a well-planned and well-executed controlled investigation dealing with asthmatic patients at a clinic. She used a balanced, incomplete block design (in which the subjects were their own controls) to compare the effects on these cases of three forms of treatment: (1) reciprocal inhibition (systematic desensitization) therapy, (2) relaxation therapy, and (3) relaxation combined with suggestion. During the first four weeks of treatment, both subjectively and objectively as measured by maximum peak flow of respired air, all three groups improved, but the desensitization group improved more than the others. After this time, progress continued in the desensitization group, while the other two began to regress. Eight weeks from the beginning of treatment, in terms of maximum peak flow, the superiority of improvement of the desensitization group was significant at the 0.001 level (Fig. 8.9).

Table 8.4.   Percentage Breakdown of Cases in Traditional "Improvement" Categories from Stress-Condition Data*

Treatment	N	Unimproved	Slightly Improved	Improved	Much Improved
Desensitization	15	—	—	14%	86%
Insight	15	7%	46%	27%	20%
Attention-Placebo	15	20%	33%	47%	—
Treatment-control	29	55%	28%	17%	—

*From Paul, Gordon L. (1966). *Insight versus desensitization in psychotherapy.* Stanford University Press. Reprinted with permission.

Table 8.5.   T-tests of Mean Fear Change Scores from Pre- to Posttreatment
in Snake Phobias.

Groups	Avoidance test	Fear thermometer	FSS No. 38	Fear survey
Combined control vs. Desensitization	2.57*	2.12*	2.19*	1.25*
Combined control vs. 15 or more	3.26†	3.44†	3.99‡	2.52*
Combined control vs. Less than 15	0.14	0.41	1.85	0.41
Less than 15 vs. 15 or more	2.33*	3.28*	5.00‡	2.26*
Pseudotherapy vs. No treatment	1.67	0.48	0.58	0.12

*p<0.05.   †p<0.01.   ‡p<0.001.
Lang, P. J., Lazovik, A. D., and Reynolds, D. (1965), Desensitization, Suggestibility and Pseudotherapy. *J. Abnorm. Psychol.* 10, 395–402.

Paul (1969, p. 63ff) made a penetrating analysis of 75 studies of the outcome of systematic desensitization. These studies involved "more than 90 different therapists and nearly 1,000 different clients." Out of 55 uncontrolled reports, all but 9 showed evidence of the effectiveness of systematic desensitization. There were eight controlled experiments which included designs that ruled out intraclass confounding of therapist characteristics and treatment techniques, of which "all found solid evidence for the specific effectiveness of systematic desensitization" (p. 145). Paul concluded that "for the first time in the history of psychological treatments, a specific therapeutic package reliably produced measureable benefits for clients across a broad range of distressing problems in which anxiety was of fundamental importance" (p. 159). Relapse and symptom substitution were notably lacking, though most of the authors were on the lookout for them.

COMMENTS ON RECENT CRITICISMS
OF SYSTEMATIC DESENSITIZATION

In the past few years both the therapeutic relevance and the mechanism of systematic desensitization have been disputed. It has been argued that the procedure has no specific efficacy and that its therapeutic results are really due to "expectancy." The strongest advocacy of this position appears in a paper by Kazdin and Wilcoxon (1976) who regard "expectancy" as the basis of nonspecific therapeutic effects. The case they present, however, is weak. First, they provide no evidence that expectancy as such is capable of therapeutic effects, but take for granted the truth of the assertion of Rosenthal and Frank (1958) that behavior change can be "due to faith in the efficacy of the therapist and his or her techniques," although Rosenthal and Frank offered no evidence to back this assertion. Ford (1978) found, to the contrary, that clients' expectations of therapeutic change were not an effective predictor of long-term maintenance of improvement. As far as systematic desensitization is concerned, the numerous experiments that Kazdin and Wilcoxon quote do not show that expectancy is a significant factor. In any event, *expectancy is not a change mechanism;* it is merely a behavioral event like ventilation, self-assertion, or autosuggestion (see also p. 53).

There is no doubt that in the neuroses, benefit flows from nonspecific events in the therapeutic interview as well as from deliberately deployed techniques. These nonspecific events are the presumptive basis of most of the effects of therapies other than behavior therapy, and probably contribute to the results of behavior therapy (see p. 326). This is clearly indicated by the

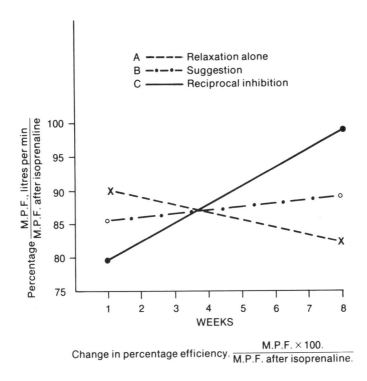

Fig. 8.9. Comparative effects of three treatment schedules on maximum peak flow of inspired air in asthmatic patients (Moore, 1965).

positive results from Paul's (1964) attention-placebo treatment. Furthermore, ignoring the nonspecific effects has been a major reason for the confusion created by some of the research that purports to show that relaxation has no effective role in systematic desensitization. It seems likely that nonspecific effects are due to a variety of interpersonal emotions that compete with anxiety. It may well be that optimistic expectations are one source of such emotions. There is no reason to believe that they are more important than the emotional response to the prestige of the therapist or to the aura of the therapeutic situation.

Another allegation is that relaxation contributes nothing to the efficacy of systematic desensitization. A great deal of the research supposedly showing this has been summarized by Yates (1975) and by Kazdin and Wilcoxon (1976).

The significance of most of this research (Crowder & Thornton, 1970; O'Donnell & Worell, 1973; Sue, 1972) is unclear, since it studies "analogue" populations with weak fears that are susceptible to elimination by minimal procedures (Bernstein & Paul, 1971) and some of it (e.g., Benjamin, Marks & Huson, 1972) has employed hopelessly inadequate relaxation. In the latter study, patients receiving desensitization did equally well whether or not the procedure was done under "relaxation." The quotation marks are used because the members of the relaxation group had had only a single session of relaxation training from a psychiatric resident, who had himself had only a single training session!

Clinically, Jacobson showed that in order to procure adequate calming, a reasonable amount of instruction and practice in relaxation is necessary. The findings of a review by Borkovec and Sides (1979) are in keeping with this. Of 25 studies of the physiological effects of progressive relaxation, they found that in those in which the relaxed subjects showed greater reduction of autonomic responses than the control group, there had been an average of 4.57 relaxation training sessions, in contrast to an average of 2.30 sessions in studies in which anxiety reductions in experimental and control were not significantly different from each other. They comment that while the theory of systematic desensitization and of relaxation's role are "solidly grounded in autonomic notions of anxiety process, yet numerous studies questioning that theory . . . have employed brief, taped relaxation training with normal subjects." (For a review of studies, see Borkovec & O'Brien, 1976).

Many of the abovementioned authors express the assumption (which is erroneously attributed to me) that relaxation is indispensable to desensitization. This has never been my view (see Wolpe, 1958, p. 193). As stated above (p. 46), and as will be further discussed in Chapter 9, *numerous* responses can compete with anxiety, including the emotional response that the patient makes to the therapist.

At present, only indirect evidence of patients' emotional responses to therapists is available. This consists partly of the clinical observation that patients whose anxieties diminish *before* formal therapy has begun often appear to be emotionally aroused by the therapist; and partly of the psychophysiological evidence that emerged in Gaupp, Stern, and Galbraith's (1972) refutation of the cognitive hypothesis of Valins and Ray (1967). Improvement was found to occur only in subjects in whom the procedure *actually* reduced physiological responding. (We have recently started a psychophysiological study in the Behavior Therapy Unit.)

Another theory is that the effect of systematic desensitization depends on "therapeutic instructions" (Leitenberg et al., 1969; Oliveau et al., 1969). In experiments conducted by these workers, snake-phobic subjects who thought they were being desensitized as a therapeutic measure improved significantly more than those who underwent the procedure in the belief that it was a physiological experiment, though the latter group did better than a control group. This contrast in outcomes was not replicated by McGlynn, Reynolds, and Linder (1971). The relevance of other "peripheral" factors such as suggestion (e.g., Efran & Marcia, 1967; McGlynn & Williams, 1970) and real-life exposure (Sherman, 1972) has also been claimed. These reports should be viewed with considerable reserve since they deal with relatively weak fears. Bernstein and Paul (1971) have pointed out that unless the fears that are the subject of an experiment have the severity that characterizes clinical phobias, they do not constitute a true analogue. Actually, the same criticism could be made of many of the studies collected by Paul (1969) that support the use of relaxation.

Gelder and his associates (1973) stated at the conclusion of a particularly well conducted clinical comparison of desensitization, flooding, and "nonspecific" factors: "The results suggest that current theories about the mechanisms underlying behavioral treatments are inadequate and in need of revision." Before "revising current theories," attention should be paid to the fact that outcome research methodology is almost universally flawed. It is marked by the virtual absence of such analyses of case material as would ensure the comparability of groups. As I have repeatedly argued in the past few years (Wolpe, 1977, 1979, 1981; see also Hersen, 1981), if unadaptive fears are to be comparable, they must have not only the same stimulus antecedents, but also the same stimulus-response structure. First of all, as we noted in Chapter 5, it is necessary to distinguish between cases in which the fear is classically conditioned and those in which it is cognitively based. To use systematic desensitization for a cognitively based fear has the same *prima facie* futility as to use penicillin for viral pneumonia. Then, in cases in which an unadaptive fear is classically conditioned, the true fear trigger is not necessarily revealed by the presenting complaint, as exemplified in a great many cases of agoraphobia, in which fear may be triggered, not by separation from the home, but by something else, such as a physical symptom like palpitations (see pp. 284ff). *The fact that these differences between cases have been gener-*

ally ignored in comparative studies of outcome means that most of these studies are rather meaningless, because apples and oranges and sausages are all mixed together in unknown quantities in the comparison groups.

Confounding is greatest where cognitive and conditioning treatments are being compared on the basis of "unselected" groups and probably least where the components of systematic desensitization are being assessed—as in the Rachman and Davison studies (see p. 140).

9

Variants of Systematic Desensitization

The advantage of having a principle is that it provides a framework from which logically parallel variations of tested procedures may be derived. If conventional systematic desensitization proves unsuitable in a particular case or class of cases, it is hoped that attempts can be made to implement in other ways the principle of reciprocally inhibiting small "doses" of anxiety at a time. And even where conventional desensitization is quite successful, it is worth experimenting with other elaborations of the principle because of the possibility that they will be more efficient or more economical.

Several variations of technique are described in this chapter. Some are held in reserve to be tried when conventional desensitization cannot or does not succeed. Others have been the subject of controlled experiments that suggest that they may be superior to conventional desensitization at least for the kinds of neurotic fears figuring in the experiments.

The desensitization variants can be divided into three categories: (1) technical variations of the standard consulting-room procedure; (2) alternative counteranxiety responses for use with imaginal stimuli; and (3) methods involving the use of real anxiety-evoking stimuli.

TECHNICAL VARIATIONS OF THE STANDARD DESENSITIZATION PROCEDURE

The essence of standard desensitization is the presentation of graded imaginal stimuli to a relaxed patient. There are two ways of carrying it out that reduce the amount of time the therapist has to spend with each patient. One way is to automate some of the procedures so that they do not need the therapist's physical presence. The second consists of group treatment of patients who have similar neurotic fears.

Mechanical Aids to Systematic Desensitization

Lang (1966) was the first to demonstrate that desensitization could be successfully accomplished by a machine. Phobias for snakes were overcome by the use of two tape recorders, one carrying hierarchy items and the other relaxation instructions. The patient controlled buttons to obtain relaxation, and repetition, change, or cessation of scene. Taking a cue from Lang's observations, Migler and Wolpe (1967) used a single specially modified tape recorder to treat a patient who was severely disturbed by inferred disapproval and derision, especially when he was speaking to a group. The patient himself recorded both the hierarchy items and the relaxation instructions under supervision. He then took the tape recorder home and completely desensitized himself in seven sessions. He was free from his original fears when followed up two years later.

The following technical details are reproduced with minor modifications from Migler and Wolpe (1967). One may use either a Wollensak T-1600 tape recorder or a Uher Universal 5000, or any other machine with the following two features. First, it must have a pause switch by which the tape motions can be instantly stopped. This switch is connected to a microswitch which the patient can hold in his hand to stop the tape motion at any time, for any duration. Second, the recorder must have two metal sensing strips on each side of the recording heads. When a metal foil which has been placed on the tape makes contact with the two sensing strips on the right side, an internal circuit is closed and the tape recorder automatically switches from playback to rewind. These two strips are, for the present purpose, bypassed by the tape and a pushbutton wired in parallel with them, so that now momentary depression of the pushbutton switches the recorder from playback to rewind. The second pair of sensing guides, to the left of the recording heads, stops the rewinding and returns to playback when another specially placed metal foil reaches these guides. This is not altered. The pushbutton and the microswitch are held together by adhesive tape, to make a combined remote control unit that the patient can hold in his hand. Depression of the microswitch (hereafter called the "pause switch") stops the playback for as long as it remains depressed. Momentary depression of the pushbutton (hereafter called the "repeat button") produces the following sequential effects: the tape recorder stops playback and switches to rewind, rewinding continues until the metal foil is detected by the sensing guides to the left of the recording head; and when rewinding has stopped, playback begins again.

In preparing the tape for desensitization Migler and Wolpe took the following steps. (They used the patient's voice throughout.)

1. Relaxation instructions were taped. (In using this section of the tape, the patient was instructed to press the pause switch after each anatomical part was named and concentrate on that part until it felt free of muscular tension, then to release the pause switch and let the tape continue.)
2. A metal foil was attached to the tape at the end of the relaxation instructions. A similar metal foil came after each scene recorded on the tape. Their function is given in steps below.
3. Just beyond the metal foil (and before the first scene) were a few brief relaxation instructions: "Relax your arms, legs, stomach, chest, neck, and all your facial muscles. Now pause until you feel relaxed." (The patient was instructed to press the pause switch at this point until he felt relaxed.)
4. Following the relaxation instructions, the tape contained instructions to visualize Scene 1 of the hierarchy: "Now imagine," etc. Pause. (The patient was instructed to press the pause switch at this point until the visualization was clear, and then to let the tape continue.)
5. Ten seconds of recorded silence followed the instruction to pause, permitting ten seconds of clear visualization. The silence was terminated by the words, "Stop visualizing it. Press the repeat button if that scene disturbed you at all." If the patient felt any negative emotional response to the scene he was to press the repeat button, which would rewind the tape back to the metal foil (Step 2 above) so that the brief relaxation instructions, the scene, and the remainder of the sequence would recur. If the repeat button was not pressed, the tape recorder continued to the next metal foil, which, like the first, was followed by relaxation instructions, after which came Scene 2 of the hierarchy, and so forth.

These elaborate arrangements made it easy for the patient to carry out the desensitization which he completed in seven solo sessions. Much simpler equipment can be used, but it calls for more effort from the patient. The first version of this was reported by Kahn and Baker (1968), in the form of a phonograph recording which the patients could use at home for any hierarchy. It contained instructions for scene presentations followed by silence into which the patient inserted his imaginary hierarchical scenes as directed beforehand by the therapist. Relaxation instructions preceded each scene, and the recording was worded in such a way that the patient could repeat a particular scene as many times as necessary.

Tape recorders are now widely used for desensitization at home. Very inexpensive ones are quite suitable. They offer far more flexibility than a phonograph recording. Denholtz (1971) has described the home use of tape recorders for both relaxation training and the presentation of anxiety-evoking scenes. Each relaxation lesson is recorded during the treatment session on the patient's own tape, which he then takes home "having been instructed to play it twice daily until his next visit. At subsequent visits, instructions are taped again, becoming progressively shorter because the patient is becoming conditioned to relaxation. Eventually the instructions are usually only 2–5 min long.'' The procedure is particularly valuable for the not uncommon patient who is simply too anxious in the presence of the therapist to be able to let go. Some of these patients learn relaxation in this way at home, and can later do it in the office.

For the purpose of homework desensitization, Denholtz usually tapes one scene from each hierarchy at each session. If, however, there is a variety of settings that belong to a particular hierarchical step, he may tape as many as three scenes for that step. It is always important to ensure that the taped scenes evoke only a small amount of anxiety, generally no more than 10 to 15 units on the *sud* scale. Relaxation instructions are renewed between scenes. The patient is told to use this tape recording daily until his next session when he will usually report no longer having anxiety to any of the taped scenes. He is then ready to move upward in the hierarchy. The use of such homework may materially reduce the amount of time the therapist has to spend with the patient.

Just as with standard desensitization, it is necessary to give adequate relaxation training. In a comparative study of audiotaped procedures by Morris and Suckerman (1974), with only two 20-minute sessions of relaxation training the results were no better than in their nonrelaxed control group. But in another inadequately relaxed group, with manifest warmth in the taped voice delivering the scenes, the outcome was significantly superior—an interesting example of the potency of ''nonspecific'' emotion (see p. 186 and 326).

Group Desensitization

If several patients suffer from the same phobia, it is reasonable to expect that, after being trained to relax, they might be desensitized simultaneously, even if the slopes of their hierarchies are not identical, provided the therapist ensures that each scene has ceased to evoke anxiety in every patient before proceeding to the next scene. Obviously, this arrangement can be very time-saving for the therapist. For example, an average of less than two hours of therapist time per client was expended by Paul and Shannon (1966) in the treatment of severe ''social evaluative'' anxiety in college students, manifested by fear and disablement in public-speaking situations. At a two-year follow-up, Paul (1968) found that the improvements achieved by this treatment had been maintained or increased.

It is possible that part of the reason why Paul and Shannon's patients were more rapidly desensitized is that exteroceptive stimuli from the other members of the group were involved in the deconditioning maneuvers. This possibility seemed in a small way to be supported by a miniexperiment I performed in 1966 during a series of behavior therapy seminars.

I invited all participants with fears of public speaking to submit to group desensitization in front of the class of 30. Eight volunteered. The treatment sessions—each lasting 15 minutes—took place at the end of a two-hour seminar. The group sat before me in the front row of the lecture room. The first session was devoted to relaxation training, with which all were already familiar, and which some had already been practicing. At subsequent sessions, imaginary scenes of speaking in public were presented to the group. The first scene was speaking to an audience of three. By the fifth desensitization session, only five of these subjects had continued with the therapy but these five were able to imagine themselves speaking to a group of 50 without anxiety. Evidence of transfer to the real situation was subsequently obtained from two of the participants. One of them reported giving a lecture to a group of 75 without any anxiety at all. Since the total time spent on the group therapy was 90 minutes, then for the five subjects who completed the course there was a mean therapist-time expenditure per patient per phobia of 18 minutes. While it is not wise to infer too much from this somewhat casual experiment, it does suggest that therapeutic change may have been accelerated by the subjects' awareness of sitting in a group while desensitization to imaginary groups was being carried out. There is a preponderance of evidence suggesting that desensitization with real stimuli is more potent than that with imaginary ones. These subjects had both.

Successful treatment in group settings has been reported for a variety of phobias, e.g., test situations (Donner & Guerney, 1969; Cohen & Dean, 1968; Ihli & Garlington, 1969). Donner and Guerney (1969) used an automated technique with the groups and, at a follow-up, Donner (1970) found that the gains had been maintained. Robinson and Suinn (1969) reported on the group treatment of spider phobias using massed desensitization sessions.

Group desensitization may also be part of a general group behavior therapy program. Each patient is first seen individually so that the therapist may take a history, perform a behavioral analysis, and decide on the goals of therapy. Group therapy is recommended for certain patients with special problems in personal interactions. One advantage of the group setting is that the therapist is able to observe the patient's behavior in response to various other people; it may elicit unforeseen behavior patterns. The procedures mainly used are modelling, behavior rehearsal, and desensitization.

ALTERNATIVE COUNTERANXIETY RESPONSES FOR USE WITH IMAGINAL STIMULI

Therapist-Evoked Responses

As noted earlier, the psychotherapeutic interview itself evokes emotional responses in many patients. Sometimes the emotion is anxiety, but more often, it would seem that it is a mixture of hopeful expectation, confidence in the expert, and other positive emotions conditioned to doctors and their consulting rooms. Altogether, it probably corresponds roughly to the psychoanalyst's "positive transference," without the presumed projection onto the therapist of a father-image. When such emotional responses occur, they may inhibit anxiety responses that are verbally evoked during the interview if these are not too strong (Wolpe, 1958, p. 193). These interview-induced emotions are probably the chief basis for the very similar success of all therapies other than behavior therapy (Eysenck, 1952, 1965. See also p. 326). Of course, behavior therapists profit from them as well, but probably only to an extent corresponding to the amount of change found in the "attention-placebo" group of Paul's (1966) controlled study.

The therapist-evoked emotions are inadvertent and their effects unsystematic. It is possible, however, to make systematic use of them. In subjects who are unable to learn to relax or who are afraid of "letting go," it is still worth presenting hierarchical scenes in the hope that therapist-evoked emotion will inhibit the anxiety. These emotions are apparently the usual basis of successful desensitization without relaxation. In addition, they probably play a leading part in desensitization *in vivo* (see below).

Relaxation Substitutes

There are several procedures that produce much the same autonomic effects and subjective calmness as is obtained by muscle relaxation. They are: autogenic training, transcendental meditation, yoga, and biofeedback. In a general way, if a person is well practiced in any of the first three of these, that skill can replace muscle relaxation for purposes of systematic desensitization.

Autogenic Training. This procedure, which is widely practiced in Europe, was developed by Schultz and Luthe (1959). It makes use of repeated suggestions of heaviness and warmth. To begin with, the heaviness suggestions are repeated five times by the therapist, and then the subject repeats them several times to himself. Warmth suggestions are incorporated later. There is evidence that the heaviness suggestions produce muscle relaxation, and the warmth suggestion vasodilatation.

There have been few studies comparing the effects of relaxation and autogenic training. Nicassio and Bootzin (1974) found that in the treatment of insomnia the two procedures were equally effective and superior to control groups.

Transcendental Meditation. The idea behind this procedure is "to turn the attention inwards to the subtler levels of thought, until the mind . . . arrives at the source of the thought" (Mahesh Yogi, 1969, p. 470). The technique consists of giving the patient a word (e.g., "rama") to attend to continuously while seated in a quiet room with his eyes closed. If other thoughts intrude, he must desist from these and return to the word. He has been told to expect calm and relaxation to result from regular practice of this discipline.

Wallace (1970) reported physiological changes during transcendental meditation, including decreased metabolic rate, increased skin resistance, and diminished heart rate, all of which are also produced by muscle relaxation. Benson (1975) has made extensive use of the method, especially in cases of hypertension. Boudreau (1972) reported its use in the treatment of a college student who had several disabling phobias. At first, systematic desensitization was tried without noticeable improvement. Then the patient indicated that he was adept at transcendental meditation. He was instructed to practice meditation following imaginal phobic scenes for a half-hour every day and also at the actual appearance of fear-evoking situations. Marked improvement followed. Within one month, the avoidance behavior to enclosed places, being alone, and elevators had disappeared. Once his tension level had decreased, he did not experience abnormal physiological sensations, and this reassured him as to his physical and mental state.

Yoga. This is a broad class of practices of which transcendental meditation is an example. To the extent that these lead to control of autonomic responses, their potential as a means to breaking unadaptive emotional habits is obvious. Boudreau (1972) has described the case of a 40-year-old schoolteacher whose severe suffering from excessive perspiration was only partially alleviated by assiduous practice of muscle relaxation. She then took a summer course of training in yoga exercises. She practiced the yoga exercises for a half-hour daily, with additional practice during tense moments. After three months of this technique, her mild perspiration decreased to below one hour every day while her excessive perspiration disappeared.

Electromyographic Biofeedback. The original work with this method was conducted by Budzinski and Stoyva (1969), who observed that it was effective in accelerating and possibly deepening muscle relaxation. Comparative studies of the two methods have yielded conflicting results. For example, Chesney and Shelton (1976) found that progressive relaxation produced superior clinical effects in tension headaches, but Reinking and Kohl's (1975) biofeedback subjects achieved lower tension levels than those who underwent relaxation training. From a survey of comparative studies, Qualls and Sheehan (1981) concluded that, on the whole, electromyograph biofeedback compares favorably.

The data do not permit a general judgment to be made one way or the other —for several reasons, one of which is the differences in relaxation training schedules in the various studies. What is of practical importance is that electromyograph biofeedback is an additional resource and a reasonably convenient one. Inevitably, there will be some patients who will respond better to it than to muscle relaxation. Other modes of biofeedback have special relevance in the treatment of some psychosomatic disorders (p. 292ff).

Responses Triggered by Electrical Stimulation

Desensitization Based on Inhibition of Anxiety by a Conditioned Motor Response This technique (Wolpe, 1954) has been used very little, although it has a solid experimental basis in an experiment reported by Mowrer and Viek (1948). They found that if a noxious electrical stimulus applied to an animal was consistently switched off whenever the animal performed a particular motor response (e.g., jumping up in the air), the animal developed conditioned inhibition of the *autonomic* responses that were evoked at the same time. By contrast, the experimental twin that received exactly the same duration of noxious stimulation whose termination was unrelated to the animal's motor behavior failed to develop any inhibition of the emotional response.

In clinical application of this finding, the patient with an anxiety hierarchy is asked to imagine a scene in the usual way and to signal when the image is clear. The therapist then passes a fairly mild shock into the forearm, in response to which the patient has previously been instructed to flex his arm. The worst case of agoraphobia that I have ever seen was successfully treated by this method and is described in detail elsewhere (Wolpe, 1958, p. 174). It generally required 15 to 25 arm flexions to bring the anxiety response to a disturbing scene down to zero.

In that particular case, flexion of the arm seemed indispensable for weakening the anxiety response. But since we now know that weak electrical stimulation without a motor response can also weaken anxiety habits, we may question how much the motor response really contributed to the change that was noted. However, there is some clinical data that suggests that muscle activity can be an anxiety-inhibiting agent (Wolpin & Raines, 1966; Farmer & Wright, 1971).

External Inhibition. The therapeutic possibilities of this phenomenon (Pavlov, 1927, p. 46) became apparent to me in 1964 while I was observing Dr. William M. Philpott perform a rather elaborate procedure to eliminate conditioned anxiety with the aid of mild electric shocks. The patient was lying on a couch with his eyes closed and electrodes strapped to his forearm. He was given a scene to imagine, and, when he indicated that it was clearly formed, Dr. Philpott called out words on the following pattern: "Muscles of the arms, respond to the will; relax." Some controlled experiments that I conducted shortly afterwards at the University of Virginia showed that the verbal patter was irrelevant and that the weak electrical stimuli could produce all the effects demonstrated by Philpott. It seemed that the kind of interference typical of external inhibition was at work.

In brief, the technique is as follows: encircling the patient's forearm are two saline-soaked gauze strips, 1½ inches wide, one just above the wrist and the other about 3 inches higher. Each strip is held in place by a stainless-steel alligator clip connected to the source of current—a 90-volt dry cell whose output is controlled by a 50,000 ohm variable resistor. (Silver electrodes may be used instead of the gauze strips.) Pulses are delivered by the therapist pressing on a soft pushbutton switch for about half a second. The level of current correct for the patient is that which is strongly felt *without being aversive.* In some cases a very weak pulse suffices; in others no therapeutic effects occur until the electrical stimulus is strong enough to produce vigorous contraction of the forearm muscles. (It has frequently been noted that if the patient has pervasive anxiety, 8 to 10 pulses per minute will gradually reduce it, so that in 20 or 30 minutes it may be brought down from 60 *suds* or more, sometimes to zero.)

Once the appropriate level of electrical stimulation has been established, the desensitizing procedure can begin. First, the weakest item in the hierarchy is presented alone to the patient's imagination once or twice in order to determine how many *suds* it evokes. He is then asked to imagine the scene again and to signal by raising his index finger when it is well defined, at which point the therapist administers two brief stimuli of the predetermined strength, separated by about a second. After about five seconds, the patient is instructed again to imagine the scene, signaling as before. After a series of 5 to 20 repetitions, a check is made on the status of his reaction to the scene by presenting it without any shock.

An early case to be treated by this method was a woman whose many-faceted neuroses had been largely overcome by the usual behavior therapy methods. An important remaining neurotic problem was a phobia for driving alone. Originally, she had been unable to drive up her own driveway without feeling anxious. With conventional desensitization, she had progressed steadily, though slowly, until she was able to drive three-quarters of a mile without any discomfort. But a disturbing incident half a mile from home had set her back to that distance. Rather than resume the desensitization that had been so tedious, I decided to try external inhibition. Mild stimulation proved to be completely ineffective, but shocks strong enough to cause muscle contraction while she visualized herself at that critical place half a mile from home led to decreasing anxiety. With 20 repetitions of the scene, the anxiety decreased to zero. The procedure was then repeated for the three-quarter-mile point. When she later tested herself at that point, she found herself completely free from anxiety. Continuing with this method produced much more rapid progress than had previously been achieved with conventional desensitization.

Responses Evoked by Verbally Induced Imagery

Falling under this heading are three methods: emotive imagery, induced anger, and direct suggestion. In the first of these, an emotional state counteractive to anxiety is evoked by the setting into which the anxiety-evoking stimuli are to be introduced; in the latter two, the counteractive emotion depends on deliberate and insistent verbal inputs, and the setting is mainly background.

Emotive Imagery. This is the name of a procedure first described by Lazarus and Abramovitz (1962) in which hierarchical stimuli are presented to the patient in an imaginary situation in which other elements evoke responses that are antagonistic to anxiety. These responses thus take the place of relaxation as the source of inhibition of anxiety.

One of their cases was a 12-year-old boy who greatly feared darkness. In the room he shared with his brother, a light constantly shone at night next to his bed. He was especially afraid in the bathroom, which he only used if accompanied by another member of the household. Attempts at relaxation training had failed. The child had a passion for two radio serials: "Superman" and "Captain Silver." He was asked to imagine that Superman and Captain Silver had appointed him their agent. Subsequent procedure was as follows:

> The therapist said, "Now I want you to close your eyes and imagine that you are sitting in the dining room with your mother and father. It is nighttime. Suddenly, you receive a signal on the wrist radio that Superman has given you. You quickly run into the living room because your mission must be kept a secret. There is only a little light coming into the lounge from the passage. Now pretend that you are all alone in the lounge waiting for Superman and Captain Silver to visit you. Think about this very clearly. If the idea makes you feel afraid, lift up your right hand."

An ongoing scene was terminated as soon as there was any indication of anxiety. When an image aroused anxiety, it would either be repeated in a more challengingly assertive manner, or altered slightly so as to appear less threatening. At the end of the third session, the child was able to picture himself alone in the bathroom with all the lights turned off, awaiting a communication from Superman. There was complete transfer to the real situation. A follow-up 11 months later revealed that the gains had been maintained.

The technique has also been used with adults. For example, a man with a claustrophobia that was especially related to theaters and restaurants was instructed to imagine himself seated in a theater (at the aisle in the back row, initially) watching a striptease. The sexual arousal inhibited the weak anxiety response and was the basis for the beginning of a deconditioning program.

Induced Anger. This procedure, which Goldstein, Serber, and Piaget in their original report (1970) found effective in six out of ten cases, consists of getting the patient to pair anger-arousing imagery (augmented by appropriate vocal and motor behavior) with fear-arousing imagined scenes (or real stimuli in the consulting room). Later, the patient uses the images to arouse anger in spontaneously occurring fear-producing real-life situations. The concern that such treatment might leave patients angry instead of fearful has not been borne out by experience. They merely become indifferent to the previously disturbing stimuli, supporting the viewpoint that the essential therapeutic process is the conditioning of inhibition of fear responses to the particular stimuli.

One of their cases was Mr. F., aged 23, who complained of fears of riding public conveyances, walking in certain neighborhoods, and being in the presence of seemingly aggressive people. These fears more or less confined him to his home. He ventured out only to attend therapy sessions, taking a roundabout route on foot to avoid public transport and certain streets.

Although some progress was made in systematic desensitization to the fear of buses, none occurred in the area of interpersonal situations. When asked to imagine even very weak interpersonal scenes, Mr. F. would reach near-panic states which completely undid the previously achieved relaxed state. He was then asked to imagine being accosted on the street by an aggressive man (a reconstruction of an actual past event). When he felt afraid, he was to imagine punching the man. Mr. F. found that he was unable to imagine this effectively because each imagined episode of attack led to a sequence in which his attempted blow missed. But by starting the imagining simply with talking back to the man, Mr. F. could gradually increase the amount of aggressiveness until he was eventually able to imagine effectively punching, kicking, and finally chopping the man up with an axe. With each increase of aggression, less fear and more anger was felt. At one point, he said, "I feel like screaming and actually hitting something." He was given a large pillow and encouraged to do so and vocalize according to his feelings. Thereafter, his images of being accosted on the street were accompanied by actual screaming of obscenities, pounding on the pillow, and imaginary counteraggression. After three sessions of ten repetitions per session of scenes appropriate to his fears, Mr. F. reported complete freedom of fear in most of the situations which had previously been frightening and said that he was traveling freely wherever he desired. He still felt somewhat fearful at plays and some movies if there were a number of people in the audience who seemed to him to epitomize aggressiveness. He was instructed to continue to attend these places and upon becoming anxious, to imagine getting up on the stage and mowing down the audience with a machine gun. He did so and developed other variations of imagined aggression which led to his being able to attend theaters with complete absence of fear. *No hostile feeling took the place of the fear;*

the result was complete indifference to the audience. At a six-month follow-up Mr. F. reported that he was free of fears, was planning marriage, and was going to attend graduate school in a distant city.

In another of their cases, the anxiety-evoking stimuli were countered by expressing the anger *in vivo*. This was a 34-year-old woman with a history of severe and constant anxiety coupled with feelings of dizziness and unsteadiness in the legs. She felt relatively calm only when sitting down at home in the presence of her husband or close friends. She was fearful of losing her balance, or, if away from home, of being unable to return. Behavior analysis showed that her anxiety was most severe at the anticipation of an anxiety-evoking situation. Standard desensitization had failed because the patient did not become anxious at imaginary scenes; *in vivo* desensitization had failed because the fear aroused by the real situations was too great to be inhibited by her muscle relaxation. It was then that the patient was taught the expression of anger, later to be used contiguously with anxiety-producing stimuli. She was shown how to express righteous indignation at the top of her voice: "I'm not afraid! I don't want to be afraid! It is stupid and unfair—I will not be afraid!" She accentuated this verbal behavior by punching a pillow in front of her. Three training sessions were given and the patient was requested to practice at home for half-an-hour a day. She was instructed to expose herself to various situations that disturbed her, such as standing alone in a locked room for ten minutes and using the anger responses she had practiced whenever she had any awareness of the disturbance. Therapy was terminated after a total of 19 sessions. Six months later she was free of all symptoms.

Case 29

The value of this method was impressively shown in the case of Yolanda, a 23-year-old girl who was severely afflicted with agoraphobia. Three months previously, after seeing a play in downtown Philadelphia, she had returned to her car which was parked in the street. She was just about to start it when she felt a bump from the car that had been parked behind her. A moment later, the driver of that car was at her window screaming abuse and threatening to take legal action. Although entirely innocent, she "felt anxious and helpless." She behaved "nicely" and did not protest. On driving away from the scene she noticed that she was extremely nervous, and thereafter she felt some degree of anxiety whenever she drove a car. Two weeks later, driving on a lonely but familiar road, she had a sudden sharp panic, which subsided in a few minutes but left her feeling uncomfortable for the rest of the day. From that time forward, she became increasingly fearful of driving and of being alone. Within a week she could not be alone even at home without anxiety. Its diurnal range was now 50–75 *suds*.

Treatment began with explaining to Yolanda the nature of her illnesss to counteract her fear of "going crazy," and then introduced assertiveness training, which was clearly fundamentally important, but not expected to help much in overcoming the present incapacitating fear. I attempted, with moderate success, to teach her progressive relaxation, but could not lower her anxiety enough to make desensitization feasible. The administration of carbon dioxide showed that only about one-quarter of Yolanda's continuous anxiety was "free-floating." Next, I attempted to control the anxiety with Valium, but found that a significant decrease required a dose that produced unacceptable drowsiness. During the next two months Yolanda became markedly more assertive. Although a certain amount of improvement in her general state was achieved by a systematic program of *in vivo* desensitization, progress was slow, and it became apparent that her orbit of comfortable movement had stopped short at the lawn surrounding the clinic. A program of flooding *in vivo* during the next three weeks produced a great deal of distress and no improvement. It was followed with paradoxical intention (p. 247). Yolanda followed my instructions to the letter; but instead of her anxiety flattening out and diminishing, it rose gradually and distressfully in the course of 1½ hours on each of two successive days. The net effect of this was to make her feel extremely angry at me for having subjected her to such torture.

The exploitation of this anger provided the long-sought breakthrough. I had Yolanda make increasing excursions away from the clinic on foot, in the course of which she was to express her anger at me, out loud when socially feasible, and subvocally when not. This was gratifyingly effective. Anxiety decreased progressively, enabling her to go farther and farther with comfort. The same strategy was equally successful in increasingly prolonged solo car trips. Within three weeks, Yolanda was so much improved that she was able to participate comfortably in her own graduation. Her remaining problems were later handled by a combination of techniques with complete success.

Direct Suggestion. Rubin (1972) has described a variant of systematic desensitization that depends on inducing various responses, often including relaxation, by strong verbal suggestion. It seems likely that suggested counteranxiety responses are the key feature of this technique.

Rubin starts with a detailed explanation of how the patient acquired his anxiety habit through learning and how the eliciting stimuli, when juxtaposed with a different response, will come to evoke the latter and weaken the anxiety. He tells the patient not actually to imagine the indicated scene until a prearranged signal is given. Scenes are generally presented without regard to their hierarchical position, but a weaker scene is used if the chosen one is found to be too distressful.

Rubin's technique may be illustrated by reference to one of his cases—a 36-year-old woman who had conditioned anxiety reactions to numerous situations, including sitting at the dining table, applying cosmetics, sitting down to work, and going to the beauty shop. All of these reactions had ramified from an occasion two years previously when she had been seized with trembling of her hands while drinking coffee in a restaurant at the moment when she became aware of a posterior cervical spasm. An important background fact was that five years previously her mother had suffered a stroke which had rendered her aphasic. The thought that the cervical spasm might foreshadow a stroke had crossed the patient's mind. The following is an edited continuation of Rubin's statement after he had explained to her how serial conditioning had eventuated from the original anxiety experience:

> Now I am going to describe a series of scenes to you. Please listen carefully while I describe them, but do not attempt to visualize until I have given you the signal of counting to three. You will indicate that visualization is taking place by raising your index finger and dropping it when visualization is complete.
>
> The very first scene that I would like you to visualize is one in which you are sitting down to eat in your own kitchen. You have prepared a delicious-looking filet mignon and you are quite hungry. As you sit there eating the filet, you feel quite comfortable and relaxed, and it is such a wonderful feeling to enjoy the food and feel relaxed. You are really not worried or concerned. You do have a feeling of some pain and discomfort in the back of your head and neck, but in spite of this you feel good. It is such a wonderful feeling to sit there feeling relaxed and enjoying the food. When I count to three, you may begin to visualize and indicate this to me by raising the index finger of your left hand. Keep it elevated until visualization is completed. (p. 276)

As long as the patient indicated satisfactory visualization, the description was augmented by comments similar to those that were given initially. Additional scenes were now offered—applying cosmetics, being seated while at work, visiting and eating at other people's homes, eating in restaurants, and other situations which would ordinarily provoke anxiety. The following excerpts from the transcript dealing with visiting the beauty shop show how the therapist used his own experiences to augment the intended effects.

> You go to the hairdresser's. You are familiar with the place and you enter feeling very comfortable and relaxed. I know that when I go to the barber, it is an opportunity for me to relax and, frequently, I almost doze off. Sometimes, because of the position I am in, I develop some pain and discomfort in my head and neck. However, it doesn't disturb or frighten me, and that is exactly the way I want you to feel. So, when I give you the proper signal, I want you to picture youself in the beauty shop feeling very comfortable and relaxed. You have some discomfort in the back of your head and neck, but it doesn't worry or disturb you. You realize that it has no significance. It certainly does not indicate that you are going to have a stroke, and so, when I count to three, please start feeling calm and relaxed. (p. 276)

The patient was seen four times, improving markedly, so that she was able to return to work. A follow-up nine months later revealed that all of the improvement had been maintained.

This technique makes the hypnotist's traditional repertoire available to the practice of behavior therapy. The classical mode of hypnotic therapy, consisting of "suggesting away" symptoms or reactions, and leaning largely on posthypnotic suggestion, has been a notoriously unreliable route to enduring change. Rubin's technique brings directly suggested responses into direct opposition with anxiety responses.

Case 30

I have occasionally used this procedure, dispensing with the preliminaries. The first case I treated markedly benefited from a single session. He was a 45-year-old executive who had just been promoted to a $50,000-a-year position which entailed a great deal of flying. Unfortunately, during the previous ten years he had been severely aerophobic following a hair-raising flying experience. Because he had come from Boston and was due to fly to Nashville a few days later, I decided to try counterconditioning by direct suggestion. I elicited from him aspects of being in a plane that he enjoyed—a feeling of freedom, the decor, and the reassuring tones of the captain's voice. I then had him close his eyes and imagine that he was sitting in a stationary chamber with the decor of a plane and strongly responding to those pleasant stimulations. When he indicated that he was having the required feelings at considerable strength, I had him imagine that the chamber was airborne, at first moving slowly near the ground and then as in actual flight. He was able to sustain this image without any anxiety for about three minutes. I then instructed him to practice the image several times a day, and told him that when he boarded the plane, he was to focus his attention on the pleasant aspects and respond exclusively to them. After the scheduled flight, he telephoned from Nashville to say that he had had slight anxiety initially and then none at all. Four months later, he informed a behavior therapist in Boston to whom I had referred him for other problems about the "miraculous cure" of his fear of flying in a single session, since when he had been flying freely.

Physical Activity Responses

This heading refers mainly to Oriental defense exercises. Desensitization based on the activity of reading (Everaerd, 1970; Stoffelmayr, 1970) may belong to the same category. As noted previously (p. 140), Farmer and Wright (1971) found that muscle activity can be used to desensitize subjects with high body-image scores.

In two cases who could not be satisfactorily treated by standard desensitization, Gershman and Stedman (1971) used Oriental defense exercises as the source of reciprocal inhibition of anxiety, on the reasonable supposition that "if a therapist identifies a counterconditioner which is idiosyncratic to a patient it is likely to have special therapeutic efficacy." One of their cases was a man who routinely practiced karate to keep himself in physical condition. His fear of flying was treated by having him imagine flying situations in hierarchical order, and, at each presentation, engage in vigorous karate exercises. In two sessions, anxiety to all items was reduced to zero on the *sud* scale. In their other case, Kung Fu exercises were rapidly effective in overcoming a severe claustrophobia by having the patient initiate them immediately upon being locked in a room. The periods of his confinement were progressively increased from ten seconds to one hour, and the duration of "Kung Fu-ing" progressively diminished though, if the patient at any time felt a twinge of anxiety, he could again resort to the exercises to dissipate it. Six-month follow-ups found both of these patients free from the anxiety habits that had been treated. It seems likely that motor competition was the basis of the changes, but the role of concomitant emotional arousal cannot be ruled out.

Stoffelmayr's (1970) case was a 30-year-old woman who complained of "retching and gagging" in response to the insertion of her dentures. This was successfully treated by arranging for reading aloud and later other activities to compete with the retching response. At a six-month follow-up, the patient was still able to retain dentures without any discomfort. Everaerd (1970) described a patient whose anxiety was triggered by awareness of his heart rate, and in whom standard desensitization and the use of external inhibition had failed. Prescribed reading proved to be an effective means to desensitization to his heart beat. Subsequently, his spoken descriptions of other disturbing situations seemed also to act as anxiety inhibitors. The patient was free of his symptoms 18 months after treatment.

Responses Produced by Relief from Distress

These substitutes for relaxation conform to the anxiety-relief paradigm (Wolpe, 1958, p. 180) which had its original use for combatting anxiety in real-life settings. That paradigm was suggested by an experiment performed in Poland by Zbrozyna (1953). An auditory stimulus was presented to an eating animal just before withdrawing the food on a number of occasions; the stimulus was subsequently found to inhibit feeding even in the middle of a meal. It seemed reasonable to expect that a stimulus repeatedly associated with the termination of a noxious stimulus might acquire anxiety-inhibiting properties, an expectation that was supported by the observation that approach responses are conditioned to a stimulus consistently presented at the termination of electrical stimulation (e.g., Coppock, 1951; Barlow, 1956).

Anxiety Relief I reported (Wolpe, 1958, p. 181) significant therapeutic value in the "anxiety-relief" conditioning obtained by pairing the word "calm" to the cessation of a moderately unpleasant electrical stimulus applied to the patient's forearm. The patient is instructed to say this word aloud when he strongly desires the stimulus to stop. Its termination produces a feeling of relief which, upon repetition, often becomes conditioned to the word "calm," but this apparently only happens in individuals who experience some degree of emotional disturbance besides the sensory discomfort produced by the stimulus. In these people, the feeling of relief when the shock stops may be quite marked. The feeling may be increased and the conditioning facilitated by the administration of drugs that augment sympathetic responses, such as amphetamines (Eysenck, 1963). If, subsequently, the patient utters the word "calm" subvocally in disturbing life situations, his anxiety level may be reduced, and conditioned inhibition of the anxiety habit may result.

Originally, this kind of conditioning was used solely in the context of actual anxiety-evoking situations, but Meichenbaum and Cameron (1974) have reported two studies in which it was used with verbally cued anxiety responses to reduce persistent fear of harmless snakes. In comparison with a self-instructional rehearsal group and a waiting-list control group, the anxiety-relief group showed significantly more improvement. In a second study, one anxiety-relief group terminated shock by emitting coping self-statements (e.g., "Relax, I can touch the snake: just one step at a time") instead of the single cue word, "calm." In another anxiety-relief group, avoidant thoughts (e.g., "It's ugly, it's slimy, I won't look at it") were paired with relief from shock. The two anxiety-relief groups—whether they used coping statements or avoidant statements—were equally effective in reducing fears. This showed that the content of the cue statement is irrelevant to the efficacy of the procedure. Yet, amazingly, Meichenbaum and Cameron deduced from their findings that the "plausability of a conditioning explanation for treatment efficacy is seriously called into question"! They expressed the belief that their clients improved because they were "developing a set of self-instructional coping skills which they could employ to deal with the stressor of shock and that these skills were in turn employed in overcoming their fear of snakes"!

Aversion Relief. The essence of this method, which was first employed by Thorpe et al. (1964), is to present a phobic stimulus to the subject at the moment that he presses a button to terminate a continuous unpleasant electrical stimulation. Solyom and Miller (1965) and Solyom (1969) have made extensive use of the following modified procedure.

The patient, who has prepared a tape recording consisting of both past and potentially anxiety-provoking events, is seated in an armchair, separated from the experimenter by a one-way screen. Items from this tape recording are presented to him, one at a time, through earphones. After a period of silence of about 30 seconds, an unpleasant electrical stimulation is administered to the patient's finger. By pressing a button, he terminates the electric shock and at the same time sets off an anxiety item from his tape. For example, a cat-phobic patient might, upon pressing the button, hear her own voice saying, "I see a grey cat," simultaneously with the cessation of the shock. The intensity of shock is determined for each individual by selecting the midpoint between his shock reception and shock tolerance thresholds. Solyom and Miller (1965) summarized the treatment of eight patients, of whom six were free from fears after a mean of 19.5 treatment sessions—without symptom substitution at follow-up.

Respiratory Relief. A method that appears to have emerged independently is respiratory relief (Orwin, 1971). The patient is asked to hold his breath voluntarily as long as he can and to signal when he can no longer maintain it. At that moment, the phobic stimulus is presented to his imagination so that the relief that ensues on the resumption of breathing can compete with the anxiety. Orwin states that six patients rapidly lost lifelong phobias. Four spider-phobic patients were able to touch a spider in one or two 30-minute sessions. One of them subsequently allowed a large house spider to run over her hands and arms without concern. The phobic constituents of chronic obsessional conditions were also "surprisingly easily controlled by respiratory relief" and all patients showed marked improvement.

The technical simplicity of the method makes it tempting to investigate, but the few attempts I have made to use it have not been encouraging.

Sensory Contrast. Cabanac (1971) has shown that physical stimuli can be made pleasurable by applying them against a suitable background state— e.g., localized cold against general hotness. This observation offers the possibility of a less stressful alternative in the domain of relief from distress. Nobody has as yet attempted to exploit it therapeutically. It is included here in the hope that somebody will.

Pharmacological Inhibition of Anxiety by Carbon Dioxide–Oxygen Inhalation

The powerful effect that carbon dioxide–oxygen has in reducing pervasive anxiety (p. 225) has made it appear to be a potentially valuable agent for overcoming specific anxiety habits as well. Philpott (1967) reported that he had been able to achieve desensitization by presenting hierarchical stimuli while the patient inhaled the gas so as to maintain a moderate degree of hyperventilation for several seconds.

I have had occasion several times to attempt desensitization with carbon dioxide by this method. Marked effects were obtained in each case, and it was possible to present scenes much higher up the hierarchy than would be possible using relaxation. In a case of classroom phobia, apparent recovery was obtained in two sessions. In an unusual phobia for certain configurations of the opposite sex that had resisted all other available methods, it took eight sessions to obtain marked reduction in anxiety responses to the stimuli concerned presented *in vivo* during inhalations that lasted from two to three minutes. The indications are that this gas is a particularly powerful anxiety inhibitor and deserves extensive clinical study.

DESENSITIZATION TO EXTEROCEPTIVE STIMULI TO ANXIETY

While it is obviously very convenient to conduct systematic desensitization with imaginal stimuli, it is not always feasible, most often because of patients who do not imagine realistically. Exteroceptive stimuli must then be used. These may be either actual feared objects or pictorial representations of them. The former have been by far the more widely used. A variety of counteranxiety responses have been involved, as will be indicated. The procedures fall into two main classes: (1) *in vivo* desensitization, in which graded exteroceptive stimuli are presented to the patient on the general lines of conventional desensitization, and (2) *modelling,* in which the patient observes a fearless subject make increasingly intimate contact with a feared object.

Desensitization *In Vivo*

It is a matter of routine to ask patients to try to expose themselves to real situations which they have been desensitized to in imagination. For example, a person with a fear of driving is asked to go out driving up to the last desensitized point. I used to regard this as a consolidating maneuver and a means of getting feedback. A controlled study by Garfield, Darwin, Singer, and McBrearty (1967) indicates that it actually accelerates desensitization. Sherman (1972) has reported a similar finding, but because he worked with weak fears, the applicability of his findings to clinical conditions is uncertain (Bernstein & Paul, 1971). Cooke (1966), however, found that in snake phobias, desensitization proceeded with the same speed, whether imagined or real stimuli were used.

The successful use of real-life graduated exposures in an institutional setting was first reported by Terhune (1948), who worked empirically, without awareness of the learning principles involved. The first account of *in vivo* therapy that was directly based on the desensitization paradigm was in connection with two agoraphobic cases treated by Meyer (1957). It was followed in 1960 by Freeman and Kendrick's report of the overcoming of a cat phobia by getting the patient to handle pieces of material progressively similar to cat fur, exposing her to pictures of cats, then a toy kitten, followed by a real kitten, and eventually grown cats. A phobia for earthworms was treated in a similar way by Murphy (1964); and Goldberg and D'Zurilla (1968) overcame fears of receiving injections by the use of slide projections of the stages of activity involved in an injection. Dengrove (1968) used moving film to overcome phobias for bridges.

The above treatments relied on interpersonal and other "natural" events to evoke anxiety-inhibiting emotional responses, and this often suffices. There was graded exposure of the patient to real fear-evoking stimuli while the therapist was present in the double role of guide and anxiety inhibitor. In a case of my own, a woman whose anxiety level was related to distance from a "reliable" person was brought by her husband to meet me in a public park in the quiet of the early morning. In the course of about ten meetings, I effected increasingly distant separations, the anxiety of separation presumably having been inhibited by her emotional responses to me.

Desensitization *in vivo* has its chief indication as the prime method in the 15 or 20 percent of patients in whom imaginal stimuli are useless for desensitization because they do not arouse emotional responses similar to those produced by the corresponding real situations. The *in vivo* stimulus requirements are not always obvious. Special "dramatic" or technical arrangements sometimes have to be contrived. For example, in treating a patient whose fear of public speaking is based on a fear of humiliation, I may have him intentionally give wrong answers to simple arithmetical problems. The anxiety this at first produces fades away with repetition. I then introduce more difficult problems, some of which he is really unable to answer correctly; and then I may increasingly deride his errors. Witnesses may be introduced to watch the sequence of failures.

Case 31

A case that called for technical inventiveness was a young woman whom I saw in 1967. She was practically confined to her home by the fear that she would die if her heart beat too fast. She was admitted to the hospital, and when conventional desensitization had proved inapplicable, I arranged the following series of procedures in collaboration with Dr. John S. Jameson: (1) the induction of tachycardia by stepping on and off a stool an increasing number of times; (2) tachycardia produced by intravenous injections of increasing doses —up to 1 cc of epinephrine hydrochloride 1 : 1000; (3) epinephrine injections accompanied by "feedback" from an oscilloscope that grossly exaggerated the tachycardia; (4) inhalations of amyl nitrite (3 cc capsules crushed in a handkerchief); and (5) locking her up for increasing periods up to two hours in an isolated room in the basement of the hospital. Following these measures the patient was greatly improved, though not "cured." She started working regularly and in a seven-year follow-up made only an occasional telephone call to boost her confidence. In the last two of those years she phoned only about three times, and after that was not heard from again.

Case 32

This was a case in which desensitization *in vivo* occurred in the first place inadvertently and was later deliberately continued. The patient, who had an 11-year-long fear of confinement in social situations, was being treated in front of 20 members of a Behavior Therapy Institute I was conducting in Heiloo, Holland, in 1966. After training in relaxation and an elaboration of his hierarchies was prepared, he was asked, at his fourth interview, to visualize being in moviehouses with increasing difficulty of egress; but none of this evoked the slightest anxiety. I then told him that it would be necessary for us to work with real stimuli. He replied, "Something remarkable has already happened, doctor. During my first session here I was very nervous in the group, but every day my nervousness has decreased, and today I don't feel nervous at all." He had been unwittingly desensitized (perhaps flooded) to the audience of 20. As it happened, 160 psychologists were expected to be present the next day, and I decided to make use of them for continuing the treatment. Accordingly, the next morning in a large lecture hall, I had the patient at first sit with me on the platform while the original 20 institute members sat in the forward rows of seats. As the patient reported no anxiety, I gave a prearranged signal for 20 more people to enter the hall. When they did so, he reported anxiety and was instructed to relax. After a minute, he stated that he felt comfortable, and then another 20 people were permitted to enter. Again the anxiety that appeared was relaxed away. The same procedure was repeated until all 160 people were seated. The patient spent the remainder of the afternoon seated comfortably in the front row of the audience. Subsequently, further *in vivo* operations were arranged—such as jamming him in the front row of spectators at a tennis tournament. These measures resulted in marked improvement of his neurosis in a ten-day period.

Graded exposure that depends on "natural" competition with anxiety is not always successful; "deliberate" competition must then be sought. Usually the calmness of muscle relaxation is used, and occasionally anxiety-relief conditioning.

Modelling

This group of methods, which was introduced by Bandura (1968), shows signs of being a significant practical advance in the treatment of certain phobias. In the first study reported (Bandura, Grusec, & Menlove, 1967), young children who were very fearful of dogs were assigned to one of four groups, each receiving eight brief treatment sessions. One group observed a fearless peer-model exhibit progressively more fear-arousing interactions with a dog. The setting was a highly positive party context designed to counteract anxiety reactions. When the jovial party was well under way, the fearless model, a four-year-old boy, entered the room leading a dog, and performed a prearranged sequence of interactions with the animal for approximately three minutes. Further sequences occurred at each subsequent session, the fear-provoking properties of the displays being gradually increased from session to session by simultaneously varying the physical restraints on the dog, the directness and intimacy of the approaches, and the duration of interactions between the model and the dog. A second group of fearful children observed the same graduated performances, but outside the party context. A third group observed the dog in the party activities, but was never exposed to either the dog or the modelled displays. Following completion of the treatment program, and again a month later, each child's phobic behavior toward two different dogs was measured separately. The two groups of children who had observed the peer-model interact nonanxiously with the dog displayed significantly greater approach behavior toward both the experimental and an unfamiliar animal than did the children in the dog exposure or the control conditions, who did not differ from each other. The party context added only slightly to the favorable outcome of modelling. Two-thirds of the children receiving the modelling treatment were eventually able to remain alone in the room confined with the dog, but relatively few children in the two control conditions could do this.

Bandura, Blanchard, and Ritter (1968) studied the effects of modelling on snake-fearful adults. Their groups were exposed to four conditions. The first group observed a graduated film depicting young children, adolescents, and adults engaging in progressively more fear-provoking interactions with a large king snake. They were taught to induce and to maintain anxiety-inhibiting relaxation throughout the period of exposure. The rate of presentation of modelling stimuli was regulated by the client through a projector equipped with remote-control starting and reversing devices. Clients were instructed, whenever a particular sequence provoked anxiety, to reverse the film to the beginning of the aversive sequence and to reinduce deep relaxation. They then reviewed the threatening scene repeatedly until it was completely neutralized before proceeding to the next item in the hierarchy. The second group of clients received a form of treatment in which, after observing intimate snake-interaction behavior repeatedly modelled by the therapist, they were aided through demonstration to perform progressively closer approaches to a snake. The third group received conventional desensitization. As in the other conditions, the treatment was continued until the clients' anxiety reactions were totally extinguished, or the maximum time allotment of six hours of treatment (not including relaxation training) was completed. A control group received before-and-after assessments without any intervening treatment. The final assessments showed that live modelling combined with guided participation was the most effective treatment, eliminating the snake phobia in 92 percent of subjects. The desensitization and symbolic-modelling groups also showed substantial change, but the control group was unchanged. A one-month follow-up assessment revealed that the beneficial changes were maintained and had transferred to real-life situations. Ritter (1968) found a similar superiority for modelling with guided participation in the treatment of snake-phobic children.

Bandura (1968) proposed that the guided participation group achieved more marked changes because of "positive reinforcement of a sense of capability through success," which he later (Bandura, 1977) expanded to his general theory of psychotherapeutic change being a function of expectations of self-efficacy, a theory that we found untenable (p. 53; see also Wolpe, 1978). It seems that the superior results of guided participation are due to its providing *in vivo* desensitization in cases of classically conditioned fear, and reassuring information in cognitively based cases.

10

The Treatment of Inhibited Sexual Responses

Uninhibited sexual responding is correlated with intense pleasurable arousal, especially during sexual intercourse. While in some cases, chronic sexual inhibition is due to failure of physical development or to physical pathology, in the great majority of cases it is the result of conditioning. Usually anxiety responses have become conditioned to stimuli associated with sexual responding, and, being incompatible with the latter, inhibit it. An inhibitory effect may also result from other emotions, like shame or disgust. Temporary inhibitions may, of course, be caused by intercurrent stresses or interfering stimuli of many kinds, such as loud voices in the next room.

Anxiety is eminently adverse to sexual responding because it inhibits the very autonomic response elements that make up the sexual response. Preorgasmic sexual arousal is predominantly parasympathetic in character (Langley & Anderson, 1895; Masters & Johnson, 1966), while anxiety is predominantly a sympathetic function. Therefore, the more intensely anxiety is aroused, the more inhibition of the early sexual response there will be (Wolpe, 1958). Reciprocally, sexual responses may be used for overcoming the anxiety habits that inhibit them. As always, such utilization depends upon arranging for the sexual response to be strong enough to dominate the anxiety response, so that by inhibiting it, it will diminish the anxiety-response habit. Napalkov and Karas (1957) have shown that experimental neuroses in dogs can be overcome by counterposing sexual excitation to neurotic anxiety. Clinical neuroses have been successfully treated on the same basis, as will be described below. Of course, other inhibitors of anxiety can also be used to treat the anxiety that affects sexual responding.

As might be expected, it is usually in connection with anxieties related to sexual stimuli that sexual arousal has therapeutic application. But its potential is not confined to these stimuli. The neurotic reactions of the dogs treated by Napalkov and Karas were conditioned to nonsexual stimuli. Similarly, sexual emotions can be instrumental in overcoming nonsexual human neuroses. Quite frequently, such therapeutic effects occur fortuitously in life. A fortunate twist in a person's life may provide him with an exciting new sexual relationship that has therapeutic consequences. The emotion then involved is often not purely sexual excitation, but a broad-based arousal that can be called love. A case in point was an exceptionally intelligent young woman who felt herself disparaged by all intelligent people whom she encountered, especially at social gatherings, where she became exceedingly anxious. Then she married a man with whom she had fallen deeply in love. Now, suffused with amorous feelings, constantly reinforced by reciprocation, she found that she no longer had anxiety in social contexts. Years later, when the phase of high romance was long past, she was still free from her original anxiety. The anxiety had presumably undergone conditioned inhibition because of its reciprocal inhibition in social situations when love was on the wing.

As a matter of fact, many other nonanxious emotions can also produce therapeutic changes without the intervention of a therapist. It is probable that the majority of neuroses that people acquire are mild, and that most of them are in time overcome by the competition of the intercurrent emotions aroused by life events (Wolpe, 1958, p. 198).

THE TREATMENT OF MALE SEXUAL INADEQUACY

The most common deliberate use of the anxiety-inhibiting effects of erotic arousal is in the treatment of inhibited sexual responding in the male, called impotence, which is generally manifested as inadequacy of penile erection or premature ejaculation or both. Penile erection is a parasympathetic function. The sympathetic discharges that characterize anxiety tend both to inhibit erection and to facilitate ejaculation, which is subserved by the sympathetic (Langley & Anderson, 1895). Thus, the key to the problem of impaired sexual performance is the subtraction of anxiety from the sexual encounter. Sometimes the anxiety has nonsexual antecedents, e.g., a fear of traumatization of human flesh (Wolpe, 1958, p. 152), but in the great majority of cases its stimuli are to be found within the sexual situation.

In using the sexual response as an anxiety inhibitor, one must first ascertain at what point in the approach anxiety begins and what factors control it. Perhaps the man begins to feel anxiety the moment he enters the bedroom, or perhaps it is when he is lying in bed in the nude with his wife. The basic idea of the treatment is explained to him—that the sexual response, being antagonistic to anxiety, can weaken his habitual anxiety if it can be consistently counterposed to anxiety that is relatively weak. He can arrange for this by limiting his sexual approaches always to the point where anxiety begins. He obviously has to obtain his wife's cooperation. She would certainly regard such constraints as odd if he were to institute them without explanation. The essence of her role is to avoid making him tense and anxious. She must not mock him or goad or press him to achieve any particular level of performance. Though this may mean her enduring a good deal of frustration, she may expect eventually to reap the reward of her helpfulness. Actually, many women obtain a reasonable degree of relief from digitally induced orgasms during this treatment. In the case of the man who begins to feel anxiety when just lying next to his wife in bed, he must do nothing more active until he no longer has anxiety in that situation. Usually after two or three occasions he will be able to say, "I feel perfectly comfortable, now—only sexually excited." Then, he can go on to the next stage—perhaps to turn toward her and lie facing her on his side and fondle her breasts while she remains on her back. When this can be done without anxiety, he again advances—this time perhaps to lying on top of her, but not attempting intromission. At the next step, the penis may be approximated to the clitoris or other parts of the vulva, but still without intromission. After this he is permitted a small degree of entry, and later greater degrees, followed by small amounts of movement and then greater movement. The precondition for advancing beyond a stage is the disappearance from it of all anxiety.

The details of the treatment, naturally, must be decided in individual cases. An adjuvant that is frequently of great value was suggested by Semans (1956). The wife manipulates her husband's penis to a point just short of ejaculation and then stops. After an interval, she does the same again. The procedure may be repeated several times during a session. Over several sessions, its effect is to increase the latency to ejaculation—sometimes from a few seconds to half an hour or more. It is easy to see how helpful this may be for prolonging intercourse when the time comes. Semans describes his technique, which Case 33 in part illustrates, as follows.

If fatigue is present in either partner, he or she should sleep for a brief period of time. After this, love play begins and progresses to mutual stimulation of the penis and clitoris. They must keep each other informed of the stage of sexual excitement being experienced. When the husband feels a sensation which is, for him, premonitory to ejaculation, he informs his wife and removes her hand until the sensation disappears. Stimulation soon begins again and is interrupted by the husband when the premonitory sensation returns. By continuing as described above, ejaculation can eventually be postponed indefinitely. Both husband and wife are advised that if erection subsides more than temporarily, a brief sleep or postponement of further stimulation is to be preferrred to continuing their efforts at that time. Next, each is told separately, and later together, that ejaculation occurs more rapidly when the penis is wet rather than dry. It is necessary, therefore, to use a bland cream or other means to lubricate the penis in order to simulate the moist surface of the vagina.[1]

Masters and Johnson (1970) describe a maneuver that may facilitate this technique. They found that when ejaculation seems inevitable it can be inhibited by the woman applying gentle digital pressure on the penis at the coronal sulcus between the uretha and the dorsum.

Case 33

Ever since the beginning of his coital life at the age of 16, Mr. I., a 36-year-old realtor, had suffered from premature ejaculation, which generally occurred within 15 seconds of intromission. He had married at age 24. His wife, though deriving some satisfaction from digital orgasms, had become increasingly conscious of incomplete fulfillment, and had in the past two years been showing interest in other men. About 18 months previously, Mr. I. had had about 25 consultations with a "dynamic" psychiatrist. Though he had found the probing type of approach irritating, his general confidence had been improved by the treatment, but his sexual performance had remained unchanged. In three short-lived extramarital affairs, his sexual performance had been no better than with his wife. He usually felt that he was doing the "chasing," and was being accepted on sufferance.

Mr. I.'s Willoughby score was 30, with highest loadings for humiliation, stage fright, and being hurt. He lacked assertiveness in relation to people close to him, but not at all in business affairs. A program of assertiveness training was seen as a secondary but very relevant therapeutic requirement.

Mrs. I., briefly interviewed, expressed great willingness to take part in a behavior therapy program. She stated that digital orgams satisfied her physically, but not emotionally. She felt that even a relatively small degree of prolongation of intromission would enable her to have coital orgasms. She regarded her marriage as very satisfactory in all other respects.

Therapy of the sexual inadequacy based upon use of sexual responses made combined use of two lines of approach: (1) graded penile stimulation by the technique of Semans (see above), and (2) gradual advances toward coitus. Mr. I. kept a detailed record of his performances, which he timed as accurately as possible with a bedside clock. The data of the early and middle stages of his record are reproduced below. Each figure refers to the *number of minutes of manual stimulation of the penis by his wife that brought him just short of ejaculation* for each successive sequence of stimulations.

[1]From J. H. Semans (1956), Premature ejaculation: A new approach. *Southern Medical Journal, 5,* 49: 354. By special permission obtained from author for this publication only. Not for other publication or reprint without author's permission.

First occasion (Saturday) 8, 6, 6, 6, and 3 minutes.

Second occasion (Saturday) 11, 7, 3, 4, and 4 minutes.

Third occasion (Sunday) 8, 6, 5, and 18 minutes.

Fourth occasion (Sunday) 17 minutes.

Fifth occasion (Monday) 33 minutes. At this juncture he felt confident enough
   to have Mrs. I. stimulate him as he sat astride her. The time to "preejaculation" on two successive sequences was two minutes and three minutes.

Sixth occasion (Monday) lying face to face sideways the preejaculatory point
   was reached in 10 minutes and was maintained for 20 more minutes, when
   Mrs. I. desisted because of fatigue.

At this occasion, Mr. I. reached and maintained a higher level of excitement than ever before; and this subsequently became the norm.

Seventh occasion (Monday) Same as sixth occasion, but "preejaculation"
   was reached in 14 minutes and again maintained to a total of 30 minutes.

Eighth occasion (Tuesday) Same as sixth occasion, but "preejaculation" was
   reached in 12 minutes and maintained to 30 minutes.

Ninth occasion (Wednesday) Penile stimulation while astride: 5, 12+, and
   9+ minutes.

Tenth occasion (Wednesday) Penile stimulation while astride: 12 and 11 minutes.

Eleventh occasion (Thursday) Penile stimulation while astride: 12½, 12, and
   23 minutes. After the last, Mr. I. inserted just the glans of his penis into the
   vagina, maintaining it there for 5 minutes. In the course of this time Mrs.
   I. became excited. Thereupon he withdrew, and they both had orgasms
   digitally.

Twelfth occasion (Friday) Partial insertion (glans penis) for 20 minutes during which Mrs. I. alone moved and in this way gradually manipulated the
   penis deeper. At the end of the period Mr. I. withdrew as he felt ejaculation imminent.

Mr. I. now reported with satisfaction that he was feeling very much less
anxious than before at partial insertion of his penis. He was finding that his
stimulation of his wife was the greatest factor increasing his own excitation.
The next objective was to increase both depth and duration of insertion, and
thereafter to add small amounts of movement. In the meantime at each meeting with the therapist the patient was receiving training in progressive relaxation.

Thirteenth occasion (Friday evening after meeting with therapist) Partial intercourse lasted 30 minutes—partial insertion 80 percent of the time and

full insertion about 20 percent, for about a minute at a time. During this minute Mr. I. would move constantly, without feeling any danger of ejaculation, but when Mrs. I. moved 5–10 times ejaculation would become imminent.

Fourteenth occasion (Saturday) Partial intercourse as above, 23 minutes and then Mr. I. ejaculated during an attempt to reverse positions.

Fifteenth occasion (Saturday) Fifteen minutes, much the same as the 13th occasion.

Sixteenth occasion (Sunday) Ejaculation after four minutes.

Seventeenth occasion (Monday) Forty minutes, varying between one-quarter to half insertion of penis. Ejaculation was several times imminent, but Mr. I. averted it by relaxing each time.

Now the therapist directed Mr. I. to concentrate first on prolonging full intromission, and then gradually to introduce movement, but preventing excessive excitation by avoiding stimulation of Mrs. I. He was told always to keep well within his capacity to control. After a few minutes of this it would be permissible to go on to orgasm, concentrating then on clitoral pressure by the penis.

Eighteenth occasion (Monday) Orgasm after 15 minutes of complete insertion with small movements.

Nineteenth occasion Orgasm after 29 minutes of small movements. Mrs. I. said that she too had been on the point of orgasm.

Further sexual occasions enabled gradually increasing excursions of movement, and finally a major breakthrough occurred after the 13th therapeutic interview. While Mr. I. retained his erection, Mrs. I. had four orgasms, and he ejaculated during the last of them. From this time onward there was mutually satisfactory sexual peformance that gradually improved. There were 14 therapeutic interviews in all, over 5 weeks. Mr. I.'s Willoughby score at the last interview was 13.

The course that events took in the treatment of Case 33 is typical. Some patients do not make this kind of progress because they cannot maintain the low levels of anxiety essential to success in the real sexual situations, even though these are delimited. Usually, the imagination of these patients takes them beyond the reality to the eventual "threat" of actual coitus. Systematic desensitization to the stages of the sexual approach is then indicated, or the use of tranquilizing drugs may be considered.

In occasional cases of premature ejaculation, recovery may be obtained in a much more simple way. The couple are told to have coitus as frequently as possible. The husband is instructed to try to enjoy himself as much as possible, just letting himself go and not caring how soon he ejaculates. The wife is asked to endure the situation if she can, and, of course, some cannot. It is quite helpful in cases like this to encourage the procural of orgasm in the wife by noncoital means—by manual and oral manipulations. A method that Semans (1962) reported as effective is for the women to move her clitoris rhythmically against the husband's thigh.

Although the most frequent source of male sexual failure is anxiety about sexual performance, nonsexual sources of anxiety can have the same effect. Eysenck (1960) recorded a case of impotence that was attributable to conditioned anxiety evoked by the wallpaper design in the bedroom. A case based on fear of traumatization was referred to above (p. 205). That nonsexual social anxiety can also cause sexual failure is illustrated by the following case.

Case 34

Mr. D., a prominent corporation lawyer of 44 (previously cited as Case 15, in the context of diagnosis), came for treatment with a 2-year history of difficulty in obtaining and maintaining an erection. For 12 years before this he had enjoyed a highly satisfying sex life with his wife. His problem had started with poor performances on occasions of unusual fatigue. This history led me to adopt the kind of sexual reconditioning program described above. He seemed at first to progress, but then it became evident that there was little real improvement.

I then examined his relationship with his wife more closely. Originally, she had behaved as an appendage to him. Then, about four years previously, she had consulted a therapist who had encouraged her to stand up for herself and assert her own personality. She had begun to rebel in diverse ways. He commented, "My feeling is that she has abandoned me." I perceived this feeling of rejection as the basis of his impaired sexual function. Having convinced him of this chain of causes, I encouraged him to discuss the relationship with his wife and to procure mutual agreement on what the rights and obligations of each should be. After a few weeks the communication between them had so greatly improved as to assure him that she had not abandoned him and still loved him. From her it removed the resentment that had caused her rebellion. I also needed to desensitize him to some of her acts of independence. These measures resulted in the restoration of his sexual abilities, in the setting of a much improved general relationship.

For a few of those patients who do not respond to the outpatient measures described above, a two-week course with spouse at The Reproductive Biology Research Foundation in St. Louis, Missouri (Masters & Johnson, 1970) might be worth considering. This is a highly structured opportunity for reconditioning sexual responses, although the principals are not very knowledgeable about conditioning. Although this course is widely regarded as the ultimate resource in sex therapy, it must be remembered that it is a "package": little attention is paid to the needs of individual couples, and there is no behavior analysis. I have seen several patients who underwent it without benefit and who would have been spared the expense and effort had they had the benefit of a behavior analysis beforehand. In one such patient, the problem resided in the wife's anxiety at being observed letting herself go, in every conceivable physical context, not only the sexual. The Masters and Johnson program was foredoomed to fail. Levay and Kagle (1977) surveyed the results of that program in 45 couples whom they themselves had referred. These had a distribution of sexual dysfunctions comparable to that reported by Masters and Johnson. After the two-week treatment period, couples were seen at least twice, at two weeks and at two months. Ten of the original 45 couples were judged to be unimproved or deteriorated. The remaining 35 evidenced either complete resolution of the problem or some degree of improvement. However, 19 of the latter returned for further therapy either because of deterioration of sexual function, or because of failure to make further progress in the period following treatment. The Masters and Johnson program should only be recommended in carefully selected cases, and only after more economical means have failed.

In general, patients who complain of erectile failure or insufficiency are more difficult to treat than those with premature ejaculation, for theirs is a more profound inhibition of response. In some of them, there is clearly a biological factor involved. Their number is probably much greater than has generally been assumed. Spark, White, and Connolly (1980) found that more than one-third of 105 consecutive patients with impotence had endocrine disorders. Appropriate medication restored sexual function in the great majority of them. Schumacher and Lloyd (1981) noted a surprisingly high and varied incidence of organic disease in a sample of 83 men complaining of impotence. The conclusion is obvious that medical investigation should be routinely undertaken in all cases of male sexual dysfunction, except perhaps those in whom a purely psychological basis is unequivocally clear from the start.

The onset of biologically based impotence is insidious, with erectile power diminishing over a period of months or years. The history often reveals a life-long low level of sexual function. If there is no evidence of anxiety or other reactive source of sexual inhibition, a biological causation is highly probable. The diagnosis may be settled by laboratory estimation of urinary testosterone (Cooper et al., 1970). Less directly relevant, but more easily available, is the estimation of urinary 17-ketosteroid excretion. A distinctly low testosterone assay is a strong indication for hormone therapy; but even with a moderately high reading, the patient need not be denied the possible benefits of testosterone treatment although most of those who are so treated fail to respond (Cooper et al., 1970). Other investigations proposed by Schumacher and

Lloyd (1981) are measurement of plasma levels of cortisol, progesterone, luteinizing hormone, follicle-stimulating hormone, thyroxine, triiodothyronine, thyroid binding globulin, free thyroxine, and where indicated, thyrotropin.

The first account of the beneficial use of male sex hormones in the treatment of impotence was by Miller, Hubert, and Hamilton (1938). In the course of about 30 years, I have twice succeeded in augmenting a very low sex drive by daily injections of testosterone so as to enable successful sexual performance which subsequently continued without further use of the hormone. Presumably, the sexual responses that the testosterone had facilitated had come to be conditioned to contiguous stimuli. More extensive reviews of the use of this substance have been provided by Cooper (1971), Jakobovitz (1970), and Miller 1968).

There is a subgroup of organically based cases in which no endocrine abnormality can be found. In three of my own who were put through Rubin's (1970) pupillography procedure, aberrant response profiles were found that were neither neurotic nor psychotic (Rubin, 1972). This suggests the possibility that some previously unrecognized form of autonomic imbalance may be the cause of sexual inadequacy in certain cases.

It was mentioned in the beginning of this chapter that various intercurrent stresses may cause temporary inhibition of sexual responding. Chronic stress that has nothing to do with the sexual relationship as such may in parallel fashion cause chronic sexual inhibition. Prolonged stress may come from an enduring real misery, such as an incurable illness in a child. Most often it is bound up with disharmonies in the relationship that are of a nonsexual kind. A program for mutual readjustment should then be undertaken. Sometimes two or three joint sessions with the couple on a "common-sense" basis are all that is needed. Other cases require more formal arrangements involving "contracts," score cards, and a token economy, as described by Stuart (1969). Case 35 affords an instructive example of the disruptive effects of nonsexual anxiety on sexual behavior.

A less common form of male sexual inadequacy is ejaculatory incompetence. One case was successfully treated by desensitization to the idea of the penis in the vagina (Razani, 1972). Masters and Johnson (1970) report having overcome 14 of 17 cases of this problem treated primarily by having the female partner repeatedly stimulate the penis to ejaculation.

Problems of Female Collaboration

A cooperative sexual partner is almost always an asset and indispensable to the success of most of the techniques described above. Many patients have a partner readily available. Others may wait months to find somebody sufficiently interested to be willing to make the effort and bear the discomforts involved in treatment. Sometimes, although the patient has a wife or paramour, she is unable to participate as needed, either because she is contemptuous of her mate's disability or more often, because a long history of disappointment and frustration has quenched her amorous responses. If the woman is unmoved by her husband's prefiguration of the behavior therapy program, the therapist should arrange to speak to her himself. If she can be persuaded to take the first steps, and if she is encouraged by early progress, the rest can be plain sailing.

When all reasonable efforts have failed to extract from the wife the affectional behavior needed for the therapeutic program, it is usually appropriate to encourage the husband to seek out another woman who may be more responsive to him. If moral justification is required, it may be said that if the man's sexual potency should be reinstated through his relationship with the other woman, it may lead to reconstruction of his marriage; and even if it does not, it is better both physiologically and psychologically to have outside satisfactions than to accept enforced chastity indefinitely.

Provided that reasonable safeguards are observed, it is best for a therapeutic extramarital relationship to be conducted with somebody in whom there is some wider personal interest, but when this is not possible, paid help has to be sought, since the casual "pick up" will not do. Perhaps there will some day be a roster of accredited women who will sell their services to men with sexual problems. Indeed, such women are already to be found in Los Angeles. For the most part, there is no other recourse than to seek out a regular prostitute —and it is usually no easy matter to find one who is both personally appealing and able to muster enough sympathetic interest to participate in the therapeutic program. One patient, with a 16-year history of impotence, tried about 10 prostitutes before he found a warm-hearted and considerate one with whose help his sexual anxiety was overcome and his potency restored. Others have found help more easily.

The Results of Behavior Therapy of Inhibited Male Sexual Responses

Among 18 cases I surveyed retrospectively in 1966, 14 (78 percent) recovered to the extent of achieving entirely satisfactory sexual performance. Another three cases (17 percent) attained a level that was acceptable to their partners. The mean span of time required was 11.3 weeks and the median 8.0 weeks. Table 10.1 gives some details of these cases.

THE TREATMENT OF FEMALE SEXUAL INADEQUACY

Female sexual inadequacy is usually referred to as frigidity, which is an undesirable term inasmuch as it implies emotional coldness or a total lack of sexual response, but it is too late to do away with it now. The important thing is

Table 10.1.   Results of Behavior Therapy in 18 Cases of Impotence.

Patient Number	Age	Therapeutic Time Span	Outcome and Remarks
1	31	1 week	Recovered
2	40	8 weeks	Recovered
3	46	10 weeks	Recovered
4	46	20 weeks	Recovered
5	40	4 weeks	Recovered
6	41	12 weeks (intermittent and furtive)	Much Improved
7	50	6 weeks	Recovered but no transfer to wife.
8	49	2 weeks	Recovered (major factor was removal of anxiety through wife taking contraceptive pills).
9	20	6 weeks	Recovered (major factor was resolution of doubts of masculinity raised by psycho-analytic reading).
10	49	10 weeks	Improved from almost complete erectile failure to functionally sufficient erections to make marriage possible and to satisfy and impregnate wife.
11	35	6 weeks	Markedly improved when therapist left country. Appropriate assertion towards wife major factor.
12	36	5 weeks	Recovered (Case 33)
13	44	16 weeks (infrequent opportunities)	Unimproved. No apparent sexual anxiety. Hypersensitivity of glans penis.
14	40	9 weeks	Recovered (See Case 5, Wolpe 1958)
15	35	8 weeks (preceded by 12 weeks of overcoming interpersonal fears)	Improved from no erection to strong ones. Coitus improving when therapist left country.
16	18	66 weeks (very irregular opportunities at first)	Recovered
17	53	3 weeks	Recovered with new consort. Previously no benefit in 12 weeks with uncooperative consort.
18	39	12 weeks	Recovered. At first erections occurred only after testosterone injections.

to recognize that there are all grades of inhibition of sexual response in women, from no response whatever of a sexual kind to the inability to achieve coital orgasm in spite of very high sexual arousal.

Two kinds of cases must be distinguished: Those whose lack of response is in relation to males in general, and those in whom it is relative to a particular male who is in many cases the patient's husband. The solutions required are of very different kinds.

General Inhibition of Arousal

This heading refers to inhibited sexual arousal even with a highly desirable partner. The inhibition may be either absolute or relative. Some cases have an organic basis. Occasionally, one encounters a woman whose sexual response system seems somehow to have failed to develop. She does not recall ever having known sexual arousal and gives no history of distressing sexual experiences that might have led to conditioned inhibition. It must be supposed that her deficiency is constitutional, and there seems to be no available solution to such a problem.

In other organically based cases, the woman is erotically arousable, but coitus is precluded or interfered with by pain or discomfort, often because of some painful pathological condition of the vagina, such as a zone of scar tissue or an inflammatory lesion. I once saw a women who had been psychoanalyzed for the whole four years of her marriage because of frigidity that was found by the gynecologist to whom I referred her to be due to vaginal spasm caused by a painful ulcer. A gynecological examination should be advised in every case of frigidity in which there is the slightest possibility of physical pathology.

In the great bulk of cases, general inhibition of arousal is a matter of conditioned inhibition which dates from earlier experiences that have attached negative, usually anxious, feelings to sexual stimuli. The causal experiences may have been informational, consisting of religious indoctrination or of statements from a mother who herself had unhappy or fearful sexual experiences. If the little girl has learned that sex is filthy and bestial, the negative emotions evoked by these adjectives will later, in an adult sexual context, compete with sexual arousal. In other cases, the inhibition of sexual arousal is the direct result of classical conditioning which may occur when a child is punished or frightened in the act of masturbation or sex play. Later on, classical conditioning may originate in the context of attempted rape or other sexual traumata; or it may develop from sexual arousal being repeatedly frustrated in one way or another. Often, a women who is highly arousable sexually and who has rarely or never achieved a satisfactory coital orgasm will relate that repeated frustration has created a growing revulsion toward sexual activity. Frigidity also sometimes develops, as in Case 35, out of negative experiences resulting from the depths of compassion of an extremely warm relationship.

The treatment of general frigidity depends upon what the stimulus-response analysis of the case reveals. Where there has been faulty indoctrination, it is necessary to remove the misconceptions about sex and sexual activity and to reeducate the patient. This done, one is almost always still left with a negative emotional attitude bound up with anxiety that has been conditioned to various aspects of the sexual situation. The usual treatment is then systematic desensitization whose details are determined by the identified stimulus antecedents of the anxiety. In yet other cases, frigidity is a byproduct of long-continued simmering resentment at a spouse's "failings." Sometimes the problem would be solved if the woman could make her wishes known; here the cure may lie in assertiveness training.

In each of the following four cases, frigidity was overcome by some form of desensitization. In Cases 36 and 37, typical sexual stimuli made up the hierarchy content; in Case 35 it was objects of increasing size in the vagina, and in Case 38 it was being seen at orgasm.

Case 35

A 38-year-old woman, Mrs. Y., whose relationship with her husband had for years been enviable in all respects, developed a vaginitis which made intercourse painful. But because of her great affection for her husband, she had gone on permitting intercourse; its aversiveness had resulted in her becoming completely frigid, with marked vaginismus. Even after the vaginitis had been successfully treated and intercourse was no longer painful, the vaginismus had persisted so extremely that it was impossible for the husband to gain entry. When I first saw her, this wretched state of affairs had lasted for three years.

The behavior analysis revealed that the vaginismus was part of an anxiety reaction to the entry of any object into the vagina. Treatment consisted of a combination of standard desensitization and *in vivo* desensitization. I instructed the patient to relax and to imagine, at first, a very thin rod (1/8 inch in diameter) being inserted to a depth of 1/2 inch into her vagina. This produced a small amount of anxiety. I repeated the scene until the anxiety disappeared. I gradually increased the extent of the rod's insertion up to four inches, and subsequently repeated the whole sequence with progressively wider rods. When the width of the imaginary rod had reached 1/2 inch, I arranged for the construction of a set of wax rods (bougies) that varied in diameter from 1/8 inch to 1 1/2 inches, that the patient was instructed to use at home while relaxed, starting with the insertion of the 1/8 inch bougie into her vagina, slowly, inch by inch. Thereafter, *in vivo* "shadowing" a few widths behind the imaginary diameter became the rule. When we reached about 3/4 inch diameter in imagination, movement such as would occur during coitus was introduced. This was a new source of anxiety which required many scene presentations for desensitization. Then, in-and-out movement of the bougie was started. Increasingly rapid movement came to be comfortably tolerated. At this point, I began to encourage careful experimentation with actual coitus, which became possible soon afterwards without producing vaginismus or any other manifestation of anxiety.

Case 36

This is a case of a much more common kind. Since an attempt at seduction by an uncle when she was about 15, Mrs. H., a woman of 32, had always felt a revulsion against sex. Nevertheless, she had married. She had borne four children in six years, because being pregnant was a defense against intercourse. Mrs. H. had been treated by conventional psychotherapy, drugs, and electroconvulsive therapy, all without benefit. Her psychiatrist, not a behavior therapist, had then decided to try systematic desensitization of which he had a reading acquaintance. The attempt had been a fiasco. The weakest item on the hierarchy was the sight of naked female breasts. When the psychiatrist presented this image to the patient, it had produced such a severe anxiety reaction that it was impossible to continue. Then he had referred Mrs. H. to me. I added to the weak end of the hierarchy several items that were quite remote from the bedroom. The first scene was being at a swimming pool where there was only one male present, 50 yards away, with his bare chest exposed. This man was later brought progressively closer. Next, we utilized, first at a distance of 50 yards and then closer, a completely nude male statue in a park. A later item in the hierarchy was seeing a little nude boy of four gambolling in a paddling pool. Eventually, after many steps, the patient was successfully desensitized to such images as dogs fornicating, pictures of nude males, four-letter words, and, finally, personal coital contingencies. It became possible for Mrs. H. to indulge in and enjoy sexual intercourse with her husband.

Case 37

A somewhat similar case was the subject of a week-to-week demonstration to a group of psychiatric residents. The patient, Mrs. D., was a 27-year-old woman with several other interpersonal neurotic anxiety reactions in addition to frigidity. These called for teaching her to assert herself. She caught on to the idea very quickly and soon began to implement it. After the fifth session, the main focus of therapy became the frigidity. Though she had worked as an actress, she was extremely standoffish. She had often been darkly warned by her mother about the evils of sex. These warnings had been borne out by an attempted sexual assault by a much older man about the time of puberty. After her marriage, she had found sex unpleasant and tried to avoid it as much as possible. Central to her problem was a tense abhorrence of the male sex organ. In treating this by desensitization, I started by having her imagine looking at a nude male statue in a park, from a distance of 30 feet. After "moving" progressively closer to the statue, she eventually imagined herself handling the stone penis with equanimity. The next series of scenes began with her imagining herself at one end of her bedroom and seeing her nude husband's penis 15 feet away. As desensitization proceeded, he was brought closer and closer. Then she imagined that she quickly touched the penis. With repetition, this aroused less and less anxiety. The duration of contact was increased step by step. *In vivo* assignments followed close behind the imagining. By about the 20th therapeutic session, Mrs. D. was enjoying sexual relations and having coital orgasms on about 50 percent of occasions.

Case 38

The precise details of treatment depend on behavior analysis in the treatment of frigidity just as with any other presenting complaint. This is well brought out in the case of Mrs. L., a 39-year-old mother of three children who had for many years been happily married and had enjoyed a thoroughly satisfying sex life. About seven years before Mrs. L. presented herself for treatment, her husband had begun drinking increasingly, until he was eventually almost constantly under the influence of alcohol to some extent. Mrs. L. was greatly distressed by this change, but when her husband paid no attention to her entreaties, she began to dislike him, and found sexual contact increasingly repugnant each time she submitted to his needs. After a few months, she moved out of the house and filed for divorce. Both before the divorce and after it, Mrs. L. had a number of sexual affairs but was surprised and disconcerted to note that she was quite unable to have coital orgasms. She came for treatment when she found this disability to extend to her relationship with a man with whom she was more deeply in love than she had been with anyone before in her life. Careful investigation of the details of her responses in the sexual situation revealed that the essence of the problem was a fear *of being seen* in the state of abandonment implicit in an orgasm. By contrast, she was easily able to induce masturbatory orgasms in private. In accordance with these facts, she was given a schedule of masturbating to orgasm at decreasing physical distance from her lover. First she did so in the dark, separated from him by the closed bathroom door, then with the door open. Then illumination was gradually increased, and thereafter he moved closer and closer, until eventually she was able to masturbate to orgasm in his full view. This, as expected, proved to be the necessary precondition to enable her to have orgasms during intercourse.

Brady (1966) found it helpful, in desensitizing the neurotic anxieties on which frigidity is based, to use intravenous Brevital as an adjuvant to relaxation. He had the impression that his cases improved more quickly with Brevital than if he had used relaxation alone. This requires further study. Its relevance goes beyond the context of frigidity (see p. 225ff).

There are certain women who are sexually arousable to a considerable and often marked degree, but who have never experienced full orgasm. Many of these are easily able to have frictional clitoral orgasms—some of them, even during coitus, if special efforts are made to continue clitoral stimulation at that time. Even so, the experience is often unsatisfactory because this kind of orgasm tends to have a restricted sensory locus in contrast to the widespread excitation that characterizes a full orgasm.

An effective solution to such problems may lie in the induction of "clinical orgasm" by suggestion (Rubin, 1972; MacVaugh, 1972, 1979). Rubin's schedule is quite simple and straightforward. MacVaugh's is very elaborate but has been more extensively studied and more fully described by its author. The following is a summary of MacVaugh's procedure.

First, the patient is shown that it is possible to influence emotions—to turn on, modify, and erase hate, jealousy, and love—by the presentation of appropriate cues. It is pointed out to her that an orgasm is a kind of power to trigger emotions. Then, facts about sex are described in such a way as to combat any ideas that it is unclean or sinful, and conveying that it is a mature and desirable activity which a woman should not feel ashamed to initiate. The next step consists of drawing attention to the anatomical features of the female sex organs—the sensory zones and the controlling muscles. The patient is instructed to practice contracting and relaxing these muscles. The typical sensations in the buildup of the orgasm are then described, and the comparative male and female excitation curves are shown. After this, the patient is given a list of the common colloquial words for the male and female organs, and for coitus, and is asked to read and say the words again and again until it becomes comfortable for her to do so. She is then shown how to put as much feeling as possible into their enunciation.

MacVaugh then goes on to project a series of slides portraying the stages in lovemaking of a Japanese couple, from getting out of a car, through their entrance into a pagoda and bathing together, up to lying together on a floor mattress. What is emphasized throughout is that the woman initiates and controls every stage: she takes off his shoes; she does the washing in the bath. This may be of importance because of its differences from the traditional female passivity in European lovemaking, which is especially notable in sexually inhibited women. MacVaugh (1972) claimed that his success rate rose from 25 to 90 percent after he introduced this Japanese sequence.

After obtaining evidence of responsiveness to suggestion, MacVaugh goes on to apply a hypnotic procedure and to suggest the successive steps of imaginary lovemaking with an exciting stimulating partner who has been previously chosen. He gives much attention to pelvic sensations, and later, when appropriate, suggests pelvic movements. He builds upon these finally to elicit a full orgasm. The tape recordings I have heard are utterly convincing. The climax-inducing procedure takes up to about three hours. Once a clinical orgasm has been induced, orgasmic behavior has entered the women's repertoire, available for elicitation in her real sex life. The whole of this schedule is unlikely to be always necessary, and a behavioral analysis beforehand should indicate what parts might be omitted.

A program that is less elaborate and that is especially designed for women who have never experienced orgasm from any kind of physical stimulation has been described by Lobitz and Lopiccolo (1972). It consists of the following nine steps:

Step 1: The patient is given the assignment to increase her self-awareness by examining her nude body and appreciating its beauty. She uses a hand mirror to examine her genitals and identify the various areas with the aid of diagrams in Hastings' book *Sexual Expression in Marriage* (1966). She is started on Kegel's (1952) exercises for increasing tone and vascularity of the pelvic musculature.

Step 2: She is instructed to explore her genitals tactually as well as visually. To avoid performance anxiety, she is not given any expectation to become aroused at this point.

Step 3: Tactual and visual exploration concentrate on locating sensitive areas that produce feelings of pleasure when stimulated.

Step 4: She is told to concentrate on manual stimulation of identified pleasurable areas. At this point a female therapist discusses techniques of masturbation, including the use of a lubricant.

Step 5: If orgasm does not occur during Step 4, the patient is told to increase the intensity and duration of masturbation. She is told to masturbate until "something happens" or until she becomes tired or sore.

Step 6: If orgasm is not reached during Step 5, the patient is asked to purchase a vibrator of the type sold in pharmacies for facial or body massage. In a particularly difficult case, Lobitz & Lopiccolo found that three weeks of daily 45-minute vibrator sessions were required to produce orgasm.

Step 7: Once masturbatory orgasm has been achieved, the husband is admitted to observe the procedure. This desensitizes her to displaying arousal and orgasm in his presence and also functions as a learning experience for him.

Step 8: The husband manipulates his wife in the manner she has demonstrated in Step 7.

Step 9: When orgasm has occurred in Step 8, the couple is instructed to engage in intercourse while the husband stimulates his wife's genitals, either manually or with a vibrator.

Lobitz and Lopiccolo use heterosexual erotic pictures or literature to supplement the above program. Three women in their masturbation program each reported masturbating to their first orgasm shortly after having viewed a sexually explicit film.

Another method that has produced encouraging results and that has the advantage of being usable in groups, consists of relaxation training followed by the viewing of a long series of videotaped vignettes depicting graduated sexual behaviors (Nemetz, Craig, & Reith, 1978).

Situational Frigidity

Behavior analysis often reveals that a woman who complains of frigidity is not negatively conditioned to sexual stimuli in general, but is unresponsive to the particular man with whom she consorts. The question then is why she does not respond to him. In many cases, one finds that she simply does not care for him as a person. Perhaps she did once, but does no longer. One patient had fallen in love with her husband for his wisdom and erudition, only to discover after marriage that she had been misled. When his image slumped, so did her ability to respond to him erotically. But sometimes the deficiencies are not easy to define. When there is a general lack of attraction to the spouse, I know of nothing that can be done about it. Sometimes, though, in the course of years, a pleasant, amicable association does build up feelings of affection and love.

Certainly one should always make every effort to identify sources of inhibition and to see whether change is possible. There may be something potentially changeable in the husband's behavior. Perhaps he comes home from work at irregular hours without ever telling his wife in advance or phoning her. Perhaps he gets lost in reading or in televised movies or in card playing, so that there is a minimum of communion. Such behavior can be extremely disturbing and, if persistent, may transform a woman's attitude from affection to dislike, and her sexual pattern from passion to frigidity. One patient in whom this happened had a husband who was an "empire builder," busy establishing branches of his business all over the United States. He was usually out of town. When he got home, he gave his wife scant attention, rushed out to play golf, or watched baseball or football on television. Though he protested that he loved his wife (who was very attractive), all efforts to change his behavior failed. He had a paternalistic attitude toward her and regarded her wishes as childish—a case of Ibsen's *Doll House* in the flesh. He utterly refused to accommodate himself to her needs. Since, for practical reasons, she could not leave him, it was hardly surprising that she found a lover.

Fortunately, few husbands are as immovable as this one was. Quite often, if the wife learns to behave with well-tempered assertiveness, the husband's behavior will also change favorably. In one case of situational frigidity, the husband, deeply involved in international affairs, treated his spouse essentially as a servant and caterer. He would bring home many visitors, often without notice, requiring her to prepare countless dinners and entertainments. Her behavior was extremely passive and compliant. In the context of assertiveness training I had her start structuring activities according to the principle: "If you will do things for me I will do things for you." This almost at once made his attitude toward her more pleasant. The next step was for her to make a stand regarding their way of life: "This kind of living does not suit me. I cannot have people here every night. I need some personal life, and I would like you to do something about it." He acceded to this, a much closer relationship progressively developed, and a sex life that was gratifying to both of them resulted.

This unilateral approach to readjustment of marriages is not always appropriate. Discord is often a matter of spiralling bilateral resentments. One partner's feelings are hurt, and he withdraws affection or retaliates against his spouse in some other way, provoking further negative behavior from her. It is necessary to break the vicious circle even if it has gone on for a very long while. This can best be done by some kind of contractual arrangement between the partners for mutual reinforcement. Stuart (1969, 1975) has devised a detailed program that includes a "marital contract," a written undertaking by each person to do things that the other desires, and score cards. In effect, each partner is given the opportunity to learn that positive reinforcement of the other is compensated in kind. A key procedure point is to translate general complaints into particular instances (e.g., "You criticized my cooking in front of your parents," rather than "You're always trying to hurt me"). The process of mutual reinforcement is, however, often quite difficult to institute and has generated considerable debate (Jacobson & Martin, 1976; Jacobson & Weiss, 1978; Knudson, Gurman, & Kniskern, 1980).

Finally, it must be said that a very useful self-help book for many cases of sexual dysfunction is Debora Phillips' *Sexual Confidence* (1980).

11

The Use of Chemical Agents in the Deconditioning of Anxiety

CONVENTIONAL DRUG ADMINISTRATION

When a person suffers from considerable anxiety or other emotional disturbance, either continuously or intermittently, it is often desirable to obtain amelioration by the use of a drug or combination of drugs. Many people resort to sedatives on their own, the most common being, of course, alcohol. Anxiety is often significantly diminished but not often entirely allayed by these substances in the usual doses. Apart from the fact that long-continued use carries the hazard the addiction, there seems to be no serious objection to relieving symptoms by drugs. Such relief certainly does not in itself jeopardize ultimate recovery.

As every experienced clinician knows, it is trial and error that decides what drug will be effective in an individual case. Diazepam (Valium), 5 to 20 mg, or chlordiazepoxide (Librium), 10 to 40 mg three or four times a day have well-established anxiety-reducing efficacy. When they do not succeed or produce unacceptable side effects, such as marked drowsiness, any of a considerable number of other drugs may be tried, including phenothiazine derivatives (e.g., trifluoperazine [Stelazine], thioridazine [Mellaril]), meprobamate, or hydroxyzine hydrochloride (Atarax). To these have been added various antidepressants such as tranylcypromine (Parnate) and phenelzine (Nardil), ever since Sargant and Dally's (1962) report of their efficacy in relieving the symptoms of many cases of anxiety. In certain of their cases, a combination with Librium was more effective. In my own experience, tricyclic antidepressants like imipramine may also be effective in this way, sometimes very rapidly in low dosages. A more recent addition to the antianxiety armamentarium is the beta-adrenergic blocking agent, propanolol (Granville-Grossman & Turner, 1966; Jefferson, 1964), whose action is entirely peripheral.

Symptom control by drugs does not always require dosage through the day. If anxieties are evoked only by specific predictable situations, the drug should be administered an hour or so before each expected situation—and *only* then. For example, a patient who has a fear of public scrutiny may take a tranquilizing preparation an hour before making a speech, and one who has a fear of flying may do the same before a flight. Many patients discover on their own that they can protect themselves against foreseeable anxiety sources in this way.

Symptomatic control by tranquilizing drugs of disabilities that are presumably secondary to anxiety has often been reported. Imipramine has controlled enuresis (Destounis, 1963) and encopresis (Abraham, 1963). Systematic use of this drug can achieve what Drooby (1964b) has called a "reliable truce" with certain disabilities when attempts at reconditioning are impracticable or unsuccessful. Drooby found that enuresis ceased completely or almost completely in a matter of days in every one of 45 children to whom he administered imipramine (25 mg) two or three times a day according to age. The treatment was not curative; enuresis recurred when the drug was withheld. When the drug was withdrawn after a year of use, 30 percent of the subjects remained free from enuresis—the same proportion as in an untreated control group. This means that while the drug relieved the child and his parents from the misery of enuresis, it did not impede the development of whatever processes led to recovery with the passage of time. Such usage is especially worthwhile when circumstances preclude the use of deconditioning procedures.

Drooby (1964a) also successfully used imipramine and other drugs such as Mellaril, Valium, and Nardil (v.s.) (each sometimes in combination with ergotamine) to curb anxiety and delay ejaculation in cases of premature ejaculation. Similar experiences have been reported by others (e.g., Singh, 1963). Sometimes the repeated successful performance of sexual intercourse under the influence of these drugs enables the patient later to perform satisfactorily without them.

The possibility of a new kind of symptomatic treatment seemed to emerge from the observation of Pitts and McClure (1967) that in some patients, anxiety attacks could be produced by intravenous infusions of lactate ion, and that the anxiety symptoms could be largely prevented by the addition of small amounts of calcium ion in the form of calcium chloride. From a review of subsequent research, however, and most notably the work of Grosz and Farmer (1972), Ackerman and Sacher (1974) concluded that when lactate infusions precipitate anxiety attacks, it cannot be by the mechanism proposed by Pitts and McClure. A hypothesis that does fit the data is that some anxiety neurotics have conditioned anxiety responses to certain of their somatic symptoms of anxiety.

Another kind of symptomatic control is possible in certain female patients. Emotional reactions are often accentuated (if not caused) by hormonal factors. In many women, exacerbation of symptoms occurs in the week before menstruation and may continue throughout the menstrual period. Marked amelioration may be obtained by the administration of female sex-hormone preparations. In most cases, it suffices to employ the same preparations and dosages as are used for contraceptive purposes, for example, Ovulen, Anovlar, Enovid, or Ortho-novum (Guttmacher, 1961). One is sometimes surprised to find that the improvement in symptoms is not confined to the late phases of the cycle, but extends through the whole of it. Some cases in whom "contraceptive pill" medication is not particularly successful respond well to large doses of progesterone by intramuscular injection or rectal suppository, according to Dalton (1964), who states that oral synthetic progestogens are not a satisfactory substitute.

THE REDUCTION OF PERVASIVE ANXIETY BY CARBON DIOXIDE-OXYGEN

When anxiety is pervasive ("free-floating")—that is, when it is apparently conditioned to pervasive aspects of stimulation such as space, time, and bodily sensations (Wolpe, 1958)—a remarkably effective measure is to administer to the patient one to five single, full-capacity inhalations of a mixture of carbon dioxide and oxygen. Originally, Meduna (1947) described a technique in which the patient inhaled a mixture of 30 percent carbon dioxide and 70 percent oxygen until he lost consciousness, an unacceptably heroic regimen that carries considerable risk. La Verne (1953) introduced the idea of administering a stronger mixture one breath at a time. The mixture that has become our standard consists of 65 percent carbon dioxide and 35 percent oxygen. As a matter of fact, in the Behavior Therapy Unit we have found it most satisfactory to use separate cylinders of oxygen and carbon dioxide and to mix the gases as needed (see Fig. 11.1). This enables us to take account of patients for whom the usual concentration is irritating or excessively drastic in its effects, and also provides the option of very high concentrations in refractory cases.

The following are the procedural details. The therapist first ascertains the patient's anxiety level in terms of the subjective (*sud*) scale. He then tells the patient what he proposes to do and what the probable effects will be. A fairly typical introductory speech is the following:

Fig. 11.1. Patient receiving carbon dioxide-oxygen mixture. The patient, at the end of inhalation, has just emptied the prefilled bag containing the mixture of gases.

Your constant high level of anxiety makes it difficult for your efforts at relaxing to decrease your anxiety very much. We sometimes find that we can get relaxation from inhalations of carbon dioxide and oxygen. Carbon dioxide is always in your body and in your breath. It has valuable physiological properties. It stimulates the breathing, and is frequently used to revive patients under anesthesia. Now, in these cylinders there is oxygen and carbon dioxide. I am going to give you a concentration of carbon dioxide exceeding what you normally have in your lungs. When I have filled the bag with a mixture of the two gases, I am going to ask you to inhale the mixture through this mask—just one breath. After a delay of a few seconds, you will begin to notice certain symptoms which are unusual, but not really unpleasant. You may notice that you become short of breath, that your heart quickens, your face flushes, and your extremities tingle. You may become rather dizzy, and possibly also have some other sensations. These reactions will reach a peak in five seconds or so, and then subside.

Now, this is what I want you to do. Take the mask in your hand. Watch as I fill the bag with the mixture of gases. (*Pause while the bag is filled.*) In a few seconds I am going to ask you to do the following things. First, empty your lungs; exhale as far as you can. Then apply the mask over your nose and chin quite firmly. After this, press the button on top of the mask. This releases the gas; and, mainly through your mouth, breathe in until you have about half-filled your lungs with the gas. Then remove the mask from your face.

In some cases, even half-filling the lungs with the gas mixture elicits a substantial respiratory reaction. In others, little or no effect is produced, and increasingly full inhalations are subsequently given, followed if necessary by higher concentrations of carbon dioxide. It is usually advisable not to try to fill the lungs completely the first time—especially when there is any reason to believe that the patient may be disturbed by the unusual sensations brought on by the gas. *It is always very important to inquire beforehand whether the patient has any fear of suffocation or of anesthetics.* In the case of those who have, a very slow and careful approach should be made to this method of treatment, providing an introductory "habituation program" for a few minutes at each of several successive sessions. At first, the patient is asked to do nothing more than handle the mask; then he may sniff at it held an inch or two in front of his nose while the gas mixture flows through the open valve; then he may take a short sniff out of the full bag, and thereafter increasingly deep breaths with pauses between them until he eventually inhales fully. Despite the greatest caution, a few individuals are so distressed by the sensations produced that it is never possible for carbon dioxide to be profitably employed on them.

Unless the mixture produces a notable respiratory reaction, it is unusual to find any significant lowering of the level of anxiety. When a full-capacity inhalation of the mixture fails to elicit hyperventilation, its effect can often be augmented by one or more of the following maneuvers: asking the patient to hold his breath for as long as he can after inhaling, requesting two or more inhalations in succession, or raising the concentration of carbon dioxide, to as much as 100 percent, if necessary.

After each inhalation, the therapist asks the patient to state the *sud* level of anxiety, which he records by the convenient notation illustrated in the following example:

"Carbon dioxide–oxygen (X5) 60 → 45 → 35 → 25 → 20 → 20."

This notation indicates that four inhalations brought subjective anxiety down from 60 to 20 and that a fifth inhalation had no effect. The failure of the score to go lower is the reason for terminating administration of the gas. While a level of 20 is not ideal, it is self-evident that a patient's efforts at relaxation are far more likely to reduce anxiety to zero from that level than from the original 60 *suds*.

In about four-fifths of neurotic subjects, pervasive anxiety responds to carbon dioxide inhalations (Wolpe, 1958, p. 169). On the other hand, schizophrenic anxiety seems never to decrease and sometimes gets worse, which gives the inhalations some value as a diagnostic test, simpler but far less reliable than pupillography (Rubin, 1970).

The mechanism of the anxiety-reducing effect of carbon dioxide–oxygen mixtures is not known. It has been suggested (Wolpe, 1958) that it might result from reciprocal inhibition of anxiety by the immediate responses to the gas, by the postinhalation reactive relaxation, or both. One thing that seems reasonably certain is that the effect is not a direct pharmacological one dependent upon the presence of carbon dioxide in the body, for any surfeit of the gas is dissipated in a matter of minutes (Gellhorn, 1967); yet one or two inhalations sometimes removes pervasive anxiety for weeks or months, and usually for at least a good many hours (Wolpe, 1958). Exposure to a specific anxiety-evoking stimulus situation seems always to be prerequisite to reestablishing the pervasive anxiety that has been removed by the inhalations; and it is only as long as a patient is able to avoid significant exposure that he can be free from pervasive anxiety. Only a conditioning hypothesis appears to be consonant with these facts. Leukel and Quinton's (1964) observations are pertinent. They found that the acquisition of avoidance conditioning in rats was impaired by the administration of carbon dioxide. The sooner the gas was given after the conditioning, the greater was the negative effect.

Granted that carbon dioxide has its effects due to a learning process, it is both interesting and of practical importance to know precisely how it works. The first step toward determining what components of the procedure are relevant was a controlled study by Slater and Leavy (1966), who found that neither the act of inhaling air from anaesthetic equipment nor mimicking the deep respiratory movements that carbon dioxide induces decreased pervasive anxiety, in contrast to administering the gas mixture. The possibility of a suggestive effect of *strong* stimulation remained to be considered. In an experiment conducted by Weinreb (1966), however, the strong nasal stimulation produced by sniffing aromatic spirits of ammonia failed to reduce pervasive anxiety. It was thus unlikely that the effects of carbon dioxide could be ascribed to suggestion provoked by a very strong sensory experience. On the other hand, Mack (1970) found amyl nitrite inhalations to be almost as effective as carbon dioxide. Since amyl nitrite also evokes powerful autonomic responses, these might be competitive with anxiety. It is interesting that Dexter (1982) has reported evidence that carbon dioxide mixtures may abort migraine attacks which vasodilators, like amyl nitrite, have long been known to do.

Much more experimental work needs to be done. At the moment, it seems likely that carbon dioxide diminishes pervasive anxiety by eliciting a powerful anxiety-inhibiting excitation. As noted above (p. 199), the excitatory effects of the gas can also be used to decondition specific anxiety habits. A pilot psychophysiological study (Shmavonian & Wolpe, 1972) indicated that after an inhalation, the pulse slows and skin conductance falls. A more thoroughgoing study by Ley and Walker (1973) extended these observations. They gave ten adult neurotic subjects single, full-capacity inhalations of a mixture of

65% carbon dioxide and 35% oxygen, and compressed air to a second group of ten subjects. Immediately before and two minutes after the administration of either gas, they determined subjective units of disturbance, heart rate, and systolic and diastolic blood pressure. The carbon dioxide–oxygen group showed a decrease in diastolic blood pressure, and a significantly greater decrease in subjective anxiety than the compressed-air group.

It is of interest that Haslam (1974) observed that carbon dioxide reduces the anxiety only of those patients who are made anxious by lactate infusions (Pitts & McClure, 1967). He suggested that lactate infusion might afford a screening test for patients who would benefit from carbon dioxide therapy.

For the use of carbon dioxide for the treatment of specific fears, see p. 199.

THE USE OF DRUGS FOR SPECIFIC DECONDITIONING

From reports published during the past half-century both in Russia (e.g., Pavlov, 1941) and in the United States (Dworkin, Raginsky, & Bourne, 1937; Masserman & Yum, 1946), it was evident that lasting recovery or improvement could be procured in neurotic animals by keeping them under the influence of such sedative drugs as bromides, barbiturates, or alcohol for long periods. It is likely, although this was not always specifically stated in the reports, that at various times while under the influence of the drugs, the animals were exposed to stimuli conditioned to their neurotic reactions. But none of these experimenters deliberately and systematically arranged for exposure to the stimuli to occur during the action of the drugs.

This was done for the first time in an experimental study by Miller, Murphy, & Mirsky (1957). Using electric shock as the unconditioned stimulus, they conditioned four groups of rats to perform an avoidance response at the presentation of a buzzer. For the purpose of studying extinction of the avoidance response under different conditions, the animals of two of the groups received injections of saline, and those of the other two groups injections of chlorpromazine on each of four consecutive days. One of the two saline-injected groups (Group I) and one of the two chlorpromazine-injected groups (Group II) received 15 unreinforced presentations of the buzzer on each of the four days, while the animals of the other two groups were simply returned to the living cage after receiving their injections. During these four days, Group II animals made far fewer avoidance responses (less than 5 percent of trials) than Group I (more than 70 percent of trials). On the fifth and subsequent days, when all groups were given unreinforced trials without receiving any further injections, Group II manifested a much lower percentage of avoidance responses than any of the other groups. Whereas the other groups showed an average of about 60 percent avoidance responses, Group II showed only about 20 percent; and in 11 of the 15 animals that comprised the group, the level of avoidance did not go above that observed during the four days under the influence of the drug. That this lasting therapeutic effect was related to the autonomic inhibitory action of the chlorpromazine and not to the suppression of motor responses was indicated by repeating the experiment with phenobarbital in a dosage that had previously been equated with chlorpromazine in terms of motor retardation effects. In the animals that were given phenobarbital, no diminished level of avoidance responses was found after stopping the drug. It is crucial to note that chlorpromazine had lasting effects only if the opportunity for relearning was afforded during the administration of the agent: the chlorpromazine-injected animals that were not exposed to the buzzer at that time showed undiminished avoidance to the buzzer when the drug was stopped.

It is reasonable to think that reciprocal inhibition was the mechanism of the observed relearning. The animals were, through earlier conditioning, capable of responding also to other stimuli in the environment where the buzzer was heard; but without the "protection" of the chlorpromazine the avoidance response to the buzzer would be overwhelmingly strong. In animals who had been given chlorpromazine any remnant of the avoidance response (and concomitant anxiety) could have been reciprocally inhibited by whatever responses were being evoked by other environmental stimuli at the time. Obviously, this explanation calls for systematic study, but some support for it is given by Berkun's (1957) observation that animals in whom weak anxiety-cum-avoidance responses have been conditioned, can overcome these responses by mere exposure, first to situations similar to those associated with the original conditioning, and then to the original situation.

Clearly, if the paradigm of the Miller, Murphy, and Mirsky experiment can be extended to human clinical neuroses, great therapeutic economies are possible. The crucial therapeutic events take place in life. The therapist's main role is to establish that a particular drug is effectively tranquilizing in a certain dosage. Thereafter, he can set up a systematic exposure program and need only check occasionally. But astonishingly, there has still been no systematic clinical investigation in the ensuing quarter-century since their 1957 study.

Encouraging results have emerged from experimental treatment of individual cases, as well as from some incidental observations in a study by Winkelman (1955). Winkelman gave his patients chlorpromazine for six months or more in doses sufficient to obtain marked diminution of neurotic symptoms, and then gradually withdrew the drug. He found that improvement persisted for at least six months after the withdrawal in 35 percent of the patients. Unfortunately, there was no control study to show what would happen to patients who would have been given a placebo.

Since 1956, I have repeatedly employed *in vivo* desensitization that parallels that of the above experiment of Miller et al., using a variety of drugs. The patient must consistently take the drug in advance of exposure to a disturbing situation. Some find themselves later not having the expected disturbance when exposed without the drug. To achieve this result, the drug has to be administered in such a way that no significant anxiety is ever produced by exposure to relevant situations. To take an early example: finding that the severe classroom anxiety experienced by a college student was markedly ameliorated by meprobamate, I kept him on an adequate dosage of the drug on every school day for six weeks. Then I gave him a drugfree test day on which he found his anxiety to have diminished by 40 percent from its original level. A second test after six more weeks showed a further 30 percent decrement of the anxiety—an overall improvement of about 70 percent. Among other cases in which I achieved complete recovery, I may mention a fear of physical deformities for which codeine was the drug used, a barber's chair phobia for which I used meprobamate and alcohol (see also Erwin, 1963), and an airplane phobia that was overcome by the use of alcohol on three flights of about an hour's duration each.

There were also reports by others during the 1960s of successful treatments by such means. Reference has already been made (p. 224) to the lasting effects that sometimes follow when premature ejaculation is controlled by anxiety-inhibiting drugs (Drooby, 1964a); and among some cases of stuttering treated by meprobamate by Maxwell and Paterson (1958) was that of a 25-year-old butcher who was eventually able to dispense with the drug and still maintain marked speech improvement.

It later became apparent that drugs of the diazepine group, such as Librium, Valium, and Serax, were especially valuable in treatment of this kind, because unlike meprobamate, their tranquilizing effects increase with increasing dosage, usually without much in the way of adverse drowsiness, except in high dosage. My own interest in the potentialities of this group of drugs was first aroused by Miller (1967), who reported using Librium in four phobic cases. In his first two cases, a woman with a fear of eating in public and a man with agoraphobia, doses of 50 and 75 mg, respectively, were needed. Miller states that, "The medication was taken only for the purpose of desensitization and never on a routine basis. The patients 'planned' a phobic exposure, took the medication, waited until it began to exert its effect and then exposed themselves to the phobic situation (in real life, not in fantasy). The course of the therapy was four weeks in one case and six weeks in the other." Both patients were completely free of their phobias without the use of any medication when followed up six months after the treatment.

The first case with whom I systematically employed Librium in this way was a physician in whom a year previously a severe emotional reaction to noise had been conditioned when he had been exposed to insistent hammering while trying to sleep in a hotel. The sensitivity had generalized to other noises, of which the most distressful had become automobile horns, perhaps because of their frequency. He had improved moderately on relaxation and a masking procedure involving white noise. He was then instructed to determine the dose of Librium that could entirely block his emotional response to noise, and to take this dose (which was 30 mg) in all circumstances in which he could anticipate being exposed to any considerable amount of honking. This schedule led to very marked diminution of the response without the drug in the course of four months.

Case 39

In recent years I have used mainly diazepam for drug-medication *in vivo* desensitization. It was impressively effective in Mr. S., a 52-year-old man who when first seen had been severely disabled by agoraphobia for a period of 16 years. The history of his problem is given on p. 29. The key precipitating event was that, while taking a woman home because he thought she was choking, he noticed that he himself was having trouble breathing and was very anxious. From that time onward he was fearful of venturing away from his apartment. In addition, he frequently had paroxysmal anxiety attacks of considerable severity that would last from a few minutes to several hours. He had made a practical adjustment to his symptoms by moving into an office located a block away from his apartment. Nevertheless, as he put it, "I suffered constant agony from the anxieties. I would perspire to the extent that even in the winter my shirts would be drenched."

Soon after the agoraphobia began, Mr. S. had consulted a psychoanalyst, whom he went on seeing for ten years without improvement. Then he had gone for two years to an alleged behavior therapist who had persisted for months with standard desensitization although Mr. S. repeatedly told him that imagined scenes aroused no anxiety, and had thereafter had him "force himself" to go out alone on very stressful excursions that accomplished nothing. Mr. S. had then gone to another psychoanalyst for a year who made him worse. When he stopped seeing him, Mr. S. improved somewhat. He had been out of therapy for about a year when he came to see me. He was brought to my office by his mother, since he was too fearful to drive alone.

The analysis of the case revealed a classically conditioned fear of separation from "base" that increased with distance. Since Mr. S. could not imagine realistically, he would have to be treated *in vivo*. But this could not be done on the basis of an ordinary program of *in vivo* exposures because he had a baseline anxiety level of 20–30 *suds* at all times, which would have to be under control before any therapeutic program could begin. The first step in this direction was to show him how to control hyperventilation (p. 283). The feasibility of using diazepam to control anxiety was suggested by the fact that he had been somewhat calmed by 5 to 10 mg doses that a previous therapist had prescribed. We found that 25 mg of Valium brought his baseline anxiety down to about 5 *suds*. He was then given the assignment of going one block from home in a particular direction, while under the protection of 25 mg of diazepam. This raised his anxiety level to 20; but after seven repetitions he was able to walk that distance without his anxiety rising above the baseline.

Increasing distances were then assigned one by one. When he could walk five blocks comfortably, he began to drive his car alone; within three weeks he was able to dispense with the services of his mother as chauffeur. Monitoring his own responses, he thereafter took increasingly long drives, and as he went along, he found it possible to decrease the dose of diazepam. To take a trip of 20 miles eventually required only 5 mg.

I saw Mr. S. for a total of 26 sessions over 18 months—weekly for three weeks, biweekly for six months, and subsequently monthly. He was eventually able to go any distance with only occasional mild anxiety, keeping 5 mg of diazepam in his pocket as a "precaution." At a three-year follow-up his recovery had been fully maintained.

Two points must be underlined with regard to programs of *in vivo* systematic desensitization using tranquilizing drugs. First, the effectiveness of such programs, in contrast to flooding (Chapter 12), almost certainly depends upon insuring that *high-anxiety evocation never occurs,* for whenever it does, it may be expected to recondition a substantial degree of anxiety and lose hard-won ground. Second, the hazard of addiction is small when the duration of drug treatment is thus limited. As neurotic reactions are deconditioned, the dosages required for symptomatic relief become less, so that it is often possible to dispense with medication altogether a good while before the conclusion of therapy.

IMAGINAL SYSTEMATIC DESENSITIZATION WITH INTRAVENOUS ANXIETY INHIBITORS

Methahexitone sodium, which goes under the trade names of Brietal and Brevital, has been used for some time as a means of tranquilization for the purposes of desensitization. It is regarded by some of its users (Friedman, 1966; Friedman & Silverstone, 1967) as a primary anxiety-inhibiting agent. Others, like Reed (1966) and Brady (1966), regard it as essentially an adjuvant to relaxation, and always give relaxation instructions when using it. A controlled study by Mawson (1970) suggests that methohexital is not only a self-sufficient anxiety-inhibiting agent, but is significantly more effective than relaxation.

Brady (1966) has made particular use of methohexital in cases of frigidity and has described his use of it with great clarity. After an introductory explanation, he has the patient relax comfortably in a reclining chair and starts the injection of a 1 percent solution:

> During the 2–4 minutes required for the drug to have its maximum effect, suggestions of calm and relaxation are given such as might be used to induce hypnosis. When a deeply relaxed state is attained, the patient is instructed to imagine the first or weakest scene in the hierarchy. For example, "Now I want you to imagine as vividly as possible that you and your husband are seated in the living room, fully clothed, and he is kissing you affectionately on the lips. Visualize this scene—imagine yourself there—what you might hear and what you might see. You remain calm and relaxed." The patient is permitted to visualize this scene for about 2 minutes and is then instructed to stop thinking of this scene and simply relax. After a minute of rest, the same scene is again suggested for about 3 minutes. After another rest period, and assuming that no anxiety is evident, the next scene in the hierarchy is suggested, and so forth. . . . Brevital is cleared from the body at such a rapid rate that usually the relaxant and sedative effect of the drug is appreciably diminished after 4–5 minutes. Hence, an additional amount is usually required after this time. During a typical session, a total of 50 to 70 mg. are administered. After the last suggested scene is terminated, the patient is allowed to remain recumbent in the chair for about 10 minutes (p. 73).

Four of Brady's five cases were greatly improved in a mean of 11.5 sessions. Follow-ups did not reveal relapse or new symptoms.

A drug of a much earlier vintage, thiopental sodium (Pentothal), may regain its lost prominence in psychiatry if the findings of Hussain (1971) are confirmed. Everybody who was on the psychotherapeutic scene during World War II can recall the vogue of narcoanalysis and the great hopes that were pinned on it as a shortcut to fundamental psychotherapy. The narcosis induced by intravenous Pentothal made it easy for soldiers with war neuroses to recount in vivid detail the incidents during which their neuroses had begun. It seemed to provide an immediate conduit to material trapped in the recesses of the "unconscious mind," enabling rapid derepression. In short, it promised the presumed benefits of instant psychoanalysis. The promise was not borne out by results, and the method fell out of favor. Hussain (1971) reports the treatment of 40 patients with agoraphobia and other severe phobias, 20 by desensitization and 20 by flooding. Half of each group had their first five treatment sessions under Pentothal and the second five without the drug, and in the other half the order was reversed. It was found that the Pentothal made little difference to desensitization, but very greatly increased the effectiveness of flooding. Flooding under Pentothal produced much more change than any of the other three therapeutic arrangements. It is, however, worth noting that Hussain's subjects showed virtually no change when flooded without Pentothal, a finding that contrasts strongly with those of others who have worked with this method (see Chapter 12).

Yeung (1968) has reported the successful treatment of a subway phobia and of snake phobias on the basis of a single large intravenous injection of diazepam. Pecknold, Raeburn, and Poser (1972) gave intravenous injections of this drug to two patients who were too anxious to be able to calm themselves by muscle relaxation. The drug-induced calmness in each patient was used for desensitization, but after a few sessions, it was found that the desensitization could be continued with the calmness of muscle relaxation alone.

12

Procedures Involving
Strong Anxiety Evocation

Contrasting with the desensitization strategies and the weak anxiety responses they employ are treatments that involve strong responses. The classical example is abreaction, in which strong emotional responses are stirred up by recall of the distressing experiences by which the neurotic anxiety was conditioned. In recent years, methods have emerged that evoke strong responses directly by exposing the patient either to real stimuli that are highly disturbing or to corresponding imaginary situations. These methods are the "flooding" techniques.

Flooding techniques belong very properly to behavior therapy because they aim to change the disturbed behavior by directly evoking it. Flooding can be instituted at will, and its components can be quantitatively varied. Abreaction, on the other hand, is not strictly a behavior therapy technique because all that the therapist can do is try to create conditions to trigger its occurrence. When it occurs, both its content and its outcome are unpredictable. Nevertheless, it could well turn out that abreaction and flooding work through the same processes. There is a published example of my own in which both figured (Wolpe, 1958, p. 197).

ABREACTION

Abreaction is operationally defined as the reevocation with strong emotional accompaniment of a fearful past experience. Some abreactions are followed by therapeutic changes, while others are not and may even leave the patient worse off than he was before. If we could predict which individuals would respond favorably to it, and could induce it at will, we would expedite recovery in many cases. As matters stand, the induction of abreaction is unreliable, and its effects unpredictable. It would seem, however, that in some neurotic patients the unadaptive emotional responses have been conditioned to intricate stimulus compounds that neither current nor contrived stimulus situations can adequately cover; and then attempted abreaction would have high priority (Wolpe, 1958, p. 198)—or, at least, it may be very desirable to use the recalled images of the causal situation in therapeutic endeavors.

Contrary to the common belief, the therapeutic efficacy of abreaction, as Grinker and Spiegel's (1945) experiences with war neuroses showed, bears no relation to the previous *accessibility* to recall of the abreacted experiences. The one apparent essential, to give it a chance of being beneficial, is for it to take place in a protected setting such as is afforded by the psychotherapeutic relationship (Grinker & Spiegel, 1945). This observation was the basis for the suggestion (Wolpe, 1958, p. 196) that beneficial therapeutic effects obtained during abreaction might be a special case of nonspecific therapeutic effects (see p. 326). In other words, abreaction succeeds when anxiety is inhibited by emotional responses that the therapeutic situation induces in the patient. It is suggested below that flooding may operate through the same process.

Abreactions take place in a variety of circumstances. Sometimes they arise unbidden, during history taking or systematic desensitization.

Case 40: Abreaction During Desensitization

A truck driver had, following an accident, a marked phobia for driving (in addition to considerable pervasive anxiety). After training in relaxation and the construction of a hierarchy on the theme of driving, he was asked during his first desensitization session to imagine himself sitting at the wheel of a car that was stationary and whose engine was not running. He suddenly began to verbalize the details of the accident, broke into a sweat, and became very agitated. After about a minute, when the reaction subsided, he was asked to open his eyes. When he did so, he appeared tired but relieved, and said that he was no longer afraid to drive a truck. The test of reality proved him right.

Case 41: Abreaction During History Taking

Another example of unscheduled abreaction occurred in a 50-year-old lawyer who had been vaguely tense for decades, and who had come for treatment mainly because of increasing insomnia. During instruction in assertive behavior, he began to talk of his childhood and mentioned that though his family had been very poor he would never take anything from other people. He recounted an incident at school when, being a good athlete, he had taken part in a race and had been the only contestant without spiked shoes. He had proudly refused to accept a pair as a handout from the school. He became very agitated and tearful during this narration. At the next interview, a week later, he said that he was feeling better and that the average duration of his sleep had gone up from four to six hours per night. At this interview he abreacted at telling the story of a friend in the Army toward whom he had been aggressive and who had been killed within a month of the aggressive incident. Further abreactions were subsequently deliberately induced in relation to this story under hypnosis. Each of these abreactions, though weaker than the first one, was followed by improvement. With the addition of assertive training and desensitization to receiving praise and favors, an apparently complete recovery was obtained in a total of 15 sessions.

If the therapist wishes to try to bring about an abreaction, there are several courses open to him. He may endeavor, either with or without hypnosis, to plunge the patient into reexperiencing some past situation *known* to be highly disturbing. He may also try to gain access to unknown material by asking the hypnotized patient to fantasize an unpleasant or fearful event out of the past. An impressive case of successful hypnotic abreaction of a war neurosis after 20 years was recently described by Leahy and Martin (1967). It is sometimes worth trying the "age-regression" technique in which the patient imagines himself back in past phases of his life, starting relatively recently and then going back year by year. I have used this technique very occasionally, but have not seen the dramatic effects reported by others. As Barber (1969) has shown, it produces a restimulating, not a reliving.

The most practical way of pursuing an abreaction is by means of drugs. The first drug to gain widespread interest for this purpose was pentobarbital (Pentothal) whose use in this manner was introduced by Horsley (1936), and was used widely during World War II. At that time, and for a few years following, I occasionally used it in the hope of obtaining beneficial abreactions; but though abreactions did occur often, and were sometimes very vivid and exciting, in not a single case did I find marked and lasting benefit. Perhaps drugs that *elevate* arousal are more likely to lead to therapeutic abreactions. One possibility is di-ethyl ether (in its excitatory phase). The amphetamines (notably Methedrine) can also produce abreactions, but it has not been evident from the literature that these yield any lastingly beneficial after-effects, and sometimes (as in my own limited experience) sensitization may afterwards be found to have been increased. It may be said that because these drugs favor responses of the sympathetic division of the autonomic nervous system, they might militate against the therapeutic counterconditioning that we have presumed to be the basis of beneficial abreaction.

The technique of obtaining excitatory abreaction with ether has been fully described by Palmer (1944) and by Shorvon and Sargant (1947). While the patient lies on his back on a couch, the therapist talks to him informally about events that preceded the incident on which it is hoped he will abreact. The ether-soaked mask is held a few inches from the face, and then rather rapidly approximated. In a matter of minutes the patient becomes excited and, in a successful case, begins to recite the events that led to the precipitation of his neurosis. He is encouraged to "cry, shout, and struggle"; an assistant should be at hand to restrain excessive movement. Shorvon and Slater express the consensus when they state that one is much more likely to produce emotional release in an individual suffering from a recent traumatic neurosis than in one with a longstanding illness. But even with recent cases, they acknowledge there are many failures. A case was recently described by Little and James (1964), in which a neurosis originating in battle 18 years previously was progressively overcome in 5 sessions of ether abreactions. During the course of these, the patient pieced together a tremendously disturbing sequence of events that had precipitated the neurosis, beginning with his shooting of two young German soldiers while the three of them were in a ditch taking shelter from artillery shells.

Lysergic acid diethylamide (LSD 25) is another drug that might have abreactive potentialities if its effects could be brought under control. It was introduced into psychiatry because of its ability to promote vivid imagery and strong emotional responses. Beneficial abreactions have frequently been reported (e.g., Sandison, 1954), but cannot be relied on.

FLOODING

The first account[1] of a case that was successfully "flooded" is recorded in *Recent Experiments in Psychology* (Crafts et al., 1938, p. 322). (The case was treated by a physician whom the book does not name, and the two surviving authors have been unable to identify him.) The patient, a young woman, was afraid to ride in automobiles except over familiar roads, and had an especially intense fear of bridges and tunnels. One day, the physician ordered her to be driven from her home to his New York office. The distance was nearly 50 miles, and the route involved crossing a number of high bridges and traversing the Holland Tunnel. On the morning set for the ride, the woman was in a condition of panic, with violent nausea and faintness. Her terror persisted during much of the ride but diminished as she neared the refuge of her physician's house. The return trip provoked little or no emotional disturbance, and subsequent journeys over the same route proved increasingly easy for her.

---

[1]In the previous editions of this book I erroneously attributed this case to E. R. Guthrie. I had also misremembered some of its details.

Recent interest in flooding therapy started with the work of Malleson (1959) and Stampfl (1964). Malleson treated several cases by the evocation of intense anxiety on the supposition that experimental extinction of the anxiety habits would occur. One was an Indian student who was very afraid of examinations. He was asked to tell of the awful consequences that he felt would follow his failure—derision from his colleagues in India, disappointment from his family, financial loss. Then he was to try to imagine these things happening—the fingers of scorn pointed at him, his wife and mother in tears. At first, as he followed the instructions, his sobbings increased. But soon his trembling ceased. The effort needed to maintain a vivid imagining increased, and, inversely, the emotion he could summon began to ebb. Within half an hour he was calm. Malleson instructed him to repeat the exercise of experiencing his fears. When he felt a little wave of spontaneous alarm he was not to push it aside, but to try to experience it more profoundly and more vividly. If he did not spontaneously feel fear, every 20 or 30 minutes he was to make a special effort to try and do so, however difficult and ludicrous it might seem. He was seen twice a day over the next two days until his examination. Malleson states that, being an intelligent man and an assiduous patient, he practiced the exercises methodically and by the time of the examination reported himself almost totally unable to feel frightened. He had, as it were, exhausted the affect in the situation. He passed his examination without apparent difficulty.

Stampfl's strategy, which also relies on the patient's imagination, is called implosive therapy. In his early writings, quoted by London (1964), Stampfl expressed the view that if the patient were insistently exposed to the conditioned anxiety-producing stimulus situations, and the anxiety was not reinforced (by an unconditioned stimulus), the anxiety-response habit would extinguish. He would, accordingly, arrange for the frightening stimulus to be presented in circumstances from which the subject could not escape. The resulting continuous exposure to the stimulus was expected to cause it to lose all power to elicit anxiety. Stampfl advocated using every resource to frighten the patient as much as possible and for as long as possible at each sitting. The patient was made to imagine himself realistically in the relevant fear situation, while the therapist described in great detail the most vivid horrors possible.

Although in later accounts, implosion therapists (e.g., Stampfl & Levis, 1967; Levis, 1980) have continued to stress maximal stimulation as a matter of principle, in practice they often invoke weaker stimuli in the initial phases. They prescribe an "avoidance serial cue hierarchy," and the hypothesized cues which are low on this hierarchy (that is, cues that have low anxiety loadings) are presented first. The incorporation of a gradual approach would seem to be inconsistent with Stampfl's original thesis. This is Stampfl and Levis' (1967) description of how they ascend the ladder of increasing stimulation:

Once the implosive procedure is begun, every effort is made to encourage the patient to "lose himself" in the part that he is playing and "live" the scenes with genuine emotion and affect. . . . The scenes which contained the hypothesized cues are described at first by the therapist. The more involved and dramatic the therapist becomes in describing the scenes, the more realistic the presentation, and the easier it is for the patient to participate. At each stage of the crisis an attempt is made by the therapist to obtain a maximal level of anxiety evocation from the patient. When a high-level anxiety is achieved, the patient is held on this level until some sign of spontaneous reduction in the anxiety-inducing value of the cues appears (extinction). The process is repeated, and again, at the first sign of spontaneous reduction of fear, new variations are introduced to elicit an intense anxiety response. This procedure is continued until a significant diminution of anxiety has resulted. . . . Between sessions the patient is instructed to reenact in his imagination the scenes which were presented during the treatment session. (p. 498)

The prescription of practice between sessions is noteworthy. However, its efficacy in accelerating progress has not been demonstrated.

One feature of the work of these authors is that while they base their methods on Mowrerian learning theory, they also assume the validity of psychoanalytic theorizing, and derive some of their scene material from it. Stampfl and Levis (1968) state that "castration dangers and Oedipal time conflicts are not foreign to the implosive therapy approach in that they are hypothesized to be a product of primary or secondary aversive conditioning events." Some of the scenes based upon psychoanalytic assumptions do evoke anxiety that diminishes in due course. The authors take this as evidence that such material has special therapeutic relevance. But this is not a fair conclusion, since a variety of stimulus material with the same essential elements may be expected to have similar anxiety-evoking consequences. It would be instructive to compare the effects of Freudian and non-Freudian images.

In the first edition of this book, I expressed reservations about the optimism and wide-ranging success with flooding claimed by implosive therapists (e.g., Levis & Carrera, 1967). I felt also that the method was not without risk. While I am now convinced of the wide efficacy of this method, and am satisfied that the risks are small, I still advocate a cautious attitude, for little is really known of the ingredients for success, and prolonged *in vivo* exposure does exacerbate some neuroses (see Case 45). The numerous outcome studies of recent years (Levis, 1980, p. 98) still do not include any that are unconfounded.

There are also good experimental grounds for caution. So far, nobody has cured an experimental neurosis simply by exposing the animal for long periods (hours or days) to the stimuli to which anxiety has been maximally conditioned (see, for example, Masserman, 1943; Wolpe, 1958; Appel, 1963). Goldstein (1972), in a tentative exploration of this matter, formed the impression that the anxiety response of neurotic cats to a conditioned auditory stimulus did not decline (and sometimes increased) if that stimulus was presented continuously or frequently, but that it did decline if presented following the presentation of a graded sequence of generalized stimuli.

It is quite clear that successful flooding requires *prolonged* exposure to anxiety-arousing stimulation. It is wise to employ only moderately strong anxiety-evoking stimuli to act on the patient for a relatively long term. The stimuli should continue until there is clear evidence of anxiety decrement in their presence, for this is the indication that the flooding has produced anxiety-response inhibition. If the stimulation is removed early, there is not enough time for the inhibitory process to develop, and the anxiety-drive reduction which follows removal reinforces the anxiety habit. This process, incidentally, appears to be the major reason for the resistance to extinction of neurotic habits, both animal and human (Wolpe, 1958, pp. 24–29).

The following experimental *in vivo* flooding seems to afford a clear example of a case in which moderating the stimulus input was indispensable to success.

Case 42: Multifaceted Experimental Flooding

The subject of the experiment was a woman in her late 20s with longstanding severe phobias for dead birds and for bats. She had heard of flooding and believed that it might be a rapid way of overcoming her phobias. At first, an attempt was made to induce it by images based on verbal descriptions, but very little emotion was aroused in this way. The decision was then made, with her full agreement, to subject her to real dead birds. (She agreed to the taking of repeated blood samples during the experiment so that the changes in cortisol levels provoked by the treatment could be measured.)

On the appointed day, the patient sat in a comfortable armchair, and an indwelling cannula was inserted into a vein in her left arm which was immobilized on a board to insure immobility. Baseline blood samples were taken by Dr. George Curtis for two hours. In the meantime, two dead birds, a small blackbird and a pheasant, had been prepared in accordance with the patient's description of what for her provided maximal stress—exposure of the neck by the removal of most of the feathers. The patient was then told that the blackbird would be brought in, and a vivid verbal description was given. This produced a certain amount of manifest uneasiness, and the patient reported some anxiety, but not much. She was then asked to close her eyes, whereupon the bird was brought in, held by the feet, with head dangling down, and in this position kept about seven feet away from her. She was asked to look at it, but refused. After two minutes, she shot a glance at the bird, and gave vent to a loud shriek and a great deal of generalized movement. She said that she would not look again. After gentle but firm coaxing, however, she did glance at it again with loud screams of terror and much movement. Her great reluctance to look at the bird made me try having it moved a little farther away—to about ten feet. She seemed pleased at this, and after half a minute or so, opened her eyes and looked at the bird for about three seconds, again screaming and contorting her body. She subsequently opened her eyes for progressively longer periods, and the fifth time she was able to scan the bird continuously. Even then, though she was relatively undisturbed most of the time, she would occasionally relapse into screaming. When questioned about this, she said that at those times the bird assumed an aspect which made it seem as though it was getting "under her skin," suggesting a perceptual organization process of turning on and off of the impact of a stimulus.

Eventually, these "spontaneous" outbursts ceased, and then an interesting thing was noticed. Every time the bird was jerked or the angle of presentation changed, there was a further flurry of anxiety. After about five minutes, the patient could no longer be stirred up, no matter what was done with the bird at ten feet, though rating her basal level at 20 *suds*. It seemed as though all the angles and varieties of movement had been deconditioned at ten feet. The bird was now brought closer through three stages until it was only about three feet from the patient. Again, at each approximation, there was a need to present the bird at different angles and with different movements, but the reactions were smaller and quite quickly overcome. At this point, it was suggested that she stroke the bird's feathers. She resisted this, but allowed herself to be persuaded to move her finger closer and closer, and eventually touched it. Thereafter, she was able to go on to stroking the bird with decreasing anxiety. The next step was to get her to hold the bird herself, which she finally did, without any increase in the anxiety level beyond the 20 *suds* baseline level. At a second session, anxiety fell to zero in 20 minutes.

The following cases illustrate how various are the ways in which flooding may be done and how diverse the stimulus antecedents of the anxiety. As in the case of desensitization, the applicability of flooding extends far beyond the limits of the classical phobia. Observe that, although persevering exposure to anxiety-evoking stimulation is a cardinal feature of flooding, its effective duration was quite brief in Case 44. By the contrast, we have seen equally successful cases in which, at the initial flooding session, anxiety showed its first decrease after about 45 minutes (e.g., from 90 to 80 *suds* in a case who feared to be seen urinating and who was treated *in vivo*).

Case 43: Successful Imaginal Flooding

Imaginal stimuli were employed with Dr. E., a dentist who had had an extraordinarily severe and widespread neurosis, that had in most respects responded very well to varied and sometimes prolonged applications of the commoner behavior therapy techniques, such as assertive training and systematic desensitization. But two disabling neurotic constellations remained—an inability to give dental injections because of a fear of the patient dying in the chair, and an extravagant fear of ridicule. Since attempts to desensitize Dr. E. to these were making insufferably slow progress, I decided to try flooding. Under light hypnosis he was asked to imagine giving a patient a mandibular block, then, withdrawing the syringe, standing back and seeing the patient slump forward, dead. Dr. E. became profoundly disturbed, sweating, weeping, and wringing his hands. After a minute or so, noticing that the reaction was growing weaker, I terminated the scene and told him to relax. Two or three minutes later, the same scene evoked a similar, but weaker reaction. The sequence was given three more times, at the last of which no further reaction was observed. Dr. E. said that he felt he had been through a wringer—exhausted, but at ease. At the next session, the fear of ridicule was introduced. Dr. E. imagined that he was walking down the middle of a brilliantly lighted ballroom with people on both sides pointing their fingers at him and laughing derisively. At the fifth flooding session, it was clear that nothing remained to be treated. Four years later, at an interview with Dr. E., it was evident that his recovery had been fully maintained. The same was noted 23 years later.

Case 44: Successful *in vivo* Flooding

In vivo flooding is exemplified by the case of Mrs. C., a woman with agoraphobia so severe that she was unable to go on her own more than two blocks by car without anxiety. Attempts at systematic desensitization had failed— apparently because she was unable to imagine scenes realistically. After other measures had also proved ineffective, I decided to persuade her to expose herself to flooding, which had to be *in vivo* because of the demonstrated inadequacy of her imagination. After resisting strenuously for some weeks, she agreed to take the plunge. Plans were made for her husband to place her, unaccompanied, on a commercial aircraft one hour's flight away from the airport where I would await her. When Mrs. C. in due course alighted from the plane, she walked toward me smiling. She had felt increasing anxiety for the first 15 minutes of the flight, and then gradual subsidence of it. During the second half of the journey she had been perfectly comfortable. She flew home alone the next day without trouble. This single experience resulted in a great increase in her range of comfortable situations away from home. She was now able, without anxiety, to drive her car alone three or four miles from home and to make unaccompanied trips by plane without any anxiety. Plans to build up this improvement by further treatment were foiled by distance plus other practical obstacles.

Case 45: Unsuccessful *in vivo* Flooding

The following is an example of a patient who was made worse by attempts to "flood" him. Dr. K. was a physician with a severe phobia for insane people and insane behavior. He was in military service, and soon after he began to consult me was offered a transfer to a psychiatric hospital. I encouraged this, thinking that the phobia might be overcome by flooding. On my advice, he exposed himself continuously to the presence of schizophrenic patients, sometimes for hours at a stretch. Far from decreasing, his reactions to these patients grew progressively worse, and in addition, he developed a rising level of pervasive anxiety. By the end of the second day he was so extremely anxious that he had to be relocated. He had become much more sensitive than ever before to "insane stimuli." He was now a far more difficult problem than when I had first seen him, and only with much effort was his neurosis overcome by desensitization.

Mechanism of Flooding Therapy

To make the most of flooding, we will have to understand how it works. Even though it was originally performed by Malleson and by Stampfl (see above) on the paradigm of experimental extinction, it seems most unlikely that it leads to change on the same basis as extinction. Extinction is defined as the progressive weakening displayed by a habit when the response concerned is evoked repeatedly without reinforcement. In the case of motor habits, the more strongly the response is evoked, the more rapidly it extinguishes (Hull, 1943, p. 279). In the case of conditioned anxiety, the experimentally observed relationship between the strength of the evoked response and the weakening of its habit is exactly the opposite: when anxiety is relatively weak as in most aversive conditioning, it extinguishes relatively easily; when its arousal is strong, there is no response decrement. There is uniform nonextinguishability of experimental neuroses by prolonged exposure to maximal stimulation (see Chapter 4). The clinical failures of flooding, as in Case 45, and similar cases—such as the many aerophobias that do not improve in repeated fear-filled flights—are of a piece with this. It is also relevant that whereas in snake phobius, Wolpin and Raines (1966) obtained good results by 5–10 minute periods of flooding; Rachman (1966) failed entirely with 100 two-minute floodings (over 10 sessions) with spider phobias. If extinction had been at work, Rachman should on quantitative grounds, have done much better.

Our own experience and Stampfl's clinically derived gradualness indicated that in order for flooding to succeed, the fear must be masterable. If it is, by what process does anxiety habit decrement take place? One straw in the wind is the observation that, generally, the therapist has been directly involved in the immediate therapeutic situation when flooding has diminished an anxiety response. It is possible that the anxiety is inhibited by the patient's response to the therapist, which seems also to be the instrument of non-specific therapeutic change (p. 326) and also of abreaction (p. 237). Another possibility is that if the stimulation is not so strong as to cause the subject to withdraw or "switch off" entirely, the continuing strong stimulation may lead, after a varying time, to transmarginal inhibition (Pavlov, 1927; Gray, 1964) of the response (see discussion on p. 50). The relevance and the possible mode of operation of this mechanism remain entirely unexplored. However, the suggestion made in the first edition of this book that an epinephrine rebound might be behind this, is now clearly untenable. Change of stimulus would not have renewed anxiety as it did in Case 42 if this were the mechanism.

An "explanation" of flooding that has become quite prominent of late is that it is the result of "exposure" (Marks, 1975, 1976). This is really rather a meaningless proposition since all unlearning involves exposure in some sense to the conditioned stimulus. The important point is to determine the mechanism or mechanisms, or the combination of factors, that under certain circumstances result in exposure leading to habit increment, and under others to habit decrement.

EVALUATION
OF FLOODING THERAPY

There is no question that flooding is an important addition to the behavior therapist's repertoire. It must be realized, however, that compared with desensitization it is an unpleasant procedure and therefore should not be considered the method of first choice except where it can be shown to be significantly more effective than desensitization. The results of laboratory studies (Willis & Edwards, 1969; DeMoor, 1970; Mealiea & Nawas, 1971) dealing with the uniform subject matter of small-animal phobias also indicate that flooding is less effective than desensitization and, in contrast to the latter, somewhat liable to relapse. In early comparisons involving severe clinical phobias, flooding was reported to achieve better results than desensitization (Boulougouris, Marks, & Marset 1971; Gath & Gelder, 1971). The use of untrained therapists by the former created a bias against desensitization, but the same objection did not apply to Gath and Gelder's study, in which flooding was found to be more effective than desensitization in agoraphobia, but less effective in some other phobias. More recently, a carefully controlled study by the same group (Mathews et al., 1974) found no difference in the efficacy of the two methods. As will be illustrated in Chapter 15, however, behavior analysis points to the need for individualized treatment programs in agoraphobia.

One kind of case in which flooding has come to be the treatment of choice is the obsessive-compulsive neurotic who is characterized by fear and avoidance of "contamination." We will consider this more fully in Chapter 15.

PARADOXICAL INTENTION

As far as anxiety is concerned, this method, like flooding, invokes high response levels. Paradoxical intention was developed by Victor Frankl (1960) from the theoretical standpoint of existential psychiatry, where it has had a dominating role (Frankl, 1975; Gerz, 1966). The practice of paradoxical intention is guided by the explanation that "if the patient were to try intentionally to bring on these symptoms he would not only find difficulty in doing so, but also change his attitude towards his neurosis." While rapid recovery is sometimes achieved, a good many cases require treatments given repeatedly over several months. One of Gerz's (1966) cases was a 29-year-old woman who had fears of heights, of being alone, of eating in a restaurant in case she vomited, and of going into supermarkets, subways, and cars. She was instructed to try to expose herself to the conditions that she feared. She was to try to vomit while dining out with her husband and friends, so as to create the greatest possible mess. She was to drive to markets, hairdressers, and banks "trying to get as panicky as possible." In six weeks she had lost her fears in her home situation, and shortly thereafter drove all by herself to Gerz's office, about five miles from her home. Four months later, she drove with her husband to New York City, 100 miles away, across the George Washington Bridge, back through the Lincoln Tunnel, and attended a goodbye party on the lower deck of an ocean liner. Gerz states that two years later she was free of symptoms.

Ascher (1978) has analyzed the behavioral components of paradoxical intention and has advocated its use within a framework of behavior analysis. Under such circumstances, it is a resource worth considering when the usual behavior therapy techniques are unsuccessful; but even then its effectiveness is a matter of trial and error (see Case 29). Its commonest use by behavior therapists has been in the treatment of insomnia (Ascher & Efran, 1978). In a controlled study, Ascher and Turner (1979) found that it was as effective as progressive relaxation or "stimulus control"—diminishing the impact of sleep-negative stimuli. Presumably, paradoxical intention would be effective in certain cases in which either of the other procedures failed. Solyom, Garza-Perez, Ledwidge, and Solyom (1972) conducted a pilot study to test the effectiveness of a modified paradoxical intention procedure in the amelioration of obsessive thoughts. Each of ten patients complaining of multiple obsessions was assigned a "target" thought and a "control" thought from among his own obsessions. Patients applied paradoxical intention (exaggerated attention) to the "target" thought, while control thought remained untreated. Five of the ten subjects reported that the "target" obsession was greatly reduced or eliminated, while the control obsession continued unabated.

13

Operant-Conditioning Methods

As described in Chapter 1, there is only one learning process. The distinction between respondent and operant conditioning is not in the nature of the conditioning, but in the fact that in the former nonvoluntary, especially autonomic, behavior is predominantly involved, whereas in the latter the behavior is predominantly motor. Some cognitive responses can also be reinforced by external rewards (Cautela, 1970). For recent wide-ranging accounts of operant conditioning, see Mackintosh (1974) and Rachlin (1976).

The conditioning of motor responses is certainly more obviously relatable to reinforcing events, and more clearly "under the control of its consequences" (e.g., reward or nonreward) than the conditioning of autonomic responses. The difference, however, is a matter of mode of reinforcement (p. 15ff). In fact, some autonomic responses can be brought under the control of reward contingencies (Kimmel, 1967; Miller & DiCara, 1968; Lang, 1968). But the resistance of neurotic anxiety responses to extinction is evidently due to negative reinforcement—the anxiety reduction that follows the removal of the organism from the conditioned stimuli (Wolpe, 1952).

The operant procedures that are used in clinical practice generally follow paradigms established by B. F. Skinner and his associates. If explicit applications of these paradigms do not figure very largely in the treatment of neuroses it is because neuroses are primarily autonomic habits. Nevertheless, we have noted the operant conditioning of motor responses that is part and parcel of assertive training. There are also numerous other unadaptive habits in neurotic patients in whose treatment operant procedures are central: for example, habits of interpersonal relating. Also, there is a wide range of unadaptive habits that have usually no particular relation to conditioned anxiety—such habits as nail biting, trichotillomania, enuresis, encopresis, chronic tardiness, and distractibility from assigned tasks. Because operant-conditioning methods have only a secondary role in the treatment of neuroses, they will only be reviewed here briefly. For clinical expositions, the reader is referred to Ayllon and Azrin (1968), Schaefer and Martin (1969), and Kalish (1981); for briefer accounts that introduce collections of cases, to Ullmann and Krasner (1965), Franks (1965), and Ulrich, Stachnik, and Mabry (1966).

Six operant-conditioning procedures are distinguishable: positive reinforcement, extinction, differential reinforcement, response shaping, punishment, and negative reinforcement. Consideration of punishment will be deferred to the context of aversion therapy in the next chapter. Differential reinforcement is a selective combination of positive reinforcement and extinction. Shaping is, in essence, a special case of positive reinforcement. Our discussion here will consequently be limited to positive reinforcement, negative reinforcement, and extinction.

POSITIVE REINFORCEMENT

Any state of affairs that, following a response, serves to increase the rate of responding may be called a reinforcer. When "reward" is that state of affairs, it is called a positive reinforcer. Food, water, sex, money, domination, approval, or affection are all operational reinforcers when they increase the rate (or strength) of a response in a given stimulus situation, as they will do under the appropriate conditions of hunger, thirst, and so on. Homme (1965) extended the range of reinforcers to include high-probability (preferred) behaviors on the strength of Premack's (1965) observation that these reinforce whatever low-probability behaviors they follow. When the rate of responding is increased by relief from anything aversive—pain, discomfort, or tension—we refer to this as "negative reinforcement."

Examples of the habit-building power of positive reinforcement are legion, ranging from pecking habits in pigeons to the most complex ceremonials of mankind. In the field of therapeutic behavior change, we have already noted that the motor behavior of assertion is reinforced by such consequences as the achievement of an interpersonal "victory" or the later approval of the therapist. Simple therapeutic examples are easy to find in the behavior problems of children. For example, a child may habitually scream to get what he wants because getting what he wants maintains the habit of screaming. Now, if the child is told, "You will never get it [e.g., a toy] if you scream; to get it you must say quietly, 'Please, may I have it?' "; if the new behavior is at once rewarded, this immediately increases the likelihood of his behaving in this new way on subsequent occasions. Consistently rewarding the new behavior results in displacing the old—assuming, of course, that the old behavior is not rewarded again.

The therapeutic potentialities of positive reinforcement have been strikingly demonstrated in recent years. Most of the earlier work was done on chronic schizophrenics, though it must at once be stated that "cure" of the psychosis is neither obtained nor claimed, but only change in particular habits. This is not surprising since a variety of evidence, e.g., genetic (Kallman, 1953), physiological (Rubin, 1970), and biochemical (Gottlieb & Frohman, 1972) suggests that schizophrenia is basically an organic illness (Wolpe, 1970). The organic abnormality seems to be directly responsible for some of the psychotic behavior, while at the same time predisposing the individual to the acquisition by learning of unadaptive habits that are often bizarre.

Lindsley (1956) was the first to explore the possibilities of operant-conditioning schedules in psychotic subjects. His work was later vastly extended by Ayllon and Azrin (1964, 1965). One of the clever treatment schedules devised by Ayllon (1963) is worth presenting at length. The patient was a 47-year-old schizophrenic woman who had been in a state hospital for nine years. Among other strange habits, she always wore an excessive amount of clothing—weighing about 25 pounds. In order to treat this, Ayllon had a scale placed at the entrance to the dining room. The requirement for entering (to receive food reinforcement) was a predetermined weight:

Initially, she was given an allowance of 23 lbs. over her current body weight. This allowance represented a 2 lb. reduction from her usual clothing weight. When the patient exceeded the weight requirement, the nurse stated in a matter-of-fact manner, "Sorry, you weigh too much, you'll have to weigh less." Failure to meet the required weight resulted in the patient missing the meal at which she was being weighed. Sometimes, in an effort to meet the requirement, the patient discarded more clothing than was required. When this occurred, the requirement was adjusted at the next weighing time to correspond to the limit set by the patient on the preceding occasion.

At the start of this experiment, the patient missed a few meals because she failed to meet the weight requirement, but soon thereafter she gradually discarded her superfluous clothing. First, she left behind odd items she had carried in her arms, such as bundles, cups and handbags. Next, she took off the elaborate headgear and assorted "capes" or shawls she had worn over her shoulders. Although she had worn 18 pairs of stockings at one time, she eventually shed these also.

At the end of the experiment, the patient's clothing weighed a normal three pounds and remained stable at this level. One result of dressing normally was her participation in small social events at the hospital. Another was that her parents took her out for the first time in nine years.

Anorexia nervosa is one of the few conditions classified as neurotic in which positive reinforcement has sometimes been successfully used as the main method. Some years ago, I was involved in the treatment of the first two cases for which positive reinforcement was used, one of which was reported in detail by Bachrach, Erwin, and Mohr (1965). This was a 37-year-old woman whose weight had fallen to 47 pounds despite various medical treatments. For the purposes of the operant-conditioning program, she was transferred from her attractive hospital room to a barren one that was furnished only with a bed, nightstand, and chair. Each of the three authors had one meal a day with her. The reinforcement schedule involved verbal reinforcement of movements associated with eating.

When the patient lifted her fork to move toward spearing a piece of food, the therapist would talk to her about something in which she might have an interest. The response required to elicit this conversation was then successively raised to lifting the food toward her mouth, chewing, and so forth. A similar schedule of increasing requirements was later applied to the amount of food she consumed. At first, any portion of the meal that was consumed would be a basis for a postprandial reinforcement (a radio, TV set, or phonograph would be brought in by the nurse at a signal from the experimenter); if she did not touch any of the food before her, no reinforcement would be given until the next meal. More and more of the meal had to be consumed for her to be reinforced until she eventually was required to eat everything on the plate. After two months, when she had gained 14 pounds, she was discharged to outpatient treatment, and positive reinforcement treatment was continued at home with the cooperation of her family. Eighteen months later her weight was 88 pounds.

A 16-year follow-up of this case has been reported by Erwin (1977). A number of other cases have also been successfully treated by operant methods (e.g., Hallsten, 1965; Blinder, Freeman, & Stunkard, 1970; Scrignar, 1971). Unfortunately, all too often, such cases have been summarily placed on operant schedules without adequate behavior analysis, with predictably unsatisfactory consequences. Some of these were the occasion for scathing comments by a psychoanalyst (Bruch, 1973), who extrapolated from the data to brand behavior therapy as "dangerous." As I pointed out in a rebuttal (Wolpe, 1975), it was *misuse* of behavioral principles that accounted for those results. It ill becomes psychoanalysts to be self-righteous about the failures of others. But what is important is that effective behavior therapy requires therapists who understand the complexities of conditioning and the importance of comprehending the stimulus-response structure of every problem.

While operant procedures have generally not had a wide role in the treatment of unadaptive fears, they can be very relevant in those for whose maintenance physical avoidance plays a major part. Ayllon, Smith, and Rogers'

(1970) treatment of a school phobia in an eight-year-old illustrates this. The problem was redefined as zero or low probability of school attendance. The implementation of techniques for increasing the probability involved getting the child's mother to withdraw the rewards of staying at home. Then, a home-based motivational system was used to reinforce school attendance, and refusal to attend school resulted in punishment. School attendance was generated quickly and maintained even after the procedures were withdrawn a month later. No "symptom substitution" was noticed either by the parents or the school officials within the nine months of follow-up.

Operant programs have in recent years been particularly widely applied to problem behavior in children. Much of the work has been directed at class-room behavior (e.g., Bijou & Ruiz, 1981; Homme et al., 1971; O'Leary & O'Leary, 1977; Patterson & Gullion, 1968), but psychiatric syndromes have also received a great deal of attention (see Daniels (1974) for many examples). Of special interest is a method described by Kimmel and Kimmel (1970) for treating nocturnal enuresis. The child, who may drink water and other liquids without restriction, is rewarded with cookies or other desired items for "holding in" his urine for increasing durations. At the beginning, the child is given the reward for inhibiting urination for five minutes after his first report of a need to urinate, and the period of inhibition is progressively lengthened. Apparently, a habit of inhibition of urination is established by this positive reinforcement. In three cases in which the method was used, complete cessation of bedwetting was achieved in about a week. Neale (1963) overcame several cases of encopresis by rewarding defecation at the toilet with candy. Similar cases were reported by Madsen (1965) and Tomlinson (1970). Edelman (1971) used a combination of negative and positive reinforcement to the same end.

The rewarding quality of the masturbatory orgasm appears to be a powerful agent for transferring male sexual interest from deviant objects to women (Marquis, 1970). The patient is instructed to masturbate to the point where he feels the inevitability of orgasm, using whatever fantasy is most arousing. Then he is to switch to the female fantasy that has previously been agreed on as appropriate. He is warned that he may experience some difficulty at first, but that he will not lose his sexual arousal at that point. After he has successfully shifted to the appropriate stimulus four or five times, he is instructed to start moving the introduction of the appropriate fantasy backward in time toward the beginning of masturbation. An attempt is made at the outset to get a commitment from the client never to continue picturing the inappropriate fantasy through the orgasm, whether in masturbation or overt sexual behavior. Any decrease in sexual arousal upon switching is seen as evidence that the client has exchanged fantasies too soon, and he is instructed to drop back to the original fantasy and switch at a higher level of sexual arousal. Of the 15 cases Marquis reported, five were cured, and seven much improved. The technique has not been subjected to systematic study, and the clinical reports of its efficacy are partly positive (e.g., LoPiccolo, Stewart, & Watkins, 1972: Van De Venter & Laws, 1978), and partly negative (e.g., Conrad & Wincze, 1976; Marshall, 1974).

Exploratory applications of operant-conditioning techniques to delinquent behavior (Schwitzgebel & Kolb, 1964; Burchard & Tyler, 1965) have yielded encouraging results. The former authors treated 40 adolescent delinquents by reinforcement procedures. A three-year follow-up study of 20 of them revealed a significant reduction in the frequency and severity of crime in comparison with a matched-pair control group. Burchard and Tyler produced a marked decrease in the "destructive and disruptive behavior" of a 13-year-old delinquent boy by systematically isolating him when he performed in an antisocial way and by rewarding socially acceptable behavior.

Thomas (1968) listed a number of rules for the effectiveness of positive reinforcement:

1. The response to be reinforced must first be emitted, otherwise reinforcement is impossible.
2. Reinforcement must not be delayed; in general, the more immediate the reinforcement, the better.
3. Reinforcement of every desired response emitted is most effective for establishing behavior.
4. Not reinforcing every desired response during response establishment, while less effective in achieving immediate high rates of responding, is generally more effective in producing responses that endure after reinforcement is terminated.
5. The stimuli suitable to reinforce one individual's behavior may not be the most appropriate for another. Recent research suggests that one important clue to what the reinforcing conditions are in the profile is simply the rank order of activities in which a person engages in his free time (see Premack, 1965; Homme, 1965).

Covert Positive Reinforcement

Cautela (1970, 1972, 1977; Cautela & Wall, 1980) introduced a procedure that he called "covert reinforcement." In this, the response to be reinforced and the reinforcer are both presented in imagination. Cautela reported that he had successfully employed covert reinforcement for phobias, obsessions, homosexuality, and obesity. The first step is to identify stimuli that will appropriately function as reinforcers. This can conveniently be done on the basis of the patient's responses to a reinforcement survey schedule (Cautela & Kastenbaum, 1967). Any item to which the patient indicates a high degree of pleasure is tested for visual clarity and for the ease with which the patient can conjure up its image. The patient must be able to evoke the image within about five seconds if the item is to be usable as a reinforcer.

The method is well exemplified in a case reported by Wisocki (1970). The patient had a neatness compulsion that included, among other things, the habit of folding articles of clothing again and again, smoothing them down more perfectly each time. In applying the covert-reinforcement procedure, the therapist instructed the patient to imagine herself in various situations involving two types of behavior: (1) refraining from repeating the obsessive-compulsive behavior, and (2) making responses that were antagonistic to that behavior. When the patient signalled imagining the appropriate response, the therapist immediately said "reinforcement," which was the cue for the patient to imagine a predetermined reinforcing item, such as walking in a forest, practicing ballet, or eating an Italian sandwich. Thus, the therapist would instigate a reinforcing image when the patient signalled that she was thinking, "I don't care if it is wrinkled; it doesn't matter," or if she imagined folding a laundered item quickly and putting it on top of the finished pile, even though it was a little wrinkled. This patient's obsessive-compulsive behaviors were eliminated in eight two-hour sessions. At a 12-month follow-up, there was no recurrence of the compulsive behavior.

While the covert-reinforcement procedure is often successful (and certainly gives the therapist much scope for inventiveness), it seems likely that when it is used to decondition anxiety, as in the above case, its mechanism is reciprocal inhibition and not positive reinforcement. In an analogue study on rat-fearful college students, Ladouceur (1974) found that those in whom the reinforcement *preceded* the approach response did as well (in contrast to a control group) as those given the standard sequence. Bajtelsmit and Gershamn (1976) made the same observation in students with test anxiety, having employed a more exact replication of Cautela's procedure.

NEGATIVE REINFORCEMENT

Negative reinforcement means increasing the rate or strength of a response by the contingent removal of a source of pain or tension. The therapeutic use of this strategy is sometimes complicated by the fact that the therapist has to introduce the source of pain in the first place, which may have countertherapeutic consequences.

A beautiful example of the operation of negative reinforcement is afforded by Ayllon's (1963) treatment of another habit of the patient referred to on p. 251—towel hoarding. This woman would collect and store large numbers of towels which the nursing staff would remove from her room about twice a week. Ayllon instructed the staff to stop the routine towel removal and, intermittently each day, to hand the patient a towel without comment. The patient was delighted at this new policy, and arranged her growing stock in neat piles, first on the dressing table and chair, and later on the floor and bed. When there were several hundred, the piles became unmanageable so that increasing numbers of them began to lie about the room in disorder. The patient now began to ask the staff to stop bringing the towels, but without avail. When the number reached 600, additional towels seemed to become aversive. One day, when there were 625 towels in the room, the patient seized the next towel that arrived and threw it out of the room, presumably to reduce the oppressiveness of the excess of towels somewhat. Since that towel did not come back, there was thus negative reinforcement of the act of discarding a towel. Thereafter, the patient progressively removed them and no more were given her. During the next 12 months the mean number of towels found in her room was 1.5.

Cautela (1970a) extended his covert-reinforcement idea to include covert negative reinforcement. He states that it is especially applicable to subjects who find it easier to evoke disagreeable images than pleasant ones. If the patient finds it unpleasant to be spoken to in a harsh tone, he will be asked to visualize this and, when he signals that the image is clear, to replace it by an image of the response to be increased. Great care is taken to insure that the patient can immediately withdraw from the aversive stimulus upon request and replace it with the response to be increased. If, after a number of trials, there is still an overlap, a new aversive stimulus is chosen. This technique has not been widely used, but Cautela (1970) reported success in 90 percent of his cases.

EXTINCTION

Extinction is the progressive weakening or diminishing frequency of a response when it is repeatedly evoked without being followed by a reinforcer. Its mechanism has been discussed on pp. 17ff.

A case of Ayllon and Michael (1959) is probably the earliest clinical example of a type of extinction program that is finding increasing use. The patient was a woman who for a period of two years had been entering the nurses' office on an average of 16 times a day. The nurses had resigned themselves to this activity on the ground that such efforts as pushing her back onto the ward bodily had failed in the past and because the patient had been classified as mentally defective and therefore "too dumb" to understand. In order to extinguish this particular problem behavior, the nurses were instructed not to give the patient any reinforcement (attention) for entering their office. What followed was a gradual and continuing diminution of entries to the nurses' office. The average frequency was down to two entries per day by the seventh week of extinction, at which time the program was terminated.

Behavior that is in the process of being extinguished diminishes at varying rates. As Thomas (1968) points out, resistance to extinction is often high in clinical cases because the responses have been sustained for long periods by intermittent reinforcement. For this reason, it is important that the cessation of reinforcement be abrupt and complete.

A massed practice type of extinction program was introduced by Dunlap (1932) who called it "negative practice." He described overcoming such habits as the repeated typing of errors, tics, and stuttering by persuading the subject to repeat the undesired act a great many times. The method has come to be mainly used in the treatment of tics (e.g., Yates, 1958; Jones, 1960; Rafi, 1962; Walton, 1964). In using this method, it is imperative that the undesirable response be evoked to the point of exhaustion, so that a high degree of reactive inhibition is produced. Otherwise, the tic may actually be reinforced, especially if it is not asymptotic to begin with. In any event, this is a tedious, time-consuming method. Kondas (1965) has reported that much more rapid change can be obtained if negative practice is combined with "anxiety-relief" conditioning. While the patient repeats the tic, an unpleasant electric current is continuously applied, and switching it off simultaneously with cessation of the tic sequence provides a negative reinforcement of not doing the tic.

In recent years, Nathan Azrin has been the author of numerous programs for eliminating undesirable habits, based on the concept of "habit reversal." A forerunner of these programs was Taylor's (1963) treatment of a case of compulsive eyebrow plucking. Another was Wolpe's (1958, p. 188) treatment of compulsive mimicry. The habits so far treated include enuresis (Azrin & Fox, 1974), tics (Azrin & Nunn, 1973), stuttering (Azrin & Nunn, 1974), trichotillomania (Azrin, Nunn, & Frantz, 1980), and self-destructive oral habits (Azrín, Nunn, & Frantz-Renshaw, 1980). The core of habit reversal is the elicitation of an incompatible response whenever the impulse to perform the undesirable behavior arises. For example, in a case of trichotillomania, the subject learns the inconspicuous competing response of grasping or clenching the hands for three minutes whenever hair pulling is likely to occur or even after it has been initiated. The habit-reversal programs have been widely adopted and appear to have achieved a high measure of success.

Habit reversal exemplifies the process of reciprocal inhibition as it applies to motor responses, (Wolpe, 1958, pp. 186–188; 1976, pp. 13–16; and see p. 259 for an experimental example) although Azrin and his colleagues have not explicitly recognized this.

14

Aversion Therapy

The essence of aversion therapy is to administer an aversive (unpleasant) stimulus simultaneously with an unwanted emotional response, with the object of inhibiting the latter and consequently diminishing its habit strength. For example, a painful stimulus may be employed to inhibit sexual arousal by a fetishistic object in order to weaken that arousal. Thus, aversion therapy operates by reciprocal inhibition. The chief aversive agents are strong but nondamaging electrical stimulation, nauseating drugs, and nauseating or disgusting evoked imagery. Aversion therapy must be clearly distinguished from punishment, in which the aversive stimulus follows the response of concern instead of coinciding with it. Whereas punishment is intended to discourage a response—that is, to make it less probable by reason of aversive consequences—the intent of aversion therapy is to diminish the habit strength of the target response through inhibiting it by the competition of the aversive agent. In general, punishment is employed to weaken motor habits, aversion therapy to weaken autonomic habits.

We must examine what happens when, in the presence of the stimulus to an undesired response, a strong aversive stimulus, such as strong electrical stimulation of a limb is administered. Besides eliciting an avoidance response, the shock will inhibit the undesired emotional response. Whenever it does so, a measure of conditioned inhibition of the undesired response will be established—a weakening of its habit, of the bond between the response and its stimulus. At the same time, the stimulus may be to some extent conditioned to the response constellation which the shock evoked. The amount of such conditioning is generally small or else transient (e.g., Raymond, 1964; O'Keefe, 1965). Pearce (1963) found that transvestites who had been treated by apomorphine later reported loss of interest rather than nausea at transvestite fantasies. Similarly, Rachman and Teasdale (1969) noted a lack of evidence that conditioned fear develops in studies employing shock as the aversive stimulus.

Figure 14.1 exemplifies the experimental paradigm on which all aversive therapeutic procedures are based. An animal is placed in a cage that has an electrifiable grid on its floor. Food has been dropped audibly into a food box within easy reach, and the animal has eaten it. With repetition he has acquired the habit of approaching the food box when he hears the sound of the food dropping into it. Appropriate autonomic responses accompany the approach—salivation, increased gastric motility, etc. Now, suppose that we decide to use aversion to eliminate that food-approach habit. One day, as the animal is approaching the food that he has heard drop, we pass a strong shock into his feed through the grid on the floor of the cage. The shock inhibits the conditioned approach. It produces "pain," anxiety, and motor withdrawal. Each time that happens, some weakening occurs of the food-approach habit, and at the same time, some conditioning of avoidance takes place. After several repetitions of the maneuver, the sound of food dropping into the food box exclusively evokes an anxiety-and-avoidance response in place of the approach response to food. It should be noted, however, that there may be an "interphase" when eating is inhibited and anxiety and avoidance not yet quite established. This "interphase" is probably the end point of most aversion therapy.

The first formal use of aversive therapy seems to have been Kantorovich's (1929) treatment of alcoholic patients by painful electric shocks in relation to the sight, smell, and taste of alcohol. In 1935, L. W. Max reported over-

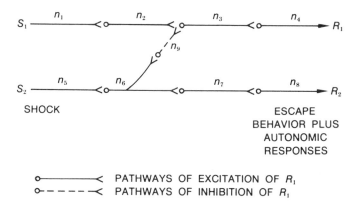

Fig. 14.1. S_1 is the stimulus to an undesired response (R_1), and S_2 a stimulus to an aversive response. When S_1 and S_2 are presented simultaneously, if S_2 is relatively strong, R_2 will be elicited, and R_1 inhibited by impulses from the inhibitory neurone, n_9. At the same time, S_1 will be conditioned to R_2 (pathway not shown).

coming a homosexual's fetish by administering very strong shocks to the patient in the presence of the fetishistic object. Unfortunately, his promised detailed account of this historic case never found its way into print. Nevertheless, Max's report served to encourage others to repeat his procedure, and instigated my own maiden attempt, in South Africa, to treat a patient with it (Wolpe, 1954). The following is a summary of that case.

Case 46: Aversion Therapy of Food Craving

The patient was a 32-year-old woman who, among other neurotic problems, was preoccupied with warding off impulses to indulge in "eating sprees," impulses which invariably in a day or two proved irresistible. Her cravings involved two kinds of "forbidden" food—doughnuts and similar sweets, and salty foods. The former were disallowed because they made her fat (and she had a particular horror of obesity), and the latter because rheumatic heart disease had several times sent her into cardiac failure, so that a salt-limited diet had been prescribed. She would try to avoid these foods by various stratagems, such as not keeping them in her apartment, and getting her African servant to lock her in the apartment when he went off at night. But at times her impulse was overpowering, so that she would go out, buy food, and eat. As she went on gorging, she would have a rising feeling of disgust and despair that would culminate in a state of prostration.

I had her list all items of food that figured in her obsession, and selected an item from the list. I then attached electrodes to her forearm, told her to close her eyes and to signal by a hand movement each time she clearly formed the mental image of the selected food. At the signal, I passed a strong faradic shock into her forearm. Ten shocks were used at a session. After two sessions, she found that thinking of these foods at any time conjured up an image of the shock equipment, which produced anxiety. With further treatment, thoughts of the foods progressively decreased. After five sessions, she felt free of their burden for the first time in 16 years. She began to enjoy company and to buy clothes, which she had not done for years.

Aversion therapy has been applied to a considerable number of behavioral problems, such as fetishism (Raymond, 1956), homosexuality (Freund, 1960; James, 1962; Feldman & MacCulloch, 1965), transvestism (Glynn & Harper, 1961; Blakemore, 1965), and the addictions—alcoholism, drug addiction, and smoking (McGuire & Vallance, 1964; Getze, 1968). A large number of clinical reports have been critically surveyed by Rachman and Teasdale (1968).

It is important to note that the foregoing problem behaviors yield pleasurable experience with inappropriate objects, and that the approach behavior is motivated by this. Simultaneous aversive stimulation inhibits the pleasurable emotion and leads to the elimination of its habit. It is this that provides the answer to what Rachman and Teasdale (1968, p. xii) termed "a major puzzle" about aversion therapy—why patients refrain from their deviant behavior after they leave the hospital. If the object of deviation no longer arouses pleasure, there is no impulse to approach it.

Only occasionally is aversion the behavioral treatment of first choice. In many instances, it will be found that the homosexual or other undesired behavior for which aversion therapy might be considered has a basis in neurotic anxiety, which should always be treated first. If the anxiety is eliminated, the behavior which is secondary to it may be expected to cease without requiring any special attention. On the other hand, if aversion therapy is mistakenly administered as the primary treatment of such a case, the "deviant" behavior will usually persist with little change; and even in those in which it is brought to halt, the continued existence of the underlying anxiety provides a basis for relapse or "symptom substitution." For example, some years ago I was consulted about a woman whose compulsive eating had been overcome by aversion therapy but who had thereafter become severely depressed. It was soon apparent to me that her central problems were neurotic anxiety habits, and that the depression was the result of her having been deprived of what was for her the anxiety-reducing activity of eating.

DESCRIPTION OF TECHNIQUES

Electrical Stimulation

Because electrical stimulation has an unfavorable public image, it has in recent years been employed with great circumspection. It does lend itself, however, to being easily quantified and precisely timed in relation to the behavior to be modified. Depending upon the circumstances of the case, one may administer the stimulus either in the presence of relevant objects or situations, or else in relation to evoked imagery or pictorial representations. Either faradic or alternating current should be used because these can, if necessary, be kept at steady levels for prolonged periods. The electrodes are usually attached to the patient's forearm. The baseline level of current is determined by gradually increasing it until the patient reports it to be distinctly unpleasant. The starting point for treatment is then usually a level that is about 25 percent stronger. The most satisfactory electrode is the concentric electrode (Tursky et al., 1965) which greatly minimizes the risk of burning the skin. Wet electrodes of saline-soaked gauze are also quite satisfactory. Ordinary electrocardiographic silver electrodes may be used if necessary. The aversive use of electrical stimulation varies in its details, but always follows the general lines of the obsessional eating case described above.

Real stimuli have figured in the treatment of transvestism (Blakemore et al., 1963) and of compulsive gambling (Barker & Miller, 1968). One of the latters' patients had been gambling steadily on "fruit machines" for 12 years. A machine borrowed from an inn was installed in the hospital. Shocks at about 70 volts were administered to the patient's forearm. While standing gambling continuously for three hours (his usual practice), he withstood a minimum of 150 shocks delivered by a third party at random to all stages of the gambling procedure from insertion of the discs to "payout." He received 672 shocks altogether, designed to produce a tolerable degree of discomfort during 12 hours' "gambling treatment," although he lost all desire to gamble after six hours. He did not resume gambling for 18 months, when, following a period of stress, he relapsed. Six hours' booster treatment, using the same technique, prevented further gambling for at least six months.

Feldman and MacCulloch (1965, p. 238) made extensive use of pictorial representations in their program for treating homosexuality. Rachman (1961) used both photographs and imagination in the treatment of a man who was sexually aroused by women's buttocks and bloomers. His five aversive-conditioning sessions incorporated photographs of women in bloomers and imagined scenes of bloomers and of women with attractive buttocks. Electric stimuli were applied to the fingers 10 to 15 times for each stimulus at each session. After the final session, the patient said that he no longer felt attracted by buttocks, and disposed of his collection of pornographic photographs.

Abel, Levis, and Clancy (1970) reported an elaborate "goal-gradient in reverse" technique in which tape-recorded descriptions of behavior were used in the treatment of sexual deviations. In three cases of exhibitionism, two of transvestism, and one of masochism, tapes were made involving descriptions of each subject's individual deviant behavior divided into three sequential segments. Five of the six subjects were placed on a schedule on which, at first, the final segment of the tape was followed by shock, and at later sessions the second, and ultimately the first segment. At each session, the shocked tape runs were followed by runs in which the patient avoided shock by verbalizing normal sexual behavior in place of the deviant segment. The sixth subject was given shocks out of relation to taped material, as a control. Treatment was evaluated by measuring penile responses to sexually deviant and nondeviant tapes, clinical interviews, and behavior reports. In the experimental subjects there was reduction of erectile responses to deviant tapes, but sustained responses to nondeviant tapes. Deviant responses became weaker and less frequent, and the improvement was maintained at follow-up 18 weeks later.

A technique in which aversion apparently works through the juxtaposition of unconditioned and conditioned aversive responses with both exteroceptive and imaginally evoked cognitions was introduced by Feingold (1966). His patient was a girl of eleven who persistently kept her mouth open and thus made it unfeasible for her dentist to perform certain necessary procedures. The girl and her parents were instructed to bring the therapist a record of each occasion on which her mouth was noticed to be open. Then, when she came to see him, she was given as many uncomfortable shocks to the leg as there were recorded occasions of open mouth. The number of shocks needed decreased from 48 to zero in the course of 12 sessions after which the mouth remained closed in a normal way, and the delighted dentist was able to proceed with his work. The following is my own solitary experience with this technique.

Case 47

Ron was a high-school junior who, despite high intelligence, was receiving low grades because he could not sit down to study in the evening. He felt he ought to be working between 7 and 11 p.m. He was asked to keep a record of his work each evening and was told that he would receive an unpleasant shock for each half-hour between 7 and 11 p.m. during which, in the course of the week, he did not work. At the end of the first week, he received four shocks, at the end of the second three, and after that no more were necessary. His report of improved work habits was supported by his mother's report of a rise in grades from C to A minus. It is presumed that the technique owed its efficacy to anxiety having become conditioned to the idea of not working.

Small portable shock equipment has made it possible to program aversive events in the life situation of the patient. There is no alternative to this when the target behavior cannot be evoked to order in the consulting room. For example, particular situations elicit rituals that cannot be conjured up by imagining the situations. Again, the patient may inhibit a ritual by self-stimulation at the appropriate time. I had one case in which such self-stimulation was an effective interim measure in the treatment of kleptomania.

Aversion Therapy of Narcotic Addiction

The repetitive occurrence of powerful impulses to take narcotic drugs like morphine, demerol, and methadone depends on learned responses of the autonomic nervous system (Himmelsbach, 1941). Although the drug habit always includes motor acts, often with a socially motivated component, treatment that concentrates on motor acts without paying attention to autonomic events misses the essence of the problem. Once a narcotic habit has been established, the individual evocations of the autonomic responses that underlie the abstinence syndrome (or craving) must be in response to some antecedent stimulus. Antecedent stimuli to craving may be in the external environment (exteroceptive), or in a specific internal state (interoceptive), or both (e.g., Wikler, 1968). It is reasonable to suppose that the stimuli might be detached from the craving response by repeatedly inhibiting evocations of the latter—for example, by simultaneous electrical stimulation.

I had the opportunity to make a preliminary test of this supposition (Wolpe, 1965) in the treatment of a physician with a Demerol addiction of five years' standing. He had an apparently endogenously based craving for the drug. This arose about once a week and required 1,000 to 1,500 mg of the drug to allay it. By using a portable shocker, he was able to overcome three successive cravings separated by days, after which he remained abstinent for 12 weeks. Similar treatments, often more lastingly successful, were subsequently reported by Lesser (1967), Liberman (1968); and O'Brien, Raynes, & Patch, (1972) of the inhibition-of-craving treatment of addiction.

An experimental test (Wolpe, Groves, & Fischer, 1980) was made possible by the appearance on the scene of the "narcotic antagonists." Intravenous injections of naloxone that were given to methadone-maintenance subjects induced craving reactions 30 to 45 minutes in duration. Continuous electric current was "titrated" against the craving in such a way as to diminish it, and was found with repetition to eliminate it. This happened with respect to increasing dosages of naloxone. As shown in Figure 14.2, several subjects were eventually more or less symptomfree with doses of intravenous naloxone of the order of .65 milligrams—more than four times the initial dose. In no case, however, did we reach a point where a further increase of naloxone was totally unable to induce withdrawal reactions, but we decided to try methadone withdrawal after learning from Jasinski (1976) that naloxone produces more powerful withdrawal effects than methadone withdrawal. Two out of three subjects experienced "painless" withdrawal from methadone. These were the only ones who had continued the treatment far enough for withdrawal to be feasible. The treatment was not very uncomfortable and the subjects were reasonably well paid. Addicts really cherish their addictions and are not enthusiastic about treatments to overcome them. The true crux of the problem of narcotic addiction is *to motivate participation* in treatment.

Aversion Therapy by Drugs

The treatment of alcoholism by an aversion method based on the nauseating effects of drugs was introduced many years ago by Voegtlin and Lemere (1942), and has been the subject of many subsequent reports (e.g., Lemere and Voegtlin, 1950). It consists of giving the patient a nausea-producing drug, such as tartar emetic, emetine, apomorphine, or gold chloride, and then having him drink a favored alcoholic beverage. The combination of alcohol and emetic is given daily for a week to ten days, after which the effectiveness of the procedure is tested by giving the patient alcohol alone. If there is sufficient conditioning, the very sight of alcohol will produce nausea. Boost-

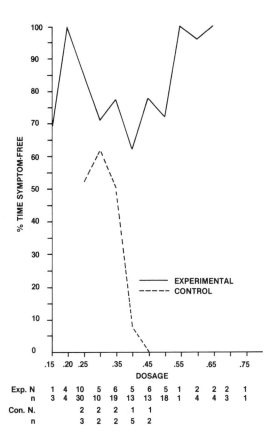

Fig. 14.2. Percentage of time symptom-free.

er treatments are given two or there times during the following year. Lemere and Voegtlin (1950) found that 38 percent of 4,096 patients had remained abstinent for 5 years or longer and 23 percent for 10 years or longer after a course of treatment. The method is, however, extremely time-consuming, tedious, and messy, and requires long-term accessibility of the patients. Trying it out in private practice in about a dozen patients in 1949, I found it so difficult and unrewarding that I gave it up in a few months.

Drug-induced aversion for a behavior problem was first reported by Raymond (1956). The patient was a 33-year-old man who had been arrested for acting out destructive fetishes toward perambulators (baby carriages) and handbags. The fetishistic acts gave him a pleasurable erotic sensation. For purposes of treatment, "a collection of handbags, perambulators and colored illustrations was obtained and these were shown to the patient after he had received an injection of apomorphine and just before nausea was produced." Treatment was given every two hours, day and night. At the end of the first week, treatment was temporarily suspended and the patient was allowed to go home to attend to his affairs. Returning eight days later to continue the treatment, he reported jubilantly that he had for the first time been able to have intercourse with his wife without the use of the old fantasies. His wife said that she had noticed a change in his attitude to her, but was unable to define it. Treatment was resumed, save that emetine hydrochloride was used whenever the emetic effect of apomorphine became less pronounced than its sedative effect. After several more days' treatment the patient said that the sight of the objects made him sick. Six months later, it was suggested that he have a booster course of treatment, to which he agreed although he did not consider it necessary. Nineteen months after the beginning of therapy, he stated that he had not again required the old fantasies to enable him to have sexual intercourse, nor had he masturbated with these fantasies. His wife said that she no longer worried about him and that their sexual relations had greatly improved.

Raymond carried out the above treatment under deprivation of food and rest, a condition that is almost certainly unnecessary, as Raymond himself later seemed to recognize (Raymond & O'Keefe, 1965). Its omission has not apparently marred the efforts of other therapists. Glynn and Harper (1961), Lavin et al. (1961), and Morganstern, Pearce, and Rees (1965) all successfully treated cases of transvestism with apomorphine, the last-named authors having entirely overcome the habit in seven of thirteen cases.

Another physiologically acting group of aversive agents are curarelike drugs, such as succinylcholine (Scoline) (Sanderson, Campbell, & Laverty, 1963). These drugs, given in sufficient dosage, produce a temporary respiratory paralysis which, added to the patient's inability to speak or move in any way, is "a most terrifying experience." If alcohol is presented to the patient just at the height of his terror, a conditioned response of fear and aversion to the drug may be established. The initial effects of this heroic treatment were good but did not endure (Laverty, 1960). Of 12 cases treated in this way by Farrar, Powell, and Martin (1968), only two were abstinent at a one-year follow-up.

There is a general comment to be made about all aversion treatments of alcoholism. At best, they result in the patient "recovering" on the condition that he no longer partakes of any alcohol at all. This does not amount to a restoration to normality. A cured patient would be one who could take a drink like anybody else. Such results may be attainable with individualized programs that involve positive reinforcement (e.g., Sobell & Sobell, 1973; Brady & Pomerleau (1975).

Covert Sensitization

"Covert sensitization" is the label Cautela (1966, 1967) has applied to the technique of pairing a verbally suggested aversive response with an imagined stimulus. It has been successful in a variety of conditions, notably obesity, homosexuality, and alcoholism. In the last-named condition, Ashem and Donner (1968) have recently noted that six out of fifteen alcoholics were abstinent six months after this treatment in contrast to none in an untreated control group—supporting to a limited extent an enthusiastic report by Anant (1967) of complete success in all of 26 patients without any relapse at a 15-month follow-up.

Cautela (1967) gives the following exposition of his instructions in relation to an obese patient in whom he wished to inhibit the eating of apple pie. The patient is relaxed and his eyes are shut:

> I want you to imagine you've just had your main meal and you are about to eat your dessert, which is apple pie. As you are about to reach for the fork, you get a funny feeling in the pit of your stomach. You start to feel queasy, nauseous, and sick all over. As you touch the fork, you can feel food particles inching up your throat. You're just about to vomit. As you put the fork into the pie, the food comes up into your mouth. You try to keep your mouth closed because you are afraid that you'll spit the food out all over the place. You bring the piece of pie to your mouth. As you're about to open your mouth, you puke; you vomit all over your hands, the fork, over the pie. It goes all over the table, over the other peoples' food. Your eyes are watering. Snot and mucous are all over your mouth and nose. Your hands feel sticky. There is an awful smell. As you look at this mess you just can't help but vomit again and again until just watery stuff is coming out. Everybody is looking at you with shocked expressions. You turn away from the food and immediately start to feel better. You run out of the room and, as you run out, you feel better and better. You wash and clean yourself up, and it feels wonderful.

It seems that the first report of the systematic use of aversion-evoking imagery was by Gold and Neufeld (1965), who used repulsive male images to overcome a 16-year-old boy's habit of soliciting men in public toilets. Davison (1967) used covert sensitization as part of a program to eliminate a sadistic fantasy. Kolvin (1967) used it to treat a fetish and an addiction to the sniffing of gasoline.

Other Aversive Agents

Anything that is unpleasant is a potential source of aversive conditioning. Philpott (1967) claimed to overcome obsessional thinking by getting a patient to hold her breath as long as possible each time an obsessional thought obtruded itself. Lublin (1968) has described two aversive inhalation techniques for the smoking habit. One consists of puffing stale warm cigarette smoke from a machine into the face of the subject while he is smoking his own cigarette. In the other, the subject has to puff regularly at a cigarette, in time to the ticking of a metronome, inhaling every six seconds on the first cigarette and then puffing without inhaling every three seconds on a second cigarette. (This strikes a familiar chord. Parents have for generations done something like this to make their children desist from smoking.) They state that both methods are very aversive; hardly any subject ever finished a whole cigarette. Of 36 patients who had an average of six half-hour sessions, 16 stopped smoking completely; and all of these are reported to have stayed off cigarettes, some for as long as a year. However, none of the numerous antismoking treatments is really satisfactory. For a comprehensive review and bibliography see Orleans et al. (1981a, 1981b).

In 1956, I treated two cases of obesity by approximating a vile-smelling solution of asafetida to their nostrils while they were handling, smelling, and tasting attractive items of food. (Both of these patients also received reciprocal inhibition therapy for interpersonal anxieties to which they responded well.) Temporary control of overeating was achieved in one, and lasting control in the other who to this day has a sylphlike figure. Kennedy and Foreyt (1968) described a very similar procedure using more sophisticated equipment to deliver noxious butyric acid gas.

Other physical stimuli that have been used for purposes of aversive conditioning are intense illumination and white noise. White noise was successfully employed in an unusual and interesting fashion by William Philpott in a case that I referred to him in 1964. The patient was a 30-year-old woman who for 15 years had had an extreme sensitivity to a variety of sharp sounds, such as bells, the jangling of keys, and a hammer on metal. Apart from this set of reactions, no unadaptive responses whatever were revealed in the analysis of her behavior. What Philpott did was feed white noise at high intensity to her ears through earphones while he jangled a bunch of keys before her eyes. Thus, while she saw the moving keys, their sound was completely masked by the white noise. The subject's hyperacusis was entirely overcome by this treatment. A follow-up inquiry in 1967 revealed that she had remained well and experienced no recurrence of this affliction.

Serber (1970) reported the use of shame as an aversive agent for cases of transvestism, voyeurism, pedophilia, and exhibitionism. The subject necessarily had to be embarrassed at performing his deviant act in front of witnesses. He was made to perform it for 15 to 35 minutes in the presence of increasing numbers of observers. A voyeur, for example, would be placed on the observer side of a one-way mirror to look at someone undressing behind the mirror, while observers in an adjoining room would openly observe the patient observing. Though five of the seven patients whom Serber treated were free of the deviant behavior at a six-month follow-up, most of them later relapsed.

The reader who wishes to inquire more fully into the theoretical and experimental studies of an avoidance behavior should consult the work of Church (1963), Solomon (1964), Azrin and Holz (1966), Rachman and Teasdale (1968, 1969), and Campbell and Church (1963). However, the reader should note that all these authors' discussions relate to the punishment paradigm; whereas, as we have already noted, aversion therapy depends on reciprocal inhibition of a target response by the aversive agent.

The following practical guidelines for aversion therapy in emotionally based habits are derived and adapted from those provided by Azrin and Holz (1966) for the different purpose of eliminating motor habits by punishment:

1. The stimulus should be as intense as necessary in order to block the pleasurable response totally.
2. The aversive stimulus should be delivered contemporaneously with the response.
3. The aversive stimulus should not be increased gradually, but introduced at a previously determined high intensity.
4. The frequency of administration should be as high as possible; ideally, the stimulus should be given with every evocation of the response to be eliminated.
5. An alternative emotional target should be available which will not be punished, but which will produce the same or greater reinforcement as that to the response being eliminated. For example, a fetishist or exhibitionist needs to achieve normal sex relations.
6. *Aversion therapy should not be administered before seeking out the possible anxiety bases of the unadaptive behavior and treating them if found.* This course of action will frequently make it unnecessary to inflict pain on the patient. For example, in both Case 55 (in Chapter 15) and Case 59 (in Chapter 16), aversion therapy was in the cards, but was not indicated.

15
Some Notable Syndromes

We will consider in this chapter some common categories of neurotic reactions within which considerable variations of stimulus-response structure are found, and some categories for which distinctive and sometimes unique methods are applicable.

NEUROTIC DEPRESSION[1]

Depression is a term that is applied to constellations of behavior among whose most characteristic elements are motor and verbal retardation, crying, sadness, loss of mirth response, loss of interest, self-devaluation, sleeplessness, and anorexia (Beck, 1967). Bleuler (1911) condensed these into the "melancholic triad" of depressive affect, inhibition of action, and inhibition of thinking.

In the second edition of this book (see also Wolpe, 1971), I voiced agreement with the widely held belief that learned helplessness (Seligman, 1968, 1975) provides an experimental model for externally caused clinical depression. It seemed to me that learned helplessness was an extension of experimental neurosis: the latter is produced by 5 to 20 inescapable and unpredictable shocks, and the routine in the former is to give the animal 64 of them. So it was "natural" to think of learned helplessness as a more advanced effect of the same agent. Only in the past few years did I realize that the two phenomena are unrelated for reasons given below.

Seligman, as Buchwald, Coyne, and Cole (1978, p. 183) noted, treats de-

---

[1]What follows is mainly a condensed version of a recent article (Wolpe, 1980).

pression as though "there is a single continuum running from happiness to severe depression," a view that is shared by some clinical authorities (e.g., Kline, 1974, p. 30). But a symptom-intensity continuum is no more indicative of a common basis for depressions than for fevers or tremors. Depression has many causes that, like the causes of fever or of tremor, are by and large unrelated to one another. The usual way of classifying clinical depressions is into the biological (or endogenous) and the neurotic (Depue & Monroe, 1978), but a third category of situational ("normal") depression needs to be recognized.

Situational depressions occur to all of us under circumstances in which it seems "normal" to be depressed. One may be depressed after a failure, a loss, or a deprivation. Sometimes the cause is relatively trivial, like losing a valued object, such as a favorite scarf or an old pocket knife; or the cause may have a social context, such as realizing that something one has said may have needlessly hurt another's feelings. Depressions that are set off by a single event generally fade within hours, days, or weeks, as the precipitating circumstances become increasingly remote, and new objects, persons, or goals compete for attention. Chronic states of threat, however, such as the prolonged illness of a spouse or child, or a continuous economic threat may result in a long-lived depression. Thus, even a long and quite severe depression may be justified by reality, a fact that clinicians usually overlook. For example, the wife of a physician who had migrated from South Africa to England was delighted at her new country, having been romantically predisposed to it by long immersion in its literature. After three years, her husband was compelled by professional considerations to move to the United States. She became greatly depressed, and what was actually a response to a situational deprivation was treated as a psychiatric illness.

Biological depressions have a variety of causes. Prolonged cases are most often associated with manic-depressive illness which may be unipolar or bipolar (Leonhard, 1959; Perris, 1966). The causative biological process may start "out of a clear sky" or may be triggered by a stressful experience (Thomson & Hendrie, 1972). There are numerous other biological bases for depressions that are usually short-lived, for example, abnormalities of the menstrual cycle; common drugs such as digitalis (Greenblatt & Shader, 1972), chlorpromazine, reserpine, and other tranquilizers (Hoch, 1959), and the aftermath of influenza (Ewald, 1928). Biological depressions fade and disappear as a function of remission of the relevant biological process, which may be facilitated by biological treatments.

Neurotic depression is also often called *reactive depression,* but the latter label, I believe, should be dropped because, as we have noted, situational depressions are in reaction to circumstances and even endogenous depressions are often triggered by stress. As will be seen, neurotic depression is a function of anxiety, to which it is linked in several ways. It often has a fluctuating character that depends on the varied strength of evoked anxiety—a relationship that is very different from the precipitation by stress of some endogenous depressions (Thomson & Hendrie, 1972) which takes place by mechanisms that are still to be identified.

Although endogenous and neurotic depressions both fall comfortably within the definition of depression given above, there are some differences between them. Endogenous depressives are more liable to have early morning wakening, retardation, ideas of guilt, and self-reference (e.g., Forrest, 1964). A very consistent difference is in sedation threshold, that is, the amount of a barbiturate injected intravenously at a given rate that produces unresponsiveness to verbal stimulation. The threshold is low for psychotic (endogenous) depressions and high for neurotic depressions (Shagass, 1956; Shagass & Jones, 1958; Shagass, Mihalik, & Jones, 1957; Shagass, Muller, & Acosta, 1959). Similarly, the evoked potentials of neurotic subjects, whether depressed or anxious, are alike, but very different from those of psychotic depressives (Shagass et al., 1978). Several other objective modes of differentiation have been reviewed by Shagass (1981). Unfortunately, these findings have been largely ignored by both clinicians and researchers. Their recognition and use would do much to reduce the confusion that is endemic in this area of psychiatry. Meanwhile, careful behavior analysis will usually enable a clear diagnosis of the nature of a person's depression.

Why Learned Helplessness has no Relevance to Neurotic Depression

My belief that learned helplessness was an advanced stage of experimental neurosis required the assumption that the two phenomena were in the same continuum of change of response. In fact, completely different response classes figure in the two types of experiments. Experimental neuroses consist of *conditioned autonomic* responses; learned helplessness consists of failure of *motor* responses to noxious stimulation, that is, lapsing of *unconditioned* responding.

The following is the sequence of events in the paradigmatic helplessness experiment. First, the animal, ensconced in a hammock, receives 64 randomly spaced unavoidable shocks to one of its extruded feet, each of five seconds' duration and 6.0 ma intensity. After making a variety of responses, the animal responds progressively less to the shocks, and finally ceases to respond—receiving the later shocks with outward passivity. (Note that it is only in terms of motor responding that the animal can positively be said to be passive, since autonomic responses seem never to have been studied in these experiments.) Then, on the next day, the animal is placed in a shuttle box and a severe pulsating shock of 50 seconds duration is introduced to the grid on which he stands. There is a shoulder-height barrier over which the animal could easily escape to the "safe" compartment (which is what experimentally naive animals almost always do). Two-thirds of the experimental animals do not cross the barrier to escape but "sit or lie, quietly whining until shock terminates" (Seligman, 1974). This is what happens 24 hours after inescapable shock, "but if intervals longer than 48 hours elapse, responding is normal." The shuttlebox helplessness may be prolonged to last a week or more by such means as repeating the hammock procedure.

Learned helplessness is not like neurotic depression if it dissipates in time. Seligman (1975) regards the dissipation as paralleling the course of clinical depression, and as a point in favor of his model; but, in fact, while such dissipation is characteristic of situational and endogenous depression, *it is not at all a feature of neurotic depressions*, which persist indefinitely or recur repeatedly until their anxiety-habit base is deconditioned. Miller and Weiss (1969) have cogently argued that the disappearance of the "helplessness" within 48 hours points to *physiological* after-effects of the unpredictable hammock shocks having a role in the production of helplessness. *Learned* patterns of behavior are not known to extinguish merely as a function of the passage of time. When learned helplessness is made to persist a week or more —for example, by repetitions of the hammock sessions (Seligman & Groves, 1970)—it must be presumed that a learning of the pattern has occurred, perhaps as a special case of the development of conditioned inhibition on the basis of reactive inhibition (Hull, 1943). It is likely that there is very little *conditioned* inhibition of excape response after a single hammock treatment.

A feature of the helplessness phenomenon that even more seriously invalidates attempts to extrapolate it to neurotic depression is the fact that the failure to make appropriate escape responses occurs *solely under the condition of electrical stimulation*. A dog that has been receiving shock in the shuttle box without moving "will come bounding across to escape" when the shock session ends (Maier & Seligman, 1976). There is no human reactive depression whose manifestations are conditional upon the presence of noxious stimulation. In the one variety of human depression in which an insistent and uniform source of disturbance does exist—depression that is caused by bereavement —the long duration (Clayton & Darvish, 1978) contrasts starkly with the characteristic brevity of learned helplessness in the animal.

Learned helplessness is a fascinating phenomenon, but the point here is that it is irrelevant to *neurotic* depression. Although Seligman points to numerous extensions of the model (many of which do not involve electrical stimulation), a bridge to neurotic depression is nowhere in sight. Aside from helplessness experiments in other animals, Seligman draws attention to long-term effects of inescapable shocks, such as interference with escape behavior in cats (Seward & Humphrey, 1967) and in fish (Behrend & Bitterman, 1963; Padilla, Padilla, Ketterer, & Giacalone, 1970; Pinckney, 1967); and the disruption of adult food-getting behavior when inescapable shocks have been given to weanling rats (Brookshire, Littman & Stewart, 1961). Any *long-last-*

ing effects of inescapable shocks probably depend on the presence of conditioned emotional reactions, a proposition supported by the finding of Brookshire, Littman, and Stewart (1962) that the development of helplessness was prevented by administering promazine along with the inescapable shocks.

Nevertheless, learned helplessness has obvious affinities with situational depressions, and may have relevance to some chronic phenomena, such as "brainwashing," of which Patricia Hearst may be a good example.

Depression in Experimental Neuroses

In the experimental neuroses described on pp. 37–40, depression of response, manifested as motor retardation, was frequently observed. Even after 24 to 48 hours of starvation, no neurotic animal would eat readily available food on the floor of the experimental cage. The food on the floor would remain untouched for hours (or indefinitely; see Masserman, 1943, p. 68). One can scarcely conceive of a more striking manifestation of motor retardation than a starving animal's inhibition of eating. General inhibition of movement was also found in some animals. These crouched passively in a corner of the experimental cage whenever they were in it. What is particularly to be noted is that the inhibited behavior was related to conditioned anxiety, and was not dependent on the presence of any kind of electric shock, as is the case in learned helplessness. The depressed behavior invariably diminished and disappeared in correlation with the successful elimination of the anxiety by a counterconditioning program in which feeding was counterposed in a systematic way to a rising gradient of anxiety-evoking stimuli (pp. 44–45).

THE CLINICAL VARIETIES OF
NEUROTIC DEPRESSION AND THEIR TREATMENT

If, in line with the experimental neuroses, human neurotic depression is a function of anxiety, there should be clinical evidence of this, and indeed there is. Clancy et al. (1978) documented a high incidence of depression secondary to anxiety neurosis. The ubiquitousness of anxiety in reactive depression has been directly shown by psychophysiological measurement (McCarron, 1973); and Suarez, Crowe, and Adams (1978) found that reactive depressives have raised electrodermal responsiveness to stress in the direction of anxiety. The presence of anxiety is indirectly manifested in the fact that sedation thresholds are very much the same in anxiety states and reactive depressions (in contrast to endogenous depressions) (Shagass, 1957; Shagass & Jones, 1958).

In order to examine the therapeutic implications of the apparent dependence of neurotic depression upon underlying anxiety, I examined the data from a series of 25 of my own cases. The material was assembled in the following way: out of the 88 neurotic cases tabulated in *Psychotherapy by Re-*

ciprocal Inhibition (1958), there are six in whose diagnostic summary the word "depression" appears, and these comprise cases 1 through 6. The remainder were the first 19 treated cases with depression as a major presenting feature that an assistant encountered in a random search through my files. There were 4 males and 21 females ranging in age from 21 to 60.

Examination of the material (Table 15.1) revealed that every case had been treated by the deconditioning of anxiety. The anxiety was found to be related to depression in four distinct contexts, on the basis of which one might refer to "types" of neurotic depression. Two or more types were frequently combined. For convenience, the 25 cases were broken down on the basis of *predominating* type, as follows:

Type I. As a consequence of severe and prolonged anxiety that is directly conditioned (11 cases).

Type II. As a consequence of anxiety based on erroneous, self-devaluative cognitions (6 cases).

Type III. In the context of anxiety-based inability to control interpersonal situations (8 cases).

Type IV. In the context of excessively prolonged and severe responses to bereavement (no cases). Case 17 was the only one in whose depression bereavement was a factor.

The different types are considered below.

Type I: *Neurotic Depression as a Consequence of Severe, Directly Conditioned Anxiety*

Patients with neuroses that include high degrees of anxiety (which may be either continuous or intermittent) often also report depression whose fluctuations are usually to a great extent correlated with the intensity of the anxiety. In some cases, the depression becomes the dominant emotional tone, seeming to substitute for the anxiety. Where there is pervasive ("free-floating") anxiety, pervasive depression may take its place. The substitution of depressed affect for anxious affect may conceivably be due to certain "overstressed" autonomic pathways becoming inhibited and the excitation rechanneled to different pathways. (Such an inhibition may be similar to that which Pavlov [1941, p. 176] describes in the context of protective [transmarginal] inhibition.) Some cases of this type display an inhibition of activity that is severe enough to invite the label "helplessness," but it is secondary to conditioned anxiety as in the experimentally neurotic cats. In our series, there were 11 cases that were predominantly of this type.

Reactive depression of this type responds well to the deconditioning of anxiety by systematic desensitization, or by whatever other method is appropriate. In correlation with the diminution of anxiety, the depressions become

Table 15.1. Twenty-five Cases of Reactive Depression

Case No.	Sex	Age	Type	Treatment	No. of Sessions	Length of Follow-up	Outcome
1.	M	32	III	Assertion.	21	5 years	+
2.	F	35	I	Assertion, relaxation.	22	22 years	+
3.	F	36	I	Assertion, systematic desensitization.	31	9 months	+
4.	M	40	I	Systematic desensitization.	17	0	+
5.	F	29	III	Assertion, systematic desensitization.	13	0	+
6.	F	41	III	Assertion, relaxation. Temporary improvement—aloneness.	17	2 months	–
7.	F	35	II	Cognitive correction.	16	9 years	+
8.	F	44	III	Assertion, systematic desensitization.	18	3 months	+
9.	F	40	III	Cognitive correction re: "right to criticize"; assertion.	74	8 years	+
10.	F	41	I	Assertion, systematic desensitization	57	8 years	+
11.	F	34	III	Assertion, systematic desensitization.	25	2 years	+
12.	M	31	II	Cognitive correction of fear of insanity; systematic desensitization.	36	21 years	+
13.	F	46	II	Cognitive correction re: insanity and heart disease; systematic desensitization.	45	6 months	+

276

No.	Sex	Age	Group	Treatment		Duration	Outcome
14.	F	29	III	Assertion, systematic desensitization *in vivo* to sexual situations.	41	7 years	±
15.	F	50	I	Systematic desensitization.	22	3 years	+
16.	F	29	III	Assertion.	11	2 months	+
17.	F	60	I	Valium. Flooding treatment of contamination obsession.	29	1 year	+
18.	F	48	I	Systematic desensitization.	17	2 years	+
19.	F	30	II	Cognitive correction of fear of insanity. Some assertion.	7	6 months	+
20.	M	21	II	Explication of rights. Assertive training. Modeling of expression of anger.	12	0	+
21.	F	42	II	Cognitive correction, assertion, and systematic desensitization.	31	2 years	−
22.	F	39	I	*In vivo* systematic desensitization of being seen to let go.	14	3 years	+
23.	F	55	I	Systematic desensitization.	135	4 years	+
24.	F	31	I	Systematic desensitization.	9	2 years	+
25.	F	35	I	Systematic desensitization. *In vivo* desensitization.	34	6 months	+

less frequent, less severe, and less enduring. They often finally disappear well before the deconditioning of the anxiety is complete.

For illustration, it is advantageous to take a previously published case, so that the reader may have access to further details: Mrs. Z (Wolpe, 1964), age 36 (Case 3 in Table 15.1), had a lifelong history of anxiety, depression, and social inadequacy. She had made numerous attempts at suicide. Before I saw her, she had had nine years of psychoanalysis without any benefit other than support. Behavior analysis revealed fear of disapproval, and a related fear of making her demands known or resisting those of others. Her treatment consisted of assertive training and systematic desensitization to inappropriate fears of rejection and ridicule. After 31 sessions, she felt calmer than she could ever remember feeling before. She was able to control situations with people, was no longer upset by a neurotic range of "disapprovals," and was free from depression. At a nine-month follow-up, she had maintained all her gains.

Type II: *Neurotic Depression as a Consequence of Anxiety Based on Erroneous Self-Devaluation Cognitions*

This category of reactive depressions is essentially the same as the previous one, distinguished from it only in that the anxiety is based on self-devaluative misconceptions. There were six cases of this kind in our series. (According to Beck, 1976, *all* cases of depression are due to misconception. Our analyses do not support this; in the majority of our *other* cases, recovery was not related to any program of cognitive correction.) Some had already, before treatment, realized the inappropriateness of their anxiety responses and others had learned this through therapeutic correction. In either case, recovery had to wait upon the deconditioning of anxiety.

Treatment. The treatment is, of course, cognitive correction. The seventh case in Table 15.1 affords an excellent example. This was a 35-year-old woman with a ten-year history of marked irritability and severe depressions. When the cognitive basis of her condition became apparent to her during her third session with me, the patient experienced marked emotional relief and henceforth had no further episodes of reactive depression. She proceeded to cooperate eagerly in the efforts that were made to normalize her sex life during the next few months. In nine years of follow-up, she has reported no further attacks of depression. For details see Case 18 (p. 89).

Type III: *Neurotic Depression Owing to Failure to Control Interpersonal Situations*

The helplessness inherent in the acceptance of a submissive role is a frequent cause of depression. The submissiveness results from being unable to handle other people because of conditioned anxiety-response habits. Anxiety may be aroused either at the thought of self-assertion or else at its assumed implications—such as hurting other people's feelings or appearing to be "pushy." This anxiety inhibits the person from expressing himself appropriately. If inhibition of expression extends to many interpersonal contexts, the person may be chronically depressed. There were eight cases in the present series that were either entirely or predominantly based on this kind of interpersonal failure.

As might be expected, assertiveness training figures largely in the treatment of depressions of this kind. Case 59 (p. 316) illustrates this, although depression was not his sole complaint. In some cases of exceptional fearfulness, systematic desensitization may need to precede assertive training: for example, if the patient feels very guilty after having asserted himself or if he is excessively afraid of an aggressive comeback. Anxiety about statements made or anxiety about the hostility of others must then be deconditioned before assertive training can succeed.

Type IV: *Reactive Depression Based on Exaggeration of Normal Reaction to Loss*

As noted in our consideration of situational depression, people are appropriately depressed when death or rejection deprives them of someone they love. If the depression is extravagantly great or lasts too long, it may sometimes be because of an interaction between the responses to the dire event and a physiological predisposition (Eysenck, 1970), which means that stress has precipitated an endogenous depression. In a demographic study, Clayton and Darvish (1978) found that 16 percent of new widows and widowers were depressed after 13 months; many of them had evidence of preexisting psychological illness. In other cases, prior conditioning suffices to explain the exaggerated reaction to bereavement: for example, the individual may have been sensitized by losses in the past. There was no pure case of this type in the present series, and only one (the 17th in Table 15.1) in which it combined with other factors.

When the investigation of the case suggests an endogenous element, the appropriate biological treatment should be administered. If bereavement or rejection by a lover leads to self-devaluation, cognitive correction should be undertaken. An overreaction to a deprivation based on preconditioning of anxiety to loss may be an indication for systematic desensitization. Ramsay (1977) has obtained impressive results in the treatment of prolonged mourning by flooding the patient with the poignant emotions aroused by both precious and painful memories of the lost loved one (see also Lieberman, 1978). Phillips (1978) and Wanderer and Cabot (1978) have offered behavioral programs for overcoming persistent emotional consequences of broken relationships.

The 25 cases of neurotic depression presented in Table 15.1 were treated by overcoming correlated anxiety. The results are summarized in Table 15.2.

Table 15.2. Summary of Data.*

Predominant Type of Depression	Number of Cases	Mean Time Since Onset of Depressive Symptoms	Mean Number of Treatment Sessions	Number Recovered or Much Improved
I	11	9.6 years	35.2	11
II	6	7.3 years	24.5	5
III	8	4.9 years	27.5	6
IV	—	—	—	—
Total	25	7.4 years	30.2	22

*Number of cases followed up six months or more: 19; Mean follow-up: 5.2 years. No relapses.

In 22 cases, the depression was lastingly overcome: two (Cases 6 and 21) were unimproved, and one (Case 14) was subject to repeated recurrences of depression but with much less severity than initially. These three cases were also in different degrees failures as far as anxiety-deconditioning was concerned. Of the 19 of the recovered followed up for at least six months, none relapsed (see footnote to Table 15.2).

It should be noted that the number of sessions given for each case is the total number applied to all aspects of its treatment, and not the depression alone. In many instances the depression disappeared long before the anxiety constellations were completely resolved. For example, although Case 7 had 16 sessions, her depression had ceased to be a problem after the third session.

These case data obviously do not have the force of a controlled study, but do provide a *prima facie* cae for the proposition that neurotic depression, like other manifestations of neurosis, is a function of anxiety. In most of the cases, depression had been a problem for years. The majority had previously had other kinds of psychotherapy with little or no benefit.

The resolution of neurotic depression apparently in consequence of the deconditioning of anxiety adds to the improbability we noted earlier of learned helplessness as a model for it. It is relevant to note that in one of the rare studies of helplessness that paid any attention to anxiety, Miller, Seligman, and Kurlander (1975) observed that "virtually no depressed non-anxious subjects could be obtained."

Conventional Outcome Research on Depression: An Essay in Futility

The need in outcome research for uniformity in the clinical material to which different treatments are applied is nowhere more blatantly flouted than in the field of depression. If some neurotic depressions are cognitively based and others a function of timidity, it is inappropriate to compare cognitive correction with assertive training on randomly assorted mixtures of cases. But researchers do not even separate out the three major categories we have noted; and assign to different treatment conditions undifferentiated assortments of subjects.

This was the case, for example, in an "operant reinforcement" study by Azrin and Besalel (1980) which records no attempted behavior analysis, and in which some of the "successes" may have been self-limited situational depressions, and others a consequence of nonspecific emotional deconditioning (p. 326). The latter might also account for such recoveries as have been reported in Lewinsohn's (1974) reinforcement program, at least in those cases that are actually neurotic depressions, since diagnostic distinctions are not always clearly made by Lewinsohn either.

In the much quoted article by Rush et al. (1977), which compares cognitive therapy with pharmacotherapy, there is no distinguishing between biological and neurotic depressions; and among the latter, no distinction between those that are cognitively based and those that are due to classical conditioning. (Of course, according to Beck, all depressions are cognitively based, which does not explain the successes of pharmacotherapy, to say nothing of my own data given above.) The cognitively treated group did significantly better, but the mere fact that they alone received psychotherapeutic interviewing would have given them the advantage of possible nonspecific emotional deconditioning. While these considerations are enough to invalidate that study, it is further weakened by the lack of follow-up information.

What is even more deplorable is that a very costly study that is currently being funded by the NIMH[2], is subject to the same criticisms. It compares pharmacotherapy, cognitive therapy, and "interpersonal psychotherapy." Although it also includes a pill-placebo control, it cannot hope to provide any definitive information as long as the groups consist of "depression" undifferentiated.

FEAR OF SYMPTOMS

Therapists frequently have difficulty with fear reactions that are triggered by bodily sensations. Endogenous stimuli are as susceptible to fear conditioning as exogenous ones. Quite commonly, the stimuli concerned are consequents of fear itself—rapid heart beat, headache, sweaty palms, and the various effects of hyperventilation such as dizziness, faintness, and dyspnea—so that a vicious cycle is set in motion by any stimuli that arouse fear, even "normal" fear.

A most important question here is whether the particular symptoms arouse the fear automatically on the basis of classical conditioning, or whether, as is usual, they have dreaded implications. The patient may believe that the symptoms foreshadow loss of consciousness, mental collapse, heart failure, or death. The first therapeutic requirement is then to correct the misconception, first by explaining that the symptoms are normal components of fear and by providing the strongest assurance that they cannot possibly have the dreadful consequences the patient envisions.

When such symptoms as dizziness, paresthesia, headache, or nausea suggest that hyperventilation is responsible for at least some of the symptoms, it is important to demonstrate this to the patient by causing him deliberately to hyperventilate. He is told to breathe deeply and rapidly (about one complete

[2]*Psychotherapy of depression collaborative research program,* Clinical Research Branch, NIMH, January, 1980.

cycle each second), and to report every new sensation experienced with the least possible interruption of the breathing. Usually, the characteristic sensations appear within two or three minutes. The direct realization that overbreathing is their cause removes the possibility of their being precursors of mental disorder or other problems. Furthermore, the patient can be shown how to control hyperventilation by keeping his mouth firmly shut (Lewis, 1954). This has the effect of preventing the further development of incipient hyperventilation symptoms and often of causing them to regress. Compernolle, Hogduin, and Joele (1979) have reported diminishing liability to these symptoms by a program of daily voluntary hyperventilation.

When fear of anxiety-related symptoms persists despite the patient's recognition of their benignness, it is often possible to decondition the fear by a graduated use of carbon dioxide–oxygen inhalations (p. 199). The basis of this is the considerable overlap between anxiety components and the autonomic responses to carbon dioxide inhalations. A small dose of carbon dioxide will, for example, elicit a small amount of unavoidable tachycardia; and the anxiety this elicits will presumably be inhibited by the post-carbon-dioxide relaxation (see p. 228ff).

Latimer (1977) has described the treatment by this method of a woman's fear conditioned to certain somatic symptoms of fear—notably rapid heart beat, trembling hands, and hyperventilation. The case was unusual in that, in order to produce fear, the symptoms had to be accompanied by the presence of another person and the thought that she might panic. The patient sat in a chair and held the mask that delivered the CO_2 and O_2 mixture and could control how much gas she inhaled by moving it closer or farther from her face. With each scene she was asked to begin with enough CO_2–O_2 to produce mild to moderate symptoms, and to imagine the scene and think of having a panic attack simultaneously. If she felt any anxiety over and above the effects of CO_2–O_2, she was to stop. A scene was repeated until she could imagine it with CO_2–O_2 and without anxiety for one minute. The same scene would then be repeated with moderate to maximum symptoms provoked by CO_2–O_2 and the same sequence followed. When a given scene would be imagined in conjunction with marked symptoms of CO_2 for one minute without anxiety, she moved up the hierarchy. The fear of panic was overcome in eight sessions and sustained at an eight-month follow-up.

Physical symptoms that have nothing to do with anxiety can also be conditioned to fear responses. Most often encountered is the person who has strong fear responses to physiologically produced palpitations, rapid heart beat, or pain in the chest. The first necessity is, of course, to have an internist rule out actual cardiac disease. In some cases, the internist's reassurance is all that is needed to dissipate the fear. Sometimes the cognitive reorientation thus obtained needs to be consolidated by the unequivocal identification of the actual cause of the pain. This is usually traceable to the intercostal structures or to gaseous distension of the stomach or intestines, which may be demonstrated by giving the patient a glass of orange juice to drink into which a teaspoonful of sodium bicarbonate has been freshly added. Occasionally the pain can be shown to be autosuggested. But it may continue to elicit anxiety even after the patient is thoroughly convinced that it has nothing to do with heart disease, because it many cases the pain is directly conditioned to the anxiety response. Systematic desensitization is then indicated. Usually the hierarchy will consist of the characteristic pain "placed" at decreasing distances from the middle of the chest, starting in the lower abdomen. If palpitations are a stimulus to anxiety, a hierarchy of numbers of "missed beats" may be appropriate.

When the patient is unable effectively to conjure up in imagination the symptoms that disturb him, they will need to be produced in actuality. Pain may be evoked by a sharp object or by heat, and tachycardia or palpitations by hyperventilation or inhalations of carbon dioxide. Occasionally, we have resorted to intravenous adrenaline. Since it is usually very difficult to achieve quantitative control of such induced stimulation, the mode of treatment may come to be flooding rather than desensitization.

AGORAPHOBIA

The Varieties of Agoraphobia

What is common to all cases of agoraphobia is that the patient responds with anxiety to physical distance from a place of safety or the relative inaccessibility of a "safe" person—in some instances to both. But the cases vary markedly in their stimulus-response structure and they therefore call for varied treatments. For this reason, the recent practice of offering uniform "packages" to all comers is deplorable (Barlow, 1979).

It is only in a minority of cases that agoraphobia is nothing but what it seems to be—a fear of separation. In others, the behavior analysis shows that what the patient really fears is some personal catastrophe. For example, he infers a heart attack when he feels a certain kind of pain in the chest, and the farther away he is from possible help at the time, the more anxious he becomes. The agoraphobia is thus incidental to a "hypochondriacal" neurosis (see p. 282ff). Overcoming the fear response to the symptom will usually cure the agoraphobia. In yet other cases, the fear is of what might be encountered in the outside world—crazy people or physical assault—in one particular case, the patient was afraid of roughly dressed people. A variant of such cases is the school phobic who fears what is in the school, in contrast to those who fear leaving home.

A group apart are the unhappily married women of low self-sufficiency in whom the syndrome usually appears after several years of marriage. If a woman with normal self-sufficiency is dissatisfied with her husband and her endeavors to change him or find an accommodation have failed, she is able to consider divorce or separation. The woman with low self-sufficiency does not have these options because the idea of being on her own is too frightening. She has a strong desire to leave her husband, but the projected consequences of leaving make it too fearful to translate the desire into action. In some cases, fear of the physical situation of being alone appears to be a simple generalization from the fear of the aloneness implied in the wished-for separation. Occasionally, there is a history of separation fantasies in which feelings of satisfaction are combined with a fearfulness that grows with repetition, and the generalized space-separation fear grows along with it. In all cases, there is a substantial amount of day-to-day anxiety based on an avoidance-avoidance conflict: aversion to the marriage and simultaneous aversion to the projected consequences of leaving it. This anxiety may summate with intercurrent anxiety arousals, such as may for example be produced by feelings of faintness or palpitations, to panic levels, leading to anxiety-conditioning of that moment's environment. If the person is driving a car on a highway at that time, fear of driving is liable to be conditioned.

Anxiety that is due to various causes may be especially severe when the person is away from home, providing a basis for agoraphobic conditioning. In many cases the cause of the anxiety, which may amount to panic, is biological—such as paroxysmal auricular tachycardia, functional hypoglycemia, mitral valve prolapse, vaso-vagal attack (common faint), the sudden onset of an acute febrile illness, and much more rarely, a limbic lobe seizure. It is of great importance for the therapist to recognize those patients in whom the biological event is liable to recur, for those patients are vulnerable to anxiety from that source in addition to possible conditioned anxiety. In some of these cases no conditioned anxiety develops: the patient merely has a normal fear of disabling physiological attacks whose onset he can neither control nor predict.

To subject such a person to psychological therapy is a culpable error. I have seen cases so treated for years—most recently a 48-year-old man who had been labeled agrophobic by numerous therapists for over 11 years, though his attacks had no relation to separation from home or to any other environmental factor.

In other cases, varying degrees of anxiety conditioning do take place. It may be severe and will be the only problem if the physiological attack is non-recurring. In Case 48 the conditioning was relatively mild, and the establishment of a medical diagnosis was the key therapeutic achievement. Deconditioning of agoraphobia was thereafter a subsidiary and relatively simple matter.

Similarly, where agoraphobia originates in marital conflict or nonagoraphobic fears, the treatment of these affords a fundamental solution to the problem, leading to resolution of the agoraphobia without its direct treatment. Cases 49 and 50 illustrate this.

Case 48: Agoraphobia Due to a Medical Illness

Mrs. B., a 31-year-old married woman, was referred for treatment by a psychiatrist in Connecticut for agoraphobia after a year of unsuccessful "psychodynamic" therapy. She had felt that a year was long enough and had asked him if there was any alternative.

When I saw her, she complained, in addition to agoraphobia, of numerous interpersonal anxieties, reflected in a Willoughby score of 66. She said that the agoraphobia was characterized by shortness of breath and dizziness. These attacks had begun seven years previously and were becoming worse. They also occurred at times under other circumstances and were sometimes ameliorated by eating. Mrs. B stated that the only benefit of her previous psychiatric therapy was that she now recognized her fears and was able to tell people about them. Because of the nature of her condition, I had decided to treat her as an inpatient, which facilitated our having one or more interviews each day. After the usual preliminaries of behavior analysis, relaxation training, and hierarchy construction, I began a program of systematic desensitization on a theme of separation from home at the same time that I was deconditioning her to certain social fears, such as of others displaying anger. She made a considerable amount of progress to the extent that, after the 14th session, she remarked that she was now finding it pleasant to walk down the long passage to my office during which she was finding herself singing. She continued to make progress to the extent that she was able to walk a distance of 20 blocks comfortably.

One day she arrived at my office reporting that she had had a severe agoraphobic "attack" that morning in the ward when she had been feeling perfectly calm and unworried. I decided that this attack must almost certainly have had a physiological cause and sent her to the Department of Internal Medicine for a full investigation. As nothing significant was shown, I next sent her to a neurologist who diagnosed Meniere's disease. She was placed on the appropriate medication and in the course of the next two months her agoraphobia faded out completely. Treatment of her social anxieties was continued in her home town.

Case 49: Agoraphobia Based on Marital Conflict

In this kind of agoraphobia, one must first work on the marriage, to try to make it satisfactory if possible, and, if not possible, to end it. Whatever happens to the marriage, the treatment of the case cannot be regarded as complete until the patient has also overcome her fear of being alone, which can usually be accomplished by a combination of assertive training and systematic desensitization. Frequently, it is the success of such measures that enables the patient to leave her husband.

Mrs. R. was a 26-year-old housewife who had suffered from agoraphobia for eight years. At the age of 14, she had married a man who treated her with scorn and indifference and whom she hated. She wanted to leave him, but could not. Not only was her self-sufficiency extremely low (Bernreuter Self-Sufficiency score of 13), but she was of the Catholic faith and had five children. She was very fearful of going out alone, even for a distance of a few blocks. It was with this complaint, together with several others of phobic nature, that she presented herself for treatment. The history itself provided unusually clear evidence of the relevance of the marriage to the agoraphobia. About three years previously, Mrs R. had met a man who had fallen in love with her and to whom she had felt attracted. She had gone to live with him for a month in another city, and during this time had been able to go about on her own any distance without the least discomfort. When she returned to her husband, the agoraphobia had reappeared in full force.

After it became obvious that there was no chance of improving the marriage, my efforts were directed at enabling her to make a break from her husband by training her self-assertion while desensitizing her in other areas of unadaptive anxiety. In about eight months, during which I saw her (in front of a professional group) once every two weeks, she felt herself ready for a temporary separation, which I arranged. She went to stay with a friend for two weeks. During the first week, her agoraphobia gradually faded away, and she was completely free of it in the second week. It was then necessary for her to return home in order to satisfy legal requirements for a permanent separation. Her return did not produce any recurrence of the agoraphobia because she now felt detached and free from her husband, and the thought of being alone was no longer threatening. She continued to put up with him for several more months, until arrangements for permanent separation were made, and ultimately, they were divorced. Three years later she was still free from the handicap of agoraphobia.

Case 50: Agoraphobia Primarily Due to Cognitively Based Fear of Insanity

In the case to be described a classically conditioned fear of separation had developed secondarily to a cognitively based fear of insanity. It was not possible to overcome the agoraphobia as long as the primary fear existed. Miss G., age 23, had had that fear for six years, following two attacks of anxiety within a fortnight, each set off by a feeling of desperation at the thought that she was so fat that nobody would every marry her. Because each time she had trembled uncontrollably and had had a feeling of numbness in her head and a sense of unreality, she had decided that she must be losing her mind. She became preoccupied with this idea, which fed upon itself by eliciting the trembling and other symptoms, especially when she was alone.

She had obtained some relief from tranquilizers, but psychiatric treatment of several kinds had been almost useless. An alleged behavior therapist had attempted desensitization and given her "walking assignments," without effect. Since it seemed to me that the physiological symptoms might well be due to hyperventilation, I had her hyperventilate, which produced the symptoms within a minute. This enabled me to convince her that the dreaded symptoms were caused by overbreathing, e.g., by sighing, and thus we were able to overcome her fear of losing her sanity. I also showed her how to check these symptoms by shutting her mouth. It was thereafter possible to begin a program of progressively longer journeys on her own to overcome the conditioned fear of separation.

Outcome Research on Agoraphobia

Outcome research on agoraphobia has focused on the treatment of the separation fear—a worthwhile aim, even if, as the foregoing discussion shows, it is very often not enough, and in certain cases does not succeed at all if underlying fears are not overcome first. A question that has been very much to the forefront is whether desensitization or flooding is the treatment of first choice. As Mathews, Gelder, and Johnston (1981) remark in the course of a scholarly review, "there have been some surprising twists and turns" (p. 97). The finding of Marks, Boulougouris, and Marset (1971) that flooding was superior to desensitization was not replicated in the better-controlled studies of Gelder et al. (1973), and Mathews et al. (1974), who found no significant difference. It appears (e.g., Emmelkamp & Wessels, 1975) that on the whole *in vivo* exposure is more effective than imaginal exposure. It is worth noting, however, that in all these studies the average subject is still far from free from agoraphobia after being treated, which again illustrates the need for diagnostic analysis beyond the general label.

Most agoraphobic patients report ongoing anxiety of varying degrees of severity which is distinct from the anxiety they experience in phobic situations. In addition, the anxiety within the phobic situation may at times reach an intensity that amounts to panic. Klein (1964) has claimed that panic attacks are central to most cases of agoraphobia, and has reported a number of investigations in which imipramine has been seen as the central agent of change (e.g., Zitrin, Klein, & Woerner, 1978, 1980). However, these investigations are quite complicated; both the methodology and the conclusions have been strongly criticized by Mathews, Gelder and Johnson (1981).

Ascher (1981) has provided an interesting demonstration of the efficacy of paradoxical intention in extending the ambit of agoraphobics. Subjects were instructed to go out up to a point where they considered the anxiety too great to proceed any further. They were then to focus on the most prominent physiological component of the anxiety and to try to increase this "in an attempt to court the anticipated disastrous consequence." All of ten subjects reached the criterion by this method. Five of the ten had previously had eight weeks of gradual exposure with very little progress.

More than any other category of neurosis, agoraphobia requires the therapist to have the widest possible repertoire of behavioral techniques. For an illustrative example, the reader is referred to Case 29 (p. 192). This young woman had made very little response to systematic desensitization, the use of tranquilizing drugs, flooding in imagination and *in vivo,* and paradoxical intention. Her recovery began when the anger that was aroused in her by the suffering that had been occasioned by the latter two methods was exploited therapeutically.

It is worth mentioning, finally, that a considerable number of cases of agoraphobia respond lastingly to the assiduous application of differential relaxation, which means acquiring marked skill in relaxation in general, and then the ability to relax very effectively muscles that are not in use at a particular time. This measure is particularly applicable to "pure" cases of agoraphobia (p. 284), even some that are severe and longstanding.

STUTTERING

The dependence of most stuttering on social anxiety is demonstrated by the fact that almost every stutterer speaks fluently when he is alone or in the presence of people with whom he is most comfortable. The greater the anxiety evoked by the social situation, the worse the stutter is likely to be. A behavior analysis will identify the stimulus elements in the social contexts that trigger the anxiety; and upon these will depend the therapeutic strategy. Most often, assertive training or some form of desensitization will be indicated, or both. Cases 51 and 52 provide illustrations of each.

Case 51

Mr. M. (Wolpe, 1958, p. 158) came for treatment of a severe stutter which had begun at age five. Almost every sentence was repeatedly interrupted by the stutter, and each interruption was marked by violent facial contortions. A great many interpersonal situations could arouse anxiety in him and so worsen the stutter. It was evident that anxiety associated with direct dealings with people needed attention first. Because of it he frequently endured aggression from others for long periods without protest, until sometimes his bottled-up emotions exploded in ill-directed rage. I told him that he had rights as well as duties. I drew attention to the flailing helplessness embodied in his delayed rage reactions, and emphasized the need for reactions of protest to be expressed as soon as possible if real mastery of situations was to be gained. Three days later he reported that he had been less permissive to his assistants at work and had insisted on their getting things done. He had also for the first time asked his wife to help him with work he had brought home from the office. In correlation with increasingly consistent exteriorizing of feelings in relevant contexts, he developed an increasing feeling of inner freedom and his speech lost its stutter except on occasions with his boss, and in conditions of unusual stress. The facial contortions ceased entirely. When seen two years later, he spoke without any suggestion of stutter.

Case 52

Mr. B. was a man of 25 who had stuttered quite severely since he was five years old. He said that his stutter had always been worse with strangers. It is interesting to note that his score on the Willoughby Neuroticism Schedule was 13, which is within normal limits, indicating that he was free from neurotic anxiety in many interpersonal situations.

Mr. B. was taught relaxation, and hierarchies dealing with the subject of humiliation were drawn up. After desensitization to situations involving less threatening individuals had been accomplished, scenes that featured his father began to be introduced. One of the weaker scenes was sitting with his father in a restaurant and knocking over the salt. More disturbing scenes were knocking the salt off the table; knocking over the water; making an erroneous statement. After nine desensitization sessions in the course of four months, his fear of these "humiliation" situations steadily declined and his speech was judged to have improved 90–95 percent. About a year later his improvement was found to have been maintained both as judged by me and as reported by his wife. (For further details of this case, see Wolpe, 1969, p. 23).

The deconditioning of anxiety is often all that is needed to overcome a stutter more or less completely, and lastingly. However, in some cases motor operants will keep the stutter going to some extent after the anxiety has been removed and their separate extinction will be needed. Since the modifiability of dysfluency by punishment was first convincingly demonstrated (Flanagan, Goldiamond, & Azrin, 1958; Goldiamond, 1965; Siegel & Martin, 1967), a variety of applications of operant principles have been described—for example, Leach (1969) used cash rewards for fluent speech and Shames (1969) verbal reinforcement. A very convenient method was suggested by Migler (1967), and yielded promising results in the few cases in which it was tried. It consists of forbidding the subject to complete any word that begins with dysfluency, so that only fluent behavior is rewarded, by being completed and by the social results thereof.

Meyer and Mair (1963) and Andrews et al. (1964) reexamined from a behavioral viewpoint the therapeutic potentialities of the previously disdained observation that dysfluencies are decreased when speech becomes rhythmic. Meyer and Mair used a metronome, and Andrews and Harris used verselike scanning. They obtained lasting improvement in many cases and complete fluency in some. Building on these observations and on experiments of his own, Brady (1971) elaborated a very practical treatment of stuttering. His procedure involves the use of a miniature electronic metronome worn behind the ear like a hearing aid, which it resembles.* The first step is to find conditions under which the patient can be highly fluent with the aid of a desk metronome. For a severe, chronic stutterer this may require being alone with the therapist and pacing one syllable of his speech to each beat of a loud metronome set as slow as 40 beats per minute. Almost always, conditions can be found under which the patient speaks in an easy, relaxed, and fluent manner.

Once fluent verbalizations appear, albeit at a low rate, the task is gradually and systematically to use the micrometronome to "shape" verbalizations to approximate the rate and cadence of normal speech and to help the patient extend his fluency to other situations to which anticipatory anxiety and tension have been conditioned. The series of small steps corresponds to a hierarchy of speaking situations arranged from those associated with minimal stuttering to those associated with severe stuttering. For example, the first situation on the list might be "speaking with wife" and the last "giving an impromptu after-dinner speech."

During this phase of treatment it is not uncommon for the patient to experience unexpected difficulty in some situations from time to time. If this occurs, it is essential for the patient to regain fluency in the situation as soon as possible by the same means he has used before, viz., by reverting to a slower rate of speech and, if necessary, to more strict pacing (one syllable or one word per beat). When he becomes more fluent and regains the feeling of "control" of his speech, he may gradually return to more rapid speech and less strict pacing on a trial basis. This is an important principle and sometimes requires much coaching by the therapist. Often it is helpful for the patient to rehearse this procedure in the therapist's office by simulating outside speaking situations.

Discontinuation of the metronome is done gradually, starting with the speaking situations in which the patient has the least amount of difficulty. During this phase many patients find it helpful to pace their speech to the beats of an "imaginary" metronome. If in any situation the patient finds himself having appreciable speaking difficulty, he must again immediately return to stricter pacing of his speech even though the metronome is not present. Only a few sentences may be required before control is regained. If he continues to have difficulty in this and related situations, he may need to return to the actual metronome.

Of 23 patients who completed Brady's treatment program, 21 (or over 90

*This metronome, called the Pacemaster, is obtainable from Associated Hearing Instruments, Inc., 6796 Market St., Upper Darby, Pa. (19082). Both its frequency and its volume can be adjusted.

percent) showed a marked increase in fluency and an improvement in their general adjustment as well. These clinical results persisted for follow-up periods that ranged from six months to over three years. More recently, Burns and Brady (1980) have described an additional technique called air flow or easy onset. Speech is initiated only toward the end of an easy exhalation, the first syllable begin stretched out in a smooth flowing way that blends imperceptibly with the exhalation. This method diminishes the blocks that some patients experience in getting ready to speak. Although notable effects are often rapidly obtained, it usually takes months of practice to develop normal speech out of this behavior. Azrin and Nunn (1974) reported a variant of the air-flow technique that may achieve success in fewer sessions than that of Burns and Brady.

PSYCHOSOMATIC DISORDERS*

A psychosomatic illness is a physical illness in which the subject's autonomic responses to external situations or endogenous stimuli are a causal or a contributing factor. These stimuli most commonly have their physiological effects through the elicitation of anxiety, but there are also other mechanisms (see the discussion of asthma). Anxiety was objectively defined (p. 23) as *the individual's characteristic constellation of autonomic responses to noxious stimulation.* When in a given person's anxiety-response constellation the autonomic response in a particular organ possesses unusual strength, the resulting overactivity in that organ may adversely affect its physiological function, sometimes to the extent of producing a lesion. According to Wolf and Wolff's (1947) classic statement, there are "stomach reactors, nose reactors, pulse reactors and blood pressure reactors." It is to be expected that if anxiety is a factor in the maintenance of a physical illness, that illness will diminish as the anxiety-response habit is overcome.

Among the illnesses commonly associated with emotional disturbance are asthma, peptic ulcer, irritable colon, migraine, hypertension, and neurodermatitis. A psychological factor, however, does not operate in every case that is labeled "psychosomatic." For example, midbrain lesions also can cause the autonomic activity in the stomach that leads to hyperchlorhydria and can thus be the basis of peptic ulcerations (Cushing, 1932). It is imperative in the handling of the individual case to establish a positive connection between psychological factors and the somatic illness before proceeding to psychological modes of treatment.

---

*This section consists in part of excerpts from my article, "Behavior therapy for psychosomatic disorders," *Psychosomatics,* **21,** 5, 1980.

Asthma

It is clear that asthma has a variable, muiltifactorial etiology that includes allergic, infective, emotional, and mechanical processes; any one of these or any combination may be causally implicated in a particular case (Rees, 1956, 1964). A general subdivision has been suggested on the basis of various medical criteria into cases in whom the somatic predisposition to asthma is high, and those in whom it is low—psychological factors playing a greater role in the latter (Block et al., 1964; Purcell, 1963). Resh (1970) found that the psychosomatic asthmatics could be fairly clearly differentiated from those whose illness was physiologically based.

Several reports of the successful behavioral treatment of asthma have appeared in recent years. The first significant controlled study was by Norah Moore (1965). She used a balanced incomplete block design to compare the effects of three forms of treatment: (1) reciprocal inhibition therapy, i.e., systematic desensitization; (2) relaxation therapy, and (3) relaxation combined with suggestion. For the desensitization treatment, three hierarchies were prepared: one based on an asthmatic attack, a second on any relevant situation that was productive of an allergic or infective reaction, and a third on a situation productive of a key psychological stress. The dependent variables were changes in the daily number of asthmatic attacks and maximum peak flow of inspired air. During the first four weeks of treatment, both subjectively and objectively, maximum peak flow improved for all three groups, but it improved most for reciprocal inhibition. After this time, while the reciprocal-inhibition group continued to improve, the other two began to regress. Eight weeks after the beginning of treatment, the superiority of maximum peak flow in the reciprocal-inhibition group was significant at the 0.001 level. Systematic desensitization alone had clearly produced a systematic weakening of anxiety-response habits that were causally connected with the asthma.

It has long been an intriguing question why anxiety should be a trigger to the parasympathetically mediated response of bronchial constriction. Studies by Hahn (1966) and by Mathe and Knapp (1971) have suggested an unusual profile of autonomic response to stress in asthmatics: unlike heart rate and blood pressure, their airway conductance and respiratory rate are *opposite in direction* to those of control subjects.

Besides the cases of asthma whose attacks are mediated by anxiety, there are others in whom bronchial constriction is directly conditioned to previously neutral stimuli. This was clearly demonstrated in an experiment on two patients by Dekker, Pelser, and Groen (1957), in which it was found that the isolated mouthpiece of the equipment through which the patients had inhaled allergenic aerosols had acquired through its association with the attacks elicited by the aerosols, an independent and obstinately persistent power to provoke asthmatic attacks. Khan, Staerk, and Bonk (1973) later showed, in a controlled study of 20 asthematic children, that it is possible to overcome such conditioned reactions by the opposing conditioning of bronchodilation. They conditioned bronchial constriction in much the same way as had Dekker et al., and then instituted training in bronchial dilatation through biofeedback reinforcement. They observed the bronchial relaxations on an electronic pulmonary function analyzer and rewarded them by turning on a bright red light and by praising the child. Apparently because of their acquired bronchodilatory skill, the experimental group were significantly improved in comparison with a control group, in frequency of asthmatic attacks and in amount of medication required—a superiority that persisted at a 12-month follow-up. A similar study on one case has been reported by Sirota and Mahoney (1974).

The behavioral approach to any case of asthma is thus first to determine if anxiety is a causal factor. If it is, it should be treated as dictated by the behavior analysis. If not, it may still be deemed worthwhile to attempt the conditioning of bronchodilatation on the basis of biofeedback.

Essential Hypertension

Although the etiology of essential hypertension is not fully understood, there is no doubt that conditioned cardiovascular responses to environmental stimuli are an essential component of many cases, and these are the ones that may be expected to respond to behavioral methods. Jacobson (1939) long ago demonstrated that progressive relaxation of skeletal muscles may markedly diminish both systolic and diastolic pressure. In a recent investigation (1980), he found significant lasting diminution of blood pressure in over two-thirds of 90 patients. Benson et al. (1971) obtained reductions in systolic pressure ranging from 16 to 34 millimeters in hypertensives treated by a form of transcendental meditation. A considerable number of other reports have been reviewed by Jacob, Kraemer, and Agras (1977) and by Blanchard and Miller (1977). These include studies in which biofeedback replaced or was combined with relaxation training. The effects, however, were often trivial. Jorgensen, Houston, and Zurawski (1981) have reported encouraging results by the use of Suinn's anxiety-management training method (Suinn & Richardson, 1971; Suinn, 1977) in which the patient is required, while relaxed, to visualize actual past stress situations.

Whether intermittent daily periods of relaxation can produce continuous and lasting diminution of blood pressure is questionable. Day-to-day and hour-to-hour blood pressure readings would really be needed to ascertain whether or not the effects of treatment extend to the patient's usual environment. A solution suggested by Graham, Beiman, and Ciminero (1977, 1978) is to have daily blood pressure readings taken at home. In their patient, who was treated by relaxation training, such readings revealed a drop in blood pressure at home from 155/95 to 130/80; a change that was found to have persisted 40 weeks later.

In general, one would expect relaxation training to lead to continuous diminution of blood pressure only under two sets of conditions. One is when the patient has developed a habit of constantly relaxing all muscles not in active use, as advocated by Jacobson (1938) under the label, "differential relaxation." The other is through the identification and deconditioning of unadaptive anxiety response habits. There has not to date, unfortunately, been any systematic study of the effects on hypertension of the deconditioning of neurotic anxiety. Only individual case reports are available. I myself have obtained lasting recovery or amelioration of hypertension in about ten patients over the years. One of these has been described at length (Wolpe, 1976 p. 233ff).

Migraine and Tension Headaches

Emotional tension is a common precipitant of attacks of migraine, and also of a variety of nonmigrainous headaches. Over the years I have repeatedly obtained the diminution or disappearance of headaches of both categories by the use of emotional deconditioning programs.

In a controlled study of migraine, Mitchell (1969) obtained a 66.8 percent reduction of attacks in subjects treated with desensitization and assertive therapy, but no change in no-treatment controls. In a second study, Mitchell and Mitchell (1971) confirmed the efficacy of behavior therapy but also found that relaxation alone did not differ from no treatment. It may be presumed that it was necessary to overcome the patient's emotional reactions to relevant environmental events.

Biofeedback has recently figured prominently in attempts to diminish tension headaches and migraine. Budzynski, Stoyva, and Adler (1970) treated tension headaches by having subjects relax frontalis and sometimes neck muscles by placing electrodes over these muscles and providing EMG feedback. Good results were obtained, but the fact that the subjects were asked to practice relaxation at home means that emotional deconditioning may have been the basis of change. The same comment applies to Chesney and Shelton's (1976) study in which relaxation either alone or in combination with biofeedback was shown to be more effective than biofeedback alone in the treatment of tension headaches.

Gastrointestinal Reactions

Since the gastrointestinal tract is innervated by the autonomic nervous system, it is not surprising that emotional disturbances may be correlated with disturbances of the tract at all levels, from the esophagus to the rectum.

The first systematic study of relationships between emotions and the vascular and secretory responses of the stomach was that of Wolf and Wolff (1942), who found that fear depressed gastric secretion and mobility, that hostility increased them, and that the gastric mucosa became fragile and sensitive during engorgement. Despite this promising beginning, a recent epidemiological survey by Pfeiffer et al. (1973) concluded that the causes of peptic ulceration are still obscure. Nevertheless, anxiety appears to be associated with exacerbation of some cases, and recovery from peptic ulcer has been known to follow deconditioning of anxiety-response habits (see, for example, Wolpe, 1958, p. 148ff).

Reports of the use of behavior therapy in conditions of the lower gastrointestinal tract are much more frequent. For example, Hedberg (1973) reported the case of a woman with a 22-year history of chronic diarrhea that was successfully overcome by 12 sessions of systematic desensitization, without recurrence at a two-year follow-up. Furman (1973) obtained uniformly positive results in five patients suffering from functional diarrhea by a biofeedback technique involving verbal reinforcement. Furman perceptively notes that desensitizing effects probably resulted from the relaxation training that was included in his procedure. In one of his cases, systematic desensitization was explicitly added.

The primary importance of the emotional side of things in patients with irritable bowel syndrome has been brought to the fore by Latimer et al. (1981), who found that their subjects' gastrointestinal reactions were no different from those of neurotic subjects who were similar in terms of anxiety and depression but without bowel symptoms (see also Latimer, 1981). The treatment of irritable bowel syndrome is thus the treatment of the underlying anxiety response habits.

OBSESSIONS AND COMPULSIONS

Obsessions are recurrent, persistent ideas or impulses. The word compulsion is more appropriate in those cases in which motor manifestations predominate. Some obsessional behavior has the effect of reducing anxiety, and some the effect of elevating it (Wolpe, 1958, pp. 90–91). Anxiety is the usual trigger to both varieties. There are cases in which obsessional behavior persists autonomously, after the deconditioning of antecedent anxiety, because it has become conditioned to other stimuli; but such cases are unusual.

The first target, in dealing with an obsessional neurosis—as with neuroses of other kinds—is the identification and deconditioning of antecedent anxiety. Originally, the mainstay of the deconditioning was systematic desensitization, but the amount of effort required is usually very considerable, as exemplified by Case 61, although now and again the method overcomes an obsessional neurosis with remarkable ease. For example, for a mathematics professor with an obsession for tidiness that was destroying his marriage, I used a hierarchy of increasing degrees of disarray in his living room, starting with a one-inch-square piece of paper lying on the floor in a corner. In the course of five desensitization sessions he became able to imagine all reasonable degrees of disarray without disturbance. The change transferred to his life situation, much to his wife's relief, and to the gratification of both.

But the fact that much time is usually required to desensitize the hierarchies that characterize obsessional neuroses stimulated research for more economical methods. Meyer (1966) was the first to attempt to treat these neuroses by prolonged exposure of two patients to the situation (e.g., "contamination") from which the obsessional behavior provided an escape. He prolonged the exposure by precluding the customary washing and rituals. Both of his cases improved markedly and lastingly. Subsequently, the idea was taken up by others, including Marks (1972), Rainey (1972), and Hodgson et al. (1972). The last-named, in a pilot control study comparing desensitization, flooding, and flooding preceded by modelling, found indications of marked superiority of the last over the other two methods.

These findings led to the adoption of flooding as the treatment of first choice for such cases in the Behavior Therapy Unit. Cases 53 and 54 were among the first to be so treated here: the former an obsessive fear of a future event that was treated by imaginal flooding, and the latter a fear of "contamination" that was treated by graduated flooding *in vivo*.

Case 53: Rapidly Effective Imaginal Flooding

Flooding by the use of imagery was applied to a history professor who was incapacitated by an obsessive fear of a negative response from a committee whom he was due to meet several months later to be considered for a position he greatly coveted. The therapist had him continuously imagine that he was actually meeting with this committee and receiving negative reactions all round. The scene raised his anxiety level to 100 *suds* in the first 15 minutes, and then the level gradually subsided to about 60 *suds* after an hour, when the flooding was terminated. At a second flooding with the same scene a week later, it was impossible to raise his anxiety above 40 *suds,* and in a few minutes it came down to zero and stayed there. He stated that his thoughts were now switching to alternatives; this possible defeat was no longer the end of the world. He remained markedly relieved and withstood his eventual actual rejection by the committee very well.

Case 54: Graduated Flooding *in vivo*

This case has been described in detail by Wolpe and Ascher (1976). Celia, an unmarried woman of 20, had for two years been preoccupied with avoiding and removing "contamination" by people or things associated with the college she had attended which she had regarded as beneath her intellectual potential. Her obsession had begun after a horrifying experience. One evening she had returned to her room to find her roommate conversing with another woman student who was lying on Celia's bed describing a drunken sexual experience. Suddenly Celia noticed lice crawling in that woman's hair. This revolting sight was to Celia an emotional confirmation of her negative feelings about the school. She began to avoid touching the students or any objects they might have touched. She had her roommate move from the room, and tried to exclude visitors. If anyone did enter, she would throw out any small objects they had handled and would wash the floor, the furniture, and any clothing the visitor might have touched.

Celia had a succession of conventional treatments, including lengthy hospitalizations. At the Behavior Therapy Unit, after the behavior analysis, systematic desensitization and imaginal flooding had been used without success. We then decided to try flooding with preliminary modelling, having obtained from Celia's parents various articles she had used at college and an assortment of clothing.

At her next visit, Celia was conducted into an unfamiliar office with a desk on which the articles sent by her parents were arranged. She was asked to list these in order of the increasing discomfort she would expect to have on contact. The therapist then picked up a pencil, which she had listed as the least anxiety evoking, and then tried unsuccessfully to get her to do the same thing. He then placed his hand on the desk some distance from the pencil and moved it slowly closer until he touched the pencil with the tips of his fingers. Next he gingerly lifted it from the table, and wrote with it. Then he asked Celia if she would copy what he had just done. She was too fearful to comply for two sessions, but at the third she was able to touch and handle the pencil. The contact made her feel contaminated and therefore anxious. In order to maintain the exposure, she was asked to refrain from washing for two hours, during which period her distress progressively diminished to a low level. In the course of the next few sessions, Celia came to be able to touch and use all the objects, and to wear all the clothing for increasing periods and eventually for the rest of the day without washing.

Under further guidance, she exposed herself to many other things, touching people, walls, doorknobs, and books. After several weeks she returned to her parental home and in the fall was admitted to a prestigious college. Followed up at intervals during the next three years, she eventually reported no vestiges of her obsession.

The common type of obsessive-compulsive neurosis based on fear and avoidance of "contamination," typified by Case 54, has been the main topic of recent research in this field. The most important result of this research has been to establish that the majority of such patients are markedly and lastingly benefited by programs of flooding and prevention of washing, carried out several times a week for several weeks (e.g., Rachman, Hodgson, & Marks, 1971; Meyer, Levy, & Schnurer, 1974; Marks, Hodgson, & Rachman, 1975; Rabavilas, Boulougouris, & Stefanis, 1976; Rachman et al., 1979; Foa, Steketee, & Milby, 1980; Foa & Tillmanns, 1980).

In obsessions that have antecedents other than anxiety, and in those where anxiety is an appropriate response (for example, preoccupations about death), it is necessary to try to break the thinking habit directly. The method used most often is thought stopping (Wolpe, 1958). Yamagami (1971) obtained complete recovery from an eight-year-old color-naming obsession by the exclusive use of thought stopping (p. 112).

Covert sensitization (Cautela, 1966) and covert reinforcement (Cautela, 1970) have been finding increasing use in the treatment of obsessions. The procedures are typified in a case reported by Wisocki (1970), summarized on page 255.

SEXUAL DEVIATIONS

Aversion methods have figured prominently, but decreasingly, in published accounts of the behavioral treatment of sexual deviations. While there is no doubt that these methods have an important place, they should never be the first resort. Each case must first be investigated for unadaptive anxiety responses, which will usually be found; and, if found, they should be treated first.

Male homosexuality is the most common sexual deviation, for which treatment is sought. Experience in the Behavior Therapy Unit has led to the conclusion that it is generally based on one or more of three kinds of learned habits:

1. Conditioned anxiety reactions evoked by women in contexts of emotional closeness or physical proximity.
2. Conditioned interpersonal anxiety of the kind that calls for assertive training, this conditioning having its greatest strength in these cases at the female end of the social spectrum.
3. Positive erotic conditioning to males.

Aversion therapy is appropriate only when the homosexuality rests on the last factor. If one or both types of anxiety conditioning are present, treatment should be directed to them first. If that treatment is successful, it will probably be found that there is no need for aversion therapy because sexual interest has "spontaneously" transferred to adult females (see Cases 59 and 60 in Chapter 16).

Electrical aversion is the common mode, but covert sensitization has also had its successes (e.g., Cautela, 1967; Barlow et al., 1972). The electrical aversion method of Feldman and McCulloch (1967, 1970, 1971) has the special virtue that approach attitudes to females are conditioned in tandem with the deconditioning of positive feelings to males. The patient is asked to examine a number of slides of males, both clothed and nude, and to rank them in a hierarchy of attractiveness. This hierarchy will later be worked through in ascending order of attractiveness. The patient also arranges in rank order a number of female slides to be worked through in descending order, i.e., the most attractive first. Next, a level of shock is determined that the patient finds very unpleasant.

The patient is then told that he will see a picture of a male and that several seconds later he may receive a shock. He can turn off the slide by pressing a switch whenever he wishes to do so, knowing that the moment the slide leaves the screen the shock will also be turned off. He is told that he will never be shocked when the screen is blank, and urged to leave the slide on the screen for as long as he finds it sexually attractive. The first slide is then presented. Should he switch it off within eight seconds he is not shocked, this being termed an avoidance response. At eight seconds, the shock begins and continues. If its strength is not sufficiently high to cause the patient to switch it off immediately, it is increased until he does so. The moment he presses the switch the slide is removed and the shock terminated. This is termed an "escape response." The patient is also told to say "No" as soon as he wishes the slide to be removed, in the hope that further strength will be given to the avoidance habit by this additional element. The usual course of events is: several trials in all of which escape responses are made; a sequence of trials in some of which the patient escapes, and some of which he avoids; a sequence of trials in which the patient avoids every time. When he reports that his previous attraction to the slide has been replaced by indifference or even actual dislike and when, in addition, he switches off within one to two seconds of the slide appearing, the next more attractive slide is introduced and the process repeated.

In combination with the aversive conditioning to male stimuli, Feldman and MacCulloch attempt to induce a positive attitude to females and approach behavior toward them by introducing a slide of a female at the moment of the removal of the male slide. Thus, anxiety relief is associated with the introduction of the female image. The patient can request the return of the female slide after it has been removed. The rationale of this is that the absence of a female slide means that a male slide, by now associated with shock, may reappear. The patient gradually becomes more motivated to request the return of the female slide. However, since this request is sometimes granted and sometimes not, the patient cannot predict the consequences of his asking for the return of the female slide. This is thought to aid the program designed to lead to avoidance of males and approach to females.

The rule of giving therapeutic priority to anxiety habits applies also to other forms of sexual deviation. Stevenson and Wolpe (1960) overcame two cases of homosexuality and one of pedophilia by assertive training. Case 60 records the similar treatment of homosexual pedophilia. The treatment by desensitization of exhibitionism was first reported by Bond and Hutchinson (1960). Its treatment by the deconditioning of social anxiety, mainly through assertiveness training and systematic desensitization, has been the rule in the Behavior Therapy Unit.

For a review of many facets of sexual deviations and their treatment, the reader is referred to Brownell and Barlow (1980).

CHARACTER NEUROSES

A character neurosis is usually defined as a neurosis characterized by asocial or antisocial behavior, such as sexual promiscuity, pathological lying, and kleptomania. This definition obviously also includes such sexual deviations as voyeurism, frotteurism, and exhibitionism. By definitional implication, anxiety is the antecedent of these habit patterns, and its deconditioning is the key to their elimination. This is illustrated by the examples that follow.

Case 55: Desensitization in a Case of Kleptomania

Mrs. U., a 36-year-old housewife married to a man of considerable substance, was referred to me by a probation officer because she had been caught shoplifting and was threatened with imprisonment. Since the age of 19, when she had gotten away with a suit stuffed into her shopping bag, she had stolen thousands of articles, mainly food and clothing. She said that getting something that she had not paid for gave her a feeling of satisfaction.

The crucial fact of the behavior analysis was that she felt an inner tension at either spending money or neglecting an opportunity to acquire something without spending any. Accordingly, two hierarchies were set up, the first in a coffee shop at which she would be having dinner with her three children. If the bill came to anything over $6, she would feel anxiety that increased with the amount of the excess. The theme of the second hierarchy was the awareness of not having taken something out of a shop when she easily could have, and here the anxiety increased with the value of the thing not taken. She was given training in deep muscle relaxation at which she was found to be an exceedingly apt subject.

Desensitization to the first hierarchy commenced with having her imagine that the coffee shop bill came to $7. This produced 20 *suds* that came down to 0 at the third presentation. The amount was then progressively increased until, at the second session, she could imagine spending $13 without anxiety. At this point, she was asked to imagine having sat down with her children in the restaurant and saying, "You can have anything on the menu." This produced no anxiety, in contrast to 30 *suds* when it was proposed to her before desensitization began.

To deal with the second hierarchy, she was first asked to imagine that she was outside a supermarket remembering that she had just been in a remote corner where she could easily have taken a 45¢ can of tuna but had not. This evoked 30 *suds,* which came down to zero at the third presentation. In the course of three sessions, she came to be able to imagine without anxiety having left a $60 gown in a clothing store that she could easily have taken.

The effects of the treatment became increasingly apparent in her everyday life. She stated that she had a wonderful feeling of freedom walking through the shops and not feeling driven to take things. During a two-month interval when she was seen only to discuss other matters such as the handling of her marital situation, there was no recurrence of impulses to steal. At this point, attention was turned to desensitization for her inability to spend any substantial sum of money for clothing—an aim that was largely achieved in the course of three sessions, though I would have preferred to have gone on longer. She was able to purchase almost anything she wanted with little or no difficulty. In the course of a seven-year follow-up, there was no recurrence of shoplifting, and only occasional easily controlled impulses.

Case 56: Inhibitory Training and Systematic Desensitization in the Treatment of Sociopathic Behavior

In 1967 I saw a man, aged 22, because of behavior that could be labeled "sociopathic." The prospective heir to a fortune, and the recipient of a considerable monthly income, he had spent money like water, usually in a way that was likely to impress others. He had often drunk heavily (though not so much recently) because it made him feel "like Superman." He was much given to grandiose daydreams. A few months earlier, he had walked into a motel, checked in, and then pulled a gun on the manager, saying, "This is a holdup." This manager had promptly knocked him down, taken the gun, and called the police, as a result of which he was currently on probation.

At the first interview, I noticed that he was very "quick on the trigger" in his conversational responses; in fact, he spoke almost continuously. He was also manifestly sensitive to the opinions of others, although his Willoughby score was only 24 (but his score for hurt feelings was 4 and for sensitivity to criticism 3). On the Maudsley Personality Inventory, his extroversion score was at the 89th percentile and his neurotic score at the 74th percentile, a characteristic psychopathic profile (Eysenck, 1957).

Two lines of treatment were adopted. First, an attack was made on his primary reactiveness by showing him how to slow down his responses, first in the context of his answers to simple mathematical problems. Then I showed him how to delay or withhold his responses to my statements or questions. I had him enlist the aid of his wife to control these behaviors at home. My second line of action was to obtain from him a hierarchical list of situations in which his feelings were hurt, and to subject this to systematic desensitization. He responded rapidly to both of these modes of treatment. After seven sessions, he claimed that he was in very good control of himself, and no longer so sensitive. He had taken a job as a used car salesman (at which he was very adept) and was managing well because he no longer felt a desire to "fly off the handle" if anybody irritated him, as he had been prone to do in the past. At a follow-up interview six months later, he stated that he was still doing well at selling cars and was getting on progressively with his wife. He had no trouble with drinking, having only one or two drinks in the evening and a few more occasionally at parties. A year later, he made a telephone call from a city in the Midwest to say that he was still getting on well and staying out of trouble.

OBESITY

Some cases of obesity have a biological basis, but the great majority are probably attributable to overeating that is a matter of habit. Stuart (1967) was the first to exploit this realization and to devise a program to change habit rather than to manipulate food content. His original trial was successful in all of twelve cases, for which weight loss was maintained at one-year follow-up.

The patient is instructed to weigh herself at least once a day, either on rising or on retiring. She is given no particular diet, but told that she is under no circumstances to eat except when seated at a table. It is desirable, as far as possible, to eat in the company of other people; but if eating alone she is to do nothing else—i.e., she is to concentrate on eating and not engage in additional activities, such as watching television, listening to music, or reading. Then, once or twice during each meal she is to put down her knife and fork and concentrate on the food without eating, initially for a period of two minutes. This period is increased by one minute each week, up to a maximum of five minutes. The rationale of this is to build up a conditioned inhibition of the automatic response of eating at the sight of food. It seems to have the effect of making many patients feel generally less hungry. In some cases, it turns out to be necessary to inhibit eating between meals by covert sensitization.

Although evidence of the superiority of the behavioral approach to obesity has continued to accumulate (e.g., Levitz & Stunkard, 1974; Stunkard, 1975; Wollersheim, 1970), the optimistic prospect foreshadowed by Stuart has not been sustained. Jeffery, Wing, and Stunkard (1978) found an average weight loss of 11 lbs. reported for behavioral programs, which, as they comment, is "modest when the severity of the obesity is considered." A study by Brownell et al. (1978) suggests that considerably better results may be obtainable with the help of trained spouses.

Aversion programs may at least occasionally be worth considering, but there is no escaping the fact that obesity remains a largely unsolved problem, perhaps because it seems often to have something of the character of an addiction.

16
Some Complex Cases

A neurosis may be complex in one or more of several ways, for example:

1. Multiple families of stimuli may be conditioned to neurotic reactions.
2. The reactions may include unadaptiveness in important areas of social behaviors (e.g., sexual deviations, "character neuroses").
3. The neurosis may have somatic consequences (e.g., asthma, neurodermatitis).
4. The neurosis may include obsessional behavior.
5. There may be pervasive anxiety in addition to that associated with specific stimuli.

The extended case summaries that make up this chapter are intended to illustrate how complex cases can be handled by a behavior therapist. At all times, the stimulus-response relations perceived by the therapist determine his strategies. New information frequently leads to change of direction.

FEAR OF SYMPTOMS

Case 57: Anxiety with Frequent Urination, Nausea, and Diarrhea; Obsession about Wife's Premarital Loss of Virginity

Mr. B. was a 31-year-old advertising salesman who four years previously had begun to notice himself increasingly anxious in social and business situations from which it was difficult to get away. Within a few months, even five minutes in the office of a client would produce considerable anxiety accompanied by a strong desire to urinate. If he went out and relieved himself, the urge would return after a further five minutes, and so on. The only circumstances that could be associated with the onset of Mr. B.'s neurosis were the unsettlement of having moved to a new house in town, and his concern at the unexpected break-up of the marriage of close friends whom he had regarded as ideally mated. His only previous neurotic phase had been a brief one that had occurred upon moving to a new school at the age of 16. This could conceivably have conditioned anxiety to "new places." The Fear Survey Schedule revealed very high anxiety to the following stimulus classes: strange places, failure, strangers, bats, journeys especially by train, being criticized, surgical operations, rejection, planes, being disapproved of, losing control, looking foolish, and fainting.

Mr. B.'s early history was quite conventional. A feature of interest was a strong religious training with marked emphasis on "the good and the bad." Churchgoing had played a prominent part in his childhood and adolescence. In his middle teens he had come to resent it, but had never outwardly rebelled. He had done well in school and got on well with both classmates and teachers. He had been trained in journal advertising, but was now engaged in advertising salesmanship, which he greatly liked.

As regards his sexual history, Mr. B. had been stimulated by erotic pictures at the age of ten. At 13, he had begun to masturbate, without fear or guilt. Dating and petting began at 14, and at 18 he had met his wife who attracted him by her intelligence, good looks, and responsiveness to his jokes. The courtship was broken by Mr. B. after she revealed that she had had an affair two years earlier. On reflection, he condoned the episode, and at the age of 20 married her. The relationship turned out to be a very congenial one, and sexually very satisfying to both; but Mr. B. was never really able to divest himself of the painful idea that he had been "dealt a dirty card."

At the second session, Mr. B. described how embarrassing and incapacitating he found his neurotic anxiety and the associated urge to urinate. Anxiety was greater in the presence of unfamiliar people and if there was no easy access to a toilet. Other factors that increased it were the importance of the occasion and the importance of the other person. On the whole, there was more anxiety in anticipation of a meeting than at the meeting itself.[1] Since it was evident that a desensitization program would need to be undertaken, relaxation training was started at this interview.

At his next session, five days later, Mr. B. reported that he had practiced relaxing, and that by means of it had been able to desist from urinating while at home for a period of six and a half hours despite quite a strong urge. Relaxation training was now extended, and the general desensitization strategy worked out. It was apparent that the duration of interviews with his clients was an important factor determining the strength of Mr. B.'s anxiety. It was therefore decided to treat an "interview" hierarchy, using a time dimension

[1]The therapeutic implication of this last observation will become apparent later.

for its easy quantifiability. I started the desensitization by having him imagine himself scheduled to a very brief meeting (of two minutes' duration) with the manager of an important firm. In spite of the fact that relaxation training had at this point involved only a limited part of his musculature, it was decided to begin desensitization at this session because he manifested considerable calmness. The first scene was presented to him as follows: "Imagine that you have just entered the office of a manager who has a rule that no representative is permitted to spend more than two minutes in his office." By the third presentation this scene produced no anxiety, and scenes of meetings of four minutes and six minutes were then presented in succession.

In subsequent interviews, the duration of these meetings was progressively extended, until by the ninth he could imaging being with an executive for 60 minutes without anxiety. He now found himself much better at real meetings and social situations. While visiting relatives, he urinated only three times in five hours. However, his anticipatory anxiety was almost as bad as ever. There was some measure of it several hours before a prospective meeting, but it became much more noticeable 30 minutes to one hour beforehand, and then increased rather steeply. At the ninth interview, then, desensitization of anticipatory anxiety was started. Anxiety decreased to zero in two to three presentations of each of the following scenes:

1. In his office, 60 minutes before visiting a client.
2. In his office, 30 minutes before visiting a client and preparing to leave.
3. Twenty minutes before visiting a client, entering his car to allow ample time.
4. In his car on the way to a client ten minutes before the appointed time.
5. Emerging from his car at the premises of the client's office, with eight minutes in hand.
6. Entering the waiting room of the client's office six minutes before the appointed time.
7. Announcing himself to the client's secretary five minutes before the appointed time.

At his tenth interview, a week later, Mr. B. reported considerably less anxiety in relation to anticipated business meetings. He had for the first time in many months taken his wife to a downtown restaurant. During the 25-minute ride to that restaurant he had not, as in the past, had to stop to relieve himself in a rest room. At first slightly anxious in the restaurant, he had become almost entirely calm after the first ten minutes. Desensitization to the anticipation of interviews was continued to the point that he could calmly imagine himself in the client's waiting room two minutes before he was to be called in. This hierarchy was finally disposed of at the next session. Now Mr. B. spontaneously reported that he felt far greater confidence in all respects. He had been going out to get new business—at first feeling some strain, but later increasingly comfortably. He had spent one and a half hours with a new and imposing manager of an important new client firm, with hardly any anxiety before or during the interview. He was no longer bothered at going into strange places because it no longer mattered whether or not he knew where the toilet was. For the same reason, he had ceased to fear using trains, airlines, buses, and other public transportation.

Attention was now turned to Mr. B.'s difficulty in asserting himself with strangers. Assertive behavior was instigated. To facilitate it, he was desensitized to one relevant situation—telling a waiter "This food is bad." Anxiety disappeared at the second presentation of this. Two weeks later, at his 14th interview, Mr. B. stated that he was expressing himself where required with increasing ease. For example, he had immediately and effectively spoken up at a drugstore when another customer was taken ahead of him out of turn. He had become more and more comfortable making business calls, citing as an example a one-and-three-quarter-hour interview with a particular executive. He commented that three months earlier he would in the course of so long a period have had to go out to urinate about 20 times. However, he still had to push himself to do some of the things he had become inured to avoiding.

From this point onward, the main focus of therapy was his distress about his wife's premarital affair. First, it was mutually agreed, after reference to Kinsey and others, that Mr. B.'s reactions were irrational. Then, an attempt was made to employ imagery in a way that was suggested by Ahsen's (1965) "eidetic psychotherapy," though this is based upon an extremely fanciful conceptual system. The central practical idea is to ask the patient to imagine himself behaving in a new way in a past real situation that has been emotionally distressful. The idea was employed in the present case by having Mr. B. project himself back to the time of his wife's affair and imagine that he was in the next room while she was amorously engaged with her lover in a hotel. He was to force the connecting door open and beat up the paramour. In doing this, it was supposed that angry emotions would be counterposed to the anxiety that this image ordinarily evoked. Mr. B. was enjoined to practice this imaginary sequence 50 to 100 times a day. He felt himself making progressive improvement for about two weeks, when he stated that his obsession was about 20 percent less in incidence and 40 percent less in emotional intensity. But continuing the drill for a further four weeks yielded no further benefit. After the second week, he was also asked to practice imagining attacking Mrs. B. in the premarital amorous situation, but the only effect of this was to make him feel generally hostile toward her.

I decided, therefore, to tackle the problem by systematic desensitization. In order to desensitize Mr. B. to this long-past situation, I employed images from a fictious film supposed to have been taken of his wife's premarital amorous activities by a hidden camera in her family's living room. Relaxed and with his eyes closed, Mr. B. was asked to imagine that his wife was sitting on a couch with her lover who kissed her and then put his hand on one of her breasts over her dress for exactly five seconds. He felt no anxiety at this. A fair amount of anxiety was evoked by the next scene in which the duration of contact was made eight seconds, but at the third presentation of this scene anxiety disappeared. Two presentations were required to remove anxiety from him imagining the hand over the breast for 10 seconds, and five for 20 seconds.

At the following session, six weeks later, Mr. B. again felt anxiety to the 20-second hand contact, but it disappeared at the third presentation. Two weeks later, he reported that his feelings toward his wife were more detached and that he was thinking of her less. In general, his thoughts were turning away from the past and toward the present and future. Further scenes were presented, increasing the duration of the lover's hand upon his wife's clothed breast successively to 25 seconds, 30 seconds, 40 seconds, one minute, one and a half minutes, two minutes, and three minutes, and her snuggling up to him. None of these scenes produced any disturbance. On opening his eyes, Mr. B. stated that "having got over the hump last time," he no longer cared what his wife had done in the past. Recovery from the obsession (as well as the other problems) had endured at last contact three years later.

The contrast between the marked effects of the desensitization and the limited impact of the 'eidetic' treatment appears to afford a valuable object lesson. In the desensitization, the relaxation systematically overcame the anxiety engendered by images of progressively greater liberties taken by Mrs. B.'s lover, desensitizing Mr. B. to the idea of her having permitted such liberties—which was precisely the therapeutic target. In the 'eidetic' treatment, the images mobilizing anger against the seducer produced some improvement, presumably by deconditioning anxiety for which the seducer was the stimulus. Practicing images of aggression towards the 'errant' Mrs. B. only led to hostility towards her. Since both eidetic images were off the main therapeutic target, neither could have been the vehicle for full recovery.

AUTOMOBILE PHOBIA

Case 58: Desensitization of a Multidimensional Automobile Phobia

The following is excerpted and adapted from an experimental study (Wolpe, 1962). Apart from showing the handling of stimulus complexity, the case illustrates how important it is to communicate accurately with one's patient. Mrs. C. was a 39-year-old woman who complained of fear reactions to traffic situations, and whom I first saw on April 6, 1960. Her story was that on February 3, 1958, while her husband was taking her to work by car, they entered an intersection on the green light. She suddenly became aware of a large truck that, disregarding the red signal, was bearing down upon the car from the left. She remembered the moment of impact, being flung out of the car, flying through the air, and then losing consciousness. Her next recollection was of waking in the ambulance on the way to the hospital. She was found to have injuries to her knee and neck, for which she spent a week in the hospital.

On the way home, by car, she felt unaccountably frightened. She stayed at home for two weeks, quite happily, and then, resuming normal activities, noticed that, while in a car, though relatively comfortable on the open road, she was always disturbed by seeing any car approach from either side, but not at all by vehicles approaching from straight ahead. Along city streets she had continuous anxiety, which, at the sight of a laterally approaching car less than half a block away, would rise to panic. She could, however, avoid a reaction by closing her eyes before reaching an intersection. She was also distressed in other situations that in some sense involved lateral approaches of cars. Reactions were extraordinarily severe in making a left turn in the face of approaching traffic on the highway. Execution of the turn momentarily placed the approaching vehicle to the right of her car. There was a considerable rise in tension even when the vehicle was a mile or more ahead. Left turns in the city disturbed her less because of slower speeds. The entry of other cars from side streets even as far as two blocks ahead into the road in which she was traveling also constituted a "lateral threat." Besides her reactions while in a car, she was anxious while walking across streets, even at intersections with the traffic light in her favor, and even if the nearest approaching car were more than a block away.

Questioned about previous traumatic experiences, she recalled that ten years previously a tractor had crashed into the side of a car in which she was a passenger. Nobody had been hurt; the car had continued its journey, and she had been aware of no emotional sequel. No one close to her had ever been involved in a serious accident. Though she had worked in the Workmen's Compensation Claims office, dealing with cases of injury had not been disturbing to her. She found it incomprehensible that she should have developed this phobia; in London during World War II, she had accepted the dangers of the blitz calmly, without ever needing to use sedatives.

Her early history revealed nothing of significance. In England, during World War II, she had been engaged to a pilot, who was killed. After his death, she had lost interest for a time in forming other associations. Her next serious association was with her husband, whom she had met in 1955. They had married in May 1957, about nine months before the accident. Until the accident, the marital relationship had been good. Sexual relations had been satisfactory, most often with both partners achieving orgasm. Since the accident, however, she had been negatively influenced by adverse comments that her husband had made about her disability, so that sexual behavior had diminished. Nevertheless, when coitus occurred, she still had orgasm more often than not.

In the second interview, training in relaxation and the construction of hierarchies were both initiated. Mrs. C. was schooled in relaxation of the arms and the muscles of the forehead. Two hierarchies were constructed; the first related to traffic situations in open country. There was allegedly a minimal reaction if she was in a car driven by her husband and they were 200 yards from a crossroad and if, 400 yards away, at right angles, another car was approaching. Anxiety increased with increasing proximity. The second hierarchy related to lateral approaches of other cars while that in which she was traveling had stopped at a city traffic light. The first signs of anxiety supposedly appeared when the other car was two blocks away. (This, as will be seen, was a gross understatement of the patient's reactions.) The interview concluded with an introductory desensitization session. Having hypnotized and relaxed Mrs. C., I presented to her imagination some presumably neutral stimuli. First, she was asked to imagine herself walking across a baseball field and then that she was riding in a car in the country with no other cars in sight. Following this, she was presented with the allegedly weak phobic situation of being in a car 200 yards from an intersection and seeing another car approaching that intersection on a crossroads from 400 yards away on the left. She afterwards reported no disturbances to any of the scenes.

At the third interview, instruction in relaxation of muscles of the shoulder was succeeded by a desensitization session in which the following scenes were presented: (1) the patient's car, driven by her husband, had stopped at an interesction, and another car was approaching at right angles two blocks away; (2) the highway scene of the previous session was suggested, except that now her car was 150 yards from the intersection and the other car 300 yards away. It was evident that these were evoking considerable anxiety. This made me subject Mrs. C. to further questioning, from which it emerged that she was continuously tense in cars, but had not thought this worth reporting, so trifling was this compared to the terror experienced at the lateral approach of a car. She also stated that all the car scenes imagined during the sessions had aroused anxiety, but too little, she had felt, to deserve mention. Mrs. C. was now asked to imagine that she was about to ride two blocks on a country road. This evoked considerable anxiety!

At the fifth interview, I learned that even the thought of a journey raised Mrs. C.'s tension, so that if, for example, at 9 AM her husband were to say, "we are going out driving at 2 PM," she would be continuously apprehensive, and more so when actually in the car. During the desensitization session (fourth) at this interview, I asked her to imagine that she was at home expecting to go for a short drive in the country in four hours' time. This scene, presented five times, evoked anxiety that did not decrease on repetition. It was now obvious that scenes with the merest suspicion of exposure to traffic were producing more anxiety than could be mastered by Mrs. C.'s relaxation potential.

A new strategy therefore had to be devised. On a sheet of paper I drew an altogether imaginary, completely enclosed square field, which was represented as being two blocks (200 years) long (see Fig. 16.1). At the southwest corner (lower left) I drew her car, facing north (upwards), in which she sat with her husband and at the lower right corner another car, supposed to be that of Dr. Richard W. Garnett, a senior staff psychiatrist, which faced them at right angles. Dr. Garnett (hereafter "Dr. G.") was "used" because Mrs. C. regarded him as a trustworthy person.

This imaginary situation became the focus of the scenes presented in the sessions that followed. At the fifth desensitization session, Mrs. C. was asked to imagine Dr. G. announcing to her that he was going to drive his car a half-block toward her and then proceeding to do so while she sat in her parked car. As this elicited no reaction, she was next made to imagine him driving one block toward her, and then, as there was again no reaction, one and a quarter blocks. On perceiving a reaction to this scene, I repeated it three times, but without effecting any decrement in the reaction. I then "retreated," asking her to imagine Dr. G. stopping after traveling one block and two paces to-

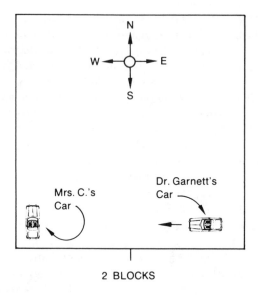

2 BLOCKS

Fig. 16.1. Imaginary enclosed square where Dr. Garnett makes progressively closer advances to Mrs. C.'s car.

ward her. This produced a slighter reaction, which decreased on repeating the scene, disappearing at the fourth presentation. This was the first evidence of change, affording grounds for a confident prediction of a successful outcome.

At the sixth session, the imagined distance between Dr. G.'s stopping point and Mrs. C.'s car was decreased by two or three paces at a time, and at the end of the session he was able to stop seven-eighths of a block short of her (a total gain of about ten paces). The following are the details of the progression. In parentheses is the number of presentations of each scene required to reduce the anxiety response to zero:

1. Dr. G. approaches four paces beyond one block (3).
2. Six paces beyond one block (3).
3. Nine paces beyond one block (2).
4. Twelve paces beyond one block, i.e., one and one-eighth block (4).

At the seventh session, Mrs. C. was enabled to tolerate Dr. G.'s car reaching a point half-a-block short of her car without disturbance; at the eighth session, three-eights of a block (about 37 yards); at the tenth, she was able to imagine him approaching within two yards of her without any reaction whatsoever.

The day after this, Mrs. C. reported that for the first time since her accident she had been able to walk across a street while an approaching car was in sight. The car was two blocks away but she was able to complete the crossing without quickening her pace. At this, the eleventh session, I began a new series of scenes in which Dr. G. drove in front of the car containing Mrs. C. instead of toward it, passing at first 30 yards ahead, and then gradually closer, cutting the distance eventually to about three yards. Desensitization to all this was rather rapidly achieved during this session. Thereupon, I drew two intersecting roads in the diagram of the field (Fig. 16.2). A traffic light was indicated in the middle, and the patient's car, as shown in the diagram, had "stopped" at the red signal. At first, Mrs. C. was asked to imagine Dr. G.'s car passing on the green light. As anticipated, she could at once accept this without anxiety; it was followed by Dr. G.'s car passing one way and a resident physician's car in the opposite direction. The slight anxiety this aroused was soon eliminated. In subsequent scenes, the resident's car was followed by an increasing number of students' cars, each scene being repeated until its emotional effect declined to zero.

At the twelfth session, the roadway at right angles to Mrs. C.'s car was made continuous with the public highway system (as indicated by the dotted lines) and now, starting off again with Dr. G., we added the cars of the resident and the students, and subsequently those of strangers. Imagining two unknown cars passing the intersection produced a fair degree of anxiety, and

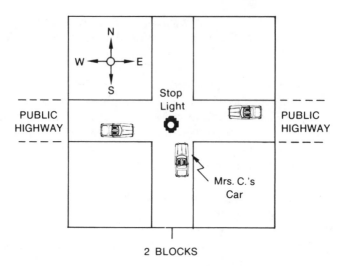

Fig. 16.2. Imaginary enclosed square with crossroads and traffic light added. Other cars pass while Mrs. C.'s car has stopped at the red light.

she required five presentations at this session and five more at the next before she could accept it entirely calmly. Once this was accomplished, however, it was relatively easy gradually to introduce several cars passing from both sides.

We now began a new series of scenes in which, with the traffic light in her favor, she was stepping off the curb to cross a city street while a car was slowly approaching. At first, the car was imagined a block away, but during succeeding sessions the distance gradually decreased to ten yards.

At this point, to check upon transfer from the imaginary to real life, I took Mrs. C. to the Charlottesville business center and observed her crossing streets at an intersection controlled by a traffic light. She went across repeatedly with apparent ease and reported no anxiety. But in the car, on the way there and back, she showed marked anxiety whenever a car from a side street threatened to enter the street in which we drove.

I now made a detailed analysis of Mrs. C.'s reaction to left turns on the highway in the face of oncoming traffic. She reported anxiety at doing a left turn if an oncoming car was in sight. Even if it was two miles away she could not allow her husband to turn left in front of it.

To treat this most sensitive reaction, I again introduced Dr. G. into the picture. I started by making Mrs. C. imagine (while hypnotized and relaxed) that Dr. G.'s car was a mile ahead when her car began to turn. But this was too disturbing and several repetitions of the scene brought no diminution in the magnitude of anxiety evoked. It seemed possible that there would be less anxiety if her husband were not the driver of the car since his presence at the time of the accident might have made him a conditioned stimulus to anxiety. Thus, I presented the scene with Mrs. C.'s brother as the driver of the car. With this altered feature, Dr. G.'s making a left turn a mile ahead evoked much less anxiety, and after four repetitions it declined to zero. We were then gradually able to decrease the distance so that she could eventually imagine making the turn with Dr. G.'s car only about 150 yards away. Meanwhile, when she was able to "do" the turn with Dr. G. three-eights of a mile away, I introduced two new left-turn series: a strange car approaching with her brother driving and Dr. G. approaching with her husband driving—both a mile away initially. Work on all three series went on concurrently. When Mrs. C. could comfortably imagine her brother doing a left turn with the strange car five-eighths of a mile ahead, I resumed the original series in which her husband was the driver, starting with a left turn while the strange car was a mile ahead. This now evoked relatively little anxiety, and progress ensued. The interrelated decrements of reaction to this group of hierarchies are summarized in Figure 16.3.

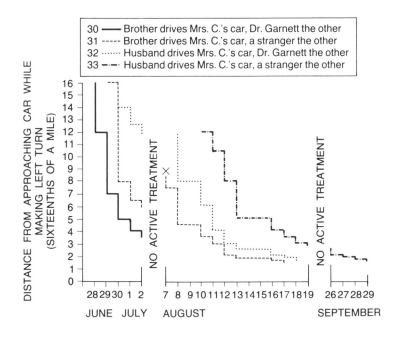

Fig. 16.3. Temporal relations of "distances accomplished" in imagination in desensitization series 30, 31, 32 and 33. X: indicates some relapse in Hierarchy 31 following a taxi ride in which the driver insisted on exceeding the speed limit. The status of Hierarchy 32 was not tested before relapse in 31 was overcome.

Other series of related scenes were also subjected to desensitization. One comprised left turns in the city in front of oncoming cars. Since cars in the city move relatively slowly, she felt less "danger" at a given distance. The series in which Mrs. C. was crossing streets as a pedestrian was extended, and she was enabled in imagination to cross under all normal conditions. She reported complete transfer to the reality. Altogether, 36 hierarchical series were used, which are detailed in the original account of this case (Wolpe, 1962).

The total effect of desensitization to these interrelated series of stimulus situations was that Mrs. C. became completely at ease in all normal traffic situations—both in crossing streets as a pedestrian and riding in a car. Improvement in real situations took place in close relation to the improvement during sessions. Her tension headaches ceased. In all, 57 desensitization sessions were conducted, comprising a total of 1,491 scene presentations. The last session took place on September 29, 1960.

Because Mrs. C. lived about 100 miles away, treatment was episodic. At intervals of from four to six weeks she would come to Charlottesville for about two weeks and be seen almost every day. Noteworthy reduction in the range of real situations that could disturb her occurred in the course of each period of active treatment, and practically none during the intervals. She was instructed not to avoid exposing herself during these intervals to situations that might be expected to be only slightly disturbing, but if she anticipated being very disturbed to close her eyes, if feasible, for she could thus 'ward off' the situation.

When Mrs. C. was seen late in December 1960, she was as well as she had been at the end of treatment. Her sexual relations with her husband were progressively improving. At a follow-up telephone call in February 1962, she stated that she had fully maintained her recovery and had developed no new symptoms. Her relationship with her husband was excellent and, sexually, at least as satisfying as before the accident. Two near-misses of accidents had had no lasting consequences. In 1969 she was still well.

HOMOSEXUALITY

Case 59: Reversal of Homosexuality After Overcoming
General Interpersonal Anxiety*

Mr. R., a 32-year-old hairdresser, was first seen in April 1954. Seven years previously he had become aware of a slowly progressive diminution in his general enjoyment of life. He had emigrated to South Africa early in 1952

---

*A shorter account of this case appears in a paper by Stevenson and Wolpe (1960).

and soon after began to suffer from a persistent feeling of tension, combined with a varying amount of depression. Over the next two years he was treated unsuccessfully by several psychiatrists who gave him electroshock therapy, injections of vitamins, and some psychoanalytic psychotherapy.

Mr. R. was born in a small town in Sweden and had an only sister, seven years younger. His father was a very good-natured religious man who never smoked, drank, or lost his temper. He was extremely submissive in all his personal relations and much dominated by his wife, a very ambitious woman who could never be satisfied. She had been very anxious for Mr. R. to do her credit by becoming someone important, and was very resentful when he did not turn out to be a particularly good scholar. She would repeatedly say how disappointed she was to have borne a son, and treated him like a girl—forbidding him to play football, for example. She used to force him to stay at home and amuse his sister when he would rather be playing with his friends. If anything went wrong, she would invariably blame him, screaming at him and often beating him. His predominant feeling toward her was fear. He also felt an impulse to please her and, particularly in later years, condoned her harshness toward him by the thought that she knew no better.

Mr. R. disliked school, was a poor scholar, and had few friends in childhood. On leaving school at 16, he was sent to work on a farm, but soon left to take up ladies' hairdressing. This greatly angered his mother, but he continued in this career despite her objections.

At the time of puberty, Mr. R. found himself attracted to men, although at first socially rather than sexually. As he became older, he experienced no sexual attraction toward women. When they occasionally made advances, he became extremely anxious and experienced no sexual arousal. By contrast, he found pleasure in the company of men and had a succession of attachments to men with whom he had sexual relations. He took the active role on about 90 percent of occasions. At the same time, he thought homosexuality sinful and shameful, and became increasingly anxious about these activities. He struggled against his inclinations and tried to fortify himself with religious advice and acts of devotion. The failure of these efforts, combined with family stresses, was almost unbearable. He sought relief by emigrating to South Africa when he was 30, hoping that a drastic environmental change might effect a psychological change. Of course, this did not happen. His homosexual behavior continued in unstable relationships, and contributed to the severe anxiety that finally brought him to treatment.

The above history required nearly five interviews. These did not discover any causal sexual trauma, did not elicit any emotions of marked intensity, and were not accompanied by any change in the patient's condition. Toward the end of the fifth interview, because it seemed clear that his excessive devotion to religious matters was responsible for many of his stresses, an effort was made to provide a different perspective and he was given a copy of Winwood Reade's *Martyrdom of Man* to read. At his sixth interview a week later, he reported having read the book, and though he was at first upset by the criticisms of religion, he felt afterwards that his ideas about it had been clarified. He saw that he had taken sin, particularly in relation to sexuality, too seriously.

His reactions in most social situations were extremely fearful and submissive. Arguments of any kind were so unpleasant that he would avoid them at almost any cost. If a customer at the beauty shop where he worked made an unjust criticism of him he would feel hurt, helpless, and tearful, but make no rejoinder. He could not retrieve the considerable sums of money he had lent to some of his friends because he was quite unable to ask for repayment, even after a year or two had elapsed since the loan.

The learning of unadaptive fears was explained to him, and their susceptibility to unlearning. The five interviews of the next two months were devoted to guiding him in the use of assertive behavior for overcoming his social fears. He proved an apt pupil and soon became much more firm and positive in all his relationships. In two months, his symptoms had almost completely disappeared and he was practically completely at ease with his customers. In the meantime, he had formed a couple of new homosexual attachments, each of which, although satisfying while it lasted, had petered out in less than a month. He asked whether I could help him overcome his homosexuality; I gave a negative answer, because Kallman's (1952) twin studies had then convinced me that it had a genetic basis and was therefore impervious to conditioning methods.

Mr. R. did not return until August 23, two months later. He had continued to advance in the handlings of his personal relationships and had been free of symptoms. The quality of his work had greatly improved and, as a consequence, his clientele had practically doubled. He had also been offered an administrative post which would begin a year later at a mission hospital in one of the African tribal reserves, and had been enthusiastically studying to equip himself for this.

When next seen on October 18, he said that he had again felt considerably depressed in the past two weeks because of uncertainties about the mission hospital job. The mission people were not particularly cooperative and if the project fell through, all his study would have been in vain. At the same time, though better than ever at hairdressing, he was becoming dissatisfied with the job because he was finding his customers boring, and he felt that it was no real service to humanity. He was told that any work that ministers to human needs is a service, and was advised to give up the idea of going to the mission. A week later, he reported feeling much relieved after having told the mission people that he had decided to withdraw. On November 29, he said that he was feeling fine and getting on very well, especially at his work, which was giving him such great satisfaction that he had abandoned the idea of changing.

He made another appointment in June 1955 to tell the following story.

Since his treatment he had given up worrying about the sexual problem and had been doing just what he pleased. He had formed a very pleasant homosexual association, but after two months had noticed that he was no longer responding to his friend sexually. A week or two later when he tried to have sex with another man to whom he felt attracted, there was a similar failure of sexual response. "It felt funny." Two or three later attempts with other men also failed and Mr. R. now felt that, "If a man were to touch me I would hit him."

A few months earlier, Mr. R. had met a girl named Jean whom he had found very likable. She had an attractive personality and many tastes and interests in common with his own, so that he had grown fond of her. He had sometimes thought, "I would marry her if I were normal." When his associations with males became unsatisfactory, he began to take Jean out. It was very pleasant, and before long he wanted to see her every day. For about three months the relationship was purely platonic, but one night after a party when they were both slightly drunk and Jean became sentimental, he kissed her and found to his surprise that it was "rather pleasant." From this time onward he began to respond to her in a sexual way. One evening he became so excited during petting that he was sure he could have had coitus. This excitement had since then recurred many times with consistent erections. Even holding Jean's hand had become exciting. Intercourse had not been attempted because she was "not that kind of girl." The reason for Mr. R.'s visit was that he wanted to know whether he dared to propose marriage. It told him that I could see no objection. The next week he reported that Jean was considering his proposal favorably, but had not yet given a definite answer. He felt wonderful and expected at any moment to wake from a dream. He had decided to move to England, and, if they married, Jean was willing to accompany him. He reaffirmed at this interview that he had previously not felt the slightest physical attraction toward women, although he had always liked their company. Unfortunately, his inexperience with courtship caused Mr. R. sadly to mishandle this affair with Jean. He blunted her interest by his unbridled eagerness. When next seen, late in July 1955 (at his 21st interview), he reported that she had rejected him, to his great disappointment, and he was leaving for England on his own. My parting advice to him was to make love only to women to whom he felt definitely attracted.

In January 1956 he wrote from London. After a party, he had taken a woman home who had suggested that he spend the night with her, but he had refused on the pretext of fatigue. A few nights later he had dinner at her apartment and, at the end of a pleasant evening, she suggested that he spend the night with her. Although strongly attracted, he felt very much afraid, excused himself, and got up to go home. But when he opened the front door it was raining heavily. He resigned himself to going to bed with her and risking the chagrin of failure. To his delight, however, his sexual performance was completely successful. At the time of writing, he had made love to this woman almost every night for a month, always with success, and with greater enjoyment than he had ever experienced with men. He was feeling jubilant. He regarded this affair as his final vindication, assuring him that he need never again feel inferior to other men.

I had follow-up interviews with Mr. R. when I was in England in 1956 and again in 1957. He continued to be free from neurotic reactions, remained exclusively heterosexual, and in 1957 began part-time courses in business administration. In January 1959 I received a letter from him stating that he had married a South American girl. His sex life was still in every way satisfactory, and his wife was expecting a baby.

This favorable sequence of events is explained as follows. Mr. R.'s anxieties evidently originated in his childhood association with his harsh, perpetually screaming mother. He was conditioned to be fearful and apologetic toward all people, but men were further than women on a gradient of generalization from his mother. During adolescence he had a pleasant feeling of warmth and affection toward men, which naturally inclined him to seek greater closeness into which entered the expression of sexual impulses. Sexual satisfaction with men reinforced his tendencies to consort with them. Direct instigation of assertive behavior with a wide range of individuals led to an extinction of his fear of people. When this had been accomplished, and he was able to survey the world of men and women without anxiety, preference for females spontaneously emerged—a preference presumably established by social role conditioning very early in his life.

HOMOSEXUAL PEDOPHILIA

Case 60: Assertive Training in a Case of Homosexual Pedophilia[2]

The patient, Dr. V., a 40-year-old physician, was seen late in June 1971 for the treatment of three problems: sexual activity with his three sons (now aged 13, 9, and 5) for about 10 years; numerous longstanding interpersonal difficulties, mainly with his wife, but also with other adults; and mild, episodic impotence with his wife for two years. What precipitated him into behavior therapy was his wife's discovery that he had persuaded his eldest son to take an active role in one of their sexual encounters, i.e., to penetrate the patient annally. Even though she had known for almost two years about the sexual activity between the patient and the boys, this new development was the last straw. The marriage had been very shaky for the past two years, but the wife

---

[2]This case report was provided by Dr. Neil B. Edwards, being condensed from a detailed account (Edwards, 1972).

now saw no possibility of reconcilation even if he were cured. He was leaving in a couple of days for a month in Europe, which was to be the beginning of a legal separation.

Dr. V., slim, athletic, and youthful in appearance, seemed initially somewhat anxious in telling his story but, as the session progressed, became quite comfortable. His pedophilic behavior with his children had started soon after he discovered that his wife had had an affair. Its frequency was variable, but averaged about once every two weeks. It involved all three sons and consisted mainly of his rubbing his penis between a boy's buttocks to the point of orgasm. Since his wife's discovery of this behavior two years back, it had been a continual source of argument. Despite her pleas he had been unable to stop. It was during these two years that he had begun to have trouble maintaining erections during their infrequent attempts at intercourse.

Regarding Dr. V.'s background, he was the elder of two children, the younger being a married sister. He described his mother as "somewhat overbearing." His father was much more quiet than his mother, but "when he did say something, people listened." He was a stern disciplinarian, yet tended to be "overly fair." The patient described himself as having the latter characteristic also.

Dr. V.'s peer heterosexual adjustment had always been, at best, tenuous. Although he dated during high school, his first sexual intercourse was at 17 when he twice had intercourse with prostitutes, contracting gonorrhea on both occasions. This was quite frightening and succeeded in turning him off sexual intercourse for several years. About one year after his second infection, he had his first pedophilic experience with the four-year-old son of a friend.

He met his wife when he was in medical school. About six months afterwards, they had intercourse. This enthused him so much that they were engaged two months later. At a brief vacation in Florida, during which "she was all for sex," they had sexual intercourse frequently. After the wedding she was less keen on sex, and almost immediately began "sitting around moping." This unexpected behavior began to turn him off. Even so, he continued "trying all sorts of ways to get sex" for a few months. Gradually, however, his efforts waned and after about a year of marriage, coitus was down to once every two or three months. Two years later she started seeing another man. Though she claimed that sex was not involved, he was very broken up by this and told her to leave. After a nine-month legal separation, they were divorced. Two months later, they remarried. Sexually she was now the aggressor! He found this irritating, so that within a year they were back to coitus once every two or three months, a frequency which continued to be the mode. It was at this stage of their remarriage that he started turning to his children for sexual outlet.

Dr. V.'s relationship with his wife was strained on several other scores also. Since the early years of the marriage they were prone to arguments. She was "bored to death," but unwilling to take up sports, reading, or any other activity. She wanted to be given a good time, but did not want to invest much of herself.

At the end of the first interview, three things were done: (1) since even when not engaging in pedophilic behavior he was troubled by pedophilic thoughts every day or two, he was shown thought stopping, and told to use it whenever the pedophilic thoughts came to his mind; (2) he was told to avoid sex with anyone during the month he was away, and to concentrate on getting to know people instead; and (3) initial instructions were given on assertive behavior, and he was told to start practicing it. He agreed to come three times a week after he got back from Europe.

On his return he reported that the thought stopping was working well, the frequency of the pedophilic thoughts having decreased to once or twice weekly. He was back with his wife and had had several good erections, but, following instructions, had not attempted intercourse. He seemed fairly well into assertive training. He was congratulated on this and instructed in the expression of positive feelings. The therapist smiled whenever he referred to his wife as "the wife," as was his wont. After about three sessions of this, he was routinely referring to her by her first name. Meanwhile, the smiling brought out some more feelings about her. What he disliked about her mainly was that she had been keeping him "one down." If she provoked him, he would be unable to assert himself, but would instead stay angry for several days, feeling dissatisfied that he was not getting things straightened out. He was now beginning to feel that he was gaining some control.

Since Dr. V. now seemed ready to approach his wife sexually, he was instructed to do so, but to assume at least equalty in control, not allowing her to domineer. At the fifth session, he reported intercourse, which he had initiated, culminating in simultaneous orgasms. He had one disturbing experience —an erection while watching cartoons with his children. He was worried that this would continue, but was assured that it was merely a habit that would extinguish.

He reported at the ninth session that he had misinterpreted a secret conversation between his wife and their eldest son as one of his wife's "subversive sessions." Although he was angry, he let it ride to see what would happen. He found later that this had been a wise decision—the son had been in some minor trouble with the police (breaking lumber at a construction site) while Dr. V. was in Europe, and was afraid to tell him about it. His wife advised the son to tell his father about it and the next day, without prodding, he did. Dr. V. told his wife of his misgivings and apologized—then congratulated her on her course of action. She continued to move toward him.

At the twelfth session, Dr. V. reported that his wife was finally convinced that her "confidence" sessions with the eldest son were subversive in terms of family interaction and that she had agreed to stop them.

The thirteenth session was the last. He reported that he had a minor lapse. He had allowed three issues to build up and had become too angry to speak out. However, having recognized this in time, he was able to express his anger to his wife, and in a couple of hours it was all over. He felt at this point that it would be a good idea for him to apologize to her for letting these things build up. He and his family were leaving for Oregon in a few days. He was advised to call periodically and, if necessary, return for consultation.

The duration of therapy was four weeks—13 sessions. In December 1971, the patient reported by telephone that he was still doing well in all areas.

WASHING COMPULSION

Case 61: A Washing Compulsion Overcome by Systematic Desensitization to Urinary "Contamination" Using Both Imaginary and Real Stimuli[3]

This case example is particularly worth noting because the well-deserved recent preference for flooding treatment in cases of this sort often leads to forgetting that other options exist—if they are needed! Among the details omitted from the account that follows is the use of assertiveness training. Anxiety from sources other than the contamination often tends to be neglected in these cases.

Mr. T. was an 18-year-old youth with a very severe washing compulsion. The basis of this was a fear of contamination by urine, and most especially his own urine, mainly because he dreaded to contaminate others with it. When the treatment to be described began, the patient was almost completely impotentiated by his neurosis. After urinating, he would spend up to 45 minutes in an elaborate ritual of cleaning up his genitalia, followed by about two hours of hand washing. When he woke in the morning, his first need was to shower, which took him about four hours. To these "basic requirements" were added many others occasioned by the incidental contaminations inevitable on any day. It is scarcely surprising that Mr. T. had come to conclude that getting up was not worth the effort, and for two months had spent most of his time in bed.

The neurosis evidently originated in an unusual domestic situation. Until he was 15, Mr. T.'s parents had compelled him to share a bed with his sister, two years older, because she had a fear of being alone. The very natural erotic responses aroused by this proximity to the girl had made him feel very guilty and ashamed. Anger toward his parents for imposing this on him led to hos-

[3]This is an adaptation of a fuller report (Wolpe 1964).

tile and, at times, destructive fantasies about them. Horrified at these, he had come to regard himself as despicable. His urine had subsequently become the prime focus of his "repulsiveness."

Treatment consisted in the first place of conventional desensitization. Since he was disturbed even at the idea of anybody else becoming contaminated with urine, the first scene he was asked to imagine was of an unknown man dipping his hand into a forty-cubic-foot trough of water into which one drop of urine had been deposited. Even this scene produced some disturbance in Mr. T. at first, but it waned and disappeared in the course of a few presentations. The concentration of urine was then gradually increased until the man was imagined to be inserting his hand into pure urine. Each scene was repeated until it no longer evoked any anxiety.

During the course of these procedures, which occupied about five months of sessions taking place about five times a week and each lasting, as a rule, about twenty minutes, there was considerable improvement in Mr. T.'s clinical condition. For example, his hand-washing time went down to about 30 minutes and his shower time to just over an hour; and he no longer found it necessary to interpose the *New York Times* between himself and his chair during interviews.

A new series of imaginary situations was now started in which Mr. T. himself was inserting his hand into increasingly concentrated solutions of urine. At first, he seemed to make some further progress, but then it became evident that there was diminishing transfer between what he could imagine himself doing and what he actually could do. Eventually, whereas he could unperturbedly imagine himself immersing his hand in pure urine, to do so in actuality was out of the question.

It was then decided to switch to desensitization *in vivo*. Relaxation was now opposed to increasingly strong real stimuli evoking anxiety. Mr. T. was, to begin with, exposed to the word "urine" printed in big block letters. This evoked a little anxiety which he was asked to relax away. The next step was to seat him at one end of a long room and present a closed bottle of urine at the other end. Again, he had to relax away the anxiety. Then, step by step, the bottle of urine was moved closer until eventually he was handling it with only minimal anxiety which he could relax away. When the bottle of urine was no longer capable of evoking anxiety, a new series of maneuvers was started. First of all, a very dilute solution of anonymous urine (one drop to a gallon) was applied to the back of his hand, and he was made to relax until all anxiety disappeared; and then, from session to session, the concentration was gradually increased. When he was able to endure pure urine, his own urine began to be used; and, finally he was enabled unflinchingly to "contaminate" all kinds of objects with his uriniferous hands—magazines, door knobs, and people's hands.

The numerous acts of desensitization outlined were completed at the end of June 1961. By then Mr. T. had achieved greatly increased freedom of movement; he was dressing daily, his hand-washing time had gone down to seven minutes, his shower time to 40 minutes, and his cleaning-up ritual was almost eliminated. In September 1961, he went back to school and was seen only occasionally until March 1962. During this time, without active treatment, he made virtually no further progress. In March 1962, he began weekly sessions as an outpatient, and then improvement was resumed. When last seen in June 1962, his hand-washing time was three minutes and his shower time 20 minutes. He said that he was coming to think of urine as "sticky and smelly and nothing else." In February 1965, he reported that hand washing took him about ten seconds, and he "wasn't even using soap." He was leading a normal life. In September 1967, a telephone call conveyed that his recovery had been maintained.

17
Evaluation of Behavior Therapy

Since behavior therapy is the clinical application of experimentally established principles of learning, its use is almost exclusively in clinical states that learning has brought into being. The commonest of these states are the neuroses, and since these are the main topic of this book, we must now evaluate behavior therapy's therapeutic effects on them. It will be seen that the evidence of behavior thearpy's superior efficacy is now very strong indeed.

Psychotherapists very easily acquire a belief in the efficacy of their own methods because, as has long been known (e.g., Landis, 1937; Wilder, 1945; Eysenck, 1952), 40 percent or more of neurotic patients improve markedly with conventional therapies (not behavior therapy) despite widely differing theories and practices. Success with this degree of frequency provides more than enough intermittent reinforcement (Skinner, 1938) to maintain habits, including therapeutic habits. But the fact that this widespread benefit is of quite uniform magnitude indicates that it is not attributable to the specific interventions of the therapies, but to some process that is common to all of them—presumably the emotional impact on the patient of the therapist, a trusted and supposedly wise and competent person to whom the patient entrusts himself. Nobody can claim potency for the particular interventions he employs unless they yield either a percentage of recoveries that is substantially above the common level, or greater rapidity of recovery.

Because there are factual grounds for believing that behavior therapy does exceed the common average in both percentage and speed of recoveries, its techniques are confidently offered in this volume. On the strength of recent reexaminations of misleading analyses of comparative studies (see p. 329ff), there is now good reason to hope that the time is approaching when behavior therapy will at last begin to displace the dominating psychoanalytically oriented approaches and their progeny of muddled eclecticisms (Smith, 1982).

THE CRITERIA OF THERAPEUTIC CHANGE

The central goal of psychotherapy, like that of any other branch of therapeutics, is the eradication or the amelioration of suffering and disability. Since the behavior therapist views the therapeutic task as the eliminating of persistent unadaptive *habits,* an appropriate way of measuring his success would be to classify and enumerate the unadaptive habits before therapy, and then, after therapy, to assess to what extent each such habit has been eliminated. Such assessment can draw upon several kinds of information: the report of the patient, clinical observation, the observations of the patient's associates, and psychophysiological studies.

The clinical criteria for therapeutic change that have been generally adopted by behavior therapists are those put forward by Knight (1941), since they cover the ground in a practical and meaningful way. Ironically, they were originally proposed for the purpose of improving psychoanalytic research, but seem never to have been used by psychoanalysts. Knight's criteria are:

1. Symptomatic improvement.
2. Increased productiveness at work.
3. Improved adjustment and pleasure in sex.
4. Improved interpersonal relationships.
5. Enhanced ability to handle ordinary psychological conflicts and reasonable reality stresses.

Symptomatic improvement is a necessary criterion for change in every case of neurosis. One or more of the other criteria are relevant in most cases, but not in all. A man with neurotic anxieties in work situations may have a completely satisfying sex life and be at ease in social situations. "Symptomatic improvement" in this context does not mean palliation by means such as drugs, but *fundamental* change in the sense that the stimuli that used to call forth inappropriate anxiety or other unadaptive responses can no longer do so *under the same conditions.* What the patient perceives as a symptom, the therapist perceives as a habit. By deconditioning the anxiety-response habit that is the basis of the symptom, he brings about a commensurate diminution of the symptom. If there have been other reactions that have depended on the presence of the anxiety, they, too, diminish or cease—whether they have appeared in the form of migraine, asthma, neurodermatitis, fibrositis, stammering, frigidity, impotence, or homosexuality. The decline of the secondary manifestations of neurosis can thus also be used as a measure of improvement. Moore's (1965) study of the treatment of asthma (p. 293) provides a good example of this.

EARLY OUTCOME DATA

From about 1955 onwards there was a steady stream of reports of the successful treatment of individual cases or small groups by behavior therapy. Many of the earlier reports were conveniently brought together in two volumes edited by Eysenck (1960, 1964). A feature of these reports that is unusual in the literature of psychotherapy is that they generally display *clear temporal relationships between specific interventions and therapeutic change,* as is also to be noted in many of the cases described in this volume.

There was also an early uncontrolled statistical comparison. In a survey (Wolpe, 1958) of my results with behavior therapy in private practice, on the criteria given above, 89 percent of 210 neurotic patients had either apparently recovered or were at least 80 percent improved, in a mean of about 30 therapeutic sessions. In the follow-ups of 45 of these patients two to seven years later, all but one had at least maintained their gains. Table 17.1 (from Wolpe, 1964), comparing the results of this study with those of a typical series from a general hospital (Hamilton & Wall, 1941), and with a psychoanalytic series (Brody, 1962) shows a substantially higher percentage of recoveries for behavior therapy. More striking than the relative percentages is the fact that the number of therapeutic sessions was very much smaller in behavior therapy. The mean number of sessions for the series reported by Brody was in the region of 600—three or four times a week for three or four years (Masserman, 1963), contrasting with a mean for behavior therapy of about 30.

Table 17.1   Uncontrolled Outcome Studies of Different Types of Therapy.

Series	No. of Cases	Apparently cured or much improved	Percentage recoveries
Behavior Therapy Wolpe (1958)	210	188	89.5
Psychoanalytic Therapy (Brody, 1962)	210*	126*	60
General Hospital Therapy (Hamilton and Wall, 1941)	100	53	53

*These figures refer only to the patients regarded as "completely analyzed." The total patient population in the psychoanalytic group was 595.

Other early reports of series of cases were by Hussain (1964) and Burnett and Ryan (1964). Hussain claimed a 95 percent "complete or almost complete removal of symptoms" in 105 patients whose disturbed habits were treated by hypnotic suggestions reportedly based on the reciprocal-inhibition principle. Burnett and Ryan treated 100 patients by relaxation training followed by desensitization to both imaginary and real situations, in groups and sometimes individually. Treatment continued for five weeks on the average. A one-year follow-up was possible on only 25 of the patients, of whom 15 (60 percent) were found to be either apparently cured or much improved. After such brief therapy, that recovery rate seemed quite noteworthy.

RECENT OUTCOME DATA

The 1970s were noteworthy for a well-controlled study (Sloane et al., 1975) that compared behavior therapy and psychoanalytically oriented methods, and for two surveys of comparative studies. The latter were Smith and Glass' (1977) study employing "metaanalysis," later extended by Smith, Glass, and Miller (1980), in which the benefits of different systems of psychotherapy methods were compared; and a review of comparative clinical studies by Luborsky, Singer, and Luborsky (1975). In the investigation of Sloane et al., subjects were evaluated by independent assessors and then sent for treatment in random sequence either to behavior therapists or to psychoanalytically oriented psychotherapists. The conclusion that Sloane et al. arrived at was that there was no significant difference between the effectiveness of behavior therapy and that of psychoanalytically oriented brief psychotherapy. The same conclusion was reached by Smith, Glass, and Miller, and by Luborsky, Singer, and Luborsky. These findings were firmly endorsed by such well-known authorities as Strupp (1978), Garfield and Bergin (1978), and Garfield (1980), and also received the acquiescence of some prominent behavior therapists, including Kazdin (1979).

The net effect of these studies was to draw a huge sigh of relief from the psychodynamically dominated establishment, at the removal of what had seemed to be an ominous threat to their teachings. They no longer felt impelled to take behavior therapy into account as a competitor or even as a serious addition to psychotherapy. All they needed to concede now was that behavior therapy probably had adjunctive value for some "superficial" problems, such as "simple" phobias and routine sexual problems (e.g., Marmor, 1980).

This revised attitude was especially evident in the psychiatric community. To take an example: for about ten years until 1975, behavior therapy symposia were constantly solicited by the organizers of the annual meetings of the

American Psychiatric Association, which also contained a fair sprinkling of other behavioral presentations. After 1975, there were no more invited symposia, and far fewer individual papers appeared on the program.

Behavior therapists involved in clinical practice found the conclusions of the Sloane, the Smith and Glass, and the Luborski studies hard to believe. They were daily observing the power of the methods they were using and knew how often these succeeded, even in many neurotic patients with whom prolonged psychoanalytically oriented psychotherapy had failed. The studies also received some criticism in the literature. Rachman (1971) called attention to flaws in the reasoning of a relevant article by Bergin (1971) . Eysenck (1978) criticized Smith and Glass, and I (Wolpe, 1981; Wolpe & Wolpe, 1981, p. 154) noted some instances where the data of Sloane and his collaborators contradicted their claim of "no significant differences." These demurrals may have given behavior therapists some solace but had little impact on the climate of opinion.

Recent reevaluations of the Sloane, the Smith and Glass, and the Luborski studies have drastically altered the picture. Andrews and Harvey (1981) made a reanalysis of the Smith, Glass, and Miller data. They obtained a copy of Smith, Glass, and Miller's data set of 475 controlled studies, *but restricted their analysis to neurotic patients who had sought treatment,* thus including only studies of persons who would normally seek psychotherapy. This reduced the data to 81 studies, comprising 2,202 patients, which Andrews and Harvey integrated statistically, using the Smith and Glass (1977) meta-analytic technique. They divided the therapies into the four "superclasses," as shown in Table 17.2: verbal, behavioral, developmental, and placebo. A

Table 17.2. Mean Effect Size for Each Type of Treatment.*		
Superclass and Class	No. of Effect Sizes	Mean (SE)
Verbal	95	0.74(0.05)
Dynamic	90	0.72
Cognitive and gestalt	5	1.20
Behavioral	110	0.97(0.06)
Behavior	103	0.99
Cognitive behavior	7	0.74
Developmental	56	0.35(0.06)
Client-centered	31	0.39
Counseling	25	0.31
Placebo	28	0.55(0.06)
Unclassifiable	3	. . .
Total	292	0.72(0.03)

*From Andrews and Harvey, 1981.

total of 292 "effect sizes" were calculated from the 81 controlled trials, based on Smith and Glass' (1977) technique. Almost 95 percent of the "effect sizes of the verbal group were 'dynamic'."

The benefits of the different superclasses of psychotherapy are graphically compared in Figure 17.1. The graphs show the results from three different cross-sections: severity as indicated by location (i.e., college, outpatient, or inpatient); hours of therapy; and time in months after therapy. On all three graphs, behavioral psychotherapy is superior to "verbal" (i.e. dynamic therapy) at every measured point. The behavioral therapies' mean effects size of 0.97 is superior to the 0.74 of the "verbal" therapies at a very significant level ($p < .001$). Andrews and Harvey can hardly be accused of bias in favor of behavior therapy, for nowhere do they make the inference from their analysis that behavior therapy should receive first preference for clinical practice and therefore in the training of clinicians. They generally bracket behavior therapy and dynamic therapy together, apparently on the rationale that because of "developments in cognitive behavior therapies . . . the conception gulf between the behavioral and verbal psychotherapies is narrowing rapidly"!

In somewhat similar fashion, a reexamination by Giles (1982a) of the survey of the outcome studies considered by Luborsky, Singer, and Luborsky (1978) challenges their much-publicized conclusion of the "equal" efficacy of behavior therapy and psychoanalytically oriented psychotherapy. In the original tally of these writers, behavior therapy was superior in six studies, and psychotherapy in none; and there were 13 ties. One might have thought that these figures gave behavior therapy an edge, instead of implying "equality." But also, on closer examination, Giles found that two of the ties actually favored behavior therapy. In his article, aptly subtitled, "Those who have won have not received prizes," Giles remarks, "Is it not curious that 8 of the 19 studies cited by Luborsky, Singer & Luborsky *all* favor behavior therapy?" Giles argues that the facts are even more compelling if one considers the positive empirical results of behavior therapy in disorders known to be refractory to other approaches, such as enuresis, sexual inadequacy, exhibitionism, pedophilia, irritable bowel syndrome, and insomnia.

Giles (1982b) reexamined Sloane et al.'s study and found that the belief that it demonstrates equivalent efficacy for behavior therapy and psychoanalytically oriented therapy cannot be sustained. Although the Sloane study, in its planning and general execution, stands alone among clinical studies, it has a number of shortcomings that, combined with the actual facts of its outcome, invalidate the "equivalency" conclusion. Because two of the independent assessors were psychydynamic and the other operant/eclectic, congruence between assessor ratings and therapist ratings was probably higher for the dynamic therapists than for the behavior therapists who often formulate their targets differently. In addition, there was little effort to assess

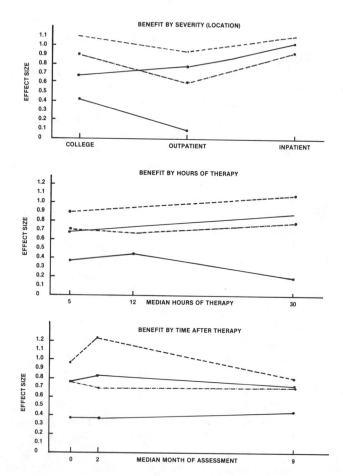

Fig. 17.1   Benefits of psychotherapy as measured by average effect size for all treatments (solid line), behavioral psychotherapy (broken line), verbal dynamic psychotherapy (dot-and-dash line), and client-centered and counseling therapy (dotted line). Results are displayed by severity as judged from location, by hours of therapy, and by time after therapy in months. From Andrews and Harvey, (November 1981) *Arch. Gen. Psychiat.*, **38**: 1205.

the reliability of the measurements—no mention of assessor training, of periodic feedback, or of interrater reliability (Poppen, 1976). The resulting error variance may have obscured differences between treatment effects (see Demaster, Reid, & Twentyman, 1977; Kazdin, 1977).

   Tabulating all of Sloane et al.'s statistically significant results, Giles found one result in favor of psychodynamic therapy and eight in favor of behavior therapy. At the 12-month assessment, only the behaviorally treated patients were rated by the assessors as significantly more improved than the controls in terms of severity of symptoms, and only the behaviorally treated patients were significantly improved over their initial baseline in work adjustment. Analytically treated patients showing low initial pathology did significantly better than those with high pathology, while lows and highs did equally well with behavioral treatment. In sum, the assertion of the equal effectiveness of the two kinds of therapy is not in accord with the data. Behavior therapy did manifestly better, despite the likely assessor bias against it.

It must be noted that the patient population of this study cannot be regarded as representative. Mainly university students, the cases were generally of a mild character. This is reflected in the fact that a high proportion of the control group (50 percent) recovered or were much improved at 4 months without having received any formal therapy. Mild neurotic cases may be expected to benefit from almost any kind of intervention.

In sum, the outcome evidence is impressively on the side of behavior therapy, making it currently the psychotherapy of choice and easily the most cost-effective. Yet the general level of its success is far below what it might be. Only a minority of the behavior therapists who have participated in the numerous studies referred to have been adequately trained in behavior therapy (Wolpe, 1981). This has two implications: (1) even inexpert behavior therapy is to be preferred to psychoanalytically oriented psychotherapy, and as a corollary, psychotherapeutic training in general should become predominantly behavioral; and (2) to the extent that adequate training in behavior therapy spreads, the standard of practice will also rise, and so will the level of its success.

The effects of the widespread insufficiency of behavior therapy training also spill over into "in-house" research in behavior therapy, especially in studies that compare the effects of different behavior therapy methods. What is most lacking is therapists' appreciation of the crucial role of behavior analysis in determining the procedures most likely to be effective in the individual case; and usually tied up with that is a lack of the skill necessary to carry out such analysis. It is usually unjustly assumed that cases with the same label are uniform (Wolpe, 1977).

In earlier chapters I drew attention to several examples of this inadequacy. In research on depression, investigators do not even, as a rule, separate the endogenous from the reactive, let alone distinguish in the latter category between depressions that are cognitively based and those that are based in different ways on emotional conditioning. Even in the commonest topic of outcome research—the treatment of phobias—the erroneous assumption of uniformity of subject matter is made. Particularly pervasive has been the failure to distinguish between fears that are cognitively based and those attributable to classical conditioning. This failure garbles the results of any treatment assessment. Consider the example of systematic desensitization: since this method contains little corrective information, it cannot be expected to have much effect on phobic cases that call for cognitive solutions. Therefore, such cases should be excluded when desensitization is being evaluated, just as viral pneumonias would be excluded in testing an antibiotic for use in pneumonia. The experiments (see p. 53ff) of Bandura and his colleagues (e.g., Bandura, Grusec, & Menlove, 1967; Bandura, Blanchard, Ritter, 1969) exemplify this mixing of sheep and goats. In the treatment of phobias, they compared desensitization with graded exposure to films of fearless models and to live modelling with guided participation. Since they did not take into account the variability of phobic problems, they did not consider that their treatments might influence their subjects in a variety of ways. It is obvious that the films and the modelling provided information that might reduce cognitively based fears. Also, a fearless model's proximity might produce reciprocal inhibition of anxiety in much the same way as the presence of a therapist (Wolpe, 1958, pp. 193–195). Without analyses of the stimulus-response structure of the individual cases, it is impossible for Bandura's experiments to yield any useful conclusions about the efficacy of the methods he used.

Formal studies of the dichotomy between cognitively based and classically conditioned anxiety are now necessary. First, we need to know the distribution of the two kinds of cases in different populations of fearful subjects; second, we need controlled studies to test the prediction that cognitively based anxiety yields specifically to cognitive correction and classically conditioned anxiety specifically to deconditioning methods. An investigation of this kind has been started in the Behavior Therapy Unit, involving two common fears in which the dichotomy is often apparent: fear of enclosed space and fear of physiological symptoms.

Of course, a great deal of further evaluative research remains to be done. We need to know how the magnitude of the nonspecific factor might be enhanced and how to make the most of the behavioral methods in current use. A wide range of additional questions have been articulated by Kazdin and Wilson (1978)—e.g., the breadth and durability of specific improvements, the duration of different treatments, and their relative efficiency and expense.

It has often been proposed in recent years (e.g., Bergin & Strupp, 1972; Feather & Rhoads, 1974; Wachtel, 1977) that psychodynamic methods should be combined with those of behavior therapy, because the different approaches may suit different problems. The weakness of this position is that there is no evidence of the specific effectiveness of any of the psychoanalytic techniques (as distinct from the nonspecific effects mentioned earlier in this chapter). Spending therapeutic time on nonbehavioristic measures may be expected to dilute behavior therapy efforts and to produce poorer results. A possible exception (still to be tested) may be the use in special cases of Wachtel's (1978) idea of persistent childhood behavior patterns.

There is really no escape from the conclusion that knowledge of the factors influencing the making and breaking of habits is of central importance in modifying and eliminating unadaptive behavior that has been learned. This knowledge has generated a steady stream of clinical methods that are increasingly vindicated by their results. While it is not the only source of effective methods—some are occasionally found empirically—it is by its nature the most fruitful. New ideas, pregnant with potential, remain to be tapped (e.g., Solomon's [1980] opponent processes and Catania's [1977] behavioral contrast). And it is time to return to the experimental neuroses, which have historically been our richest resource.

A

Willoughby Personality

Schedule

Instructions: The questions in this schedule are intended to indicate various emotional personality traits. It is not a test in any sense because there are no right nor wrong answers to any of the questions.

After each question you will find a row of numbers whose meaning is given below. All you have to do is to draw a ring around the number that describes you best.

0 means "No," "never," "not at all," etc.
1 means "Somewhat," "sometimes," "a little," etc.
2 means "About as often as not," "an average amount," etc.
3 means "Usually," "a good deal," "rather often," etc.
4 means "Practically always," "entirely," etc.

1. Do you get stage fright?—0 1 2 3 4
2. Do you worry over humiliating experiences?—0 1 2 3 4
3. Are you afraid of falling when you are on a high place?—0 1 2 3 4
4. Are your feelings easily hurt?—0 1 2 3 4
5. Do you keep in the background on social occasions?—0 1 2 3 4
6. Are you happy and sad by turns without knowing why?—0 1 2 3 4
7. Are you shy?—0 1 2 3 4
8. Do you daydream frequently?—0 1 2 3 4
9. Do you get discouraged easily?—0 1 2 3 4
10. Do you say things on the spur of the moment and then regret them?—
    0 1 2 3 4

11. Do you like to be alone?—0 1 2 3 4
12. Do you cry easily?—0 1 2 3 4
13. Does it bother you to have people watch you work even when you do it well?—0 1 2 3 4
14. Does criticism hurt you badly?—0 1 2 3 4
15. Do you cross the street to avoid meeting someone?—0 1 2 3 4
16. At a reception or tea do you avoid meeting the important person present? —0 1 2 3 4
17. Do you often feel just miserable?—0 1 2 3 4
18. Do you hesitate to volunteer in a class discussion or debate?—0 1 2 3 4
19. Are you often lonely?—0 1 2 3 4
20. Are you self-conscious before superiors?—0 1 2 3 4
21. Do you lack self-confidence?—0 1 2 3 4
22. Are you self conscious about your appearance?—0 1 2 3 4
23. If you see an accident does something keep you from giving help?— 0 1 2 3 4
24. Do you feel inferior?—0 1 2 3 4
25. Is it hard to make up your mind until the time for action is past?—0 1 2 3 4

B

Revised Willoughby Questionnaire for Self-Administration

Instructions: The questions in this schedule are intended to indicate various emotional personality traits. It is not a test in any sense because there are no right nor wrong answers to any of the questions.

After each question you will find a row of numbers whose meaning is given below. All you have to do is to draw a ring around the number that describes you best.

> 0 means "No," "never," "not at all," etc.
> 1 means "Somewhat," "sometimes," "a little," etc.
> 2 means "About as often as not," "an average amount," etc.
> 3 means "Usually," "a good deal," "rather often," etc.
> 4 means "Practically always," "entirely," etc.

1. Do you get anxious if you have to speak or perform in any way in front of a group of strangers?—0 1 2 3 4
2. Do you worry if you make a fool of yourself, or feel you have been made to look foolish?—0 1 2 3 4
3. Are you afraid of falling when you are on a high place from which there is no real danger of falling—for example, looking down from a balcony on the tenth floor?—0 1 2 3 4
4. Are you easily hurt by what other people do or say to you?—0 1 2 3 4

5. Do you keep in the background on social occasions?—0 1 2 3 4
6. Do you have changes of mood that you cannot explain?—0 1 2 3 4
7. Do you feel uncomfortable when you meet new people?—0 1 2 3 4
8. Do you day-dream frequently, i.e., indulge in fantasies not involving concrete situations?—0 1 2 3 4
9. Do you get discouraged easily, e.g., by failure or criticism?—0 1 2 3 4
10. Do you say things in haste and then regret them?—0 1 2 3 4
11. Are you ever disturbed by the mere presence of other people?—0 1 2 3 4 people?—0 1 2 3 4
12. Do you cry easily?—0 1 2 3 4
13. Does it bother you to have people watch you work even when you do it well?—0 1 2 3 4
14. Does criticism hurt you badly?—0 1 2 3 4
15. Do you cross the street to avoid meeting someone?—0 1 2 3 4
16. At a reception or tea do you go out of your way to avoid meeting the important person present?—0 1 2 3 4
17. Do you often feel just miserable?—0 1 2 3 4
18. Do you hesitate to volunteer in a discussion or debate with a group of people whom you know more or less?—0 1 2 3 4
19. Do you have a sense of isolation, either when alone or among people?—0 1 2 3 4
20. Are you self-conscious before "superiors" (teachers, employers, authorities)—0 1 2 3 4
21. Do you lack confidence in your general ability to do things and to cope with situations?—0 1 2 3 4
22. Are you self-conscious about your appearance even when you are well-dressed and groomed?—0 1 2 3 4
23. Are you scared at the sight of blood, injuries, and destruction even though there is no danger to you?—0 1 2 3 4
24. Do you feel that other people are better than you?—0 1 2 3 4
25. Is it hard for you to make up your mind?—0 1 2 3 4

C
Fear Inventory*

The items in this questionnaire refer to things and experiences that may cause fear or other unpleasant feelings. Write the number of each item in the column that describes how much you are disturbed by it nowadays.

	Not At All	A Little	A Fair Amount	Much	Very Much
1. Noise of vacuum cleaners					
2. Open wounds					
3. Being alone					
4. Being in a strange place					
5. Loud voices					
6. Dead people					
7. Speaking in public					
8. Crossing streets					
9. People who seem insane					
10. Falling					
11. Automobiles					
12. Being teased					
13. Dentists					
14. Thunder					
15. Sirens					
16. Failure					
17. Entering a room where other people are already seated					
18. High places on land					

*A 108-item inventory, by Wolpe and Lang (1969) is obtainable from Educational and Industrial Testing Service, San Diego, California 92107.

	Not At All	A Little	A Fair Amount	Much	Very Much
19. Looking down from high buildings					
20. Worms					
21. Imaginary creatures					
22. Strangers					
23. Receiving injections					
24. Bats					
25. Journeys by train					
26. Journeys by bus					
27. Journeys by car					
28. Feeling angry					
29. People on authority					
30. Flying insects					
31. Seeing other people injected					
32. Sudden noises					
33. Dull weather					
34. Crowds					
35. Large open spaces					
36. Cats					
37. One person bullying another					
38. Tough looking people					
39. Birds					
40. Sight of deep water					
41. Being watched working					
42. Dead animals					
43. Weapons					
44. Dirt					
45. Crawling insects					
46. Sight of fighting					
47. Ugly people					
48. Fire					
49. Sick people					
50. Dogs					
51. Being criticized					
52. Strange shapes					
53. Being in an elevator					
54. Witnessing surgical operations					
55. Angry people					
56. Mice					
57. Blood					
a—Human					
b—Animal					
58. Parting from friends					
59. Enclosed places					

	Not At All	A Little	A Fair Amount	Much	Very Much
60. Prospect of a surgical operation					
61. Feeling rejected by others					
62. Airplanes					
63. Medical odors					
64. Feeling disapproved of					
65. Harmless snakes					
66. Cemeteries					
67. Being ignored					
68. Darkness					
69. Premature heart beats (Missing a beat)					
70. Nude Men (a) Nude Women (b)					
71. Lightning					
72. Doctors					
73. People with deformities					
74. Making mistakes					
75. Looking foolish					
76. Losing control					
77. Fainting					
78. Becoming nauseous					
79. Spiders					
80. Being in charge or responsible for decisions					
81. Sight of knives or sharp objects					
82. Becoming mentally ill					
83. Being with a member of the opposite sex					
84. Taking written tests					
85. Being touched by others					
86. Feeling different from others					
87. A lull in conversation					

D

Bernreuter S-S Scale and Scoring Key

1. Yes No ? Would you rather work for yourself than carry out the program of a superior whom you respect?
2. Yes No ? Do you usually enjoy spending an evening alone?
3. Yes No ? Have books been more entertaining to you than companions?
4. Yes No ? Do you feel the need for wider social contacts than you have?
5. Yes No ? Are you easily discouraged when the opinions of others differ from your own?
6. Yes No ? Does admiration gratify you more than achievement?
7. Yes No ? Do you usually prefer to keep your opinions to yourself?
8. Yes No ? Do you dislike attending the movies alone?
9. Yes No ? Would you like to have a very congenial friend with whom you could plan daily activities?
10. Yes No ? Can you calm your own fears?
11. Yes No ? Do jeers humiliate you even when you know you are right?
12. Yes No ? Do you think you could become so absorbed in creative work that you would not notice the lack of intimate friends?
13. Yes No ? Are you willing to take a chance alone in a situation of doubtful outcome?
14. Yes No ? Do you find conversation more helpful in formulating your ideas than reading?
15. Yes No ? Do you like to shop alone?
16. Yes No ? Does your ambition need occasional stimulation through contacts with successful people?
17. Yes No ? Do you have difficulty in making up your mind for yourself?

18. Yes No ? Would you prefer making your own arrangements on a trip to a foreign country to going on a prearranged trip?
19. Yes No ? Are you much affected by praise, or blame, of many people?
20. Yes No ? Do you usually avoid taking advice?
21. Yes No ? Do you consider the observance of social customs and manners an essential aspect of life?
22. Yes No ? Do you want someone with you when you receive bad news?
23. Yes No ? Does it make you uncomfortable to be "different" or unconventional?
24. Yes No ? Do you prefer to make hurried decisions alone?
25. Yes No ? If you were to start out in research work would you prefer to be an assistant in another's project rather than an independent worker on your own?
26. Yes No ? When you are low in spirits do you try to find someone to cheer you up?
27. Yes No ? Have you preferred being alone most of the time?
28. Yes No ? Do you prefer traveling with someone who will make all the necessary arrangements to the adventure of traveling alone?
29. Yes No ? Do you usually work things out rather than get someone to show you?
30. Yes No ? Do you like especially to have attention from acquaintances when you are ill?
31. Yes No ? Do you prefer to face dangerous situations alone?
32. Yes No ? Can you usually see wherein your mistakes lie without having them pointed out to you?
33. Yes No ? Do you like to make friends when you go to new places?
34. Yes No ? Can you stick to a tiresome task for long without someone prodding or encouraging you?
35. Yes No ? Do you experience periods of loneliness?
36. Yes No ? Do you like to get many views from others before making an important decision?
37. Yes No ? Would you dislike any work which might take you into isolation for a few years, such as forest ranging, etc.?
38. Yes No ? Do you prefer a play to a dance?
39. Yes No ? Do you usually try to take added responsibility upon yourself?
40. Yes No ? Do you make friends easily?
41. Yes No ? Can you be optimistic when others about you are greatly depressed?
42. Yes No ? Do you try to get your own way even if you have to fight for it?
43. Yes No ? Do you like to be with other people a great deal?
44. Yes No ? Do you get as many ideas at the time of reading as you do from a discussion of it afterwards?

45. Yes No ? In sports do you prefer to participate in individual competitions rather than in team games?
46. Yes No ? Do you usually face your troubles alone without seeking help?
47. Yes No ? Do you see more fun or humor in things when you are in a group than when you are alone?
48. Yes No ? Do you dislike finding your way about in strange places?
49. Yes No ? Can you work happily without praise or recognition?
50. Yes No ? Do you feel that marriage is essential to your happiness?
51. Yes No ? If all but a few of your friends threatened to break relations because of some habit they considered a vice in you, and in which you saw no harm, would you stop the habit to keep friends?
52. Yes No ? Do you like to have suggestions offered to you when you are working a puzzle?
53. Yes No ? Do you usually prefer to do your own planning alone rather than with others?
54. Yes No ? Do you usually find that people are more stimulating to you than anything else?
55. Yes No ? Do you prefer to be alone at times of emotional stress?
56. Yes No ? Do you like to bear responsibilities alone?
57. Yes No ? Can you usually understand a problem better by studying it out alone than by discussing it with others?
58. Yes No ? Do you find that telling others of your own personal good news is the greatest part of the enjoyment of it?
59. Yes No ? Do you generally rely on your own judgment?
60. Yes No ? Do you like playing games in which you have no spectators?

Bernreuter Key*

1. <u>Yes</u> No ?	21. Yes <u>No</u> ?	41. <u>Yes</u> No ?
2. <u>Yes</u> No ?	22. Yes <u>No</u> ?	42. <u>Yes</u> No ?
3. <u>Yes</u> No ?	23. Yes <u>No</u> ?	43. Yes <u>No</u> ?
4. Yes <u>No</u> ?	24. <u>Yes</u> No ?	44. <u>Yes</u> No ?
5. Yes <u>No</u> ?	25. Yes <u>No</u> ?	45. <u>Yes</u> No ?
6. Yes <u>No</u> ?	26. Yes <u>No</u> ?	46. <u>Yes</u> No ?
7. <u>Yes</u> No ?	27. <u>Yes</u> No ?	47. Yes <u>No</u> ?
8. Yes <u>No</u> ?	28. Yes <u>No</u> ?	48. Yes <u>No</u> ?
9. Yes <u>No</u> ?	29. <u>Yes</u> No ?	49. Yes <u>No</u> ?
10. <u>Yes</u> No ?	30. Yes <u>No</u> ?	50. <u>Yes</u> No ?
11. Yes <u>No</u> ?	31. <u>Yes</u> No ?	51. Yes <u>No</u> ?
12. <u>Yes</u> No ?	32. <u>Yes</u> No ?	52. <u>Yes</u> No ?
13. <u>Yes</u> No ?	33. Yes <u>No</u> ?	53. Yes <u>No</u> ?
14. Yes <u>No</u> ?	34. <u>Yes</u> No ?	54. <u>Yes</u> No ?
15. <u>Yes</u> No ?	35. Yes <u>No</u> ?	55. <u>Yes</u> No ?
16. Yes <u>No</u> ?	36. Yes <u>No</u> ?	56. <u>Yes</u> No ?
17. Yes <u>No</u> ?	37. Yes <u>No</u> ?	57. <u>Yes</u> No ?
18. <u>Yes</u> No ?	38. <u>Yes</u> No ?	58. Yes <u>No</u> ?
19. Yes <u>No</u> ?	39. <u>Yes</u> No ?	59. <u>Yes</u> No ?
20. <u>Yes</u> No ?	40. Yes <u>No</u> ?	60. <u>Yes</u> No ?

*Underlined answer scores one point.

Bibliography

Abel, G. G., Levis, D. J., & Clancy. J. (1970) Aversion therapy applied to taped sequences of deviant behavior in exhibitionism and other sexual deviations: A preliminary report, *J. Behav. Ther. Exp. Psychiat.,* **1**:59.

Abraham, D. (1963) Treatment of encopresis with imipramine, *Amer. J. Psychiat.,* **119**:891.

Ackerman, S. H. & Sachar, E. J. (1974) The lactate theory of anxiety: A review and reevaluation, *Psychosom. Med.,* **36**:69.

Ahsen, A. (1965) *Eidetic psychotherapy,* Lahore, India, Nai Matboat Press.

American Psychoanalytic Association (1958) Summary and final report of the Central-Fact-Gathering Committee, Unpublished manuscript.

Amsel, A. (1962) Frustrative nonreward in partial reinforcement and discrimination learning: Some recent history and a theoretical extension, *Psychol. Rev.,* **69**:306.

Amsel, A. (1972) Inhibition and mediation in classical, Pavlovian, and instrumental conditioning. In R. A. Boakes & M. S. Halliday (Eds.), *Inhibition and learning,* London, Academic Press.

Anant, S. (1967) A note on the treatment of alcoholics by a verbal aversion technique, *Canad. Psychol.,* **80**:19.

Anderson, O. D. & Parmenter, R. (1941) A longterm study of the experimental neurosis in the sheep and dog, *Psychosom. Med. Monogr.* **2**, nos. 3 and 4.

Andrews, G., Harris, M., Garside, R., & Kay, D. (1964) *Syndrome of stuttering,* London, Heinemann Medical Books.

Andrews, G. & Harvey, R. (1981) Does psychotherapy benefit neurotic patients?, *Arch. Gen. Psychiat.,* **38**:1203.

Appel, J. B. (1963) Punishment and shock intensity, *Science,* **141**:528.

Arnold, M. B. (1945) The physiological differentiation of emotional states, *Psychol. Rev.,* **52**:35.

Arnold, M. B. (1960) *Emotion and Personality,* Vol. 1, New York, Columbia University Press.

Ascher, L. M. (1978) Paradoxical intention: A review of preliminary research, *Internatl. Forum Logother.,* **1**:18.

Ascher, L. M. (1981) Paradoxical intention. In A. Goldstein & E. B. Foa (Eds.), *Handbook of behavioral interventions,* New York, Wiley.

Ascher, L. M. & Efran, J. S. (1978) The use of paradoxical intention in a behavioral program for sleep onset insomnia, *J. Consult. Clin. Psychol.,* **46**:547.

Ascher, L. M. & Turner, R. M. (1979) Controlled comparison of progressive relaxation, stimulus control, and paradoxical intention therapies for insomnia, *J. Consult. Clin. Psychol.,* **471**:500.

Ashem, B. & Donner, L. (1968) Covert sensitization with alcoholics: A controlled replication, *Behav. Res. Ther.,* **6**:7.

Asratian, E. A. (1972) Genesis and localization of conditioned inhibition. In R. H. Brookes & M. S. Halliday. *Inhibition and Learning.* Academic Press.

Ax, A. F. (1953) The physiological differentation of anger and fear in humans, *Psychom. Med.,* **15**:433.

Ayllon, T. (1963) Intensive treatment of psychotic behavior by stimulus satiation and food reinforcement, *Behav. Res. Ther.,* **1**:53.

Ayllon, T. & Azrin, N. H. (1964) Reinforcement and instructions with mental patients, *J. Exp. Anal. Behav.,* **7**:327.

Ayllon, T. & Azrin, N. H. (1965) The measurement and reinforcement of behavior of psychotics, *J. Exp. Anal. Behav.,* **8**:357.

Ayllon, T. & Azrin, N. H. (1968) *The token economy: A motivational system for therapy and rehabilitation,* New York, Appleton-Century-Crofts.

Ayllon, T. & Michael, J. (1959) The psychiatric nurse as a behavioral engineer, *J. Exp. Anal. Behav.,* **2**:323.

Ayllon, T., Smith, D., & Rogers, M. (1970) Behavioral management of school phobia, *J. Behav. Ther. Exp. Psychiat.,* **1**:125.

Azrin, N. H. & Besalel, V. A. (1980) *How to use overcorrection,* Lawrence, Kan., H. & H. Enterprises.

Azrin, N. H. & Foxx, R. M. (1974) *Toilet training in less than a day,* New York, Simon & Schuster.

Azrin, N. H. & Holz, W. C. (1966) Punishment. In W. K. Honig (Ed.), *Operant behavior: Areas of research and application,* New York, Appleton-Century-Crofts.

Azrin, N. H. & Nunn, R. G. (1973) Habit reversal: A method of eliminating nervous habits and tics, *Behav. Res. Ther.,* **11**:619.

Azrin, N. H. & Nunn, R. G. (1974) A rapid method of eliminating stuttering by a regulated breathing approach, *Behav. Res. Ther.,* **8**:330.

Azrin, N. H., Nunn, R. G., & Frantz, S. E. (1980) Habit reversal vs. negative practice treatment of nervous tics, *Behav. Ther.,* **11**:169.

Azrin, H. H., Nunn, R. G., & Frantz-Renshaw, S. E. (1980) Habit reversal treatment of thumbsucking, *Behav. Res. Ther.,* **18**:395.

Bachrach, A. J., Erwin, W. J., & Mohr, J. P. (1965) The control of eating behavior in an anorexic by operant conditioning techniques. In L. Ullmann & L. Krasner (Eds.), *Case studies in behavior modification,* New York, Holt, Rinehart, & Winston.

Bailey, P. (1964) Sigmund Freud: Scientific period (1873–1897). In J. Wolpe, A. Salter, & L. J. Reyna (Eds.), *The conditioning therapies,* New York, Holt, Rinehart & Winston.

Bain, J. A. (1928) *Thought control in everyday life,* New York, Funk & Wagnalls.

Bajtelsmit, J. W. & Gershman, L. (1976) Covert positive reinforcement: Efficacy and conceptualization, *J. Behav. Ther. Exp. Psychiat.,* **7**:207.

Bandura, A. (1968) Modelling approaches to the modification of phobic disorders, *Ciba Foundation Symposium: The Role of Learning in Psychotherapy,* London, Churchill.

Bandura, A. (1969) *Principles of behavior modification,* New York, Holt, Rinehart, & Winston.

Bandura, A. (1974) Behavior theory and the models of man, *Amer. Psychol.,* **29**:859.

Bandura, A. (1977) Self-efficacy: Toward a unifying theory of behavioral change. *Psychol. Rev.,* Vol. 84, p. 191.

Bandura, A. & Adams, N. E. (1977) Analysis of self-efficacy theory of behavioral change, *Cogn. Ther. Res.,* **1**:287.

Bandura, A., Blanchard, E. D., & Ritter, B. (1969) Relative efficacy of desensitization and modeling approaches for inducing behavioral, affective and attitudinal changes, *J. Pers. Soc. Psychol.,* **13**:173.

Bandura, A., Grusec, J., & Menlove, F. (1967) Vicarious extinction of avoidance behavior, *J. Pers. Soc. Psychol.,* **5**:16.

Barber, T. X. (1969) *Hypnosis: A scientific approach,* New York, Van Nostrand Reinhold.

Barker, J. C. & Miller, M. B. (1968) Recent developments and some future trends in the application of aversion therapy. Unpublished manuscript.

Barlow, D. H. (1979) President's message, *Behav. Ther.,* **2**:8.

Barlow, J. A. (1956) Secondary motivation through classical conditioning: A reconsideration of the nature of backward conditioning, *Psychol. Rev.,* **63**:406.

Beach, F. A. (1942) Comparison of copulatory behavior of male rats reared in isolation, cohabitation, and segregation, *J. Genet. Psychol.,* **60**:121.

Beck, A. T. (1967) *Depression,* New York, Harper & Row.

Beck, A. T. (1976) *Cognitive therapy and the emotional disorders,* New York, International Universities Press.

Beck, A. T. & Mahoney, M. (1979) Schools of "thought," *Amer. Psychol.,* **34**:98.

Behrend, E. R. & Bitterman, M. E. (1963) Sidman avoidance in the fish, *J. Exp. Anal. Behav.,* **13**:220.

Benjamin, S., Marks, I. M., & Huson, J. (1972) Active muscular relaxation in desensitization of phobic patients, *Psychol. Med.,* **2**:381.

Benson, H. (1975) *The relaxation response,* New York, Morrow.

Benson, H., Shapiro, D., Tursky, B., & Schwartz, G. E. (1971) Decreased systolic blood pressure through operant conditioning techniques in patients with essential hypertension, *Science,* **173**:740.

Bergin, A. (1971) The evaluation of therapeutic outcomes. In A. E. Bergin & S. L. Garfield (Eds.), *Handbook of psychotherapy and behavior change: An empirical analysis,* New York, Wiley.

Bergin, A. E. & Strupp, H. H. (1972) *Changing frontiers in the science of psychotherapy,* Chicago, Aldine Atherton.

Berkun, M. M. (1957) Factors in the recovery from approach-avoidance conflict, *J. Exp. Psychol.,* **54**:65.

Berlyne, D. E. (1960) *Conflict, arousal, and curiosity,* New York, McGraw-Hill.

Berlyne, D. E. (1971) *Aesthetics and psychobiology,* New York, Appleton-Century-Crofts.

Bernstein, D. A. (1973) Behavioral fear assessment. In H. Adams & P. Unchil (Eds.), *Issues and trends in behavior therapy,* Springfield, Ill., C. C. Thomas.

Bernstein, D. A. & Paul, G. L. (1971) Some comments on therapy analogue research with small animal "phobias," *J. Behav. Exp. Psychiat.,* **2**:225.

Bijou, S. W. & Ruiz, R. (1981) *Behavior modification: Contributions to education,* Hillsdale, N.J., Lawrence Erlbaum.

Black, A. H. (1958) The extinction of avoidance responses under curare, *J. Comp. Physiol. Psychol.,* **51**:519.

Blakemore, C. B. (1965) The application of behavior therapy to a sexual disorder. In H. J. Eysenck (Ed.), *Experiments in behavior therapy,* Oxford, Pergamon Press.

Blakemore, C. B., Thorpe, J. G., Barker, J. C., Conway, C. G., & Lavin, N. I. (1963) The application of faradic aversion conditioning in a case of transvestism, *Behav. Res. Ther.,* **1**:29.

Bleuler, E. (1911) *Dementia praecox or the group of schizophrenias,* J. Zinken (Trans.), New York, International Universities Press.

Blinder, J., Freeman, D. M. A., & Stunkard, A. J. (1970) Behavior therapy of anorexia nervosa: Effectiveness of activity as a reinforcer of weight gain, *Amer. J. Psychiat.,* **126**:1093.

Block, J., Jennings, P. H., Harvey, E., & Simpson, E. (1964) Interaction between allergic potential and psychopathology in childhood asthma, *Psychosom. Med.,* **26**:307.

Bond, I. K. & Hutchinson, H. C. (1960) Application of reciprocal inhibition therapy to exhibitionism, *Canad. Med. Ass. J.,* **83**:23.

Borkovec, T. D. & O'Brien, G. T. (1976) Methodological and target behavior issues in analogue therapy outcome research. In M. Hersen, R. M. Eisler, & P. M. Miller (Eds.), *Progress in Behavior Modification,* New York, Academic Press.

Borkovec, T. D. & Sides, J. K. (1979) Critical procedural variables related to the physiological effects of progressive relaxations: A review, *Behav. Res. Ther.,* **17**:119.

Boudreau, L. (1972) Transcendental meditation and yoga as reciprocal inhibitors, *J. Behav. Ther. Exp. Psychiat.,* **3**:97.

Boulougouris, J. C., Marks, I. M., & Marset, P. (1971) Superiority of flooding (implosion) to desensitization for reducing pathological fear, *Behav. Res. Ther.,* **9**:7.

Bower, T. G. R. (1976) Repetitive processes in child development, *Scientific American,* **235**:38.

Bower, T. G. R. (1977) *A primer of infant development,* New York, W. H. Freeman.

Brady, J. P. (1966) Brevital-relaxation treatment of frigidity, *Behav. Res. Ther.,* **4**:71.

Brady, J. P. (1971) Metronome-conditioned speech retraining for stuttering, *Behav. Ther.,* **2**: 129.

Brady, J. P. & Pomerleau, O. F. (1975) Behavior modification in medical practice, *Penn. Med.,* **78**:49.

Bregman, E. (1934) An attempt to modify the emotional attitudes of infants by the conditioned response technique, *J. Genet. Psychol.,* **45**:169.

Brody, M. W. (1962) Prognosis and results of psychoanalysis. In J. H. Nodine & J. H. Moyer (Eds.), *Psychosomatic medicine,* Philadelphia, Lea and Febiger.

Brookshire, K. H., Littman, R. A., & Stewart, C. N. (1961) Residue of shock trauma in the white rat: A three-factor theory, *Psychol. Monogr.,* **75** (10, Whole No. 514).

Brookshire, K. H., Littman, R. A., & Stewart, C. N. (1962) The interactive effect of promazine and postweaning stress upon adult avoidance behavior, *J. Nerv. Ment. Dis.,* **135**:52.

Brownell, K. D. & Barlow, D. H. (1980) The behavioral treatment of sexual deviation. In A. Goldstein & E. B. Foa (Eds.), *Handbook of behavioral interventions,* New York, Wiley.

Brownell, K. D., Heckerman, C. L., Westlake, R. J., Hayes, S. C., & Monti, P. M. (1978) The effect of couples training and partner cooperativeness in the behavioral treatment of obesity, *Behav. Res. Ther.,* **16**:323.

Bruch, H. (1973) *Eating disorders: Obesity, anorexia nervosa and the person within,* New York, Basic Books.

Buchwald, A. M., Coyne, J. C., & Cole, C. S. (1978) A critical evaluation of the learned helplessness model of depression, *J. Abnorm. Psychol.,* **87**:180.

Budzinski, T. H. & Stoyva, J. M. (1969) An instrument for producing deep muscle relaxation by means of analog information feedback, *J. App. Behav. Anal.,* **2**:231.

Budzinski, T., Stoyva, J., & Adler, C. (1970) Feedback-induced muscle relaxation: Application to tension headaches, *J. Behav. Ther. Exp. Psychiat.,* **1**:205.

Burchard, J. & Tyler, V. (1965) The modification of delinquent behavior through operant conditioning, *Behav. Res. Ther.,* **2**:245.

Burnett, A. & Ryan, E. (1964) Conditioning techniques in psychotherapy, *Canad. Psychiat. Ass. J.,* **9**:140.

Burnham, W. H. (1924) *The normal mind,* New York, Appleton-Century-Crofts.

Burns, D. & Brady, J. P. (1980) The treatment of stuttering. In A. Goldstein & E. B. Foa (Eds.), *Handbook of behavioral interventions,* New York, Wiley.

Cabanac, M. (1971) Physiological role of pleasure, *Science,* **173**:1103.

Campbell, B. A. & Church, R. M. (1969) *Punishment and aversive behavior,* New York, Appleton-Century-Crofts.

Campbell, D., Sanderson, R. E. & Laverty, S. G. (1964) Characteristics of a conditioned response in human subjects during extinction trials following a single traumatic conditioning trial, *J. Abn. Soc. Psychol,* **68**:627.

Carmichael, L. (1946) *Manual of child psychology,* New York, Wiley.

Castelucci, V. F., Carew, T. J., & Kandel, E. R. (1978) Cellular analysis of long-term habituation of the gill-withdrawal reflex of Apoysia Californica, *Science,* **202:**1306.

Catania, A. C. (1963) Concurrent performances: Reinforcement interaction and response independence, *J. Exp. Anal. Behav.,* **6:**253.

Catania, A. C. (1969) Concurrent performances: Inhibition of one response by reinforcement of another, *J. Exp. Anal. Behav.,* **12:**731.

Catania, A. C. (1973) Self-inhibiting effects of reinforcement, *J. Exp. Anal. Behav.,* **19:**517.

Cautela, J. (1966) Treatment of compulsive behavior by covert sensitization, *Psychol. Rec.,* **16:** 33.

Cautela, J. (1967) Covert sensitization, *Psychol. Rep.,* **20:**459.

Cautela, J. (1970) Covert reinforcement, *Behav. Ther.,* **1:**33.

Cautela, J. (1970) Covert negative reinforcement, *J. Behav. Ther. Exp. Psychiat.,* **1:**273.

Cautela, J. R. (1972) The treatment of over-eating by covert conditioning, *Psychotherapy: Theory, Research and Practice,* **9:**211.

Cautela, J. R. (1977) The use of covert conditioning in modifying pain behavior, *J. Behav. Ther. Exp. Psychiat.,* **8:**45.

Cautela, J. R. & Kastenbaum, R. (1967) A reinforcement survey schedule for use in therapy, training, and research, *Psychol. Rep.,* **20:**1115.

Cautela, J. R. & Wall, C. C. (1980) Covert conditioning in clinical practice. In A. Goldstein & E. B. Foa (Eds.), *Handbook of behavioral interventions,* New York, Wiley.

Chapman, J. (1966) The early symptoms of schizophrenia, *Brit. J. Psychiat.,* **112:**225.

Chesney, M. A. & Shelton, J. L. (1976) A comparison of muscle relaxation and electromyogram biofeedback treatments for muscle contraction headache, *J. Behav. Ther. Exp. Psychiat.,* **7:** 221.

Church, R. (1963) The varied effects of punishment, *Psychol. Rev.,* **70:**369.

Clark, D. E. (1963) The treatment of monosymptomatic phobia by systematic desensitization, *Behav. Res. Ther.,* **1:**63.

Clayton, P. J. & Darvish, H. S. (1978) The course of depressive symptoms following the stress of bereavement. Paper presented at the meeting of the American Psychopathological Association.

Cohen, R. & Dean, S. J. (1968) Group desensitization of test anxiety, *Proceed., 76th Ann. Conv. Amer. Psychol. Ass.,* 615.

Compernolle, T., Hogduin, K., & Joele, L. (1979) Diagnosis and treatment of the hyperventilation syndrome, *Psychosom.,* **20:**612.

Conner, W. H. (1974) Effects of brief relaxation training on autonomic response to anxiety-provoking stimuli, *Psychophysiol.,* **11:**591.

Conrad, S. R. & Wincze, J. P. (1976) Orgasmic reconditioning in male homosexuals, *Behav. Ther.,* **7:**155.

Cooke, G. (1966) The efficacy of two desensitization procedures: An analogue study, *Behav. Res. Ther.,* **4:**17.

Cooper, A. J. (1971) Treatments of male potency disorders: The present status, *Psychosom.,* **12:** 235.

Cooper, A. J., Ismail, A., Smith, C. G., & Loraine, J. (1970) Androgen function in "psychogenic" and "constitutional" types of impotence., *Brit. Med. J.,* July 4.

Coppock, H. W. (1951) Secondary reinforcing effect of a stimulus repeatedly presented after electric shock, *Amer. Psychol.,* **6:**277.

Crafts, L. W., Schneirla, T. C., Robinson, E. E., et al. (1938) *Recent experiments in psychology,* New York, McGraw-Hill.

Crowder, J. E. & Thornton, D. W. (1970) Effects of systematic desensitization, programmed fantasy and bibliotherapy on a specific fear, *Behav. Res. Ther.,* **8:**35.

Culler, E. (1938) Observations on direct cortical stimulation in the dog, *Psychol. Bull.,* **35:**687.

Cushing, C. H. (1932) Peptic ulcers in the interbrain, *Surg. Gynecol. Obstet.,* **55**:1.

Dale, H. (1937) Transmission of nervous effects by acetylcholine, *Harvey Lec.,* **32**:229.

Dalton, K. (1964) *Pre-menstrual syndrome,* Springfield, Ill., C. C. Thomas.

Daniels, L. K. (1974) *The management of childhood behavior problems in school and at home,* Springfield, Ill., C. C. Thomas.

Darnton, R. (1968) *Mesmerism and the End of the Enlightenment in France.* Cambridge: Harvard University Press.

Darwin, P. L. & Mc Brearty, J. F. (1969) The subject speaks up in desensitization. In R. D. Rubin & C. M. Franks (Eds.), *Advances in behavior therapy, 1968,* New York, Academic Press.

Davis, A. D. (1960) Some physiological correlates of Rorschach body image productions, *J. Abn. Soc. Psychol.,* **60**:432.

Davison, G. C. (1967) The elimination of a sadistic fantasy by a client-controlled countercondi-tioning technique, *J. Abn. Psychol.,* **73**:84.

Dekker, E., Pelser, H. E., & Groen, J. (1957) Conditioning as a cause of asthmatic attacks, *J. Psychosom. Res.,* **2**:97.

Deluty, M. Z. (1976) Choice and the rate of punishment in concurrent schedules, *J. Exp. Anal. Behav.,* **25**:75.

Deluty, M. Z. (1977) Similarities of the matching law to other models of conditioning, *Psychol. Rec.,* **27**:599.

Demaster, B., Reid, J., & Twentyman, C. (1977) Effects of different amounts of feedback on observers' reliability, *Behav. Ther.,* **8**:317.

DeMoor, W. (1970) Systematic desensitization versus prolonged high intensity stimulation (flooding), *J. Behav. Ther. Exp. Psychiat.,* **1**:139.

Dengrove, E. (1968) Personal communication.

Denholtz, M. (1971) The use of tape recordings between therapy sessions, *J. Behav. Ther. Exp. Psychiat.,* **1**:139.

Depue, R. A. & Monroe, S. M. (1978) Learned helplessness in the perspective of the depressive disorders: Conceptual and definitional issues, *J. Abn. Psychol.,* **87**:3.

DeSilva, P., Rachman, S., & Seligman, M. E. P. (1977) Prepared phobias and obsessions: Ther-apeutic outcome, *Behav. Res. Ther.,* **15**:65.

Destounis, N. (1963) Enuresis and imipramine, *Amer. J. Psychiat.,* **119**:893.

Dexter, S. L. (1982) Rebreathing aborts migraine attacks, *Brit. Med. J.,* **284.**

Donner, L. (1970) Automated group desensitization: A follow-up report, *Behav. Res. Ther.,* **8**: 241.

Donner, L. & Guerney, B. G., Jr. (1969) Automated group desensitization for test anxiety, *Behav. Res. Ther.,* **7**:1.

Drooby, A. S. (1964) A reliable truce with enuresis, *Dis. Nerv. Syst.,* **25**:97. (a)

Drooby, A. S. (1964) Personal communication. (b)

Drvota, S. (1962) Personal communication.

Dunlap, K. (1932) *Habits: Their making and unmaking,* New York, Liveright.

Dworkin, S., Raginsky, B. B., & Bourne, W. (1937) Action of anesthetics and sedatives upon the inhibited nervous system, *Current Res. Anaesth.,* **16**:283.

Ebbinghaus, H. (1913) *Memory,* New York, Teachers College.

Eccles, J. C. (1975) Under the spell of synapse. In F. G. Worden, J. P. Swazey, & G. Adelman (Eds.), *The neurosciences: Paths of discovery,* Cambridge, Mass., Colonial Press.

Edelman, R. L. (1971) Operant conditioning treatment of encopresis, *J. Behav. Ther. Exp. Psychiat.,* **1**:71.

Edwards, N. B. (1972) Case conference: Assertive training in a case of homosexual pedophilia, *J. Behav. Ther. Exp. Psychiat.,* **3**:55.

Efran, J. S. & Marcia, J. E. (1967) The treatment of fears by expectancy manipulation: An ex-ploratory investigation, *Proceed., 75th Ann. Conv. Amer. Psychol. Ass.,* **239.**

Ellis, A. (1958) Rational psychotherapy, *J. Gen. Psychol.,* **59**:35.

Ellis, A. (1962) *Reason and emotion in psychotherapy,* New York, Lyle Stuart.

Ellis, A. (1970) *Address to the 1970 meeting of the Assoc. Adv. Behav. Ther.,* Miami, Fla.

Ellis, A. (1974) *Humanistic psychotherapy: The rational-emotive approach,* New York, Julian Press.

Emmelkamp, P. M. G. & Wessels, H. (1975) Flooding in imagination vs. flooding in-vivo: A comparison with agoraphobics, *Behav. Res. Ther.,* **13**:7.

Engel, B. T. (1972) Response specificity. In N. S. Greenfield & R. A. Sternbeck (Eds.), *Handbook of psychophysiology,* New York, Holt, Rinehart, & Winston.

Eppinger, H. & Hess, L. (1915) Vagotonia, *Nerv. & Ment. Dis.* Monograph 20.

Erwin, W. J. (1963) Confinement in the production of human neuroses: The barber's chair syndrome, *Behav. Res. Ther.,* **1**:175.

Erwin, W. J. (1977) A sixteen-year followup of a case of severe anorexia nervosa, *J. Behav. Ther. Exp. Psychiat.,* **8**:157.

Evans, I. M. (1973) The logical requirements for explanations of systematic desensitization, *Behav. Ther.,* **4**:506.

Everaerd, W. (1970) Reading as the counterconditioning agent in a cardiac neurosis, *J. Behav. Ther. Exp. Psychiat.,* **1**:165.

Ewald, G. (1928) Psychoses in acute infections. In O. Bumkel (Ed.), *Handbook of mental diseases,* Berlin, Springer.

Eysenck, H. J. & Prell, D. (1951) The inheritance of neuroticism. *J. Ment. Sci.,* **97**:441.

Eysenck, H. J. (1952) The effects of psychotherapy: An evaluation, *J. Consult. Psychol.,* **16**: 319.

Eysenck, H. J. (1955) Psychiatric diagnosis as a physiological statistical problem, *Psychol. Rev.,* **1**:3.

Eysenck, H. J. (1957) *The dynamics of anxiety and hysteria,* London, Routledge & Kegan Paul.

Eysenck, H. J. (1960) *Behavior therapy and the neuroses,* Oxford, Pergamon Press.

Eysenck, H. J. (1962) *Maudley personality inventory,* San Diego, Educational Individual Testing Service.

Eysenck, H. J. (1963) *Experiments with drugs,* New York, Pergamon Press.

Eysenck, H. J. (1964) *Experiments in behavior therapy,* Oxford, Pergamon Press.

Eysenck, H. J. (1965) The effects of psychotherapy, *Internatl. J. Psychiat.,* **1**:97.

Eysenck, H. J. (1970) The classification of depressive illness, *Brit. J. Psychiat.,* **117**:241.

Eysenck, H. J. (1976) The learning theory model of neurosis—A new approach, *Behav. Res. Ther.,* **14**:251.

Eysenck, H. J. (1978) An exercise in mega-silliness, *Amer. Psychol.,* **33**:517.

Eysenck, H. J. (1979) The conditioning model of neurosis, *The Behavioral and Brain Sciences,* **2**:155.

Farmer, R. G. & Wright, J. M. C. (1971) Muscular reactivity and systematic desensitization, *Behav. Ther.,* **2**:1.

Farrar, C. H., Powell, B. J., & Martin, L. K. (1968) Punishment of alcohol consumption by apneic paralysis, *Behav. Res. Ther.,* **6**:13.

Feather, B. & Rhoads, J. (1972) Psychodynamic behavior therapy: Theory and rationale, *Arch. Gen. Psychiat.,* **26**:496.

Feingold, L. (1966) Personal communication.

Feldman, M. P. & MacCulloch, M. J. (1965) The application of anticipatory avoidance learning to the treatment of homosexuality. I. theory, technique and preliminary results, *Behav. Res. Ther.,* **2**:165.

Feldman, M. P. & MacCulloch, M. J. (1967) Aversion therapy in the management of homosexuals, *Brit. Med. J.,* **1**:594.

Feldman, M. P. & MacCulloch, M. J. (1970) *Homosexual behavior: Therapy and assessment,*

Oxford, Pergamon Press.

Fenz, W. D. & Epstein, S. (1967) Gradients of physiological arousal in parachutists, *Psychosom. Med.,* **29**:33.

Flanagan, B., Goldiamond, I., & Azrin, N. (1958) Operant stuttering: The control of stuttering behavior through response-contingent consequences, *J. Exp. Anal. Behav.,* **1**:173.

Foa, E. B., Steketee, G., & Milby, J. B. (1980) Differential effects of exposure and response prevention in obsessive-compulsive washers, *J. Consult. Clin. Psychol.,* **48**:71.

Foa, E. B. & Tillmanns, A. (1980) The treatment of obsessive-compulsive neurosis. In A. Goldstein & E. B. Foa (Eds.), *Handbook of behavioral interventions,* New York, Wiley.

Fonberg, E. (1956) On the manifestation of conditioned defensive reactions in stress, *Bull. Soc. Sci. Lettr. Lodz. Class III. Sci. Math. Natur.,* **7**:1.

Ford, J. D. (1978) Therapeutic relationship in behavior analysis, *J. Consult. Clin. Psychol.,* **46**: 1302.

Forrest, A. D. (1964) Comparative trial of nortriptylene and amytriptylene, *Scot. Med. J.,* **9**:34.

Frankl, V. E. (1960) Paradoxical intention: A logotherapeutic technique, *Amer. J. Psychother.,* **14**:520.

Frankl, V. E. (1975) Paradoxical intention and dereflection, *Psychother.: Theory, Res. and Prac.,* **12**:226.

Franks, C. M. (1965) *Conditioning techniques in clinical practice and research,* New York, Springer.

Franks, C. M. & Wilson, G. T. (1979) *Annual review of behavior therapy: Theory and practice, 1979,* Vol. 7, New York, Brunner/Mazel.

Freeman, G. L. & Pathman, J. H. (1942) The relation of overt muscular discharge to physiological recovery from experimentally induced displacement. *J. Exper. Psychol.,* **30**:161.

Freeman, H. L. & Kendrick, D. C. (1960) A case of cat phobia: Treatment by a method derived from experimental psychology, *Brit. Med. J.,* **1**:497.

Freund, K. (1960) Some problems in the treatment of homosexuality. In H. J. Eysenck (Ed.), *Behavior therapy and the neuroses,* Oxford, Pergamon Press.

Friedman, D. E. (1966) A new technique for the systematic desensitization of phobic symptoms, *Behav. Res. Ther.,* **4**:139.

Friedman, D. E. & Silverstone, J. T. (1967) Treatment of phobic patients by systematic desensitization, *Lancet,* **1**:470.

Fry, W. H. (1962) The marital content of an anxiety syndrome, *Family Process,* **1**:245.

Furman, S. (1973) Intestinal biofeedback in functional diarrhea: A preliminary report, *J. Behav. Ther. Exp. Psychiat.,* **4**:317.

Gale, D. S., Sturmfels, G., & Gale, E. N. (1966) A comparison of reciprocal inhibition and experimental extinction in the psychotherapeutic process, *Behav. Res. Ther.,* **4**:139.

Gambrill, E. D. & Richey, C. A. (1975) An assertive inventory for use in assessment and research. *Behav. Ther.,* **6**:550–661.

Gantt, W. H. (1944) Experimental basis for neurotic behavior. *Psychosom. Med. Monogr.* **3,** Nos. 3 & 4.

Garfield, S. (1980) *Psychotherapy: An eclectic approach,* New York, Wiley.

Garfield, S. & Bergin, A. (1978) *Handbook of psychotherapy and behavior change,* New York, Wiley.

Garfield, Z. H., Darwin, P. L., Singer, B. A. & McBrearty, J. F. (1967) Effect of *in vivo* training on experimental desensitization of a phobia, *Psychol. Rep.,* **20**:515.

Gath, D. & Gelder, M. G. A. (1971) *Treatment of phobias—Desensitization versus flooding.* Paper delivered to Dept. Psychiatry, Temple Univ. Medical School, November 8, 1971.

Gaupp, L. A., Stern, R. M., & Galbraith, G. G. (1972) False heart rate feedback and reciprocal inhibition by aversion relief in the treatment of snake avoidance behavior, *Behav. Ther.,* **3**:7.

Geer, J. H. (1965) The development of a scale to measure fear, *Behav. Res. Ther.,* **3**:45.

Gelder, M. G., Bancroft, J. H. J., Gath, D. H., Johnston, D. W., Mathews, A. M., & Shaw, P. M. (1973) Specific and non-specific factors in behavior therapy, *Brit. J. Psychiat.*, **123**:445.

Gellhorn, E. (1967) *Principles of autonomic-somatic integrations,* Minneapolis, University of Minnesota Press.

Gershman, L. & Stedman, J. (1971) Oriental defense exercises as reciprocal inhibitors of anxiety, *J. Behav. Ther. Exp. Psychiat.*, **2**:117.

Gerz, H. O. (1966) Experience with the logotherapeutic technique of paradoxical intention in the treatment of phobic and obsessive-compulsive patients, *Amer. J. Psychiat.*, **123**:548.

Gesell, A. (1946) The untold genesis of infant behavior. In L. Carmichael (Ed.), *Manual of child psychology,* New York, Wiley.

Getze, G. (1968) Adverse appeal to senses cuts smoking, *Los Angeles Times.* Reprinted by Z. Wanderer, Center for Behavior Therapy, Beverly Hills, California.

Giles, T. R. (1982) Bias against behavior therapy in outcome reviews: Those who have won have not received prizes (submitted for review). (a)

Giles, T. (1982) Behavior therapy vs. psychotherapy: A review of the Sloane, et al. study and of the behavioral outcome literature, *Amer. Psychol.* (under review). (b)

Gleitman, H., Nachmias, J., & Neisser, U. (1954) The S-R reinforcement theory of extinction, *Psychol. Rev.*, **61**:23.

Glynn, J. D. & Harper, P. (1961) Behavior therapy in transvestism, *Lancet,* **1**:619.

Gold, S. & Neufeld, I. (1965) A learning theory approach to the treatment of homosexuality, *Behav. Res. Ther.*, **2**:201.

Goldberg, J. & D'Zurilla, T. J. (1968) A demonstration of slide projection as an alternative to imaginal stimulus presentation in systematic desensitization therapy, *Psychol. Reps.*, **23**:527.

Goldfried, M. R. (1980) Toward the delineation of therapeutic change principles, *Amer. Psychol.*, **35**:991.

Goldfried, M. R. & Goldfried, A. P. (1975) Cognitive change methods. In F. H. Kanfer & A. P. Goldstein (Eds.), *Helping people change,* New York, Pergamon Press.

Goldiamond, I. (1965) Stuttering and fluency as manipulable operant response classes. In L. Krasner & L. P. Ullmann (Eds.), *Research in behavior modification,* New York, Holt, Rinehart, & Winston.

Goldstein, A. (1972) Flooding vs. extinction in the elimination of conditioned fear in cats. Unpublished manuscript.

Goldstein, A., Serber, M., & Piaget, J. (1970) Induced anger as a reciprocal inhibitor of fear, *J. Behav. Ther. Exp. Psychiat.*, **1**:67.

Goodson, F. A. & Brownstein, A. (1965) Secondary reinforcing and motivating properties of stimuli contiguous with shock onset and termination, *J. Comp. Physiol. Psychol.*, **48**:381.

Gottlieb, J. S. & Frohman, C. E. (1972) *A probable biologic mechanism in schizophrenia,* mimeo.

Gourevitch, M. (1968) Eloge de François Leuret, *Inform. Psychiat.*, **44**:843.

Graham, L. E., Beiman, I., & Ciminano, A. R. (1977) The generality of the therapeutic effects of progressive relaxation training for essential hypertension, *J. Behav. Ther. Exp. Psychiat.*, **8**:161.

Graham, L. E., Beiman, I., & Ciminano, A. R. (1978) Self-control progressive relaxation training as an alternative nonpharmacological treatment for essential hypertension: Therapeutic effects in the natural environment, *Behav. Res. Ther.*, **16**:371.

Granville-Grossman, K. L. & Turner, P. (1966) The effect of propranolol on anxiety, *Lancet,* **1**:788.

Gray, J. A. (1964) *Pavlov's typology,* Oxford, Pergamon Press.

Gray, J. A. (1976) The behavioural inhibition system: A possible substrate for anxiety. In M. P. Feldman & A. Broadhurst (Eds.), *Theoretical and experimental bases of the behaviour therapies,* London, Wiley.

Greenblatt, D. J. & Shader, R. I. (1972) Digitalis toxicity. In R. I. Shader (Ed.), *Psychiatric complications of medicinal drugs,* New York, Raven Press.

Grings, W. W. & Schandler, S. L. (1977) Interaction of learned relaxation and aversion, *Psychophysiol.,* **14:**275.

Grings, W. W. & Uno, T. (1968) Counterconditioning: Fear and relaxation, *Psychophysiol.,* **4:** 479.

Grinker, R. R. & Spiegel, J. P. (1945) *War neuroses,* Philadelphia, Blakiston.

Grosz, H. J. & Farmer, B. B. (1972) Pitts' and McClure's lactate anxiety study revisited, *Brit. J. Psychiat.,* **120:**415.

Groves, P. M. & Thompson, R. F. (1970) Habituation: A dual-process theory, *Psychol. Rev.,* **77:**419.

Guensberger, E. (1981) Are experimental neuroses pathological states?, *J. Behav. Ther. Exp. Psychiat.,* **12:**115.

Guthrie, E. R. (1935) *The psychology of human learning,* New York, Harper & Bros.

Guttmacher, A. F. (1961) *Complete book of birth control,* New York, Ballantine.

Hahn, W. (1966) Autonomic responses of asthmatic children, *Psychosom. Med.,* **28:**323.

Haggard, E. A. & Freeman, G. L. (1941) Reactions of children to experimentally induced frustration. *Psychol. Bull.,* **38:**581.

Hall, S. B. (1927) The blood pressure in psychoneurosis: An investigation of 71 cases, *Lancet,* **2:**540.

Hallam, R. S. & Rachman, S. (1976) Current status of aversion therapy. In M. Hersen, R. Eisler, & P. Miller (Eds.), *Progress in behavior modification,* Vol. 2, New York, Academic Press.

Hallsten, E. A. (1965) Adolescent anorexia nervosa treated by desensitization, *Behav. Res. Ther.,* **3:**87.

Hamilton, D. M. & Wall, J. H. (1941) Hospital treatment of patients with psychosomatic disorders, *Amer. J. Psychiat.,* **98:**551.

Hampe, E., Noble, F., Miller, L. C. & Barrett, C. I. (1973). Phobic children one and two years post treatment. *J. Abnorm. Psychol.* Vol. **82,** 3:446–453.

Harris, B. (1979) Whatever happened to little Albert? *Am. Psychol.,* **34,** 2:151–160.

Haslam, M. E. (1974) The relationship between the effect of lactate infusion on anxiety states and their amelioration by carbon dioxide inhalation, *Brit. J. Psychiat.,* **125:**88.

Hastings, D. W. (1966) *Sexual expression in marriage,* New York, Bantam.

Hedberg, A. G. (1973) The treatment of chronic diarrhea by systematic desensitization: A case report, *J. Behav. Ther. Exp. Psychiat.,* **4:**67.

Hernstein, R. J. (1970) On the law of effect, *J. Exp. Anal. Behav.,* **13:**243.

Hersen, M. (1973) Self-assessment of fear, *Behav. Ther.,* **4:**241.

Hersen, M. (1981) Complex problems require complex solutions, *Behav. Ther.,* **12:**15–29.

Herzberg, A. (1941) *Active psychotherapy,* London, Research Books.

Himmelsbach, C. K. (1941) The morphine abstinence syndrome: Its nature and treatment, *Ann. Intern. Med.,* **15:**829.

Hinde, R. A. (1966) *Animal behaviour,* New York, McGraw-Hill.

Hoch, P. H. (1959) Drug therapy. In S. Arieti (Ed.), *American handbook of psychiatry,* New York, Basic Books.

Hodgson, R., Rachman, S., & Marks, I. M. (1972) The treatment of chronic obsessive-compulsive neuroses: Follow-up and further findings, *Behav. Res. Ther.,* **10:**181.

Homme, L. E. (1965) Perspectives in psychology—XXIV, Control of coverants, the operants of the mind, *The Psychol. Rec.,* **15:**501.

Homme, L. E., Csanyi, A. P., Gonzales, M. A., & Rechs, J. R. (1971) *How to use contingency contracting in the classroom,* Champaign, Ill., Research Press.

Horsley, J. S. (1936) Narco-analysis: A new technique in shortcut psychotherapy, *Lancet,* **1:**55.

Hull, C. L. (1943) *Principles of behavior,* New York, Appleton-Century.

Hurwitz, H. P. M. (1956) Conditioned responses in rats reinforced by light, *Brit. J. Animal Behav.*, **4**:31.

Hussain, A. (1964) Behavior therapy using hypnosis. In J. Wolpe, A. Salter, & L. J. Reyna, *The conditioning therapies*, New York, Holt, Rinehart, & Winston.

Hussain, M. Z. (1971) Desensitization and flooding (implosion) in treatment of phobias, *Amer. J. Psychiat.*, **127**:1509.

Huttunesn, M. O. (1973) General model for the molecular events in synapses during learning, *Perspectives in Biology and Medicine*, **17**:103.

Ihli, K. L. & Garlington, W. K. (1969) A comparison of group versus individual desensitization of test anxiety, *Behav. Res. Ther.*, **7**:207.

Jacob, R. G., Kraemer, H. C., & Agras, W. S. (1977) Relaxation therapy in the treatment of hypertension, *Arch. Gen. Psychiat.*, **34**:1417.

Jacobson, E. (1938) *Progressive relaxation*, Chicago, University of Chicago Press.

Jacobson, E. (1939) Variation of blood pressure with skeletal muscle tension and relaxation, *Ann. Intern. Med.*, **12**:1194.

Jacobson, E. (1940) Variation of pulse rate with skeletal muscle tension and relaxation, *Ann. Int. Med.*, **13**:1619.

Jacobson, E. (1964) *Anxiety and tension control*, Philadelphia, Lippincott.

Jacobson, N. S. & Martin, B. (1976) Behavioral marriage therapy: Current status, *Psychol. Bull.*, **83**:540.

Jacobson, N. S. & Weiss, R. L. (1978) Behavioral marriage therapy: III. The contents of Gurman et al. may be hazardous to our health, *Family Process*, **17**:149.

Jakobovitz, T. (1970) The treatment of impotence with methyl-testosterone thyroid, *Fertility and Sterility*, **21**:32.

James, B. (1962) Case of homosexuality treated by aversion therapy, *Brit. Med. J.*, **1**:768.

Janet, A. (1925) *Psychological healing, historical and clinical study*, New York, Macmillan.

Jasinski, D. R. (1976) Personal communication.

Jasinski, D. R., Martin, W. R., & Haertzen, C. A. (1967) The human pharmacology and abuse potential of N-allyneroxymorphove (naloxone), *J. Pharm. Exp. Ther.*, **157**:420.

Jeffrey, R. W., Wing, R. R., & Stunkard, A. J. (1978) Behavioral treatment of obesity: The state of the art 1976, *Behav. Ther.*, **9**:189.

Jersild, A. T. & Holmes, F. B. (1935) Methods of overcoming children's fears, *J. Psychol.*, **1**:35.

John, E. (1941) A study of the effects of evacuation and air raids on children of pre-school age, *Brit. J. of Educational Psychol.*, **11**:173.

Jones, H. G. (1960) Continuation of Yates' treatment of a tiquer. In H. J. Eysenck (Ed.), *Behavior therapy and the neuroses*, Oxford, Pergamon Press.

Jones, M. C. (1924) Elimination of children's fears, *J. Exp. Psychol.*, **7**:382. (a)

Jones, M. C. (1924) A laboratory study of fear. The case of Peter, *J. Genet. Psychol.*, **31**:308. (b)

Jorgensen, R. S., Houston, B. K., & Zurawski, R. M. (1981) Anxiety management training in the treatment of essential hypertension, *Behav. Res. Ther.*, **19**:467.

Kahn, M. & Baker, B. L. (1968) Desensitization with minimal therapist contact, *J. Abn. Psychol.*, **73**:198.

Kalish, H. I. (1981) *From behavioral science to behavior modification*, New York, McGraw-Hill.

Kallman, F. (1952) Comparative twin studies on the genetic aspects of male homosexuality, *J. Nerv. Ment. Dis.*, **115**:283.

Kallman, F. (1953) *Heredity in health and mental disorder*, New York, Norton.

Kandel, E. R. (1979) Psychotherapy and the single synapse: The impact of psychiatric thought on neurobiological research, *N. Engl. J. Med.*, **19**:1028.

Kantorovich, N. V. (1929) An attempt at associative reflex therapy in alcoholism, *Psychol. Abst.*, No. 4282, 1930.

Kazdin, A. E. (1977) Artifact, bias, and complexity of assessment: The ABC's of reliability, *J. Appl. Behav. Anal.,* **10**:141.

Kazdin, A. E. (1979) Fictions, factions, and functions of behavior therapy, *Behav. Ther.,* **10**: 629.

Kazdin, A. E. & Wilcoxon, L. A. (1976) Systematic desensitization and nonspecific treatment effects: A methodological evaluation, *Psychol. Bull.,* **23**:729.

Kazdin, A. E. & Wilson, G. T. (1978) Criteria for evaluating psychotherapy, *Arch. Gen. Psychiat.,* **35**:407.

Kegel, A. H. (1952) Sexual functions of the pubococcygens muscle, *West. J. Surg. Obstet. Gynol.,* **60**:521.

Keltner, A. & Marshall, W. L. (1975) Single trial exacerbation of an anxiety habit with 2nd order conditioning and subsequent desensitization. *J. Behav. Ther. & Exp. Psychiat.,* **6**:323.

Kennedy, W. A. & Foreyt, J. (1968) Control of eating behavior in an obese patient by avoidance conditioning, *Psychol. Rep.,* **22**:571.

Kent, R. N., Wilson, G. T., & Nelson, R. (1972) Effects of false heart-rate feedback on avoidance behavior: An investigation of "cognitive desensitization," *Behav. Ther.,* **3**:1.

Khan, A. U., Staerk, M., & Bonk, C. (1973) Role of counterconditioning in the treatment of asthma, *J. Psychosom. Res.,* **17**:389.

Kimmel, H. D. (1967) Instrumental conditioning of autonomically mediated behavior, *Psychol. Bull.,* **67**:337.

Kimmel, K. D. & Kimmel, E. (1970) An instrumental conditioning method for the treatment of enuresis, *J. Behav. Ther. Exp. Psychiat.,* **1**:121.

Klein, D. G. (1964) Delineation of two drug-responsive anxiety syndromes, *Psychopharmacologia,* **5**:397.

Kline, N. S. (1974) *From sad to glad,* New York, Ballantine.

Knight, R. P. (1941) Evaluation of the results of psychoanalytic therapy, *Amer. J. Psychiat.,* **98**:434.

Knudson, R. M., Gurman, A. S., & Kniskern, D. P. (1980) Behavioral marriage therapy: A treatment in transition. In C. M. Franks & G. T. Wilson, *Annual review of behavior therapy— Theory and practice,* Vol. 7, New York, Brunner/Mazel.

Kolvin, I. (1967) Aversive imagery treatment in adolescents, *Behav. Res. Ther.,* **5**:245.

Kondas, O. (1965) The possibilities of applying experimentally created procedures when eliminating tics, *Studia Psychol.,* **7**:221.

Krasnogorski, N. I. (1925) The conditioned reflexes and children's neuroses. *Amer. J. Dis. Child.,* **30**:754.

Kuhn, T. S. (1962) *The Structure of Scientific Revolutions.* Chicago, University of Chicago Press.

Lacey, J. I., Bateman, D. E., & Van Lehn, R. (1953) Autonomic response specificity: An experimental study, *Psychosom. Med.,* **15**:8.

Lacey, J. I. & Lacey, B. C. (1958) Verification and extension of the principles of autonomic response specificity, *Amer. J. Psychol.,* **71**:50.

Lader, M. (1975) *The psychophysiology of mental illness,* London, Routledge and Kegan Paul.

Lader, M. (1976) Physiological research in anxiety. In H. M. van Praag (Ed.), *Research in neurosis,* Utrecht, Bohn, Scheltema & Holkema.

Lader, M. H. & Mathews, A. M. (1968) A physiological model of phobic anxiety and desensitization, *Behav. Res. Ther.,* **6**:411.

Lader, M. H. & Wing, L. (1966) *Physiological measures, sedative drugs and morbid anxiety,* Maudsley Monograph No. 14, London, Oxford University Press.

Ladouceur, R. (1974) An experimental test of the learning paradigm of covert positive reinforcement in deconditioning anxiety, *J. Behav. Ther. Exp. Psychiat.,* **5**:30.

Lande, S. (1981) The cognitive habit inventories: A method of differentiating phobic types. Unpublished manuscript.

Landis, C. (1937) A statistical evaluation of psychotherapeutic methods. In L. Hinsie (Ed.), *Concepts and problems of psychotherapy,* New York, Columbia University Press.

Lang, P.J. (1968) Appraisal of systematic desensitization techniques with children and adults. II. Process and mechanisms of change, theoretical analysis and implications for treatment and clinical research. In C. M. Franks (Ed.), *Assessment and status of the behavior therapies and associated developments,* New York, McGraw-Hill.

Lang, P. J. (1970) Stimulus control, response control and the desensitization of fear. In D.J. Levis (Ed.), *Learning approach to therapeutic behavior change,* Chicago, Aldine.

Lang, P. J. & Lazovik, A. D. (1963) The experimental desensitization of a phobia, *J. Abn. Soc. Psychol.,* **66**:519.

Lang, P. J., Lazovik, A. D., & Reynolds, D. (1965) Desensitization, suggestibility and pseudo therapy, *J. Abn. Psychol.,* **70**:395.

Lang, P. J., Melamed, B. G., & Hart, J. (1970) A psychophysiological analysis of fear modification using an automated desensitization procedure, *J. Abn. Psychol.,* **76**:221.

Langley, J. N. & Anderson, H. K. (1895) The innervation of the pelvis and adjoining viscera, *J. Physiol.,* **19**:71.

Lathrop, R. G. (1964) Measurement of analog sequential dependency, *Human Factors,* **6**:233.

Latimer, P. (1977) Carbon dioxide as a reciprocal inhibitor in the treatment of neurosis, *J. Behav. Ther. Exp. Psychiat.,* **8**:83.

Latimer, P. R. (1981) Irritable bowel syndrome: A behavioral model, *Behav. Res. Ther.,* **19**:475.

Latimer, P., Campbell, D., & Latimer, M. (1979) Irritable bowel syndrome: A test of the colonic hyperalgesia hypothesis, *J. Behav. Med.,* **2**:285.

Lautch, H. (1971) Dental phobia. *Brit. J. Psychiat.,* **119**:151–8.

LaVerne, A. A. (1953) Rapid coma technique of carbon dioxide inhalation therapy, *Dis. Nerv. Syst.,* **14**:141.

Laverty, S. G. (1966) Aversion therapies in the treatment of alcoholism, *Psychosom. Med.,* **28**: 651.

Lavin, H. I., Thorpe, J. G., Baker, J. C., Blakemore, C. B., & Conway, D. G. (1961) Behavior therapy in a case of transvestism, *J. Nerv. Ment. Dis.,* **133**:346.

Lazarus, A. A. & Abramovitz, A. (1962) The use of "emotive imagery" in the treatment of children's phobias, *J. Ment. Sci.,* **108**:191.

Leach, E. (1969) Stuttering: Clinical application of response-contingent procedures. In B. B. Gray & G. England (Eds.), *Stuttering and the conditioning therapies,* Monterey, Calif., Monterey Institute for Speech and Hearing.

Leaf, W. B. & Gaarder, K. R. (1971) A simplified electromyograph feedback apparatus for relaxation training, *J. Behav. Ther. Exp. Psychiat.,* **2**:39.

Leahy, M. R. & Martin, I. C. A. (1967) Successful hypnotic abreaction after twenty years. *Brit. J. Psychiat.,* **113**:383.

Leitenberg, H., Agras, W. S., Barlow, D. H., & Oliveau, D. C. (1969) Contribution of selective positive reinforcement and therapeutic instructions to systematic desensitization therapy, *J. Abn. Psychol.,* **74**:113.

Lemere, F. & Voegtlin, W. L. (1950) An evaluation of the aversion treatment of alcoholism, *Qrt. J. Stud. Alcoh.,* **11**:199.

Leonhard, K. (1959) *Aufteilung der Endogenen Psychosen,* 2nd ed., Berlin, Haug.

Leschke, E. (1914) Quoted by J. G. Beebe-Center (1932) in *The psychology of pleasantness and unpleasantness,* New York, Van Nostrand.

Lesser, E. (1967) Behavior therapy with a narcotics user: A case report, *Behav. Res. Ther.,* **5**: 251.

Leukel, F. & Quinton, E. (1964) Carbon dioxide effects on acquisition and extinction of avoidance behavior, *J. Comp. Physiol. Psychol.,* **57**:267.

Leuret, F. (1846) *De traitement moral de la folie,* Paris, quoted by Stewart (1961).

Levay, A. N. & Kagle, A. (1977) A study of treatment needs following sex therapy, *Amer. J. Psychiat.,* **134**:970.

Levis, D. J. (1980) Implementing the technique of implosive therapy. In A. Goldstein & E. B. Foa (Eds.), *Handbook of behavioral interventions,* New York, Wiley.

Levis, D. J. & Boyd, T. L. (1979) Symptom maintenance: An infrahuman analysis and extension of the conservation of anxiety principle, *J. Abn. Psychol.,* **88**:107.

Levis, D. J. & Carrera, R. N. (1967) Effects of ten hours of implosive therapy in the treatment of outpatients: A preliminary report, *J. Abn. Psychol.,* **72**:504.

Levis, D. J. & Hare, N. (1977) A review of the theoretical and rational and empirical support for the extinction approach of implosive (flooding) therapy. In M. Hersen, R. M. Eisler, & P. M. Miller (Eds.), *Progress in behavior modification,* New York, Academic Press.

Levitz, L. S. & Stunkard, A. J. (1974) A therapeutic coalition for obesity: Behavior modification and patient self-help, *Amer. J. Psychiat.,* **131**:423.

Lewinsohn, P. M. (1974) Clinical and theoretical aspects of depression. In K. S. Calhoun, H. E. Adams, & K. M. Mitchell (Eds.), *Innovative treatment methods in psychopathology,* New York, Wiley.

Lewinsohn, P. M., Steinmetz, J. C., Larson, D. W., & Franklin, J. (1981) Depression-related cognitions: Antecedent or consequence?, *J. Abn. Psychol.,* **90**:213.

Lewis, B. I. (1954) Chronic hyperventilation syndrome, *J. Amer. Med. Assoc.,* **155**:1204.

Lewis, D. (1875) *Chastity: Or our secret sins,* Philadelphia, Maclean.

Ley, R. & Walker, H. (1973) Effects of carbon dioxide-oxygen inhalation on heart rate, blood pressure and subjective anxiety, *J. Behav. Ther. Exp. Psychiat.,* **4**:223.

Liberman, R. (1968) Aversive conditioning of a drug addict: A pilot study, *Behav. Res. Ther.,* **6**:229.

Liddell, H. S. (1944) Conditioned reflex method and experimental neurosis. In J. McV. Hunt (Ed.), *Personality and disorders,* New York, Ronald Press.

Lieberman, S. (1978) Nineteen cases of morbid grief, *Brit. J. Psychiat.,* **132**:159.

Lindsley, O. R. (1956) Operant conditioning methods applied to research in chronic schizophrenia, *Psychiat. Res. Rep.,* **5**:118.

Little, J. C. & James, B. (1964) Abreaction of conditioned fear after eighteen years, *Behav. Res. Ther.,* **2**:59.

Lloyd, D. P. C. (1946) Facilitation and inhibition of spinal motorneurons, *J. Neurophysiol.,* **9**:421.

Lobitz, W. C. & LoPiccolo, J. (1972) New methods in the behavioral treatment of sexual dysfunction, *J. Behav. Ther. Exp. Psychiat.,* **3**:265.

Locke, E. A. (1971) Is "behavior therapy" behavioristic? An analysis of Wolpe's psychotherapeutic methods, *Psychol. Bull.,* **76**:318.

London, P. (1964) *The modes and morals of psychotherapy,* New York, Holt, Rinehart & Winston.

LoPiccolo, J., Stewart, R., & Watkins, B. (1972) Treatment of erectile failure and ejaculatory incompetence of homosexual etiology, *J. Behav. Ther. Exp. Psychiat.,* **3**:233.

Lubeskind, J. C. & Paul, L. A. (1977) Psychological and physiological mechanisms of pain. In Rosengweiz, M. R. & Porter, L. W. (Eds.), *Ann. Rev. Psychol.,* **28**.

Lublin, I. (1968) Aversive conditioning of cigarette addiction. Paper read at 76th Meeting of Amer. Psychol. Assoc., San Francisco.

Luborsky, L., Singer, B., & Luborsky, L. (1975) Comparative studies of psychotherapy: Is it true that "Everyone has won and all must have prizes"?, *Arch. Gen. Psychiat.,* **32**:995.

Macfarland, J. M., Allan, L., & Honzek, M. (1954) *A developmental study of the behavior problems of normal children,* Berkeley, University of California Press.

Mack, K. (1970) Unpublished data.

Mackintosh, N. J. (1974) *Psychology of animal learning,* New York, Academic Press.

MacVaugh, G. (1972) *Frigidity: Successful treatment of one hypnotic imprint session with the Oriental relaxation technique,* New York, Medcon Inc.

MacVaugh, G. S. (1974) *Frigidity: What you should know about its cure with hypnosis,* New York, Pergamon Press.

Madsen, C. H. (1965) Positive reinforcement in the toilet training of a normal child: A case report. In L. P. Ullmann & L. Krasner (Eds.), *Case studies in behavior modification,* New York, Holt, Rinehart, & Winston.

Mahesh Yogi, M. (1969) *Maharishi Mahesh Yogi on the Bhagavad-Gita: A new translation and commentary,* Baltimore, Penguin.

Mahoney, M. J. (1977) Reflections on the cognitive-learning trend in psychotherapy, *Amer. Psychol., 32*:5.

Maier, S. F. & Seligman, M. E. P. (1976) Learned helplessness: Theory and evidence, *J. Exp. Psychol. Gen., 105*:3.

Malleson, N. (1959) Panic and phobia, *Lancet, 1*:225.

Malmo, R. B. & Shagass, C. (1952) Studies of blood pressure in psychiatric patients under stress, *Psychosom. Med., 14*:82.

Marks, I. M. (1969) *Fears and phobias,* London, Heinemann.

Marks, I. M. (1972) Flooding (implosion) and allied treatments. In W. S. Agras (Ed.), *Learning theory application of principles and procedures to psychiatry,* New York, Little, Brown.

Marks, I. M. (1975) Behavioral treatments of phobic and obsessive-compulsive disorders: A critical appraisal. In M. Hersen, R. M. Eisler, & P. M. Miller (Eds.), *Progress in behavior modification,* New York, Academic Press.

Marks, I. M. (1976) Current status of behavioral psychotherapy: Theory and practice, *Amer. J. Psychiat., 133*:253.

Marks, I. M., Boulougouris, J., & Marset, P. (1971) Flooding versus desensitization in the treatment of phobic patients: A crossover study, *Brit. J. Psychiat., 119*:353.

Marks, I. M., Hodgson, R., & Rachman, S. (1975) Treatment of chronic obsessive-compulsive neurosis by *in vivo* exposure, *Brit. J. Psychiat., 127*:349.

Marmor, J. (1980) Recent trends in psychotherapy, *Amer. J. Psychiat., 137*:409.

Marquis, J. N. (1970) Orgasmic reconditioning: Changing sexual object choice through controlling masturbation fantasies, *J. Behav. Ther. Exp. Psychiat., 1*:263.

Marshall, W. L. (1974) The classical conditioning of sexual attractiveness, *Behav. Ther., 5*:298.

Martin, I. (1961) Somatic reactivity. In H. J. Eysenck (Ed.), *Handbook of abnormal psychology,* New York, Basic Books.

Marzillier, J. S. (1980) Cognitive therapy and behavioural practice, *Behav. Res. Ther., 18*:249.

Mash, E. J. & Terdal, L. G. (1976) *Behavior therapy assessment,* New York, Springer.

Masserman, J. H. (1943) *Behavior and neurosis,* Chicago, University of Chicago Press.

Masserman, J. H. (1963) Ethology, comparative biodynamics, and psychoanalytic research. In J. Scher (Ed.), *Theories of the mind,* New York, The Free Press.

Masserman, J. H. & Yum, K. S. (1946) An analysis of the influence of alcohol on the experimental neuroses in cats, *Psychosom. Med., 8*:36.

Masters, W. H. & Johnson, V. E. (1966) *Human sexual response,* Boston, Little Brown.

Masters, W. H. & Johnson, V. E. (1970) *Human sexual inadequacy,* Boston, Little Brown.

Mathe, A. A. & Knapp, P. H. (1971) Emotional and adrenal reactions to stress in bronchial asthma, *Psychosom. Med., 33*:323.

Mathews, A. M., Gelder, M. G., & Johnson, D. W. (1981) *Agoraphobia: Nature and environment,* New York, Guilford.

Mathews, A. M., Johnson, D. W., Shaw, P. M., & Gelder, M. G. (1974) Process variables and the prediction of outcome in behavior therapy, *Brit. J. Psychiat., 123*:445.

Mawson, A. B. (1970) Methohexitone-assisted desensitization in treatment of phobias, *Lancet, 1*:1084.

Max, L. W. (1935) Breaking up a homosexual fixation by the conditioned reaction technique: A case study, *Psychol. Bull., 32*:734.

Maxwell, R. D. H. & Paterson, J. W. (1958) Meprobamate in the treatment of stuttering, *Brit. Med. J., 1*:873.

McGeogh, J. A. (1932) Forgetting and the law of disuse, *Psychol. Rev., 39*:352.

McGeogh, J. A., McKinney, F., & Peters, H. (1937) Studies in retroactive inhibition. IX. Retroactive inhibition, reproductive inhibition and reminiscence, *J. Exp. Psychol., 20*:131.

McGlynn, F. D. Reynolds, E. J., & Linder, L. H. (1971) Systematic desensitization with pretreatment and intratreatment therapeutic instructions, *Behav. Res. Ther., 9*:57.

McGlynn, F. D. & Williams, C. W. (1970) Systematic desensitization of snake-avoidance under three conditions of suggestion, *J. Behav. Ther. Exp. Psychiat., 1*:97.

McGuire, R. J. & Vallance, M. (1964) Aversion therapy by electric shock: A simple technique, *Brit. Med. J., 1*:151.

Mealiea, W. L. & Nawas, M. M. (1971) The comparative effectiveness of systematic desensitization and implosive therapy in the treatment of snake phobia, *J. Behav. Ther. Exp. Psychiat., 2*:85.

Meduna, L. J. (1947) *Carbon dioxide therapy,* Springfield, Ill., C. C. Thomas.

Meichenbaum, D. H. (1975) Self-instructional methods. In F. H. Kanfer & A. P. Goldstein (Eds.), *Helping people change,* New York, Pergamon Press.

Meichenbaum, D. H. & Cameron, R. (1974) The clinical potential of modifying what clients say to themselves, *Psychotherapy: Theory, Research, and Practice, 11*:103.

Mesmer, A. (1779) Quoted by C. L. Hull (1933) *Hypnosis and suggestibility,* New York, Appleton-Century.

Meyer, V. (1957) The treatment of two phobic patients on the basis of learning principles, *J. Abn. Soc. Psychol., 58*:259.

Meyer, V. (1963) Paper read at Behavior Therapy Seminar, University of London.

Meyer, V. (1966) Modifications of expectations in cases with obsessional rituals, *Behav. Res. Ther., 4*:273.

Meyer, V., Levy, R., & Schnurer, A. (1974) The behavioral treatment of obsessive-compulsive disorders. In H. R. Beech (Ed.), *Obsessional states,* London, Methuen.

Meyer, V. & Mair, J. M. (1963) A new technique to control stammering: A preliminary report, *Behav. Res. Ther., 1*:251.

Migler, B. (1967) Personal communication.

Migler, B. & Wolpe, J. (1967) Automated desensitization: A case report, *Behav. Res. Ther., 5*:133.

Miller, G. E. (1967) Personal communication.

Miller, N. E. & DiCara, L. V. (1968) Instrumental learning of vasomotor responses by rats: Learning to respond differentially in the two ears, *Science, 159*:1485.

Miller, N. E. & Dollard, J. (1941) *Social learning and imitation,* New Haven, Yale University Press.

Miller, N. E., Hubert, E., & Hamilton, J. (1938) Mental and behavioral changes following male hormone treatment of adult castration hypogonadism and psychic impotence, *Proc. Soc. Exp. Biol. Med., 38*:538.

Miller, N. & Weiss, J. M. (1969) Effects of somatic or visceral responses to punishment. In B. A. Campbell & R. M. Church (Eds.), *Punishment and aversive behavior,* New York, Appleton-Century-Crofts.

Miller, R. E., Murphy, J. V., & Mirsky, I. A. (1957) Persistent effects of chlorpromazine on extinction of an avoidance response, *Arch. Neurol. Psychiat., 78*:526.

Miller, W. R., Seligman, M. E. P., & Kurlander, H. M. (1975) Learned helplessness, depression, and anxiety, *J. Nerv. Ment. Dis., 161*:347.

Miller, W. W. (1968) Afrodex in the treatment of male impotence: A double blind crossover study, *Current Therapeutic Research, 10*:354.

Mineka, S. & Kihlstrom, J. F. (1978) Unpredictable and uncontrollable events: A new perspective on experimental neurosis, *J. Abn. Psychol.,* **87**:256.

Mitchell, K. R. (1969) The treatment of migraine: An exploratory application of time limited behavior therapy, *Technology,* **14**:50.

Mitchell, K. R. & Mitchell, D. M. (1971) Migraine: An exploratory treatment application of programmed behavior therapy techniques, *J. Psychosom. Res.,* **15**:137.

Moore, N. (1965) Behavior therapy in bronchial asthma: A controlled study, *J. Psychosom. Res.,* **9**:257.

Morganstern, F. S., Pearce, J. F., & Rees, W. (1965) Predicting the outcome of behavior therapy by psychological tests, *Behav. Res. Ther.,* **2**:191.

Mowrer, O. H. & Jones, H. M. (1945) Habit strength as a function of the pattern of reinforcement, *J. Exp. Psychol.,* **35**:293.

Mowrer, O. H. & Vick, P. (1948) Experimental analogue of fear from a sense of helplessness, *J. Abn. Soc. Psychol,* **43**:193.

Murphy, I. C. (1964) Extinction of an incapacitating fear of earthworms, *J. Clin. Psychol.,* **20**: 396.

Napalkov, A. V. (1963) Information process of the brain. In N. Wiener & J. C. Sefade (Eds.), *Progress in brain research, Vol. 2: Nerve, brain and memory models,* Amsterdam, Elsevier.

Napalkov, A. V. & Karas, A. Y. (1957) Elimination of pathological conditioned reflex connections in experimental hypertensive states, *Zh. Vyssh. Nerv. Deiat.,* **7**:402.

Neale, D. H. (1963) Behavior therapy and encopresis in children, *Behav. Res. Ther.,* **1**:139.

Nemetz, G. H., Craig, K. D. & Reith, G. (1978) Treatment of female sexual dysfunction through symbolic modeling, *J. Consult. and Clin. Psychol.,* **46**:62.

Nicassio, P., & Bootzin, R. (1974) A comparison of progressive relaxation and autogenic training as treatments for insomnia, *J. Abn. Psychol.,* **83**:235.

O'Brien, J., Raynes, A., & Patch, V. (1972) Treatment of heroin addiction with aversion therapy, relaxation training and systematic desensitization, *Behav. Res. Ther.,* **10**:77.

O'Donnell, C. R. & Worell, L. (1973) Motor and cognitive relaxation in the desensitization of anger, *Behav. Res. Ther.,* **11**:473.

Ohman, A., Eriksson, A., & Olofsson, C. (1975) One-trial learning and superior resistance to extinction of autonomic responses conditioned to potentially phobic stimuli, *J. Comp. Physiol. Psychol.,* **88**:619.

Ohman, A., Erixon, G., & Lofberg, I. (1975) Phobias and preparedness: Phobic versus neutral pictures as conditioned stimuli for human autonomic responses, *J. Abn. Psychol.,* **84**:41.

Olds, J. (1962) Hypothalmic substrates of reward, *Physiol. Rev.,* **42**:554.

Olds, J. (1975) Mapping the mind onto the brain. In F. G. Worden, J. P. Swazey, & G. Adelman (Eds.), *The neurosciences: Paths of discovery,* Cambridge, Mass., Colonial Press.

Olds, J., Disterhoft, J. F., Segal, M., Kornblith, C. C., & Hirsh, R. (1972) Learning centers of rat brain mapped by measuring latencies of conditioned unit responses, *J. Neurophysiol.,* **35**:202.

O'Leary, K. D. & O'Leary, S. G. (1977) *Classroom management,* New York, Pergamon Press.

Oliveau, D. C., Agras, W. S., Leitenberg, H., Moore, R. C., & Wright, D. E. (1969) Systematic desensitization, therapeutically oriented instructions, selective positive reinforcement, *Behav. Res. Ther.,* **7**:27.

Orleans, C. T., Shipley, R. H., Williams, C., & Haac, L. A. (1981) Behavioral approaches to smoking cessation. I. A decade of progress 1969–1979. *J. Behav. Ther. & Exp. Psychiat.,* **12**: 125.

Orleans, C. T., Shipley, R. H., Williams, C., & Haac, L. A. (1981) Behavioral approaches to smoking cessation. II. Topical bibliography 1969–1979. *J. Behav. Ther. & Exp. Psychiat.,* **12**:131.

Orwin, A. (1971) Respiratory relief: A new and rapid method for the treatment of phobic states,

Brit. J. Psychiat., **119**:635.

Osgood, C. E. (1946) Meaningful similarity and interference in learning, *J. Exp. Psychol.,* **38**: 132.

Osgood, C. E. (1948) An investigation into the causes of retroactive inhibition, *J. Exp. Psychol.,* **38**:132.

Osgood, C. E. (1953) *Method and theory in experimental psychology,* London, Oxford University Press.

Ost, L. & Hugdahl, K. (1981) Acquisition of phobias and anxiety response patterns in clinical patients. *Behav. Res. & Ther.,* **19**:439.

Padilla, A. M., Padilla, C., Ketterer, T., & Giacalone, D. (1970) Inescapable shocks and subsequent avoidance conditioning in goldfish, *Carrasius Auratus. Psychonom. Sci.,* **20**:295.

Palmer, H. A. (1944) Military psychiatric casualties, *Lancet,* **2**:492.

Patterson, G. R. & Gullion, M. E. (1968) *Living with children: New methods for parents and teachers,* Champaign, Ill., Research Press.

Paul, G. L. (1964) Modifications of systematic desensitization based on case study. Paper presented at the meeting of the Western Psychological Association, Portland, Oregon.

Paul, G. L. (1966) *Insight versus desensitization in psychotherapy,* Stanford, Calif., Stanford University Press.

Paul, G. L. (1968) Two-year follow-up of systematic desensitization in therapy groups, *J. Abn. Psychol.,* **73**:119.

Paul, G. L. (1969) Physiological effects of relaxation training and hypnotic suggestion, *J. Abn. Psychol.,* **74**:425.

Paul, G. L. & Lentz, R. J. (1977) *Psychosocial treatment of chronic mental patients,* Cambridge, Mass., Harvard University Press.

Paul, G. L. & Shannon, D. T. (1966) Treatment of anxiety through systematic desensitization in therapy groups, *J. Abn. Psychol.,* **71**:124.

Pavlov, I. P. (1927) *Conditioned reflexes,* G. V. Anrep (Trans.), New York, Liveright.

Pavlov, I. P. (1941) *Conditioned reflexes and psychiatry,* W. H. Gantt (Trans.), New York, International.

Pavlov, I. P. (1955) *Selected works* (in English), Moscow, Foreign Languages Publishing House.

Pearce, J. F. (1963) *Aspects of transvestism,* M. D. Thesis, University of London.

Pecknold, J. C. Raevurn, J., & Poser, E. G. (1972) Intravenous Diazepam for facilitating relaxation for desensitization, *J. Behav. Ther. Exp. Psychiat.,* **3**:39.

Perris, C. (1966) A survey of bipolar and unipolar recurrent depressive psychoses, *Acta. Psychiat. Scand.,* Supplement 194.

Pfeiffer, C. J., Fodor, J., & Geizerova, H. (1973) An epidemiologic study of the relationships of peptic ulcers in 50- to 54-year-old urban males with physical, health, and smoking factors, *J. Chronic Dis.,* **26**:271.

Phillips, D. (1978) *How to fall out of love,* Boston, Houghton Miflin.

Phillips, D. (1980) *Sexual confidence,* Boston, Houghton Miflin.

Phillips, L. W. (1971) Training of sensory and imaginal responses in behavior therapy. In R. D. Rubin, H. Fensterheim, A. A. Lazarus, & C. M. Franks (Eds.), *Advances in behavior therapy,* New York, Academic Press.

Philpott, W. M. (1964) Personal communication.

Philpott, W. M. (1967) Personal communication.

Pinckney, G. (1967) Avoidance learning in fish as a function of prior fear conditioning, *Psychol. Rep.,* **20**:71.

Pitts, F. N. & McClure, J. (1967) Lactate metabolism in anxiety neurosis, *New Eng. J. Med.,* **277**:1329.

Poppen, R. (1970) Counterconditioning of conditioned suppression in rats, *Psychol. Rep.,* **27**: 659.

Poppen, R. (1976) Psychotherapy versus behavior therapy, *J. Behav. Ther. Exp. Psychiat.*, **7**: 101.

Potter, S. (1971) *The complete upmanship,* New York, Holt, Rinehart, & Winston.

Premack, D. (1965) Reinforcement theory. In D. Levine (Ed.), *Nebraska symposium on motivation,* Lincoln, University of Nebraska Press.

Purcell, K. (1963) Distinction between subgroups of asthmatic children: Children's perceptions of events associated with asthma, *Pediatrics,* **31**:486.

Qualls, P. J. & Sheehan, P. W. (1981) Electromyograph biofeedback as a relaxation technique: A critical appraisal and reassessment, *Psychol. Bull.,* **90**:21.

Rabavilas, A. D., Boulougouris, J. C., & Stefanis, C. (1976) Duration of flooding sessions in the treatment of obsessive-compulsive patients, *Behav. Res. Ther.,* **14**:349.

Rachaim, S., Lefebvre, C., & Jenkins, J. O. (1980) The effects of social skills training and behavioral and cognitive components of anger management. *J. Behav. Ther. & Exp. Psychiat.,* **11**: 3.

Rachlin, H. (1976) *Behavior and learning,* San Francisco, Freeman.

Rachman, S. (1961) Sexual disorders and behavior therapy, *Amer. J. Psychiat.,* **118**:235.

Rachman, S. (1966) Studies in desensitization: III. Speed of generalization, *Behav. Res. Ther.,* **4**:7.

Rachman, S. (1971) *The effects of psychotherapy,* Oxford, Pergamon Press.

Rachman, S. (1974) *The meaning of fear,* Middlesex, England, Penguin Books.

Rachman, S. (1977) The conditioning theory of fear-acquisition: A critical examination, *Behav. Res. Ther.,* **15**:375.

Rachman, S. (1978) *Fear and courage,* San Francisco, Freeman.

Rachman, S., Cobb, J., Grey, S., McDonald, B., Mawson, D., Sartory, G., & Stern, R. (1979) The behavioral treatment of obsessional-compulsive disorders, with and without clomipramine, *Behav. Res. Ther.,* **17**:467.

Rachman, S., Hodgson, R., & Marks, I. M. (1971) Treatment of chronic obsessive-compulsive neurosis, *Behav. Res. Ther.,* **9**:237.

Rachman, S. & Teasdale, J. D. (1968) Aversion therapy. In C. M. Franks (Ed.), *Assessment and status of the behavior therapies and associated developments,* New York, McGraw-Hill.

Rachman, S. & Teasdale, J. (1969) *Aversion therapy and behavior disorders,* London, Routledge & Kegan Paul.

Rafi, A. A. (1962) Learning theory and the treatment of tics, *J. Psychosom. Res.,* **6**:71.

Raimy, V. (1976) Changing misconceptions as the therapeutic task. In A. Burton (Ed.), *What makes behavior change possible?,* New York, Brunner/Mazel.

Rainey, C. A. (1972) An obsessive-compulsive neurosis treated by flooding *in vivo, J. Behav. Ther. Exp. Psychiat.,* **3**:117.

Ramsey, R. W. (1977) Behavioral approaches to bereavement, *Behav. Res. Ther.,* **15**:131.

Rathus, S. A. (1972) An experimental investigation of assertive training in a group setting, *J. Behav. Ther. Exp. Psychiat.,* **3**:80.

Rauter, U. & Braud, W. (1969) Forced activity and conflict behavior. *Psychonom. Sci.,* **16**:117.

Raymond, M. J. (1956) Case of fetishism treated by aversion therapy, *Brit. Med. J.,* **2**:854.

Raymond, M. (1964) The treatment of addiction by aversion conditioning with apomorphine, *Behav. Res. Ther.,* **1**:287.

Raymond, M. & O'Keefe, K. (1965) A case of pin-up fetishism treated by aversion conditioning, *Brit. J. Psychiat.,* **111**:579.

Razani, J. (1972) Ejaculatory incompetence treated by deconditioning anxiety, *J. Behav. Ther. Exp. Psychiat.,* **3**:65.

Razran, G. (1971) *Mind in evolution,* Boston, Houghton Miflin.

Reed, J. L. (1966) Comments on the use of methohexitone sodium as a means of inducing relaxation, *Behav. Res. Ther.,* **4**:323.

Rees, L. (1956) Physical and emotional factors in bronchial asthma, *J. Psychosom. Res.,* **1**:98.

Rees, L. (1964) The importance of psychological, allergic, and infective factors in childhood asthma, *J. Psychosom. Res.,* **7**:253.

Reinking, R. H. & Kohl, M. L. (1975) Effects of various forms of relaxation training on physiological and self-report measures of relaxation, *J. Consult. Clin. Psychol.,* **43**:5.

Resh, M. (1970) Asthma of unknown origin as a psychological group, *J. Consult. Clin. Psychol.,* **35**:424.

Ritter, B. J. (1968) The group treatment of children's snake phobias using vicarious and contact desensitization procedures, *Behav. Res. Ther.,* **6**:1.

Robinson, C. & Suinn, R. (1969) Group desensitization of a phobia in massed sessions, *Behav. Res. Ther.,* **7**:319.

Rosen, G. M. & Ornstein, H. (1976) A historical note on thought stopping, *J. Consult. Clin. Psychol.,* **44**:1016.

Rosen, G. M., Rosen, E., & Reid, J. R. (1972) Cognitive desensitization and avoidance behavior, *J. Abn. Psychol.,* **80**:176.

Rosenthal, D. & Frank, J. D. (1958) Psychotherapy and the placebo effect. In C. F. Reed, I. E. Alexander, & S. S. Tomkins (Eds.), *Psychopathology: A sourcebook,* Cambridge, Mass., Harvard University Press.

Rozhdestvenskaya, V. I. (1959) Strength of nerve cells as shown in the nature of the effect of an additional stimulus on visual sensitivity. In B. M. Teplov (Ed.), *Typological features of higher nervous activity in man,* Vol. 2, Moscow.

Rubin, J., Nagler, R., Spiro, H. M., & Pilot, M. L. (1962) Measuring the effect of emotions on esophageal motility, *Psychosom. Med.,* **24**:170.

Rubin, L. S. (1964) Autonomic dysfunction as a concomitant of neurotic behavior, *J. Nerv. Ment. Dis.,* **138**:558.

Rubin, L. S. (1970) Pupillary reflexes as objective indices of autonomic dysfunction in the differential diagnosis of schizophrenic and neurotic behavior, *J. Behav. Ther. Exp. Psychiat.,* **1**:185.

Rubin, M. (1972) Verbally suggested responses as reciprocal inhibition of anxiety, *J. Behav. Ther. Exp. Psychiat.,* **3**:273.

Rush, A. S., Beck, A. T., Kovacs, M., & Hollon, S. (1977) Comparative efficacy of cognitive therapy and pharmacotherapy in the treatment of depressed outpatients, *Cognitive Ther.,* **1**:17.

Ryle, G. (1949) *The concept of mind,* London, Hutchinson.

Salter, A. (1949) *Conditioned reflex therapy,* New York, Creative Age.

Salter, A. (1952) *The case against psychoanalysis,* New York, Holt, Rinehart, & Winston.

Salzer, H. M. (1966) Relative hypoglycemia as a cause of neuropsychiatric illness, *J. Natl. Med. Assoc.,* **58**:12.

Sanderson, R. E., Campbell, D., & Laverty, S. G. (1963) Traumatically conditioned responses acquired during respiratory paralysis, *Nature,* **196**:1235.

Sandison, R. A. (1954) Psychological aspects of the LSD treatment of the neuroses, *J. Ment. Sci.,* **100**:508.

Sargant, W. & Dally, P. (1962) The treatment of anxiety states by anti-depressant drugs, *Brit. Med. J.,* **1**:6.

Sartory, G., Rachman, S., & Gray, S. (1977) An investigation of the relation between reported fear and heart rate, *Behav. Res. Ther.,* **15**:435.

Schaefer, H. H. & Martin, P. L. (1969) *Behavioral therapy,* New York, McGraw-Hill.

Schultz, J. H. & Luthe, W. (1959) *Autogenic training: A psychophysiological approach in psychotherapy,* New York, Grune & Stratton.

Schumacher, S. & Lloyd, C. (1981) Physiological and psychological factors in impotence, *The Journal of Sex Research,* **17**:40.

Scrignar, C. B. (1971) Food as the reinforcer in the outpatient treatment of anorexia nervosa, *J. Behav. Ther. Exp. Psychiat.,* **2**:31.

Sechenov, I. M. (1965) *Autobiographical notes,* Baltimore, Caramond/Pridemark.

Seitz, P. F. D. (1953) Dynamically oriented brief psychotherapy: Psychocutaneous excoriation syndrome, *Psychosom. Med.,* **15**:200.

Seligman, M. E. P. (1968) Chronic fear produced by unpredictable shock, *J. Comp. Physiol. Psychol.,* **66**:402.

Seligman, M. E. P. (1970) On the generality of the laws of learning, *Psychol. Rev.,* **77**:406.

Seligman, M. E. P. (1971) Phobias and preparedness, *Behav. Ther.,* **2**:307.

Seligman, M. E. P. (1974) Depression and learned helplessness. In R. J. Friedman & M. Katz (Eds.), *The psychology of depression,* Washington, D.C., Winston.

Seligman, M. E. P. (1975) *Helplessness: On depression, development, and death,* San Francisco, Freeman.

Seligman, M. E. P. & Groves, D. (1970) Non-transient learned helplessness, *Psychonom. Sci.,* **19**:191.

Semans, J. H. (1956) Premature ejaculation, a new approach, *South. Med. J.,* **49**:353.

Semans, J. H. (1962) Personal communication.

Serber, M. (1970) Shame aversion therapy, *J. Behav. Ther. Exp. Psychiat.,* **1**:213.

Serber, M. (1972) Teaching the nonverbal components of assertive training, *J. Behav. Ther. Exp. Psychiat.,* **3**:179.

Seward, J. & Humphrey, G. L. (1967) Avoidance learning as a function of pretraining in the cat, *J. Comp. Physiol. Psychol.,* **63**:338.

Shagass, C. (1956) Sedation threshold: A neurophysiological tool for psychosomatic research, *Psychosom. Med.,* **18**:410.

Shagass, C. (1957) Neurophysiological studies of anxiety and depression, *Psychiat. Res. Reprints,* **8**:100.

Shagass, C. (1981) Neurophysiological evidence for different types of depression, *J. Behav. Ther. Exp. Psychiat.,* **12**:99.

Shagass, C. & Jones, A. L. (1958) A neurophysiological test for psychiatric diagnosis: Results in 750 patients, *Amer. J. Psychiat.,* **114**:1002.

Shagass, C. Mihalik, J., & Jones, A. L. (1957) Clinical psychiatric studies using the sedation threshold, *J. Psychosom. Res.,* **2**:45.

Shagass, C., Muller, K., & Acosta, H. (1959) The pentothal "sleep" threshold as an indicator of affective change, *J. Psychosom. Res.,* **3**:253.

Shagass, C., Roemer, R. A., Straumanis, J. J., & Amadeo, M. (1978) Evoked potential correlates of psychosis, *Biol. Psychiat.,* **13**:163.

Shagass, C. & Schwartz, M. (1963) Psychiatric correlates of evoked cerebral cortical potentials, *Amer. J. Psychiat.,* **119**:1055.

Shames, G. H. (1969) Verbal reinforcement during therapy interviews with stutterers. In B. B. Gray & G. England (Eds.), *Stuttering and the conditioning therapies,* Monterey, Calif., Monterey Institute for Speech and Hearing.

Shaw, B. F. (1977) Comparison of cognitive therapy and behavior therapy in the treatment of depression, *J. Consult. Clin. Psychol.,* **45**:543.

Sheffield, F. D. & Roby, T. B. (1950) Reward value of a non-nutritive sweet taste, *J. Comp. Physiol. Psychol.,* **43**:471.

Sherman, A. R. (1972) Real-life exposure as a primary therapeutic factor in the desensitization treatment of fear, *J. Abn. Psychol.,* **79**:19.

Sherrington, C. S. (1906) *Integrative action of the nervous system,* New Haven, Yale University Press.

Shirley, M. M. (1933) *The first two years, Vol. 3, Personality manifestations.* Inst. Child Welfare Monogr. No. 8, Minneapolis, University of Minnesota Press.

Shmavonian, B. M. & Wolpe, J. (1972) Unpublished data.

Shorvon, H. J. & Sargant, W. (1947) Excitatory abreaction with special reference to its mechanism and the use of ether, *J. Ment. Sci.,* **93**:709.

Siegel, G. M. & Martin, R. R. (1967) Verbal punishment of disfluencies during spontaneous speech, *Lang. and Speech,* **10**:244.

Simonov, P. V. (1962) Stanislavskii method and physiology of emotions, mimeo.

Simonov, P. V. (1967) Studies of emotional behavior of humans and animals by Soviet physiologists. Paper read at a Conference on Experimental Approaches to the Study of Behavior, New York.

Singh, H. (1963) Therapeutic use of thioridazine in premature ejaculation, *Amer. J. Psychiat.,* **119**:891.

Sirota, A. & Mahoney, M. (1974) Relaxing on cue: The self-regulation of asthma, *J. Behav. Ther. Exp. Psychiat.,* **5**:65.

Skinner, B. F. (1938) *The behavior of organisms,* New York, Appleton-Century-Crofts.

Skinner, B. F. (1953) *Science and human behavior,* New York, Macmillan.

Skinner, B. F. & Lindsley, O. R. (1954) Studies in behavior therapy. Status reports II and III, Office of Naval Research, Contract N5 ori-7662.

Slater, S. L. & Leavy, A. (1966) The effects of inhaling a 35% carbon dioxide, 65% oxygen mixture upon anxiety level in neurotic patients, *Behav. Res. Ther.,* **4**:309.

Sloane, R. B., Staples, F. R., Cristol, A. H., Yorkston, N. J., & Whipple, K. (1975) *Psychotherapy versus behavior therapy,* Cambridge, Mass., Harvard University Press.

Smart, R. G. (1965) Conflict and conditioned aversive stimuli in the development of experimental response, *Canad. J. Psychol.,* **19**:208.

Smedlund, J. (1978) Bandura's theory of self-efficacy: A set of common sense theorems, *Scand. J. Psychol.,* **19**:1. (a)

Smedlund, J. (1978) Some psychological theories are not empirical: Reply to Bandura, *Scand. J. Psychol.,* **19**:101. (b)

Smith, D. (1982) Trends in counselling and psychotherapy. *Amer. Psychol.* **37**:802.

Smith, M. L., Glass, G. V., & Miller, T. I. (1980 *The benefit of psychotherapy,* Baltimore, Johns Hopkins University Press.

Snyder, S. H. (1978) The opiate receptor and morphine-like peptides in the brain. *Am. J. Psychiat.,* **135**:645.

Sobell, M. B. & Sobell, L. C. (1973) Individualized behavior therapy for alcoholics, *Behav. Ther.,* **4**:49.

Sokolov, Y. N. (1963) *Perception and the conditioned reflex,* S. W. Waydenfeld (Trans.), Oxford, Pergamon Press.

Solomon, R. L. (1964) Punishment, *Amer. Psychol.,* **19**:239.

Solomon, R. L. (1980) The opponent-process theory of acquired motivation: The costs of pleasure and the benefits of pain, *Amer. Psychol.,* **35**:691.

Solyom, L. (1969) A case of obsessive neurosis treated by aversion relief, *Canad. Psychiat. Assoc. J.,* **14**:623.

Solyom, L., Garza-Perez, J., Ledwidge, B. L., & Solyom, C. (1972) Paradoxical intention in the treatment of obsessive thoughts: A pilot study, *Comprehensive Psychiat.,* **13**:291.

Solyom, L. & Miller, S. (1965) A differential conditioning procedure as the initial phase of the behavior therapy of homosexuality, *Behav. Res. Ther.,* **3**:147.

Sommer-Smith, J. A., Galeano, C., Pineyrua, M., Roig, J. A., & Segundo, J. P. (1962) Tone cessation as conditioned signal, *Electroenceph. Clin. Neurophysiol.,* **14**:869.

Spark, R. F., White, R. A., & Connolly, P. B. (1980) Impotence is not always psychogenic, *J. Amer. Med. Assoc.,* **243**:750.

Stampfl, T. G. (1964) Quoted by London (1964).

Stampfl, T. G. & Levis, D. J. (1967) Essentials of implosive therapy: A learning-theory-based psychodynamic behavioral therapy, *J. Abn. Psychol.,* **72**:496.

Stampfl, T. G. & Levis, D. J. (1968) Implosive therapy, A behavioral therapy, *Behav. Res. Ther.,* **6**:31.

Steketee, G. & Roy, G. (1977) Unpublished data.

Stetten, D. (1968) Basic sciences in medicine: The example of gout, *New Engl. J. Med.,* **278**: 1333.

Stevens, S. S. (1957) On the psychophysical law, *Psychol. Rev.,* **64**:153.

Stevens, S. S. (1962) The surprising simplicity of sensory metrics, *Amer. Psychol.,* **17**:29.

Stevenson, I. & Wolpe, J. (1960) Recovery from sexual deviation through overcoming non-sexual neurotic responses, *Amer. J. Psychol.,* **116**:737.

Stewart, M. A. (1961) Psychotherapy by reciprocal inhibition, *Amer. J. Psychiat.,* **188**:175.

Stoffelmayr, B. E. (1970) The treatment of a retching response to dentures by a counteractive reading aloud, *J. Behav. Ther. Exp. Psychiat.,* **1**:163.

Stratton, G. M. (1897) Vision without inversion of the retinal image, *Psychol. Rev.,* **4**:341.

Strupp, H. (1978) Psychotherapy research and practice: An overview. In S. Garfield & A. Bergin (Eds.), *Handbook of psychotherapy and behavior change,* New York, Wiley.

Stuart, R. B. (1969) Operant-interpersonal treatment for marital discord, *J. Consult. Clin. Psychol.,* **33**:675.

Stuart, R. B. (1975) *How to manage the blues, tension, anger or boredom,* Manhasset, N.Y., Weight Watchers.

Stunkard, A. J. (1975) From explanation to action in psychosomatic medicine: The case of obesity, *Psychosom. Med.,* **37**:195.

Suarez, Y., Crowe, M., & Adams, H. E. (1978) Depression: Avoidance learning and physiological correlates in clinical and analog populations, *Behav. Res. Ther.,* **16**:21.

Sue, D. (1972) The role of relaxation in systematic desensitization, *Behav. Res. Ther.,* **10**:153.

Suinn, R. M. (1977) *Manual—Anxiety management training,* Fort Collins, Colo., Suinn.

Suinn, R. M. & Richardson, F. (1971) Anxiety management training: A non-specific behavior therapy program for anxiety control, *Behav. Ther.,* **2**:498.

Sushinsky, L. W. & Bootzin, R. R. (1970) Cognitive desensitization as a model of systematic desensitization, *Behav. Res. Ther.,* **8**:29.

Symonds, C. P. (1943) The human response to flying stress, *Brit. Med. J.,* **2**:703.

Taylor, F. G. & Marshall, W. L. (1977) A cognitive behavioral therapy for depression, *Cognitive Ther. and Res.,* **1**:59.

Taylor, J. G. (1955) Personal communication.

Taylor, J. G. (1959) Personal communication.

Taylor, J. G. (1962) *The behavioral basis of perception,* New Haven, Yale University Press.

Taylor, J. G. (1963) A behavioral interpretation of obsessive compulsive neurosis, *Behav. Res. Ther.,* **1**:237.

Terhune, W. S. (1948) The phobic syndrome, *Arch. Neurol. Psychiat.,* **62**:162.

Thomas, E. J. (1968) Selected sociobehavioral techniques and principles: An approach to interpersonal helping, *Social Work,* **13**:12.

Thorpe, J. G., Schmidt, E., Brown, P. T., & Castell, D. (1964) Aversion relief therapy: A new method for general application, *Behav. Res. Ther.,* **2**:71.

Tomlinson, J. R. (1970) The treatment of bowel retention by operant procedures: A case study, *J. Behav. Ther. Exp. Psychiat.,* **1**:83.

Turner, R. M., DiTomasso, R. A., & Murray, M. R. (1980) Psychometric analysis of the Willoughby personality schedule. *J. Behav. Ther. Exp. Psychiat.,* **11**:185–194.

Tursky, B., Watson, P. D., & O'Connell, D. N. (1965) A concentric shock electrode for pain stimulation, *Psychophysiol.,* **1**:296.

Ullmann, L. P. & Krasner, L. (1965) *Case studies in behavior modification,* New York, Holt, Rinehart, & Winston.

Ulrich, R., Stachnik, T., & Mabry, J. (1966) *Control of human behavior,* Glenview, Ill., Scott-Foreman.

Valins, S. & Ray, A. A. (1967) Effects of cognitive desensitization on avoidance behavior, *J. Pers. Soc. Psychol.,* **7**:345.

Van de Venter, A. D. & Laws, D. R. (1978) Orgasmic reconditioning to redirect sexual arousal in pedophiles, *Behav. Ther.,* **7**:155.

Van Egeren, L. F., Feather, B. W., & Hein, P. L. (1971) Desensitization of phobias: Some psychophysiological propositions, *Psychophysiol.,* **8**:213.

Voegtlin, W. & Lemere, F. (1942) The treatment of alcohol addiction, *Qrt. J. Stud. Alcoh.,* **2**:717.

Wachtel, P. L. (1978) On some complexities in the application of conflict theory to psychotherapy, *J. Nerv. Ment. Dis.,* **166**:475.

Wade, T. C., Malloy, T. E., & Proctor, S. (1977) Imaginal correlates of self-reported fear and avoidance behavior, *Behav. Res. Ther.,* **15**:17.

Wagner, A. R. & Rescoria, R. A. (1972) Inhibition in Pavlovian conditioning: Applications of a theory. In M. S. Halliday & R. A. Boakes (Eds.), *Inhibition and learning,* New York, Academic Press.

Wallace, R. K. (1970) Physiological effects of transcendental meditation, *Science,* **167**:1751.

Walton, D. (1964) Experimental psychology and the treatment of a tiquer, *J. Child Psychol. Psychiat.,* **2**:148.

Wanderer, Z. & Cabot, T. (1978) *Letting go,* New York, Putnam.

Watson, J. B. (1970) *Behaviorism,* New York, Norton.

Watson, J. B. & Rayner, P. (1920) Conditioned emotional reactions, *J. Exp. Psychol.,* **3**:1.

Watts, F. N. (1979) Habituation model of systematic desensitization, *Psychol. Bull.,* **86**:627.

Weinreb, S. (1966) The effects of inhaling spirit of ammonia upon anxiety level in neurotic patients, mimeo.

Weitzman, B. (1967) Behaviour therapy and psychotherapy, *Psychol. Bull.,* **74**:300.

Wenger, M. A. (1966) Studies of autonomic balance: A summary, *Psychophysiology,* **2**:173.

Wikler, A. (1968) Interaction of physical dependence and classical and operant conditioning in the genesis of relapse. New York, Association for Research in Nervous and Mental Disease Proceedings, **46**:280.

Wilder, J. (1945) Facts and figures on psychotherapy, *J. Clin. Psychopath.,* **7**:311.

Willis, R. W. & Edwards, J. A. (1969) A study of the comparative effectiveness of the systematic desensitization and implosive therapy, *Behav. Res. Ther.,* **7**:387.

Wilson, G. T. & O'Leary, K. D. (1980) *Principles of behavior therapy,* Englewood Cliffs, N.J., Prentice-Hall.

Winkelman, N. W. (1955) Chlorpromazine in the treatment of neuropsychiatric disorders, *J. Amer. Med. Assoc.,* **155**:18.

Wisocki, P. A. (1970) Treatment of obsessive-compulsive behavior by covert sensitization and covert reinforcement: A case report, *J. Behav. Ther. Exp. Psychiat.,* **1**:233.

Wolberg, L. (1948) *Medical hypnosis,* New York, Grune & Stratton.

Wolf, S. & Wolff, H. G. (1942) Evidence in the genesis of peptic ulcer in man, *J. Amer. Med. Assoc.,* **120**:670.

Wolf, S. & Wolff, H. G. (1947) *Human gastric functions,* New York, Oxford University Press.

Wollersheim, J. P. (1970) Effectiveness of group therapy based on learning principles in the treatment of overweight women, *J. Abn. Psychol.,* **76**:462.

Wolpe, J. (1948) An approach to the problem of neurosis based on the conditioned response. Unpublished manuscript, M. D. Thesis, University of the Witwatersrand.

Wolpe, J. (1949) An interpretation of the effects of combinations of stimuli (patterns) based on current neurophysiology, *Psychol. Rev.,* **56**:277.

Wolpe, J. (1950) Need-reduction, drive-reduction, and reinforcement: A neurophysiological view, *Psychol. Rev.,* **57**:19.

Wolpe, J. (1952) Objective psychotherapy of the neuroses, *South Afr. Med. J.,* **26**:825. (a)

Wolpe, J. (1952) Experimental neurosis as learned behavior, *Brit. J. Psychol.,* **43**:243. (b)

Wolpe, J. (1952) The formation of negative habits: A neurophysiological view, *Psychol. Rev.,* **59**:290. (c)

Wolpe, J. (1953) Theory construction for Blodgett's latent learning, *Psychol. Rev.,* **60**:340.

Wolpe, J. (1954) Reciprocal inhibition as the main basis of psychotherapeutic effects, *Arch. Neur. Psychiat.,* **72**:205.

Wolpe, J. (1958) *Psychotherapy by reciprocal inhibition,* Stanford, Calif., Stanford University Press.

Wolpe, J. (1961) The systematic desensitization treatment of neuroses, *J. Nerv. Ment. Dis.,* **112**:189. (a)

Wolpe, J. (1961) The prognosis in unpsychoanalyzed recovery from neurosis, *Amer. J. Psychiat.,* **118**:35. (b)

Wolpe, J. (1962) Isolation of a conditioning procedure as the crucial psychotherapeutic factor, *J. Nerv. Ment. Dis.,* **134**:316.

Wolpe, J. (1963) Quantitative relationships in the systematic desentization of phobias, *Amer. J. Psychiat.,* **119**:1062.

Wolpe, J. (1964) Behavior therapy in complex neurotic states, *Brit. J. Psychiat.,* **110**:28. (a)

Wolpe, J. (1964) Unpublished data. (b)

Wolpe, J. (1965) Conditioned inhibition of craving in drug addiction: A pilot experiment, *Behav. Res. Ther.,* **2**:285.

Wolpe, J. (1969) Behavior therapy of stuttering: Deconditioning the emotional factor. In B. B. Gray & G. England (Eds.), *Stuttering and the conditioning therapies,* Monterey, Calif., Monterey Institute for Speech and Stuttering.

Wolpe, J. (1970) Emotional conditioning and cognitions: A rejoinder to Davison and Valins, *Behav. Res. Ther.,* **8**:103.

Wolpe, J. (1971) The behavioristic conception of neurosis: A reply to two critics, *Psychol. Rev.,* **78**:341.

Wolpe, J. (1973) *The practice of behavior therapy,* 2nd ed., New York, Pergamon Press.

Wolpe, J. (1975) Foreword. In R. B. Sloane, F. R. Staples, A. H. Cristol, N. J. Yorkston, & K. Whipple (Eds.), *Psychotherapy versus behavior therapy,* Cambridge, Mass., Harvard University Press.

Wolpe, J. (1976) *Theme and variations: A behavior therapy casebook,* New York, Pergamon Press.

Wolpe, J. (1977) Inadequate behavior analysis: The Achilles heel of outcome research behavior therapy, *J. Behav. Ther. Exp. Psychiat.,* **7**:1.

Wolpe, J. (1978) Cognition and causation in human behavior and its therapy, *Amer. Psychol.,* **33**:437. (a)

Wolpe, J. (1978) Self-efficacy theory and psychotherapeutic change: A square peg for a round hole, *Adv. Behav. Res. Ther.,* **1**:231. (b)

Wolpe, J. (1979) The experimental model and treatment of neurotic depression, *Behav. Res. Ther.,* **17**:555.

Wolpe, J. (1980) Behavior therapy for psychosomatic disorders, *Psychosom.,* **21**:329.

Wolpe, J. (1981) Behavior therapy versus psychoanalysis: Therapeutic and social implications, *Amer. Psychol.,* **36**:159. (a)

Wolpe, J. (1981) The dichotomy between directly conditioned and cognitively learned anxiety, *J. Behav. Ther. Exp. Psychiat.,* **12**:35. (b)

Wolpe, J. (1981) Perception as a functioning of conditioning, *Pavlovian Journal of Biological Science,* **16**:70. (c)

Wolpe, J. & Ascher, L. M. (1976) Outflanking "resistance" in a severe obsessional neurosis. In H. J. Eysenck (Ed.), *Case histories in behavior therapy,* London, Routledge & Kegan Paul.

Wolpe, J. & Flood, J. (1970) The effect of relaxation on the galvanic skin response to repeated phobic stimuli in ascending order, *J. Behav. Ther. Exp. Psychiat.,* 1:195.

Wolpe, J. & Fried, R. (1968) Psychophysiological correlates of imaginal presentations of hierarchical stimuli. I. The effect of relaxation. Unpublished manuscript.

Wolpe, J., Groves, G. A., & Fischer, S. (1980) Treatment of narcotic addiction of inhibition of craving: Contending with a cherished habit, *Comprehensive Psychiat.,* 21:308.

Wolpe, J. & Lang, P. J. (1964) A fear survey schedule for use in behavior therapy, *Behav. Res. Ther.,* 2:27.

Wolpe, J. & Lang, P. J. (1969) *Fear survey schedule,* San Diego, Calif., Educational and Industrial Testing Service.

Wolpe, J. & Theriault, N. (1971) Francois Leuret: A progenitor of behavior therapy, *J. Behav. Ther. Exp. Psychiat.,* 2:19.

Wolpe, J. & Wolpe, D. (1981) *Our useless fears,* Boston, Houghton Miflin.

Wolpin, M. & Pearsall, L. (1965) Rapid deconditioning of a fear of snakes, *Behav. Res. Ther.,* 3:107.

Wolpin, M. & Raines, J. (1966) Visual imagery, expected roles and extinction as possible factors in reducing fear and avoidance behavior, *Behav. Res. Ther.,* 4:25.

Woody, C. D. & Engel, J., Jr. (1972) Changes in unit activity and thresholds to electrical microstimulation at coronal-pericruciate cortex of cat with classical conditioning of different facial movements, *J. Neurophysiol.,* 35:230.

Yamagami, T. (1971) The treatment of an obsession by thought-stopping, *J. Behav. Ther. Exp. Psychiat.,* 2:133.

Yates, A. J. (1958) The application of learning theory to the treatment of tics, *J. Abn. Soc. Psychol.,* 56:175.

Yates, A. J. (1975) *Theory and practice in behavior therapy,* New York, Wiley.

Yerkes, R. M. (1939) Sexual behavior in the chimpanzee, *Human Biol.,* 2:78.

Yeung, D. P. H. (1968) Diazepam for treatment of phobias, *Lancet,* 1:475.

Young, J. Z. (1973) Memory as a selective process. Australian Academy of Science Report: Symposium on Biological Memory.

Young, J. Z. (1975) Sources of discovery in neuroscience. In E. G. Worden, J. P. Swazey, & G. Adelman (Eds.), *The neurosciences: Paths of discovery,* Cambridge, Mass., Colonial Press.

Zbrozyna, A. W. (1953) Phenomenon of non-identification of a stimulus operating against different physiological backgrounds in dogs, *Lodskie Towanzystwo Naukowe,* 3, No. 26.

Zbrozyna, A. W. (1957) The conditioned cessation of eating, *Bull. Acad. Polonaise Sci.,* 5:261.

Zitrin, C. M., Klein, D. F., & Woerner, M. G. (1978) Behaviour therapy, supportive psychotherapy, imipramine and phobias, *Arch. Gen. Psychiat.,* 35:307.

Zitrin, C. M., Klein, D. F. & Woerner, M. G. (1980) Treatment of agoraphobia with group exposure *in vivo* and imipramine, *Arch. Gen. Psychiat.,* 37:63.

Author Index

Subject Index

About the Author

Joseph Wolpe, M.D., who was born and educated in South Africa, is Professor of Psychiatry at Temple University Medical Center and Editor of the *Journal of Behavior Therapy and Experimental Psychiatry*. After World War II, he pioneered the field of behavior therapy and came to be considered the founder of behavior therapy of the neuroses. Experiments he performed in animals pointed the way to the counterconditioning methods, such as systematic desensitization, that have been so effective in clinical neuroses. His first book, *Psychotherapy By Reciprocal Inhibition* (1958), described his early experimental and clinical research. In 1979 he was awarded the American Psychological Association's prestigious Distinguished Scientific Award for the Applications of Psychology.

Pergamon General Psychology Series

Editors: Arnold P. Goldstein, Syracuse University
Leonard Krasner, SUNY at Stony Brook